My Brother the Boxer

To: David

A true boxing fan!

To: David

A true Horatio fan!

[signature]

My Brother the Boxer
The Terry Daniels Story

Jeff Daniels

Copyright © 2015 by Jeff Daniels
All rights reserved.

ISBN: 1515005011
ISBN 13: 9781515005018

The stories in this book were based on facts, newspaper articles, and/or personal experiences. Names of some people and places were changed for confidentiality.

DEDICATIONS

This book is dedicated to the team of coaches, trainers, personnel and amateurs who sacrificed their time and energy to become good at, and appreciated, the art of boxing.

This book was written in loving memory of Bill and June Daniels who helped their "little hooligans" grow up to lead responsible and meaningful lives.

"You become a champion when you fight one more round. When things are tough, you <u>fight</u> one more round."

James J. Corbett
Heavyweight Champion

"A man can only be beaten twice – once when he dies and once when he quits."

Anonymous

CHAPTER 1

New Orleans, January 15, 1972 – Yank Durham, Joe Frazier's manager, was standing in the entrance of Rivergate Auditorium surrounded by a reporter and a camera crew taping a last-minute interview before the main event of the evening – a title fight between Smokin' Joe Frazier and Terry Daniels.

Durham wore his gray suit, black shirt and silver-colored tie. It fit his 6' 0" body frame perfectly and blended well with his slightly graying Afro hairstyle. He flashed his big smile as he looked into the camera, and assured the reporter that his fighter was in great shape and would defend his title in true championship style. He was proud of the fact that he was the manager of the *undisputed* Heavyweight Champion of the World.

Back in March 1971, Frazier defended his title in a grueling 15-round unanimous decision against the undefeated Muhammad Ali in Madison Square Garden. Both fighters were admitted to the hospital after what the press called "The Fight of the Century."

Century Telesports Network was carrying tonight's fight on home TV in over twenty countries in front of an estimated 70 million viewers. It would be the first time a Heavyweight Championship Fight would be seen on home television since 1967. The whole world wanted to see if Frazier had truly recovered from his momentous fight with Ali and the pummeling they gave each other.

When asked about his fighter's weight going from 208 pounds to 215 pounds since the Ali fight, Durham replied, "He is solid as a rock;

you saw him at the weigh-in this afternoon. Joe trains harder than any other fighter I manage – and they are all world-class contenders!"

Tom Harmon, the former football All-American and Heisman Trophy winner turned sports broadcaster, interviewed the 28-year-old Frazier at the weigh-in. He asked the champion what strategy he was planning to use and if he would like to share it with the television audience.

"Well, my opponent is strong and is the same height as me," Joe said, "and I usually like a guy a little taller so I can work on his body before landing some hard shots to the head. But my strategy will be to just stay on him with hard shots everywhere from the start of the fight, and not let up until it's over."

Inside the auditorium, Frazier sat in his locker room, having his hands wrapped while listening to Motown hits on his portable eight-track stereo. He had his own routine that never changed before each fight: start getting the trunks on 45 minutes before the fight; push-ups to get the blood flowing, followed by sit-ups to firm up his stomach; jump-rope and shadow boxing to work up a sweat, then relax to music while having his hands wrapped by his trainer.

Down the hall was his opponent – Terry Daniels, ranked 10th in world heavyweights by the World Boxing Association (WBA). He was well known by boxing fans in Cleveland, Ohio, and Dallas, Texas, but was unknown to the *world* until a few months ago when Durham announced to the press that "The hard puncher from Dallas, Texas," would be Frazier's next challenger.

Harmon also interviewed Terry at the weigh-in, and asked the handsome 25-year-old boxer if he thought he had the power in his punch to beat the undefeated champion, who had a record of 27-0 (23 by KO). He replied, "No I don't *think* I do – I *know* I do. If it lands, it's all over."

Terry was 5' 11," weighed in at 191.5 pounds with his muscle-bound physique, and came with a professional record of 28-4-1 (25 by KO). Despite Frazier's 24-pound edge, Terry felt he had the determination to knockout his opponent and claim the heavyweight championship belt.

A few days earlier Terry read an article about the fight in a morning paper. It described the last heavyweight title fight held in New Orleans, in 1892. At the time the champion was the popular "Boston Strongman" John L. Sullivan, and the challenger was a slender 178-pound dynamo named James "Gentleman Jim" Corbett. The underdog, Corbett, knocked out Sullivan in the 21st round.

Terry predicted to the press that this would be an upset too. He had maintained that confidence since arriving for the fight on January 3rd. The New Orleans *Times-Picayune* ran an article with a photo on the cover of the sports page showing Terry between two beautiful models holding a mock newspaper with the headline stating, "Daniels Cools Frazier in the Fifth, New Champ!"

Back in Terry's hometown of Willoughby, Ohio, his family was preparing for the championship fight in their ringside seats – in front of the television set. His father, Bill Daniels, had decided against pulling Terry's three brothers out of school and staying at an overpriced hotel in New Orleans with the rest of the crowd in town for the fight *and* Super Bowl VI which was the next day.

Bill chose to join some friends and watch the fight at his favorite restaurant, LaVelle's, on Mentor Avenue. His boys Jeff and Denny and his daughter Debbie would watch it with their mother, June, at home. His other son, Tom, was in Athens, Ohio, and was preparing to watch the fight in his apartment with his wife.

At 52 years of age, Bill had a hard time convincing himself that his oldest son was about to step into the ring with one of the toughest fighters in the world. Deep down, he feared for his boy's life. He couldn't shake the guilt that ate away at him over the years.

As he sat there with a drink in his hand, he shared his feelings with a close friend. "If I had encouraged him more to excel in any other profession, instead of ridiculing him for not taking the direction I expected him to take, maybe Terry wouldn't even be here."

Terry's brothers and sister, on the other hand, were thrilled to see this "Cinderella" story for their big brother come to life. Tom was 21 and a senior at Ohio University. Jeff was 18 and a senior in high school. Denny was 15 and Debbie 13. The tension in the air was built by the news media over the past six weeks, and now the fight would be shown live on Cleveland's Channel 5 at 10:30 p.m.

Jeff and Denny had gone into the kitchen to refill their glasses of soda pop and bowls of popcorn. The Daniels boys had endured hundreds of questions from reporters, friends and neighbors in the past several weeks about their big brother's fight against the tough champion from Philadelphia. The answer to all of their questions would be presented in the next 10 minutes.

They put their snacks down on the coffee table and sat down with their mother and younger sister. Jeff stared ahead at the car commercial on the TV screen, but couldn't focus on the words. He took a deep breath to try to settle his nerves; when he exhaled, he said in a quiet voice, "Terry, how in the *world* did you get here?"

CHAPTER 2

Willoughby, Ohio, summer 1964 (Eight years earlier) – "Jeff and I are leaving to tend to the horses, Mom!" Terry yelled up the stairs.

"Okay, Honey. You boys be careful, and don't forget, we're doing burgers on the grill tonight!"

Terry and Jeff had volunteered to take care of the family horses on Saturday, while Tom, Denny and Debbie spent their day with friends. Their father had a passion for horses, and he purchased two large draft horses years ago because they always reminded him of his upbringing in Lake County. He kept his horses boarded at a friend's house at nearby Waite Hill village.

To encourage his kids to help the stable maintenance crew from time to time, he had purchased a 9-year-old quarter horse a year ago. The kids loved her and renamed her Pollyanna, after the Disney movie.

Bill had also purchased a 6-year-old gelding a week ago from a friend who owned a stable of polo ponies and a large home construction company. His friend tried to get Bill interested in polo, but he said he was too busy running his own companies.

Even though there was an eight-year age difference between them, 10-year-old Jeff always looked forward to spending time with his big brother, Terry, who worked on their father's road construction company throughout the summer. Most evenings he was either playing baseball in the American Legion League, or out on a date, and didn't have that much time to spend with his younger siblings any more.

But this summer was different. Terry had graduated from Willoughby South High and would soon be attending college at Southern Methodist University in Dallas, Texas. Jeff knew that Terry would be leaving in a few weeks, and was determined to take advantage of any time he could spend with him.

The boys sat in the front seat of their '62 Ford station wagon, and Terry finished his extra thick bologna sandwich. As he turned the key in the ignition the radio speaker blasted out *Walk Like a Man*, by the Four Seasons, and he realized he'd left the volume turned up to the max after his date the night before.

"Wow!" Jeff said as he turned it down.

"No leave it up," Terry said, "I like this song."

Terry loved all kinds of music. His favorites were The Chiffons, *He's So Fine*, The Angels, *My Boyfriend's Back*, and all the songs about drag racing from Jan & Dean and the Beach Boys. The Cleveland AM stations with all the rock and pop hits of the time were WHK and KYW, and the boys always knew which buttons to push on their parents' cars when they were in the front seat.

They pulled out of their driveway onto Johnnycake Ridge and drove west until they got to a bridge that crossed the Chagrin River. Across the bridge on the left was Waite Hill Road and on the right was the entrance to Daniels Park – named after Terry's great-grandparents after they passed away.

They turned left and made their way up the winding hillside until they reached the top of the hill. There was a flat-sided sandstone rock in the ground that marked the entrance of an old driveway just at the curve on the top of the road that read, Drury Lane 1896. Terry and Jeff would always see who could say the date the fastest when they saw the stone (one of those "little brother" games they'd play that eventually turned into a habit).

It was noon and the mid-July sun was heating up the landscape. The bright green leaves on the oak and maple trees brought the vibrant colors of Ohio to life. It was a beautiful day.

Waite Hill was the home to many older estates of prominent people in the Cleveland area. Large castle-like homes sat 50 to 100 yards off the road and were surrounded by stone walls or old picket fences.

When the boys arrived at the stables, the routine was to shoot a little game of basketball first at the small blacktop court that Bill had put in for his friends, then saddle up the horses and give them a ride.

One thing Jeff liked best about hanging out with Terry was that he would always show him how to play a sport. If Jeff started to go off and play it his way, Terry would correct him without calling him "stupid" like some of Jeff's friends' older brothers did.

Another thing that he admired about him was the way he exuded confidence. Terry was good at just about everything, but he was humble. He didn't go around trying to prove that he was superior, and Jeff knew that's why he was so popular in school.

After shooting some hoops and cleaning out the stalls, they put the blankets and saddles on the horses. Jeff was determined to be the first to ride the new horse, Twister. He was even dressed for the part with cowboy boots and a set of pearl-handled cap guns.

Before helping Jeff up in the saddle, Terry said, "Maybe I ought to test this gelding out first. Your feet don't even reach the stirrups."

"No way! How about I ride him for awhile and then we switch?"

"Okay. Mr. Nemec told Dad that Twister was a good polo pony, but he got hurt last year and now he can't run so fast, so I guess you'll be alright. We can wait for Dad if you want."

"Nah, we'll be back by the time he gets here and we can switch then. I think Twister will be just fine with me," Jeff said while gripping the reins with one hand and petting the horse's mane with the other.

"Okay, partner," Terry said as he swung his right leg over Pollyanna's back.

They walked the horses on a trail that led from the estate to a large open field of tall grass across the road. Once in the open field, they worked the horses up to a slow trot, then headed for the woods.

Terry laughed as Jeff bounced in the saddle next to him.

"You better hold on to those reins and saddle horn a little tighter or you'll lose those nice cap guns out here," he said.

They crossed the field in a slow trot. When they reached the woods, the horses stopped to graze, but Terry wanted to bring them to a canter, then gallop.

Without warning, Terry went into his "Hollywood" mode, pointed into the woods and said, "Jeff look, Indians!" He pulled on the reins and coaxed Pollyanna into a gallop.

Jeff's horse immediately followed Terry's and he started laughing, "Yahoo!"

But what felt like a light gallop on a nice leisurely afternoon turned into a full speed race with Twister passing Terry in seconds.

What they hadn't realized, since they didn't wait for their dad to get there, was that Jeff was riding a trained athlete. For the last three years the horse was accustomed to passing other horses while pursuing a small white ball in an open field, at full speed.

Jeff knew something was wrong, and in panic mode he pulled back hard on the reins several times, yelling "Whoa!"

He turned his head in desperation and saw Terry, who looked like a large dot getting smaller. Terry was yelling to him, "Hold on Jeff, I'm coming!"

Jeff noticed the quarter-mile field was quickly coming to an end and he was heading for the picket fence that separated the field from the road.

His dad had taught him what to do when a horse gets out of hand. "You run him into a fence and he'll think it's time to stop." But Twister had no intention of stopping, rather, he was picking up speed to jump the fence!

Jeff pulled on the left rein and Twister turned left like a race cart making a sharp turn, then headed down the fence line toward a big white house. Twister's head was bobbing up and down at full speed. Terry was desperately trying to catch up, but Jeff had a good 50 yards on him.

The horse galloped across the front yard of the house, taking large divots from the moist turf, and headed toward the main road. Jeff caught a split-second glimpse of himself in the picture window of the house, seeing an elderly gentleman in the living room who was smoking a pipe and looking up from his newspaper. His jaw dropped and the pipe fell out of his mouth when he saw the terrified look on Jeff's face.

In desperation, Jeff guided Twister across the road and onto a stretch of grass that was lined by a picket fence and silver maple trees. He let go of the reins and reached out for a large branch on one of the trees. He misjudged the height and thickness of the branch and it hit him squarely in the chest. The blow knocked him off the horse and pounded him to the ground like a sack of feed grain.

"Boom!" was all he heard, and he felt the air rush out of his body. Twister didn't miss a step and kept galloping full speed, straight down the road.

Jeff tried to breathe for what seemed like minutes, and he looked like a fish flopping out of water.

As he inhaled his next breath he found himself airborne and in the arms of his big brother. "Oh my gosh, are you all right, Jeff?" Terry nervously asked.

As he blinked through the bright sunlight he was nose to nose with Terry's frightened face. He tried to talk, but all he could do was cry uncontrollably. He hugged his big brother like he would never let him go.

"Are you okay, buddy? You hurt? It's okay, I got you now," Terry said, with a frightened look on his face.

The owner of the house drove up in a shiny new Cadillac, rolled down the passenger window and asked, "You kids okay?"

They both nodded and he drove down the road to look for their runaway horse. He found him a quarter-mile away, leisurely munching on the grass on the side of the curb. The gentleman walked the horse back to where they were resting. Terry thanked him, took the reins of both horses with Jeff in his other arm, and began walking back to the estate.

When they got to the stables, they were met by their dad. He saw Jeff sobbing and hugging Terry, and the horses walking along behind.

"What the *hell* is going on?" he asked.

Terry quickly gave him the story and apologized for not waiting for him to get there before they saddled up. He transferred Jeff to Bill's arms and said he would get the saddles off and take the horses into the corral. It was Terry's way of trying to avoid his dad's wrath, at least momentarily.

Bill, with his frowning eyebrows and dark brown eyes, stared piercingly at Terry as he quickly walked the horses back to the stalls.

Bill turned his attention back to Jeff and asked, "Are you okay, Hon? You hurt anywhere? Here, we'll sit down over here and check you out real quick."

He put Jeff down in an Adirondack chair that sat by the side of the house under a large oak tree; then gently touched his arms and legs to see if he had any broken bones. Jeff wiped the tears from his eyes and said, "I feel like I got leveled in one of our football games in the backyard – only when it happened, I thought I was going to die!"

When Bill was satisfied that nothing was broken, he tested him for a concussion.

"How many fingers do I have up?" he asked, holding up his index and middle fingers, directly in front of Jeff's face.

"Two," Jeff replied.

Then Bill held up both his index fingers and said, "Okay, follow the one that's moving," while moving his right hand from side to side, followed by the left. He looked very serious and Jeff tried not to laugh, but he couldn't hold it in and just burst out laughing.

Terry came back from the stables, heard Jeff laughing and said, "You're okay now Jeffro?"

He nodded and they spent the rest of the afternoon tending to the other horses.

That evening at the dinner table, Terry told the story in great detail to the rest of the family. They all had a good laugh over it, except for his mother. She shook her head, like she always did after hearing stories about the daily heroics of her boys and said, "It's a wonder you didn't break your neck!"

CHAPTER 3

Aside from a week's camping vacation with his family at his Uncle Warren's place in Utica, New York, Terry rarely got time off unless it rained. And it had to be a torrential downpour for the road crew to get a day off. Weekends were generally free and he would work out in his basement with dumbbells and do calisthenics before taking a girl out on a date.

He would also drive over to South High and run laps on the track, even in the rain. He had not lost track of his long-term goal – playing football at Southern Methodist University. He was committed to his dreams. Terry lettered in football his junior and senior years in high school, and was an outstanding running back and linebacker. He suffered a knee injury in the fourth game of his senior season, but he had received recruiting letters from top colleges in the northern states. Finishing in the top tenth of his class with a 4.0 grade-point average also helped.

He told his friends and family that he'd had enough of the northern winters and made contacts with athletic offices at Southern California and SMU in Dallas, Texas. Both showed an interest in him.

The Daniels family were devoted Methodists and attended the Willoughby United Methodist Church. The minister at the church had overheard Terry's interest in attending a southern college and encouraged him to look into the advantages of SMU.

Terry wasn't interested in becoming a Methodist minister, but he *was* interested in the Southwest Conference, which consisted of some of the toughest teams in the nation: Texas, Arkansas, Texas Tech, Rice, Texas Christian, Baylor, Texas A&M, and SMU.

He had heard that SMU was rebuilding their football team and wanted to be a key player in the process. He also wanted to spend his winters in the warm Texas sunshine.

Terry and Tom shared a bedroom, and one night before turning in, Terry confessed to Tom his real reason for choosing a school so far south.

"If I stay close to home, Dad's gonna expect me to work in the companies after I graduate, and I don't want to do that. I want to blaze my own trail like Grandpa Doc.

"I figure I can get a better perspective down south, besides, Dad and Uncle Peps will always be calling the shots until they retire. And you know, they get along like oil and water, and I don't want to be stuck in the middle."

In 1918, their grandfather, Lyle "Doc" Daniels, took advantage of farmland he and his brother Willard owned near a railroad crossing in Willoughby. They decided to go into business together using the money they inherited from their parents.

They had cement silos built near the tracks to hold large quantities of coal, a much-needed commodity for the cold winters near Lake Erie. They called their corporation The Daniels Brothers Coal Company.

As time passed, Doc and his brother changed to the more economical and cleaner commodity of fuel oil, and changed their name to The Daniels Brothers Fuel Company. The company grew, and by the 1960s, Doc and Willard had over 5,000 customers.

Daniels Fuel, as the locals called it, diversified its profits into other companies that benefited from the explosive growth in population in Lake County in that time. Road construction was in high demand and Doc purchased land in nearby Painesville and Fairport Harbor. He had a shipping dock built in Fairport to allow Canadian ships to deliver various sizes of stone, and a 40-acre plant in a valley in Painesville.

The plant manufactured asphalt, or "blacktop" as it came to be known, and Doc used it to form the Northeastern Road Improvement Company in Willoughby. Other companies used concrete to build roads, especially when it came to the new freeways. "But blacktop always covers concrete," he used to say.

Doc also had a passion for golf, although he never had time to be good at it, he did have a 9-hole golf course built on land that the company owned between Route 84 and Route 20. Unfortunately, he never did get a chance to enjoy it when he retired. He had a stroke and passed away a month before the Sequoia Golf Course opened in April 1964. He was 70 years old.

All of his grandchildren loved him very much too, and when they were of age, he always found work for them in his companies. When Terry was 12, his grandpa gave him a summer job as a flagman on his road crew. By the time he turned 16, Terry was mature enough and strong enough to fill any position where the crew needed him.

The job paid well, and *that* was the motivation that took the sting out of getting up at 6 each morning to be at the fuel oil garages by 7 a.m. The company had two road crews and a few years before his grandfather died, Doc passed the baton of foreman from himself to his two sons – Lyle Jr. and Bill, Terry's dad. Lyle Jr. was nicknamed "Peps" when he was younger by the men on the road crew, because the only thing they ever saw him drink was Pepsi cola.

Peps was two years younger than Bill, but wouldn't let anybody know it by the way he acted. He always viewed himself as the leader of Doc and Clara Daniels' family children, even though he was in the middle of six. Whatever direction his older brother Bill went, he would go the other way, and say his way was *better*.

Doc and Clara's house was close to the city limits of Willoughby and Mentor, and while growing up, their kids could elect to go to either city's schools. When Bill chose to go to Mentor High School, Peps chose Willoughby. That way, if one of them accomplished anything in the field of athletics, and they did, they could take credit for doing it on their own. Bill excelled in baseball for the Mentor "Cardinals," while Peps was an outstanding running back in football for the Willoughby Union High School "Rangers."

When World War II broke out, Bill elected to serve in the Army Air Corps while Peps chose the Navy, and on it went, until they eventually headed up the two crews of the road construction company.

Bill rarely argued with his brother, however, he was the oldest boy among the six children in the Daniels family and he felt he never had to prove to anyone who he was or what he stood for. He, like his father and brothers, worked hard for the family corporations and expected his boys to do the same.

Terry was the oldest in his family, and a natural leader. He was grateful that he had a great start in life, but at age 18, he told his friends that his life was just beginning. He was determined to make things happen for himself going forward, on his terms.

CHAPTER 4

The first Saturday afternoon in August, Terry asked his mother if he could borrow the station wagon for his date that night. He and his girlfriend Barb were planning on going to the Mentor Drive-In to see *A Hard Day's Night,* starring The Beatles.

His mom laughed and said, "The Beatles made a movie? I thought you didn't like The Beatles?"

"Well I don't, but Barb does," Terry replied. "We're going to meet Danny Iafelice and his date there."

Jeff was playing a game of Stratego with Denny in the living room and overheard them mention *The Beatles.*

"Oh boy, Terry can you take me too?" Jeff asked.

Denny followed and said, "Yeah, me too?"

"What!? No, not this time guys," Terry said.

"Come on Ter, you don't even like 'em," Jeff pleaded. "Mom, can you take us? Please!"

June looked at Terry and said, "Oh Honey, I've had them all week and could use a break. Why don't you let them go in their pajamas and we'll fix up the sleeping bags with their pillows? You know how much they love The Beatles, and after the movie is over they'll probably fall asleep."

"Mom, I leave for football practice next week! This will be the last weekend Barb and I can go out and have some fun," Terry said.

"Come on Ter, we'll be good for you, and like Mom said, we'll go to sleep right after the movie," Jeff said. "The second one's probably a stupid surfer movie anyway."

"Yeah!" Denny chimed in.

Beatlemania was sweeping the countryside, and Willoughby was no exception. Just about all their friends from school, *including* their brothers and sisters, idolized the Fab Four. Even the die-hard fans of Elvis were converting.

WHK and KYW were constantly competing to see who could play the most Beatle hits in one day. It was even rumored that the group would stop in Cleveland while doing their U.S. tour that summer.

The walls of the bedroom that Denny and Jeff shared were covered with Beatles pictures and articles from the teen magazines, but they rarely got to see them just being themselves. And now they could watch them in a full-length movie – they were excited!

"Ah jeez...Alright," Terry said. "But you better behave, I won't hesitate to smack you one if you don't."

"We won't!" they both said in unison.

They got to ride in the back as promised, with sleeping bags and pillows. Jeff even coerced Terry into letting his friend Cliff go with them. Danny and his date met them at the entrance and followed them in his car. The place was packed, and they parked in the last set of rows.

The evening was fun for all. Terry was surprised to hear Cliff and Jeff singing some of the songs together, and laughed as they tried their best to harmonize like John and Paul. Barb wasn't amused, however. She hushed them to be quiet. Terry followed up by quietly saying, "Don't forget what I told you guys."

They did settle back in their pillows just after *Beach Blanket Bingo* started. It turned out to be the last evening Jeff and Denny had with their big brother before he packed his bags and went off to college the following Friday.

Bill and Tom drove Terry to Dallas after the family gathered in the front yard to say their tearful goodbyes. His mom hugged and kissed Terry for the last time and said, "We'll keep you in our prayers every night, Honey."

They walked to the end of their yard and waved as the station wagon drove farther down Johnnycake Ridge before disappearing around the corner.

* * *

The trip to Dallas was long, but they made good time because they took turns driving and drove straight through. Tom called home around noon the next day from the players' dormitory to let the family know they made it.

When Jeff answered the phone he asked how it was going. Tom said, "The coach has all the players staying in the same dormitory until school starts, and Dad and Terry are still unpacking. We're waiting for the maids to finish cleaning the room that Terry's assigned to, so I thought I would call and let you guys know."

"Wow, they got maids cleaning their dorm rooms?"

"Jeff, this place is awesome!" Tom said. "If it wasn't 90 degrees in the shade every day, I'd say it's just about perfect."

Terry had met the head coach, Hayden Fry, on a trip to SMU when he was on spring break the past April. Coach Fry was impressed with Terry's scholastic and academic achievements and told him he was looking forward to having him on his football team. Before he left his office, the coach noticed Terry's blue and gray high school letter jacket and asked, "How did a school in Ohio come to pick 'Rebels' as a mascot?"

Terry smiled and said, "The town I'm from, Willoughby, decided to build two new high schools in 1960 – one on the north end and one on the south end of the city limits. Someone came up with the mascot name, Willoughby South High Rebels."

Coach Fry shook his head and said, "Now, don't tell me the school on the north end chose 'Yankees.'"

Terry chuckled and said, "No, they kept the original school's mascot, 'The Rangers.' I guess I'll have to get used to answering that question when I wear this jacket on campus."

Most of the players were checked in by Saturday afternoon. The freshman players, along with their families, were introduced to the head freshman coach, Herman Morgan. Coach Morgan and Assistant Coach Dudley Parker gave them all a tour of the football facilities at SMU.

During dinner, Bill struck up a conversation with the two coaches when he learned that they both served in the Army Air Corps in World War II, as did he. Terry and Tom watched as the men seemed to enjoy each other's war stories.

"Dad fits right in down here, doesn't he?" Tom said to his big brother.

"Yeah, but then again, where *doesn't* Dad fit in?"

Bill and Tom said their goodbyes to Terry that evening and checked into a small motel outside of Dallas. They got on the road early Sunday morning with plans to drive straight through so his dad could be back to work Monday afternoon. Big brother Terry was officially starting a whole new adventure in the Lone Star State.

The family received their first letter from him a week later. He said the practices were much more intense than those in high school. But he felt he was able to handle every drill they could throw at him.

The heat was a big factor to deal with, but he said it didn't seem any hotter than when he worked next to the asphalt trucks on the road crew. The asphalt they dumped came out at over 300 degrees Fahrenheit.

His three-page letter ended with him stating that he would give them a call when summer practices would be winding down. Unfortunately, the excitement of playing college football would prove to be short-lived for Terry.

CHAPTER 5

Denny and Jeff had just returned home from back-to-school shopping at the Great Lakes Mall with their mom when the phone rang. June asked Jeff to get it because she was in the middle of peeling potatoes for dinner.

"Oh, hi Terry!" he said excitedly. "Wow, I didn't think we'd hear from you till Sunday. How's it going?"

"Not too good Jeff, I got hurt in practice today," he said. "I just left the hospital a little while ago."

"You got hurt? Oh, my gosh! Are you okay?" Jeff said.

June looked up from the sink, quickly wiped her hands and walked over to the phone as Jeff handed it to her.

Terry was in the middle of a sentence when June put the phone to her ear and said, "I'm sorry, start over. What happened, Honey? Are you okay?"

"Well, I got hurt in practice today. I was on the kickoff team," he said. "I was one of the first guys downfield and was closing in on the receiver when this kid came up on my blind side and hit me with a block below my knee. The same one I hurt last year."

"Oh, my God," she said. Jeff tried to listen by putting his head up close to the phone, but she nudged him away.

"I thought it was broken," Terry continued. "Man did that hurt! The coaches and the trainer got me on my feet after a minute but I couldn't put any weight on it, so they helped me off the field and called an ambulance.

"The doctor said the x-rays didn't show any major damage to the bone, but he couldn't rule out a hairline fracture. The pins were still in place, but he said I overstretched or tore some tendons. He wrapped an ice pack around it and told me not to put any pressure on it for the next two weeks. He would take another look then."

"Oh, Sweetie I'm so sorry," June said. "Do you want to come home and go back after Christmas break?"

"No. School starts next Monday and they gave me some crutches. I'll manage."

"Did the doctor say you'd be able to play football?" she asked.

"He said this year is out and probably no more football. The risk of breaking it might result in me possibly losing it." She muffled a gasp, putting her hands to her mouth.

Terry lay back in his bed with his knee propped up after the call. He started to feel the effects of the pain pills and mumbled to himself, "Ah…I'm screwed, and my dreams of being an All American running back are too. I've worked so hard to get here, and now this. God, are you listening? Please send me an answer."

* * *

On Saturday, September 12, Terry was moved into his room at McIntosh Hall, and was prepared to start his first semester at SMU on Monday morning – with crutches.

His new roommate was Ed Fincher, from El Dorado, Arkansas. The two of them hit it off instantly.

Terry met with his guidance counselor who rearranged his classes to minimize travel between them. A school nurse supplied him with a backpack to help him carry his books. Together they helped make his first day in the classrooms less stressful.

During the week, Terry felt his upper body strength improving from using the crutches and carrying the extra load of books on his back. Although his knee was still tender, he managed to make it to all of his classes on time.

By the time Saturday morning arrived, he and Ed were ready to go to the freshman football game at the stadium. The varsity traveled to Florida to take on the Gators, while the freshmen played their game at home. Terry watched his teammates from the sideline, while Ed and his buddies viewed the game from the stands.

Freshman kicker Dennis Partee won the game in the last minute by kicking a 32-yard field goal and starting the freshman Ponies off with a victory of 17-14. Later in the day, they learned from ABC Sports that the varsity was not as lucky. They were trounced by Florida 24-8. Nonetheless, the 1964 college football season was underway, and all eyes were on the Southwest Conference to see if Darrell Royal's Texas Longhorns could win their fourth straight SWC championship. Coach Hayden Fry knew his Mustangs had their work cut out for them.

The following week, Terry received a "care package" in the mail from home. His mom sent a box of Ritz crackers and a small jar of peanut butter, along with a few letters from the kids, in a box stuffed with newspaper. Jeff included news clippings from *The Cleveland Press* with his letter and told Terry about The Beatles playing in Cleveland Public Hall on September 15.

On Saturday, Coach Fry and his varsity team traveled to Columbus, Ohio, to take on the Buckeyes of Ohio State in front of a sellout crowd of over 80,000. It was the fifth time the teams had met with SMU winning the first game in 1950 by a close score of 32-27, but succumbing to OSU every game thereafter.

Tom and Jeff were excited to know that Terry's school was battling one of Woody Hayes' powerhouse teams, and watched the game on ABC Sports.

It seemed a little unusual for them to be supporting an opposing team against OSU, but they cheered after SMU scored and went for the two-point conversion to put the Mustangs ahead in the first quarter 8-7. The lead was short-lived, however, and by the end of the game

Coach Fry had to walk across the field and shake Coach Hayes' hand in defeat 27-8.

A week later, Terry revisited the doctor's office. It had now been 34 days since his injury, and the doctor was impressed with the progress he had made. The bone did not seem to be fractured, and the swelling had subsided. He gave him a knee brace and told him to start putting pressure on it. It wouldn't be long before he could go without crutches.

That was the good news, Terry thought, but not participating in football anymore really brought him down. His family also felt the depression in his tone the next time they spoke with him on the phone.

Terry was not a quitter, and committed himself to think positively by praying every day and concentrating on his academic schedule.

Each class he took had a professor who instilled discipline in the students to complete their assignments in a timely and orderly fashion, and Terry loved the new challenges of his college courses, which included history, English and math. He especially liked one of his pre-requisite courses in theology entitled, *The History of the Methodist Church*, taught by Herndon Wagers, PhD. Terry found it fascinating.

The Perkins School of Theology at SMU was recognized as one of the strongest seminaries in the world with a faculty of approximately 40 outstanding scholars from several denominations and a student body from 35 states and 10 foreign countries. Terry adapted well to the biblical studies that were added to his other courses.

One evening after studies he told his roommate Ed, about a time when his parents were called to school when he was in the fourth grade: "Mom got a call from the principal requesting my folks meet with him in his office after school. They both thought it was odd that he wanted to talk with them at the end of the school year given the fact that I had been a good student as far as they knew. But Dad took off from work early and they showed up as requested.

"Mom asked if I'd done something wrong and the principal said no, but added that I wasn't being challenged enough. When Dad asked what he meant, he said that I got my class assignments done before any of the other kids, and that I appeared bored.

"He said he discussed it with my teacher and they both agreed that I should skip the fifth grade and go into sixth the following year.

"Mom talked it over with Dad on the way home and Dad didn't like the idea of all the kids in my graduating class being older than me. He convinced her that I was better off where I was, and said the teachers would just have to give me more to do in class to keep me busy."

Terry's ability to quickly complete his class assignments at SMU gave him more time to watch the football team practice, and by the first week in October, he was able to jog a slow pace around the track while doing so.

Eddie Lane, the head trainer for the team, walked across the field and approached Terry as he was passing by. "Hey Terry, how's the knee holdin' up?" he asked.

Terry stopped and said, "It's getting better, Eddie. I think I'll be able to work up to a full sprint by the end of this month."

"Yeah, well you better let me take a look at it before you push yourself too quickly. I've seen a lot of guys ruin their knees by trying to do too much too soon. Stop by the training room after practice," he said.

Later, when Eddie saw Terry in the locker room he said,

"Have a seat on the end of the table, Terry." He cupped his left palm under Terry's knee and straightened his leg out with his other hand, while gently turning his foot from side to side.

He said, "Well Terry, the tendons seem to be doing better, but they're still gonna take more time to heal. I'd say take it real easy on the joggin' for the next few weeks and make sure you ice it down every night. I think you'll be okay."

"Not well enough for football though, right?" Terry said.

Eddie shook his head and said, "No, and that is a shame, but I want you to start exercising at a gym downtown. It's a boxing gym."

"A *boxing* gym?"

"Yeah, it's a great aerobic workout and will not only strengthen your legs, but your upper body too. I think you'll like it," he said.

"It's sponsored by The Police Athletic League, the PAL they call it, and it's located in downtown Dallas. An officer by the name of Tony Minnelli runs it. Coach Fry and I have sent players to him before. He's a full-time policeman and spends his spare time training inner-city kids."

"Sounds interesting," Terry said.

"I think you're quite an athlete, Terry, and you kinda remind me of Tony in a way too. You both have big hands and plenty of power to back 'em up," Eddie said. "I'll give him a call at home tonight and tell him to keep an eye out for ya'."

"Okay, Eddie, I'll give it a shot," Terry said.

Terry and his friends didn't follow boxing because it seemed to have lost its luster by the late 1950s. Rocky Marciano retired as the only undefeated heavyweight champion in 1956, then a popular light-heavyweight champion from Cleveland, Joey Maxim, retired in 1958. The Cleveland newspapers seemed to run out of exciting fighters to grab the headlines for several years thereafter.

Floyd Patterson carried the title for a few years, but never commanded the headlines like the previous champions. Nor did his successor, Sonny Liston. Known to the public as "The Ugly Bear," he was a brute of a fighter with a personality to match.

Television still carried the Friday night fights, albeit to a dwindling crowd, and by the early '60s, professional wrestling was gaining more popularity than pro boxing. On February 25, 1964, however, a new heavyweight champion was crowned, promising to turn the boxing world on its head.

Cassius Marcellus Clay, Jr. shocked the world when he scored a technical knockout (TKO) over the current champion, Sonny Liston, in the seventh round on national TV. Every newspaper in the English-speaking world had a picture on the cover of its sports section of Clay being hoisted in the air by one of his corner men, with his mouth wide open and his arms extended in the air in an animated fashion. The news media now had a new heavyweight champion known as a true showman.

In Texas, professional and amateur boxing never lost its prevalence. The sport ranked in popularity with football and baseball, particularly in the Dallas/Fort Worth area, and Terry was about to discover a whole new world.

CHAPTER 6

The following week, Terry took a bus from the campus to the gym, carried his gym bag across the street and entered a building with a large emblem above the door in the shape of a police badge. The large golden letters on the sign read Police Athletic League.

The door opened to a small glassed-in, bullet-proof entranceway that had another thick wooden door. Terry tried turning the big brass doorknob, but it was locked. He looked through the glass windows and saw an elderly gentleman sweeping the floor of a workout room filled with dumbbells and weightlifting equipment. Terry rapped lightly on the window to get the man's attention.

The man turned and said loudly, "Ya' gotta press the buzzer!" while pointing to the door. Next to the knob was a small black buzzer, so Terry pushed it and a bell rang.

The door opened and Terry said, "I'm here to see Officer Minnelli."

The gray-haired man took the stub of a stogie out of his mouth, pointed to the end of the room and said, "He's upstairs in the gym. Go through that door and take the first door on your right."

"Thanks," Terry said, and walked through the dimly lit workout room to the door. He entered another hallway which led to the main-floor locker room. The walls were covered with fight posters, wanted posters, police announcements, and a few *Playboy* centerfolds.

When he opened the door to the gym upstairs, a strong smell of leather, sweat, and cigarette smoke hit his nostrils. He entered into a changing area filled with lockers, benches, and a couple of training tables. A wall was removed and exposed the entire warehouse-sized gym to the locker room, which helped management keep an eye on anyone entering or leaving.

Terry gazed into the gym, which was filled with a dozen young men working on speed bags, heavy bags, skipping rope, and shadow boxing in front of a mirror. In the center was a slightly elevated ring where two boys in headgear and gloves were trading punches. A middle-aged man stood with one arm draped on the top rope and a stopwatch in his other hand. He was watching the two boxers spar in the center of the ring.

"Time!" the man yelled. He turned and saw Terry and said to the boys in the ring, "Okay, you two cool off. Willey and Hernandez get laced up, you're next!"

Terry knew the man had to be Officer Minnelli and introduced himself. Tony, as he preferred to be called, was 5' 9" and weighed a solid 220 pounds. He had a tan complexion, with a dark receding hairline and five o'clock shadow decorating his face. He wore a green undershirt that covered his protruding rock-hard stomach, and large gym shorts that exposed his dark hairy legs.

He let the stopwatch dangle from his neck; extended his large meaty hand and said, "Terry? I'm Tony. How you doin'?"

"I'm fine, Tony," Terry said as he gripped his hand firmly. He briefly glanced at Tony's flat nose, which had obviously been on the receiving end of quite a few punches.

"Your coach told me you'd probably be stoppin' by tonight. Why don't you get changed and I'll show you around the gym?"

"Okay," Terry said, and before he turned, he caught the eye of one of the boxers exiting the ring. He was a dark-haired boy about Terry's age with a slender build, 6 feet tall, and wore a sweat-soaked t-shirt with a picture of the grill of a truck and a head of a bulldog. It read *Built Like a Mack Truck*. The boy gave Terry an evil stare as he made his way over to a wall with jump ropes.

Terry went to an open locker and quickly changed into his gym clothes. He wore a gray t-shirt with blue lettering that read *SMU*

Mustangs, with a blue football insignia underneath the letters. He slipped on his knee brace and laced up his Converse high-tops.

Tony looked down at Terry's knee as he walked from the changing area and said, "Eddie told me about your football injury, that's a bitch. He said they were sad to lose you."

"Yeah, I guess the only *good* thing was that I didn't break it," Terry said. "The doctor said if I had, it would have been impossible to heal right."

"Well, I got some exercises for you that will help strengthen that knee, but I want you to train at a slow pace for the first two weeks. You look in good physical shape otherwise. You ever box before?"

"Not really. My buddies in high school brought some gloves over to my house a few times and we took turns sparring in my basement, but nothing serious."

"Well, you won't be putting any gloves on for at least three solid weeks and that's only if you work hard and follow my instructions. The coaches have sent a few players over here that thought they were really tough stuff, got in the ring thinking they were gonna be the next champ. They were underprepared and over-confident. They walked outta here and never came back, and I don't like to waste my time," Tony said unapologetically.

"We got one of the best boxing gyms in Texas," he continued, "Manuel Navarro won the National Golden Gloves title in the 118 division last year, and we trained him since he was in high school."

He pointed to the dark-haired boy with the Mack Truck shirt who was skipping rope and said, "That's Dickie Wills. He won the Heavyweight Novice Division in the city Golden Gloves last year and I think he'll win the Open Division this year. "

"So how does the Golden Gloves tournament work?" Terry asked.

"Well, the Golden Gloves tournament actually got its start in my hometown, Chicago, back in the '20s and it was established to determine who the best amateur fighter was in each weight category through a tournament," Tony said.

"So it's kind of like high school wrestling, where you have teams and each kid advances in the sectional, district, and state championship tournament?" Terry asked.

"Yeah, kinda like that, only each city has to have a Golden Gloves charter to sponsor a tournament, then the kids that win go on to a state championship. Each state champion then goes on to the national Golden Gloves tournament which is held in a different city each year. They usually have the nationals around the second week in March. Next year, the kids will be goin' to Kansas City."

A strong looking teenager overheard them while he was rapidly hitting a heavy bag, stopped and said, "That's where I'll be headed, coach!"

Tony smiled and said, "You keep workin' hard Tommy, and you'll have a good shot at bein' the welterweight champ, but that bag you're hittin' can't hit back! Why don't you rest a round, then get the gloves on and show me what you got in the ring?"

"That's Tommy Lopez," he said to Terry. "I met him for the first time a couple years ago when I got a call to check out a family disturbance. The address was in a tough neighborhood on the south side of town. When I pulled my cruiser to the front of the house, I saw Tommy in the front lawn tryin' to punch his old man.

"I got out and told them both to back off, and I approached his father first. He said he wanted his kid to show him some respect. The guy had been drinkin' and the booze on his breath about knocked me over. I looked at Tommy and saw that his cheek was red and swollen; he was cryin' and told me that his old man beats on his mom every time he comes home from drinkin' at the bar. He was sick of it.

"I looked at the guy and told him I would give him a warning this time, but if I saw that he's hitting his wife and kid, I'd run him in. The old man said he was sorry and went to sleep it off. Before I left, I pulled Tommy aside and told him to stop by my gym some time.

"He came by a few days later and started workin' out. That was two years ago and he rarely misses a day. He won the Welterweight Novice Division last year and he's got a good shot at winnin' the Open this year too."

"Wow, that's great," Terry said. "I bet you see a lot of that kinda stuff, huh?"

"Are you kiddin' me? *All the time.* And not just in the poor neighborhoods. But ya' know, this is what the PAL is all about, we get kids off the streets and give 'em somethin' to do with their time; somethin' productive; somethin' they can be proud of.

"Not all of 'em hang in there, but the ones that do turn out to be pretty good boxers – and pretty good men."

Tony introduced Terry to his other trainers, who spent the rest of the hour showing him different drills to practice. Terry could already feel the excitement of learning a new sport.

A loud buzzer went off letting everybody know it was closing time. Tony clapped his hands loudly and said to the boys, "Alright, listen up! Before you guys start checkin' outta here, I want you to know that this weekend the summer Olympics start in Japan and they're gonna be televised on ABC. They'll be runnin' the Games from October 10th through the 24th. They'll be showin' the best amateur fighters in the world and I want you guys to make it part of your homework. That's all I got, so have a good night."

Over the next two weeks, Terry stuck to a rigid schedule of attending classes, going to the gym between 4:30 p.m. and 6:30 p.m. weekdays, and completing his homework assignments at night. The weekends were reserved for college football and the parties that followed.

SMU had strict rules about students drinking on campus, so most of the parties were held at someone's apartment off campus. Terry got sick after sloshing down several shots of tequila one night, and it curbed his appetite for strong alcohol. That turned out to be a good thing, because his training had intensified and alcohol interfered with his timing and reflexes.

He managed to catch a few boxing matches while the Olympics were on, even though the time difference in Tokyo made it difficult. An announcer reported that the heavyweight division of the U.S. boxing team was hindered because the number-one man, Buster Mathis, broke a bone in his hand a few days before his first match and an alternate took his place.

On Tuesday afternoon, October 20, 1964, ABC televised the semifinals in the heavyweight division. In the blue corner, representing the Soviet team was Vadim Yemelyanov, and in the red corner, representing the U.S. was the alternate – Joe Frazier. Terry watched the match in his dorm along with a few other guys.

The Russian towered over the short, stocky Frazier, picking away at his opponent with his left jab. Terry was impressed at how Frazier bobbed and weaved continuously with his hands held tightly to his cheeks and dodged most of the Russian's punches while scoring a few of his own.

In the middle of the second round, Frazier unleashed a vicious left hook to the Russian's jaw and dropped him on his butt. The referee quickly stuck his arm into Frazier's chest and ordered him to a neutral corner, then started his count while the Russian grabbed hold of the middle rope and pulled himself up to his feet.

As Terry watched the fight with friends, one of them yelled, "Wow! That colored boy sure can punch!"

The ref ordered the boxers back to the center of the ring and said, "Box!"

Frazier ran from his corner and smothered Yemelyanov with six or seven unanswered punches. The ref pulled the U.S. boxer off his opponent and waved the fight over.

Frazier was met in the ring by his coaches, proudly hugging him and raising his hand in victory.

Terry and his friends were on their feet applauding and slapping each other's hands in favor of the stunning U.S. upset. Suddenly, he looked at the clock on the wall and said, "Oh shit, I gotta get to my English class!" He grabbed his books and took off running out the door. He ended up getting reprimanded by his prof for being 15 minutes late, but it was worth it.

At the gym the next day, Tony and the rest of the boys were still talking about the fight. He told everyone to watch the final gold medal match when Frazier would be matched against a German.

Terry watched it with his buddies in the dorm again, and saw Joe Frazier, from Beaufort, South Carolina, win the only gold medal for the U.S. boxing team by defeating Hans Huber with a major decision.

The following Monday, Terry could hardly wait to get to the gym. He had worked hard the past two weeks on basic boxing techniques, and was ready to test his skills in the ring. He desperately wanted to start sparring, just to see what it was like.

After working up a good sweat he said to one of the coaches, "Hey Al, where's Tony today?"

Al Stewart was a retired police officer in his early 60s. He had limited experience with boxing, but was an expert in martial arts. He held a third degree black-belt in Karate and trained other Dallas policemen in the art of self-defense. He liked helping Tony with the boys in the gym and specialized in helping them develop maximum power in their punches.

Al said, "He had a guy coming over to work on his roof after his shift today, I guess he's still there."

"Well, how 'bout I get the gear on and try a few rounds sparring with one of the guys?" Terry asked.

"That's Tony's call, you know that, Terry."

"Come on Al, I'm in good shape, and I'm getting tired of just hitting the heavy bag. I gotta get in the ring sometime. Might as well be now," Terry said.

"I'll go a few rounds with him," said a stocky red-haired teenager with a sheepish grin on his face.

"Well, I suppose it wouldn't hurt you to go a few rounds with Randy here, he's a novice too. You've got, what is it, four fights under your belt so far, Randy?" Al said.

"Yes, sir. I'm three and one, but Tony said he's gonna get me a rematch at the next show with that kid I lost to over the summer. I lost to him on a split decision, but I thought I won, and so did Tony," Randy said.

"Okay, you guys, get your gloves and headgear on, and make sure you're wearing cup protectors. You'll go in after Tommy and Hector are through."

Randy Tyler was a senior in high school and was training hard for the Dallas Golden Gloves High School Heavyweight Division. He met Tony his junior year when he was called into the principal's office for fighting in school. Tony convinced Randy to use his anger at the boxing gym rather than risk being expelled, and Randy took his advice.

Terry had recently read an article in *The Ring* magazine that said the art of boxing can teach every young man what he is truly made of, both physically and mentally. It stated that once one masters the art of "hitting and not getting hit in return" he gains the respect of others, and more importantly, gains respect of himself. Perhaps more so than any other sport.

One thing Terry didn't realize until reading the article is that even in amateur boxing, a person could actually die in the ring. This is the single most important distinction from any other amateur sport.

When Terry stepped through the ropes and into the boxing ring for the first time his heart started pounding faster as he anticipated testing the skills he had worked so hard to perfect. Having the headgear on for the first time felt awkward, forcing him to repeatedly push it up in order to see clearly.

"Here, get some Vaseline on your face," Al said as Terry turned to him.

Al stood in the center of the ring and said, "Okay, you both got your mouthpieces in? Then touch gloves...time!"

He clicked his stopwatch and backed away to let the boys start their sparring session.

Randy showed his skill from sparring with different heavyweights for the past six months, but he was leery of the new football player from SMU. He started moving slowly to his left and threw the first punch with his left jab and tagged Terry on the top of his headgear.

"Keep your hands *up*, Terry. We're in no hurry now, Randy, we're only going two three-minute rounds to get the feel of the ring," Al said.

Terry flicked his left jab out while Randy darted his head aside, making Terry miss. Randy countered with a double jab tagging Terry solidly on the nose with the second punch.

What the – Terry mumbled to himself.

"Keep that right hand *up* Terry," Al said. "Keep moving to your left; don't stand in one place too long."

Randy took advantage of several openings and landed some punches on Terry's head and stomach. He threw a left-right-left combination to his head connecting with all three punches, then dropped two double left hooks to his mid-section.

Al stepped between them and had Randy back off. He could see the frustration developing on Terry's face. "Keep working the jab, Terry. When he comes in on you like that, you have to stick your left jab in his face to throw him off," he said.

Terry's heart was pumping harder and adrenaline was heating up his veins. He bit down on his mouthpiece and decided to throw a left-right combination of his own, but Randy easily moved back from his jab and caught the right in his glove. Both fighters were working up a sweat and it was only one minute into the round.

"Time!" yelled Al as he clicked his stopwatch and approached Terry. "When you throw that left-right combination, you always make it a left-right-*left*, otherwise you drop your left hand after throwing your right and leave your head open. Got it?"

Terry nodded, and pushed his headgear up so he could see. "Time," Al said and started the stopwatch again. Both Terry and Randy moved in and out while circling to their left for the rest of the round. Randy scored on most of the punches he threw while Terry continued to miss his target.

After three minutes elapsed, Al clicked his stopwatch and yelled, "Time!"

"Man, this is harder than it looks," Terry said to Al as he came back to his corner breathing heavily.

Al washed the mouthpiece with water in a bucket and said, "It's way different when you actually get in the ring with a moving target that knows what he's doin', isn't it? I just want you to concentrate on keeping your hands at eye level and arms close to your body. Keep shuffling to your left. You never want to give a man a standing target. Okay?"

"Time," he said and both fighters came to the center of the ring to start the second round.

Randy started to smile as he saw the frustration on Terry's face. He decided to step up the pace a little by throwing some quick jabs to the top of Terry's head, lightly touching his headgear, but enough to throw his rhythm off. Randy was in control of this college boy and he was enjoying it.

The gym had no air conditioning and the ceiling fans did very little to keep the Texas air circulating. The sweat pouring from Terry's body added to the frustration he felt with every punch he took. His blood began to boil and he said to himself, *That's enough of this shit!*

He threw a double jab to Randy's head and anticipated he would move to his left. Before Randy could counter, Terry followed with a solid right hand to Randy's nose. POW! Randy's eyes widened and the smile disappeared from his face. He stepped back slightly while Terry continued to move in with a left hook and three body shots, all throwing Randy off balance.

Randy clinched Terry's arms and swung him around into the corner of the ring, then started a flurry of punches in retaliation. Terry kept his hands up and arms tucked tight to deflect most of Randy's punches.

"Move outta that corner, Terry!" Al yelled.

Terry tried shuffling to his left, then to his right, but Randy was determined to pin him in and score punches. In desperation, Terry dipped below Randy's waistline and up his left side landing a right hook to Randy's left ear. Then he shuffled out into the center of the ring.

"Good Terry! Way to work your way outta there," Al said.

The fighters returned to the center of the ring and were breathing heavily. They exchanged jabs while moving to the left but both were running out of gas.

"Time!" Al yelled. "Good workout, both of you. Okay, take your gear off and I want 10 minutes of skipping rope. Finish with a hundred sit-ups."

As Terry removed his gear he mumbled under his breath, "What the hell have I gotten myself into?"

CHAPTER 7

The fall semester at SMU moved along smoothly for Terry. He wrote in a letter to the family that he couldn't believe it was already Thanksgiving weekend. He told them that he would be staying on campus to watch the final football game.

Terry never mentioned to the family that he was training at a boxing gym because he didn't want to worry his mother. Tony was impressed with his improvement in sparring and Al was impressed with the power in his punches. They told him over the holiday weekend that he was ready for his first amateur fight.

They had lined up a boxing card at a local high school the weekend before school let out for the Christmas break and wanted to match him up with a novice light-heavyweight from Fort Worth. Terry told them that he was just in it for the workout and didn't really take it seriously enough to enter a ring in front of a live audience. Even his buddies at school didn't know about it. Two nights later, however, Terry had a change of mind.

It was a Tuesday night. Terry had finished his homework assignments and headed over to his football buddy's apartment to watch a movie and drink a few beers. Jim met him at the door with a Coors in his hand and said in a Texas drawl, "Hey Tirri. How you doin', buddy? Come on in."

Jim played second string guard for the Mustangs and shared a two-bedroom apartment with Larry who played defensive back. The two of them decided to celebrate the end of the season and invited

Terry to their place for a little R & R before study time intensified for finals, just two weeks away.

"Here are the pretzels and chips you told me to bring," Terry said while tossing the bags on to the coffee table.

Larry removed his feet from the table when the bags landed and said, "And here's a nice cool one for you in return," while tossing Terry a beer from the cooler.

Terry pulled the ring top off his beer and sat down on the big cushioned sofa. "So, what's on the tube tonight?" he asked.

Jim pulled up a big padded chair with a partly chewed seat cushion and said, "It's an Elvis movie, *Kid Galahad*. Sorry, the dog got hungry," as he pointed to the hole in the cushion.

"Oh, I haven't seen that movie," Terry said.

"Me neither," Larry added.

"I saw it a few years ago at the drive-in," Jim said, "it's pretty cool. Elvis plays a boxer and starts out gettin' his ass kicked, but ends up knockin' guys out. It's a good movie so I won't say any more."

Terry took a swig of beer, chuckled and said, "No shit?"

The movie starred Gig Young, Charles Bronson, and Elvis Presley as the main character. Elvis gets the nickname, Kid Galahad, after coming from behind in his first pro fight and knocking his opponent out with a wicked right cross to the chin. Charles Bronson, a corner man, gives Elvis the name from a book he read, about a good-looking prince who proves to be a fierce fighter for his king.

The boys were enjoying the movie while munching on pretzels and guzzling down beers, and talked during the commercials about SMU's 1-9 season. They watched as Elvis' character got progressively better in the ring and the movie intensified when a couple of Mafia thugs broke Charles Bronson's hands.

Gig Young, who played the owner of the boxing training camp, tried to help his corner man, but he was outnumbered by the thugs. Then Elvis came down from the upstairs bedroom to save his friends.

"Yeah, get 'em Galahad!" Jim yelled.

"Look at him take those two guys on," said Larry. "Let's see what y'all can do when you go up against a real boxer you sons a bitches!"

Terry cheered right along with them but held back on making any comments about his training. He didn't want any of his classmates, other than his roommate Ed, to know about it until he could prove himself.

He felt the rush of adrenaline start to reduce the buzz he was getting from the beer and asked Larry for one more.

"Nah, I just downed the last one," Larry said. "Why don't we pool our money and I'll run down to the carry-out and get us a couple more six-packs?"

"Ah, that's okay," Terry said, "The movie's about over. I'll wait till the end and then call it a night."

The boys watched the climax of the movie, when Elvis came from behind and won the big pro fight, and of course, also won over the pretty girl. Terry thanked them both and called it a night.

Walking back to his dorm, he looked up at the clear star-filled Texas sky and started wondering if people would cheer for him in the ring like they did for Kid Galahad. It was quite a vision, one he never thought about before. He had been cheered on in football and baseball, but this was something else all together. *Terry Daniels – Kid Galahad?*

He came upon a stop sign on the corner of Mockingbird Lane and Bishop and did a little shadow boxing with it. He started feeling the adrenaline fill his veins again and he paused to gaze up at the stars. He felt disappointed every time he thought about his football career coming to a screeching halt, and about having to gimp around campus on crutches for weeks.

Stepping into a boxing ring is something none of his relatives or close friends ever dreamed of doing. Could this be a new journey for him? Could he make his family proud of "the first one to go to college?"

He got back to his room and told his roommate, "I think I'll tell Tony to count me in on that boxing match."

CHAPTER 8

The amateur boxing show was being held at the gymnasium of Woodrow Wilson High School in Dallas the Saturday before finals at SMU. The card was eight matches: six in the High School Division; one in the Novice Division; and one in the Open Division. Terry was the novice fight and was matched with a boy from Fort Worth named Berry Walters in the 175 pound Light-heavyweight Division.

In addition to Terry, Tony and Al had three more boys from the PAL on the card: Randy Tyler was re-matched with another senior in the High School Heavyweight Division; Tommy Lopez in the Open Welterweight division, and Dickie Wills in the Open Heavyweight Division.

The show was going to be one of the last boxing cards in the Dallas area before the Golden Gloves tournament started in the third week in January.

Terry rode the city bus over to the match along with Tony, Al, and the rest of the boys, and arrived at the school an hour before the show started. Once he told his friends about the show, word spread quickly. He wondered how many would show.

He expected his roommate Ed and a couple of other guys from the dorm, and certainly Jim and Larry would show up to see Kid Galahad, but he wasn't sure about anyone else.

The bus dropped the team off at the front of the school and Tony led them down the sidewalk to a back entrance. They each carried a gym bag and walked up to a door where a policeman was standing along with another gentleman wearing a short-sleeved white shirt and black tie. The cop nodded hello to Tony and unlocked the door while the other gentleman extinguished a cigarette he was smoking and shook hands with Tony.

"We sold a lotta tickets and it looks like we're gonna have a full house tonight, Tony," the gentleman said. "Good luck to you fellas."

Terry walked through the door and up a set of steps with the rest of the PAL team. The musty smell of the hallway lockers reminded him of his junior high school; in fact, the design of the school looked similar.

They walked down a hallway past the steel double doors that led to the back of the gymnasium. Two small wired windows allowed the boys to glance at the inside of the gym. In it, they saw the boxing ring set up on the basketball court with sets of chairs 20 rows deep all around it. People were starting to straggle in through the front entrance, taking their seats.

Tony continued to lead the team into the locker room, where he was greeted by other coaches and their boys. He guided them to a row of lockers where they all could stay together as a team.

Terry noticed a difference between amateur boxing and wrestling right away. In amateur wrestling, your opponent and his team met and dressed in different locker rooms, but in boxing all the participants got dressed in the same locker room. The coaches were all nonchalant with each other, but the boys made very little eye contact with anyone they didn't already know.

This made it uncomfortable for any amateur boxer, especially when it was his first bout. The boxers had to quickly size up the boy *they thought* was in their weight class and determine if he was their opponent. If they did peg the right one: Was he taller or shorter? More muscular? Did he look like a genuine tough guy or a pushover?

"There's no sense in us changing and getting wrapped up yet," Dickie said to Terry as he put his gym bag down next to his.

"They'll take a 30-minute intermission before they put you and me up last. They always leave the heavyweights 'til last so they can keep the crowd here and milk 'em for as much as they can get from the concession stand."

Dickie Wills never talked much with Terry at the PAL gym, so it caught him off guard when he offered some advice. Terry was eager for any advice he could get. Dickie was two years older than Terry; was 6' 0" and weighed 185 pounds. Not a true heavyweight, but then again, neither was Terry. He didn't resemble a true boxer either. He combed his slick black hair like Elvis and wore dark-rimmed "Buddy Holly" glasses. He smoked cigarettes and always had a pack of Marlboros rolled up in one of his short-sleeved white t-shirts.

If an opponent didn't know Dickie and tried sizing him up before the fight, he most likely would think he was just an average Texas cowboy. But that always worked in Dickie's favor. He was a well-conditioned boxer and used his fists like they were shot out of a cannon. The element of surprise always worked in his favor.

Dickie grew up in Pampa, Texas, and moved to the Dallas area when he was 18. Those who knew him said he had at least 100 fights before he ever stepped into a ring. He, like many boys in the PAL, was headed down the wrong path until Tony came along. Tony got him into the gym and found him a job in construction, allowing Dickie to make a good living and stay out of trouble.

"C'mon, let's take a walk and check this place out," he said to Terry.

Tony told them they had to weigh in for the referee before they wandered off. He told them to make sure they were back in the locker room to get dressed and wrapped before the start of the third fight.

They walked down the hall to the concession stand and ordered a couple of Cokes. Terry offered to buy, but Dickie said, "That's okay college boy, I got this one. Besides, aren't you on a fixed budget goin' to that expensive school a yours?"

Terry offered some details about SMU, but was careful not to indulge in anything related to the family businesses. He didn't know Dickie that well yet and chose to keep it that way.

They sipped their Cokes out back and continued their idle chat, mostly about boxing then re-entered the gym and took seats high in the bleachers away from the crowd.

By 7 p.m. the crowd had grown to several hundred and Terry noticed a couple of blue and red SMU letter jackets coming through the door. It was Jim and Larry followed by several other football players. A few minutes later he saw his roommate, Ed Fincher, and three other guys from his dormitory. The adrenaline started heating up his veins and he could feel his heart start to pound harder.

He thought about approaching his friends, but decided to stay put and concentrate on how he was going to handle himself in the ring. It helped that Dickie was sitting next to him. He felt more at ease with someone close to his age that he could talk to about getting into the ring for a live fight for the first time.

The temperature in the school gym started to rise with all the bodies that were filling the stands, and the air was getting thick with the smell of cigarette smoke and popcorn wafting in from the hallways. The back rows of lights started to go out on each side of the gym, leaving only the lights above the ring on.

The gentleman that he saw earlier with the white shirt and tie climbed into the ring while one of the judges rang the bell several times. It was showtime!

The announcer was handed a microphone and started to tap it for a test when the P.A. system kicked in and let out a loud squeal. He waited for the feedback to adjust and said, "Welcome everybody! Welcome to tonight's amateur boxing show!"

"I'm Bobby White, and y'all probably recognize me from my car commercials on TV. I'm one of the proud sponsors of tonight's show, and the only commercial I'm gonna give is to invite ya'll down to my dealership, and if you tell me that you were here for the boxing show, I'll knock an extra $50 off my final deal for a car – new or used!"

The crowd laughed and applauded while Bobby smiled and bowed his head and said, "Well, you're gonna see some fine amateur boxers here tonight, so without further adieu I'm gonna turn it over to our main announcer, Mr. Tad Akins, and he's gonna announce our first bout. Thank you."

Bobby exited the ring while Tad announced the first of six high school-division bouts. "This high school division is excitin', man," Dickie said to Terry. "Each kid has his family and friends from school in the crowd to cheer 'em on and sometimes the fightin' carries into the crowd. I've seen a couple times where the dads got into it big-time!"

Terry smiled, but chose not to ask Dickie if his parents ever watched him box. He got the feeling that Dickie's home life wasn't all that great. He decided he'd leave it up to him to volunteer that information.

While sitting back, Terry noticed that people were still coming in and the bleachers were filling up like it was the basketball playoffs. He said to Dickie, "Man, these Texans love this stuff!"

Dickie smiled and said, "We better head on back to the locker room and get ready."

Terry heard his name called out from the crowd as he was halfway down the bleachers. One of the boys was wearing a white jacket, waving his hands in a crisscross motion to get his attention. Terry saw him with the rest of the SMU crowd and gave them a big smile and thumbs up sign.

Tony was finishing wrapping Randy's hands, and told Terry and Dickie to get their trunks on. They were next to get wrapped. Terry was given the blue and gold trunks the PAL team wore and tried them on for the first time. They were a little snug but he figured they would do.

"Did you see that dark-haired kid with the acne on his face?" Dickie asked Terry. "That's your boy from Fort Worth. My guy's from

Greenville, I fought him last year for the novice championship and this will be a tune-up for us both for the Golden Gloves next month."

"I figured that was him. Do you know anything about him?" Terry asked.

"Not really. I think Tony said he only had one fight so far, but I wouldn't worry about it. He never puts his boys in the ring if he doesn't think they're evenly matched."

Terry felt a little better, but started feeling butterflies stirring in his stomach. It reminded him of how he felt before each high school football game under the lights. He knew the nerves were normal and would subside once he got the first hit in, so that's what he concentrated on. He, Dickie and Randy jogged up the stairs to the second floor to start warming up away from the crowd.

For Terry, amateur boxing brought with it another unknown: How to mentally prepare to enter a ring and go toe-to-toe with someone you've never met and know nothing about. In any other sport he participated in, he knew a little about his opponent through personal observations, coaches or teammates.

In amateur boxing, however, the only thing he knew for sure was the kind of shape *he* was in and how much confidence he had in himself. Once the bell rang, he was on his own.

Within minutes, Tony came trotting up the stairs and said, "Okay, how you guys doin'?" The boys each nodded and Tony continued, "Boy, Tommy was takin' it on the chin from his guy the first round and part of the second, but he started settlin' down and tore into him like a Texas tornado! He got him in the corner the end of the third round and totally commanded the fight. He won a unanimous decision!"

Randy said, "All right! That's one down and three to go for the PAL!"

Terry smiled while doing a few more squat thrusts on the floor and Dickie said, "Hey man, we didn't come here to lose. Let's do it!"

Tony said, "Okay, we have about 15 more minutes before the crowd starts comin' back, so I want you guys to keep workin' up your sweat for the next five minutes; then be at the table to get your gloves on. You'll be seated in line for your bouts. I'll see ya' in five."

As Terry watched the next fight, he realized he had to get used to sitting next to his opponent before being called into the ring for his match. He thought, *"Jeez, you spend about an hour psyching yourself up to get in a ring and slug it out with someone you've never met, only to have him sit next to you while you watch the match before yours. Then you both climb into the ring together. It was a little uncomfortable to say the least. What do you say to your opponent? 'Good luck!' or 'Hey, I hope you don't hold it against me when I knock your ass outta the ring!' It got the heart pounding for sure."*

"Okay Terry, you're up," said Tony.

With a towel around his neck, Terry followed Tony up the steps to the blue corner of the ring while Berry walked in the opposite direction with his corner man entering the red corner.

Terry looked down at the crowd on the floor and then made a quick panoramic view of the stands. He tried not to focus on any one person.

"Take it to him, Daniels!" he heard someone yell, followed by hoops and hollers. He knew it was his buddies from school.

Tad stood in the center of the ring and announced, "All right folks, we're gonna move along in the Light-heavyweight Novice Division where the boys will be goin' two-minute rounds." The crowd applauded and showed they were ready for some serious leather to be thrown.

While reading from a card in his hand, Tad continued, "In the red corner, from the Buckner Gym in Fort Worth, with a record of 3-0, is Berry Walters." He pointed to Berry as he acknowledged the applause from the crowd.

Tad looked down at his card again and said, "In the blue corner, representing the Police Athletic League, and currently enrolled as a student at SMU is Terry Daniels!"

His friends stood up and let out a unified cheer igniting the rest of the crowd to applaud even louder while Tad shouted into the microphone, "This is the first boxing match for this young man!"

Terry could feel the sweat from his hands soaking the interior of his gloves. He raised his hand in acknowledgement of the crowd and felt the adrenaline pumping through his veins. A combination of fear and pride took over. He took a deep breath and tried to calm himself.

Tony knew his fighter would be tense, and turned Terry around to face him while he put his mouthpiece in.

"Okay, Terry, this is just like you worked in the gym. Get your left jab off first and score with it, and then you keep shuffling to your left," he said while smearing Vaseline on the top of Terry's forehead and cheek bones.

"Pick your shots and look for an opening to throw that big right hand of yours."

The referee went to the center of the ring and said, "Seconds down…boxers touch gloves…and box!"

Terry felt extremely nervous, but touched gloves and got the first punch off just like he had practiced. It grazed Berry's forehead and he countered with a left of his own, but Terry caught it with his right hand and shuffled to his left. The crowd from school cheered loudly from the bleachers.

Terry felt himself moving quicker than he ever did in the gym and was bobbing his head, careful not to make a standing target. He doubled up his jabs and looked to throw a combination, but Berry was doing the same, and threw a left-right-left of his own, landing the last punch on Terry's right ear.

Terry heard a loud "Bang!" in his ear when the punch hit him, but kept his hands up and backed off. The crowd was getting into the fight and started turning up the noise level with every punch the boxers threw.

Tony was yelling for Terry to take his time and work the jab, but Terry started heating up, and the crowd started working on his psyche. He felt the anger and determination he got on the football field when fighting off a blocker. He committed to making a solid hit, working on strategy.

Berry was busy popping his left jab to throw Terry off-balance, but Terry quickly picked up the rhythm and threw a thunderous left-right combination that caught Berry right on his cheekbone. The crowd gave out a big, "Oooo!" when the punch landed and followed with yells and clapping as the referee stepped between the boys. He ordered Terry to a neutral corner, and started a standing eight-count on Berry.

Terry looked wild-eyed as he stood in his corner while Tony and Al were urging him to keep taking the fight to his opponent.

The ref stopped at the count of eight, looked at Berry and said, "Can you continue, son?"

Berry nodded. The ref motioned the boys back to the center of the ring and said, "Box!"

Terry came out of his corner preparing to throw a left-right-combination, but Berry stuck him on the jaw with a stiff left jab. Both fighters mixed it up until the bell rang ending the first round.

Terry went back to his corner breathing heavily. Tony took his mouthpiece out and passed it to Al, who rinsed it off over a bucket.

"Alright, Terry, take a deep breath, you're doin' fine. I want you to concentrate on the basics. He hit you with a couple good stiff left jabs, and if it wasn't for that solid punch you hit him with early, I think he'd be ahead on points. So, keep your guard up and don't be in such a hurry to hit him – pick your shots!"

The ref said, "Seconds down," and motioned for the bell to sound Round Two.

The SMU boys were chanting and cheering Terry on while he met his opponent at the center of the ring. *"Stick and move, stick and move,"* Terry kept saying to himself.

The fighters were scoring punches on one another and the crowd loved every minute of it. Berry snuck in a right uppercut that jarred Terry's head up, but Terry countered with a left-right-left combination that buckled Berry's knees. Both were showing signs of fatigue when the round ended. Terry was sucking in as much oxygen as he could from the now smoke-filled gymnasium.

"I can't believe how winded I am! I trained hard for this," he said.

Tony gave him further instructions, smeared a little more Vaseline on his face, and wiped his chest off before tapping him on the back and sending him back into battle.

The ref signaled for the round to start and Tad shouted into the mic, "Third and final round, folks!"

Cheers came from the crowd as the boxers exchanged jabs and continued where they left off a minute ago. Berry threw a double jab and followed with a right hand, but Terry got underneath it just in time and countered with solid shots to his opponent's stomach and ribs. Both boxers were giving it their all in the last minute.

"Take it to him, Kid!" came one of the yells from the SMU group.

Terry heard Tony's voice above it all, "Ten seconds!"

He mustered up the last drops of gas in his tank and kept stabbing left jabs, followed by right hooks to Berry's head. Most of the punches missed, but the crowd was cheering louder than it had all evening.

The bell rang and the referee separated the boys. "That's it boys, good match! Go back to your corners," he said.

Terry touched gloves lightly with his opponent and said, "Good match, man."

Tony wiped Terry's face with a towel and said, "That was a great effort by you at the end, Daniels. It may have won you the match."

The ref gathered up the judges' cards and handed them to Tad, then called the boxers to the center of the ring.

"Ladies and gentlemen...The winner of his first boxing match – in the blue corner, Terry Daniels of the Dallas PAL and SMU Mustangs!"

Terry had his hand raised in victory and was thrilled just to survive the experience in front of a packed house. He could hear his buddies above the crowd yell, "Yeah, Kid Galahad! It's Kid Galahad!"

A few of his friends came down from the bleachers and were smiling and patting him on the back while he had his gloves removed by one of the handlers at the gloving table.

Before he left, a guy tapped Terry on the back and said, "Here son, this is yours. You earned it tonight." He held out a gold-colored medal on a blue and red cloth necklace and draped it over Terry's head. "The other corner gets the silver. Congratulations to you both," he said.

Terry said, "Thank you," but quickly turned to go back to the locker room to get a shirt so he could join his buddies and root for Dickie. He got to his gym bag and pulled out an SMU sweatshirt, but before he slid it over his head, he took a better look at the medal that swung from his chest. It resembled an Olympic medal with the shape of a boxer on it.

Terry looked at himself in a full-length mirror and smiled.

The locker room doors opened and in walked Berry and his coaches. Terry immediately pulled his sweatshirt down over his head, gave a little nod to them, and made his way back to the bleachers.

Dickie was one minute into the first round of his fight and the crowd was hungry. He was not about to disappoint them. He took the fight to his opponent and did not back up the entire first round.

Terry realized that Dickie was a favorite with the amateur boxing crowd of Dallas, and watched as he carefully picked apart his opponent over all three rounds and won a unanimous decision at the end. Tad Akins boomed over the speakers, "How about that for a night of amateur boxing folks? Let's give 'em a big ol' round of applause!"

Jim slapped Terry on the back and said, "Man, this is the first time I've ever attended an amateur boxing match, and Daniels, if you keep doin' what we've seen tonight, you're gonna have one heck of a fan club!"

On Sunday evening, Terry called his family at home to give them the news. Jeff answered the kitchen phone, and once he realized who it was, he covered the speaker and said, "Hey, guys, its Terry! Denny, turn down the TV, I can barely hear him!"

Denny turned down the volume on their black-and-white set playing the theme song of Davy Crockett on *The Wonderful World of Disney*. Then he took his place in line to talk with his big brother.

"What was that again? You had a *boxing match* with some guy?" Jeff said.

Bill and June were at the kitchen table reading the Sunday edition of *The Cleveland Press*, and they lifted their heads in unison when they heard it was Terry.

June made her way over to Jeff, holding her hand out to receive the phone. By now, they all knew the drill: Mom, Dad, followed by Tom or Jeff, then Denny, and Debbie last.

The longest time allotted was 20 minutes, so each one knew to get in as much as they could in three minutes. Bill was not a big fan of Ohio Bell's long distance charges.

In June's conversation the kids heard her say, "Boxing? Oh, Honey, isn't that a bit dangerous?" It came as a surprise to all of them because they knew Terry was training hard, but they were surprised to learn he was in an actual boxing match.

When it was Bill's turn to talk he didn't seem as interested in Terry's well-being as much as him keeping his grades up. "I didn't send you down there to get into a boxing ring," he said in a stern voice. "You could have done that right here in Cleveland and saved me a helluva lot of money! Your studies should be your main concern, not getting your head knocked around."

Terry's smile disappeared when he heard the reaction from his dad and said, "Jeez Dad, it's not much different than if I was in a wrestling match. It's a heck of a workout on a Saturday night too! Don't worry about my grades – I've got them covered."

He hung up the phone after listening to his little sister say, "I miss you Ter. I can't wait to see you when you come home for Christmas!"

As he walked down the hall to his room, he could only imagine the conversations they had about him at home for the rest of the evening – especially his Dad.

He later shared his conversation with Ed and said, "I bet Dad will come around when I make the Dean's List this semester. I may not be able to play football, but I'm gonna make a name for myself down here in the beautiful Lone Star State!"

CHAPTER 9

Two weeks later, on Saturday evening, Tom and Jeff rode with their dad to pick up Terry at Cleveland Hopkins Airport. His flight home for Christmas break was originally due in around 1 p.m. in the afternoon, but there was a blizzard and all the flights were delayed.

The state plows kept the freeway cleared, but traffic was moving at a slow 40 miles per hour. Bill had put chains on the back tires of the station wagon to give them traction in the snow, but they could hear the left tire chain nick the fender with a small but constant "click-click-click." Tom was in the front seat and turned up the radio to help drown out the clicking, and *I Feel Fine* by The Beatles played.

"Is that all WHK plays anymore - Beatle songs?" Bill asked.

Tom said, "Well, let's see what else is on," and proceeded to punch the buttons on the radio. Three out of the six buttons for stations had been programmed for rock 'n' roll, courtesy of Tom, and his dad got a quick medley of current stars of the popular 45 rpm records in the stores: The Supremes, The Four Seasons, and The Beatles.

"Here, look out," Bill said disgustedly, reaching and turning the dial slowly until he found what he was looking for – good old-fashioned Cleveland polka music.

Tom and Jeff didn't protest. They sat back and looked at the mountains of snow that had been piled up along the sides of the road while Frankie Yankovic and his band played one of their hits.

The traffic was slow but constantly moving and they pulled into the airport parking lot around 8:15 p.m. The ride took only 20 minutes longer than it usually did. The lot had only been plowed once, and a fresh layer of snow made the walk to the terminal sloppy, especially for Tom and Jeff since they were only wearing tennis shoes.

Bill had his boots on and said, "Don't you guys know enough to wear your boots in the winter?"

"The parking lot is usually all cleaned off Dad, but we do have our high-tops on," Jeff said.

Bill frowned and shook his head as they proceeded to the main doors of the terminal. The place was packed with people coming and going, and the electronic board listing the flight arrivals was loaded with a jumble of numbers and letters.

"What flight was he coming in on again?" Bill asked Tom.

"American, Flight 648, but I'm not sure if it's already arrived or not," Tom said.

Bill went up to an attendant and asked him for help. The attendant looked at the board and picked up a phone. After a minute he hung-up the phone and told Bill that the flight had been delayed, but was due in 20 minutes.

About a half-hour later, Bill said, "I bet that's Terry's plane that just landed. Let's see if it taxies up to our gate."

The nose of the plane slowly made its way to their gate and the crew pushed the exit stairs to open the door. The glare of the airport lights shining off the snow made it difficult to see the faces of the passengers as they disembarked, but Terry told them to look for his South High letter jacket.

Jeff pointed and said, "There he is!"

The passengers came into the terminal and up the stairs to the gate where the boys were waiting. They watched as the people walked through the door and were greeted by someone who hugged and kissed them. This was the first time Terry had ever been away from home this long and they were all looking forward to seeing his smiling face again.

He was carrying his gym bag and looking into the crowd. Jeff yelled, "Hey Terry!" and ran to greet him.

Terry flashed his dimpled smile and said, "Hey, Jeff! How are you, buddy?"

They were surrounded by Tom and Bill. "Look at that tan you got," Bill said as they made their way towards the baggage claim. "That weather still nice in Texas?"

"Yes, but not having any snow around Christmas got me a little homesick, believe it or not," Terry said.

They laughed and carried on the conversations all the way home. As they pulled into their driveway Jeff could see little Debbie's face steaming up the front-picture window. They found out she had been peering out the window for over an hour in anticipation of her big brother's arrival.

He saw her head quickly disappear when she saw them, and a moment later she opened the front door with June and Denny.

Bill went in first carrying the suitcase, followed by Terry, who was quickly mobbed by his mom and the rest of the family. The temperature outside was about 20 degrees Fahrenheit and they could feel a wave of heat hit them as they went into the house. Bill had built a fire in the fireplace before they left and they literally had a warm welcome home for big brother.

By the time they were settled in, it was 10:30 p.m., too early to go to bed. Tom, Denny and Jeff begged Terry to play a game of cards and June said, "OK, but only if you go to bed by one. We have to get up for second service tomorrow morning."

Terry agreed and sat down at the dining room table while Tom got a deck of cards. They wanted to play their favorite game called, *I Doubt You.* It was a simple game that Terry taught them years ago when camping, and required each player to take turns getting rid of their cards face down as they were called.

Little Deb sat on Terry's lap and every now and then she would laugh, giving away Terry's chance to lie about the card he laid down. The rest of the boys would shout, "I doubt you!" and he'd bear hug Deb telling her not to give his cards away. They laughed because Terry was good at keeping a straight face, and it was always a challenge to doubt him.

The evening wore down and Terry won the last game. He was able to convince Debbie to help sucker them into doubting him and have *them* pick up a pile of cards. Bill and June were staying occupied in the living room finishing the Sunday newspaper. They smiled at each other every time they heard the kids laugh in the other room. It was fun to have their oldest home again.

* * *

Getting dressed for church on Sunday was always a chore for the Daniels boys, and being able to attend the second service helped. Terry got tired of tying Jeff and Denny's ties every Sunday, so the Christmas before he had given each of them clip-on ties. It helped to get them ready on time. It also silenced their dad's station wagon horn that would blast from the driveway to remind them they were late.

Terry sat with his mom and dad in the congregation, while the rest of his siblings went to their Sunday school classrooms and met friends from school. The Sunday school classes, church pews, and parking lot were always filled to capacity, and this always brought a smile to the minister's face.

When Jeff's class was dismissed, he walked down the hallway to meet the rest of his family. But when he approached the sanctuary, he noticed something that would soon become a regular scene: A line had formed to shake hands with the minister, and then a second line formed to shake hands with Terry.

Jeff watched his brother, not fully understanding what was going on. This was the first time people were drawn to Terry in an inexplicable way. He was wearing a white shirt and tie that accentuated his Texas tan, and his brown hair had grown out, giving him a movie-star appearance. The folks wanted to hear the stories about the boy from Willoughby who had his college football career cut short, then scored a victory in his first boxing match in Dallas, Texas.

As 10-year-old Jeff wormed his way through the crowd and nuzzled up to his side, Terry put his arm around him and continued the conversations – unlike other big brothers that would brush off their little brothers while acting cool and talking to grownups.

Whenever the family would go to the second service, the usual routine was to have Sunday brunch at June's sister's house, across town. The kids loved the smell of fresh-brewed coffee and cinnamon rolls when the kitchen door swung open, and were always greeted by their Aunt Mary with hugs and kisses.

Bill's cousin, Jerry "Skeet" Daniels, married June's sister not long after June and Bill got married and had three children of their own: Jerry Jr., who was a year younger than Terry; Nancy, who was a year older than Tom, and Joy, who was the same age as Jeff.

Entertainment always followed brunch. Joy had four years of piano lessons and Jeff had three years of accordion lessons. Everyone listened as they rehearsed the songs they would perform for their school's Christmas show the following week. Terry said he was impressed at how Jeff had improved on the accordion, and remarked about Joy's skillful piano playing.

June said, "Jeff's accordion teacher told me that he thought Jeff was one of his best students and would be entering him in the Ohio State Accordion contest next March."

Later, Terry called his buddies after dinner to see what their plans were over the holiday. When he spoke with Danny Iafelice, all Danny wanted to hear about was how Terry managed to get into a real boxing match down in Dallas. Terry told him the story and included the fact that he would be entering the Dallas Golden Gloves the second week in January.

Danny said, "Hey, if you're interested in working out over the holiday, my neighbor is a coach at a boxing gym in Collinwood. If you want, I'll get you his number and you guys could hook up. His name is Tommy Morris."

Terry wanted to have fun while he was home, but he was also determined to do well in his first boxing tournament. He got Tommy's number Monday afternoon and gave him a call. Morris was a good boxer in the U.S. Navy in his younger days. He worked full time in the Pipefitters Union and trained amateur boxers on a part-time basis. He told Terry that he knew of him from reading about him in the newspaper.

Tommy said, "I've followed your athletic and academic achievements in the papers over the years and knew you would be accepted to any college of your choice. Danny said you were president of student council and nominated to the National Honor Society. I thought baseball and football were more your speed. What are you doing in the boxing arena?"

Terry smiled and said, "You sound like my dad," and went on to tell him how he was referred to the gym in Dallas.

"Well, you certainly have the build for a boxer," Tommy said. "So, if you're interested, I got some kids training at the gym for a show the end of January. You're welcome to join us."

"Sounds good Tommy; I'll meet you at your house. I don't want my parents to know about the gym, especially my dad. He's not too crazy about me boxing while I'm going to school, so I'm keeping it under wraps for now."

Terry also told his brothers not to bring it up in front of their parents, at least until he had a chance to see how he'd do in the Golden Gloves.

The next morning after breakfast, Terry offered to drive the kids to the mall to do some last-minute Christmas shopping. Bill had left a note informing them that they had to tend to the horses before they went anywhere. He said his part-time help was out of town for a few days and they would have to clean out the stalls.

Terry told his brothers, "That's okay, we got four boys on our team and it won't take us anytime at all."

Debbie blurted out, "Hey what about me? I wanna go see the horses and go to the mall too, you know!"

"That's right," June said, "you boys can take your little sister with you. I've got to be at my artist's table by three anyway. She can give them a few carrots to munch on through the fence. Just make sure she keeps her distance from them!"

June Daniels was known in the Cleveland area as an accomplished artist. Her ink sketches, watercolor and oil paintings were hanging in homes all over the surrounding counties. Known as "The Silhouette Lady," she rented a booth at the mall during the Christmas holidays and people would stand in line to have a hand-cut portrait of their child. They marveled at how quickly and accurately she could cut and paste the black picture on white matted paper.

The kids bundled up and plowed into the station wagon. Terry figured they could go directly to the mall from the stables. He didn't want to waste time because he wanted to get them back home, then drive over to Tommy Morris' house in time to go to the gym.

Bill had let the horses out in the corral after he fed them so all the boys had to do was clean out the stalls and put fresh straw down. While Terry, Tom and Jeff shoveled out the stalls, Denny and Debbie ran to the outside of the fence to feed the horses the carrots. The boys were working on their second wheelbarrow of manure when they heard a scream from outside.

Terry dropped his pitchfork and ran to the corral with Tom and Jeff close behind. They found Debbie screaming, "Get him off me! Help!"

While Debbie was feeding Pollyanna, one of the draft horses trotted up behind her. When the horse looked down at her mop of light brown hair, he started to nibble on the top of her scalp thinking it was a little pile of hay.

Terry grabbed the bridle of the horse and pulled him away from her. The horse reared his head up with a small handful of hair in his mouth while Debbie screamed bloody murder, but was able to pull away safely. Terry gave the big Goliath a good tug on the leather bridle as his dad had taught him, to show him who was boss. The kids watched as the dappled gray stud stood at attention for their big brother.

Debbie was half crying and half giggling when she realized she wasn't in danger. Terry picked her up in his arms after the horses trotted off and gave her a big hug and a kiss. She smiled back while wiping her eyes and said, "Can we go to the mall now?"

The Great Lakes Mall was located in Mentor, four miles from the Daniels' home, and was open to the public in 1961. It provided the convenience to shoppers to buy from a variety of stores, most of which were under one roof, and gave the people the comfort of heat in the winter and air-conditioning in the summer.

Terry and his siblings were able to get their shopping done in less than three hours, and on the drive home he reminded them not to tell their Mom or Dad that he was going to workout at a boxing gym for a few hours. "Just tell them I went to Danny's house and would be home around 6:30," he said.

He met up with Tommy Morris at his house. "We're gonna' pick up a few kids in Wickliffe – Danny's cousin and another kid, and then head to the gym," Tommy said.

The gym was on the third floor of an older building that had a drug store and apartments in it. It was great for boxing with a full-sized ring and plenty of equipment. Tommy shared the rent with his friend who was also a good boxer in his younger days, Larry Wagner.

Larry was a couple of years younger than Tommy and trained several teenage boys at the gym, including Larry's younger brother, Billy. Billy was a year younger than Terry and was a senior at St. Joseph High School in Cleveland. He was a good athlete in school, and had the makings of another Wagner boy becoming a good boxer.

Terry heard the sound of a buzzer and then a bell echo through the ceiling as they went up the last set of steps and it reminded him of the PAL gym in Dallas. Tommy introduced him to everybody and gave Terry a good workout.

On the way home he told Terry that he looked pretty good for a beginner, and encouraged him to work hard on the basics before he entered the Golden Gloves tournament next month. He also advised him to drop a few pounds and enter the tournament as a light-heavyweight.

"Taking on guys that can outweigh you is not the way to go as a novice. You're better off learning the basics and then going up against guys the same weight as you," he said.

Terry said he appreciated the advice and told him he would do his best getting to the gym during the holidays.

"Good," Tommy said as he pulled into his driveway, "and go easy on the parties while you're home, college boy!"

CHAPTER 10

Everyone in the Daniels household kept occupied during the holidays. There was sled riding on the steep hills of the Manakiki Golf Course, ice skating and hockey games on ponds throughout the Willoughby area, and countless snowball fights with friends and neighbors.

June stayed busy every night at her booth at the mall, while Bill and the rest of the managers at the fuel-oil company worked the snow-filled days making sure the trucks kept running on time.

Another enjoyable Christmas was celebrated at the Daniels' home, and Terry received a surprise Christmas present from his cousin, Frank Daniels, who gave him two tickets to the Cleveland Browns championship game.

The Browns played the Baltimore Colts for the NFL championship at the Cleveland Municipal Stadium on Sunday, December 27, 1964. Terry took a friend of his from high school and endured the sub-zero temperatures while watching the Browns upset the Colts, 27-0. They were the 1964 NFL Champions!

Later in the week, Terry took Tom and Jeff to see the new James Bond movie, *Goldfinger*, at the Vine Theatre. Terry knew the guy at the ticket booth and he let Jeff in, even though he was underage.

When the movie let out, Jeff said he'd never forget the scene with the naked girl who was sprayed in gold paint. "Yeah, well don't let Mom hear you say that," Terry replied.

By the time Sunday arrived, the kids were sad to know that their big brother would be on a plane back to Dallas. Terry said goodbye to his family and friends. This time it wasn't as tearful because they'd had so much fun, and knew he would write and call on a regular basis. Tom, Denny and Jeff also looked forward to hearing from Terry with the results of his first Golden Gloves tournament, which was just a few weeks away.

The new year of 1965 was officially starting for Terry on Monday, back on the campus of SMU in Dallas, Texas.

* * *

Terry and the rest of the SMU students had an extra day to recover before classes resumed on Tuesday, January 5. The professors welcomed them back with homework assignments but Terry took it all in stride. The Texas weather helped. It was 40 degrees and a little rainy, but was a welcome relief from the frozen Ohio tundra.

Once 4:30 p.m. hit, he was on the bus to the gym. Tony and Al were glad to see that he kept in shape over the holidays. Tony said, "I hope you're ready to work hard, 'cause I want all my boys ready for the tournament."

"I've got my schedule all worked out and I'm looking forward to it," Terry replied.

The two hours spent at the gym every day seemed to take its toll on some of the boys, but Terry was eating it up. He felt himself growing stronger by the day from the aerobic workouts, and the cool breeze from the Texas winter air that circulated in the gym made the training schedule much more tolerable.

Days later, Terry was getting the gear on to spar with Rufus. It would be the second time the two had worked in the ring together. Rufus was from a family of six boys; he was in the middle at age 19. His two older brothers were serving time in the county jail and he was headed in the same direction until Tony met him.

Tony was called to a street fight in progress in front of a drug store in downtown Dallas, and saw Rufus taking on two other boys when he pulled up in his squad car. Tony stopped the fight and arrested Rufus for fighting on a public street. He took the names of the other boys and gave them a stern warning.

"What chu' goin' arrestin' me for?" Rufus said as he was being put in the back seat of Tony's squad car, "I was just defendin' myself!"

"But you were the one throwing all the punches," Tony replied.

When they got back to the police station, Tony learned that the other boys were from a gang and were trying to pressure Rufus into joining. Rufus had seen what a gang had done to his two older brothers, and was fighting them off as best he could.

"Same old shit," Tony said to another officer. "But my gut tells me that this young man needs some guidance."

He decided to let Rufus brood about it for an hour in a cell, then said, "C'mon, I'll give you a ride home in my squad car."

On the way home, Tony learned a little more about Rufus' family and his frustration in staying out of a gang while trying to find a job since graduating high school. He decided to make him an offer.

He told him about his boxing gym and how he could see the potential in him even though Rufus had never participated in any high school sports.

"You know anything about cars?" Tony asked.

"A little I guess. I would help my Daddy work on our car now and then. Why?" Rufus said.

"I got a friend with a gas station a few miles from here; he could use an extra hand. You interested?"

"Yes, sir," Rufus replied, "and I could ride my bike there. I wouldn't need nobody to depend on gettin' me there."

Rufus directed him to a street of large duplex homes that were built in the '30s just off the freeway. He told Tony to pull over to the sidewalk curb.

Tony put the squad car in park, turned to Rufus in the back seat and said, "Okay, I'll talk to my friend tomorrow and let you know. Meanwhile, here's my card with the address of the gym on the back. I want to see you there at 4:30 tomorrow. I'm gonna hold off filing this charge against you for now, and I won't be callin' your folks unless you bullshit me and don't show up."

Rufus smiled and said, "No, sir. I'll be there - lookin' forward to it!"

"All right, and don't be worried about those gang punks. You tell them you got a record now with the police and we got their names. If you get in any trouble with them I'll throw all your asses in jail!" Tony growled.

The next day, Rufus made good on his word and Tony on his. And except for holidays or sickness, Rufus hadn't missed a day of work or a workout at the gym since.

* * *

On Tuesday, January 19, 1965, Terry went to the weigh-ins for the Golden Gloves tournament. The boxers were required to have a physical signed by a licensed Texas physician and a completed entry form, which listed their personal information and the gym they represented.

Terry stepped on the scale and the bar settled at 175 pounds, the exact limit for light-heavyweights. He signed and submitted his entry along with Rufus and six other boys for the Light-heavyweight Novice Division.

The annual Regional Championship Golden Gloves Tournament was set to take place Thursday through Monday, January 21-25 at the Memorial Auditorium in downtown Dallas. A total of 164 boys, representing 12 different gyms were entered and the tournament expected thousands of spectators. Mike told Terry, "The Golden Gloves drew in over 4,000 people per night last year, and that's more than the pro bouts bring in."

Terry walked away and said, "4,000 people per night – holy shit!"

Later he told his roommate Ed that his entry form was officially in for the Golden Gloves tournament and Ed said, "Wow! You're really goin' through with it? Well, you can be sure that we'll have a big rootin' section for you."

Word spread quickly around campus and several students planned to spend their weekend at the Memorial Auditorium. When Terry arrived, he was instructed to go to the locker rooms with Al and the rest of the team while Tony organized the lineup for the evening. His energy level was high and his palms were starting to sweat. His nerves were on "wire alert," so he didn't waste any time changing. He wanted to start loosening up right away.

Tony came over to Terry, handed him a program and said, "You can take it easy for a while Daniels, I don't want you to work up a sweat too soon, your bout is number 35 out of 44. You got six guys in your division including Rufus, so if one of you loses your first match, you'll be able to fight the loser of the third match in your division. If you win tonight, you'll be in the semifinals Saturday with the finals on Monday."

"Six guys?" Terry asked. "There were eight signed up at the weigh-in. What happened to the other two?"

"Probably cold feet, it happens a lot in these tournaments. These guys get all psyched up, show up to the final weigh-ins, get a good look at their competition and then don't show. It's happened to me a few times over the years and it pisses me off," Tony said.

"Like I've said before," he continued, "its one thing to be a good street fighter or good in the gym, but to climb into the ring in front of a crowd in a place like this takes a little extra stones between your legs, and some guys chicken out at the last minute."

Terry nodded and said, "Well, who's this Mannie Ortega I'm up against? Do you know anything about him?"

"Not really," Tony replied, "He's from a gym in Alvarado. We'll get a good look at him before you get laced up and discuss a little strategy before you have to get in line. You got about an hour before you have to get wrapped and taped, so take it easy back here before you start warmin' up."

Terry walked to the far back of the locker room and looked for a place to lie down, away from all the commotion. He found a door marked *Dressing Room* tried the handle and found it was unlocked. He stepped inside and clicked on the light.

The room was filled with mirrored dressing tables and chairs. The floor was a thick carpet and looked to be rather new, so he locked the door and lay down using his gym bag as a pillow. The walls were well insulated and he could barely hear the crowd.

He stretched out and closed his eyes, because he knew the best thing he could do right now was to slow his heart rate down and relax. He took a deep breath through his nose and exhaled through his mouth several times while picturing himself on a beach in Miami. He slowly lulled himself to sleep.

He awoke to hear his name being called throughout the locker room. He heard the doorknob turn a few times followed by a pounding. His eyes popped open, bringing him back to reality.

"Daniels! You in there?" Tony yelled.

Terry immediately jumped to his feet and shouted, "Yeah, hang on!"

He opened the door and Tony said, "I've been lookin' all over for you! We gotta get you wrapped and to the glove table. They're on fight number 23!"

"Ah, shit! I must have fallen asleep," Terry said.

Tony frowned and said, "Oh good. I told you to relax for an hour, not hibernate for the winter! Now we only got a short time to get you wrapped and loosened up, so let's go, Sleepy Bear."

Terry grabbed his gym bag and followed his coach onto the floor of the auditorium. An explosion of heat, smoke, and the pungent odor of sweat and leather hit him in the face when he walked through the double-steel framed doors.

He hadn't seen anything like this before. Three rings were filled with separate fights going on at the same time. A referee was busy separating the boxers in one ring, while a ref in another was holding the ropes to protect a boxer from falling through them as his opponent was landing a flurry of punches. Bells were going off at different intervals and the crowd loved it.

Tony led him to a set of chairs where Al was waiting with a roll of white gauze. "Hey, I was getting a little concerned about you, Ter," Al said. "I thought you might have had second thoughts about this and headed back to your dorm."

"Not me, Al, I like a good challenge," Terry said.

Terry followed Tony down an aisle past the last set of floor seats and suddenly heard a girl's voice call out from the middle section of the upper level, "Hey Terry! Terry…up here!"

He looked to where the voice was calling from and saw Tracie Dixon frantically waiving to him. Terry sat next to her in a calculus class. He told her about the tournament, but he didn't think she'd show.

She not only showed, but brought a few of her girlfriends. They were sitting with 20 others wearing blue and red SMU letter sweaters, jackets and sweatshirts. They whistled and cheered when they saw their local Mustang walk by in his boxing trunks.

His biceps bulked up a bit as he squeezed the towel around his neck a little tighter. He smiled and acknowledged them with a nod of his head and continued to the gloving table.

Tony pulled Terry aside after he got his gloves on and said, "Mannie Ortega is off to your left doin' a little shadow boxing."

Terry turned and saw the dark-haired Mexican-bred boy with a tan complexion throwing straight jabs and combinations while shuffling in a semi-circle.

"He's got kind of a beefy build, not really muscular like you," Tony said. "He's got a paunchy mid-section too, like he hasn't done enough sit-ups.

"Protect your head, but I want you to slip off his punches and go for his stomach and rib cage early. Remember, we got two minutes each round, so pick your shots wisely. Let's see if you can get him to drop his guard a little, and when he does, land that solid right of yours."

Terry took his seat and a few seconds later, Mannie Ortega took the seat next to him. Terry guessed him to be 19 or 20 based on the little mustache he was trying to grow, and saw he'd worked up a good sweat. They nodded hello to each other and then stared straight ahead at the action that was going on in the rings before them.

Terry was eye-level with the floor of the ring and could see small drops of blood that speckled the canvas, along with the large water spots from boxers spitting and missing the water buckets in each of the corners.

He felt the butterflies churning and wished he hadn't slept so long. The bell rang ending the bout in the center ring and a man in a bow tie said, "Okay, you two will go in that ring when the others leave."

Terry stood up and started twisting his torso while keeping his hands on the towel around his neck. When the referee raised the hand of the winner to the cheering crowd, Tony motioned him over to the red corner.

He and his opponent entered the center ring at the same time. The referee in the ring motioned to the announcer and he boomed his voice into the microphone, "Ladies and gentlemen, we now move into our first light-heavyweight fight in the novice division tonight! In the blue corner, with a record of two wins and no losses, from the Diablo Gym in Alvarado, let's welcome Manuel Ortega!"

The crowd gave the fighter polite applause and the announcer continued, "And in the red corner, with a record of one win and no losses, from the Police Athletic League in Dallas, let's welcome Terry Daniels!"

A loud cheer came from the "student body" for their new Yankee friend from Ohio, and Terry raised his left arm while turning in their direction to acknowledge the applause.

He went back to his corner to get his mouthpiece. Tony rinsed it out and said, "How you feel, Ter?"

"Well rested," he said.

"Yeah, it figures. Just remember what I told you," Tony said as the referee commanded the corner men down and the fighters to come out and touch gloves.

The bell sounded and Terry met Mannie in the center of the ring. He quickly followed with a left jab that caught his opponent on the top of the head, and the crowd responded favorably.

"Yeah Terry, take it to him!" one of the students yelled.

Mannie kept his hands up and elbows in tight and did not seem in a hurry to lead into Terry, so Terry kept his jab popping and slowly pushed him backward. He sensed Mannie was a little leery of him so he made sure to keep the lead in the fight by doubling up his jab and following with a right hand.

Tony always taught his boxers to get the first punch off quickly. "It's just like ballroom dancin'," he would say, "one person leads and the other follows, and I want *leaders* in my gym!"

Terry continued to drive his opponent into the corner of the ring with short left and right shots that landed on Mannie's gloves as he protected his face. Suddenly, a man in Ortega's corner shouted in Spanish, "Get out of the corner and hit him with combinations!"

Mannie ducked his head and pushed Terry off him while quickly returning punches in left-right combinations, several of which caught Terry on the head and shoulder.

The cheers from the crowd intensified for the fight in the center ring.

Terry was getting mad, mostly at himself for letting this guy tag him with a few punches, taking command of the fight away from him. Mannie's punches didn't have much of a sting, and Terry could feel adrenaline heating up his veins.

The bell rang ending the first round and the SMU crowd led the cheers. Al started to put the stool in the corner, but Terry said he didn't need it. During the last fight he saw Cassius Clay in, he noticed "The Champ" stood in his corner between rounds and Terry thought that was cool. Since the Heavyweight Champion of the World did it, he would do it too.

Tony gave Terry a big swig of water and said, "That was a good combination to his body at the end of the round. I want you to move in on him slowly, leading with your jabs; then dig into that belly of his. And don't drop your right!"

"Okay," Terry said. He took some deep breaths and filled his lungs with secondhand smoke that hung in the auditorium like a thick fog. The bell rang and Mannie was on guard while his corner man was chanting instructions in Spanish so fast he sounded like a 78-speed record.

Mannie tried to take the lead by throwing a left-right-left combination, but Terry slipped off the right and dug a solid left hook to his rib cage, weakening his opponent's finishing left punch. As Mannie's left dropped slightly, Terry's right hand followed off his left hook lead and found his opponent's nose.

Terry's torso was bent from the left hook and this allowed his right hand to be cocked and ready to hit his target with power behind it. The velocity of the punch snapped Mannie's head back and the crowd let out an "Oooo!" followed by a roar.

Mannie looked a little stunned while backing up, and Terry sensed it. He moved in for the kill by quickly following up with a left hook to the head as his opponent tried desperately to tie him up. But Terry hit him again with a short right to his jaw and Mannie went down like a ton of bricks!

The SMU crowd led the audience in loud cheers while the ref ordered Terry to a neutral corner. He started his count as the downed fighter slowly pushed himself off the canvas to one knee, then got to his feet barely beating the count at nine.

The ref sensed the intensity of the crowd and decided to let the fight continue even though he probably would have stopped it any other time. He looked back at Terry who looked like a tiger ready to pounce on his prey, then stepped back into the center ring and said, "Box!"

Mannie threw a left jab at Terry's head out of desperation, but Terry had already committed in his mind to the left-right-left combination and caught the dazed Mexican solidly on his temple with the last left hook. The impact from the punch spun the guy around and he hit the canvas for the last time.

The referee stepped in front of Terry and waved the fight over. The auditorium echoed the roar from the crowd. Flash cubes went off and the bell rang several times indicating the fight was over.

Terry's heart was pounding rapidly, but his breathing came down to a normal pace, and he had barely broken a sweat. "Maybe that rest before the fight helped," he laughingly said to Tony and Al as they greeted him in his corner. Tony reminded his boxer to go over and shake hands with his opponent. Terry turned and bumped into the referee who was coming over to raise Terry's hand.

He stood with the ref in the middle of the ring while the announcer turned his microphone up to the max and said, "In the center ring, we have a winner by a knockout in 31 seconds of the second round – in the red corner, Terry Daniels!"

His friends whistled and hollered with delight as their fellow Mustang turned and waved to them flashing his dimpled smile.

CHAPTER 11

The next morning, the *Dallas Morning News* had the results of the Golden Gloves tournament on the cover page of the sports section. At the end of the article it listed the stats for the night showing six PAL fighters advancing to the semifinals at the Memorial Auditorium: Dickie Wills, Open Heavyweight; Terry Daniels, Novice Light-heavyweight; Rufus Cutler, Novice Light-heavyweight; Tommy Lopez, Open Welterweight; Jesse Valdez, Novice Light-middleweight, and Randy Tyler, High School Heavyweight.

The boys met Tony at the gym that evening to ride the bus over to the tournament and their coach said, "You guys are really showing everyone how hard you have worked here in the gym. This is the most we've had make it to the semifinals in some time, and I want you to know that I'm proud of each and everyone of yeas'.

"Now let's go catch our bus. Oh, and Daniels…I hope you took a nice nap at home today because you sure as hell are not gonna sleep through your match tonight!"

Terry smiled while the boys chuckled and headed out the door to the city bus stop.

The article in the paper must have aroused the interest of more Dallas sports fans, because when they walked in, the place was packed. Tony led the team through the locker room and said, "We're gonna use this room tonight. It's where Daniels got his beauty rest last night. We'll have a little more privacy in here."

Terry's opponent was from a gym in Farmers Branch, about 30 minutes north of Dallas. He'd beaten his opponent by way of a TKO in the third round the night before. Tony said that he saw the fight and wasn't impressed with either fighter. In fact, he thought the other guy simply ran out of gas and quit in the middle of the third round.

Terry was feeling a little more confident tonight, but the butterflies were churning again, so he changed into his trunks and his hooded sweatshirt. He asked Dickie if he wanted to find some place in the halls of the auditorium to loosen up for a while, and Dickie agreed.

The bells rang and match after match continued with each boy giving his all, in hopes of making it to the Monday night finals. The crowd in the auditorium continued a chorus of boos and cheers throughout the evening for the young warriors.

Terry and Dickie worked up a good sweat and went back to the dressing room to get their hands wrapped. A few minutes later, a man stuck his head in the dressing room and said, "It's time to get your boxers to the gloving table Tony."

Terry decided to keep his sweatshirt on even though the temperature in the auditorium had heated up to a toasty 85 degrees. His small gang of fans yelled as their fellow Mustang walked down the aisle in front of them. Terry pushed his hood off and acknowledged them with a little nod of the head and a stern look.

He took off his sweatshirt and got laced up at the gloving table while Tony was rubbing his neck. Tony said, "Your guy is sittin' down over there with the sandy blond hair. His name is Ronnie Lankford from Greenville, and like I said, I don't think he's in half the shape you are.

"If he wants to take the lead first, let him. Just keep your hands up; elbows tucked in, and keep moving – you know. Let him burn up his energy in the first minute of the round, then pick your shots and wear him down in the second minute."

"I got Rufus goin' up before you," Tony continued, "so just be ready to come up to the same corner when he's done."

Terry nodded and walked over to take a seat next to his opponent.

When it was Rufus' turn to enter the ring, the predominantly white crowd let out applause of support for his white opponent. It was one of several inter-racial bouts that evening.

The citizens of Texas had let it be known to their congressmen that the majority of them were against the new Civil Rights Act that President Johnson had presented to the House and Senate. Many of them had written letters to the local newspapers informing the public that it was unjust for the government to force integration on their children in schools and families in their neighborhoods.

The mood of the country was showing tension on this matter, but the news media in Texas had been doing a good job of reporting both sides of the issue, helping to keep racial tensions at bay.

Terry was neutral on the issue at this point in his life. Although he attended a racially mixed grade school when he lived in Painesville, he'd never had a racial confrontation to make him angry one way or another.

It didn't help matters much when Cassius Clay, the new professional Heavyweight Champion of the World, was quoted in Sport Illustrated as saying, "I'm a bad-ass nigger!"

Rufus' opponent was Danny Bosworth, a southpaw for the Dallas Athletic Club. Danny was last year's high school light-heavyweight champion and had a record of four wins and one loss with two knockouts (KOs).

Rufus struggled with the awkward style of his opponent and never gave up during the match, but his opponent proved to be too powerful and won all three rounds of the fight.

The crowd gave a loud cheer when the ref raised Danny's arm and then kept the applause going to acknowledge Rufus' good sportsmanship.

Terry made his way to Tony and touched gloves with Rufus as he exited the ring. When the announcer introduced the fighters to the audience, he decided to play up to the energetic crowd by saying, "And in the red corner, from the PAL gym and a freshman at SMU here in Dallas – Terr-ree Daniels!"

On cue, his friends let out another cheer. "Sounds like you're buildin' a little fan club for yourself, Terry," Tony said while putting the mouthpiece in his fighter's mouth.

The referee called the boxers to the center of the ring as the bell rang for the start of Round One. Terry got his jab off first and on target; it caught his opponent right between the eyes. The crowd responded and Terry could feel the blood begin to boil.

He waited a split second for the 6' 1" Ronnie Lankford to respond, and when he didn't, Terry threw a left-right-left combination and scored with his first and last punch. He felt the urge to take command of the fight and nixed the idea of letting his opponent do the leading in the first round. It proved to be the right choice.

Ronnie had a look of surprise on his face and Terry sensed his opponent was going to take his time and pick his shots. Terry could feel the butterflies return, but they subsided when he connected with a solid combination to Ronnie's head. The crowd responded with cheers.

The second round ended with Terry ahead. He returned to his corner with his breathing better controlled and Tony said, "That was a good round, Terry. Don't get too aggressive this third round unless he starts to take the fight to you. You take your time and don't get careless."

Ronnie came out of his corner like a new fighter. He led with double jabs while dipping his head and taking the fight to Terry. The SMU crowd responded with yells above the rest: "Come on Terry, don't back down – let him have it!"

Terry kept shuffling to his left, then planted his feet and fired a quick left-right that stopped his opponent in his tracks. The crowd responded, and the two of them started to trade punches in the middle of the ring.

Terry pushed forward with his punches, and within seconds had Ronnie on the ropes. The spectators stepped up the cheering to another level and Terry's adrenaline flowed into his hands. He connected with a left hook and knocked Ronnie through the ropes!

The ref ordered him to a neutral corner as Ronnie collected himself with the help of one of the judges, and climbed back into the ring. Terry desperately tried putting him away, but at the final ring of the bell, both boys were standing.

Terry was awarded a unanimous decision and realized he was now one bout away from a Golden Gloves Championship trophy.

* * *

The phone rang a little after 7 on Sunday evening, and the Daniels family knew who it was. June picked it up first because she had just finished a long conversation with her sister Mary, while the kids scampered to take their place in line to talk with their big brother.

Terry told his mom how good it was to be back in school, about the mild Texas winter, and the challenge of the homework assignments from his professors. However, he saved the action of the Golden Gloves tournament till the rest of the boys got on the phone.

Tom got to talk with him first and Terry gave him the blow-by-blow description of each fight, as well as the reaction of the fans. Tom was laughing and saying, "Are you kidding me? Oh, that is so cool, Ter!" which made Denny and Jeff even more excited to hear what he had to say. They began pushing each other to jockey into position.

June said, "Would you two stop it! Tom, give your brothers a chance to talk before a fight breaks out!"

Tom said goodbye and handed the phone to Jeff, who grabbed the receiver while laughing and pushing Denny's hand away from his face. "I'll hang up if you don't stop it," he said.

They all got to talk, including Bill who had heard bits and pieces of Tom's conversation from the dining room. He was curious about the boxing tournament, but Terry assured him that he would be fine, that he had a good coach, and was looking forward to calling him after the finals.

Bill had a serious look on his face as he listened to Terry, but toward the end of the conversation, a smile slowly developed on his face as the boys heard him say, "Okay son, it sounds like you can handle yourself. Good luck tomorrow night."

The family then screamed in unison, "Goodbye Terry! Good Luck!"

Terry hung up the phone in the hallway of the dorm and came away with a good feeling knowing that his dad trusted him. He was determined once again to make his parents proud of his accomplishments in the classroom *and* in sports.

The next day in class, Tracie asked Terry if he was ready for the big fight. "That Bosworth guy looked pretty tough against that colored boy the other night," she said.

"Yeah, well after I went to the library yesterday I met my coach at the gym and we did some sparring together. He showed me what to expect from a southpaw and how to counter with some shots of my own," Terry said. "Then I can keep the pressure on *him*."

"A southpaw? Oh, you mean the way he was standin' kinda like a mirror to the guy instead of opposite like all the other boxers?" she said.

"Right. I'm ready for him. You're planning on coming aren't ya'?"

Just then, Professor Pipes rapped his yardstick several times on his desk in front of the class and said, "Miss Dixon, Mr. Daniels – can we get started *please*?"

They nodded and opened their books while the professor started writing an algebraic equation on the chalk board.

Tracie smiled at Terry with her feisty hazel eyes, and whispered in her Houston drawl, "I'll be there alright. Just don't let him hit that handsome face of yours too much."

Terry smiled back and thought maybe he *was* building a fan club after all.

The morning paper pumped up the boxing fans of Dallas for that evening's Golden Gloves finals. It featured another colorful story about the fighters.

Tony was proud that they mentioned the PAL had three boxers in the finals: Randy Tyler against a big boy named Murphy Von Hutchins for the High School Heavyweight Division; Terry against Danny Bosworth from the DAC for Novice Light-Heavyweight; and Dickie against Jorge Ortega (Manuel's older brother) from the Diablo Gym for Open Heavyweight.

The paper mentioned the fact that Terry was a freshman at SMU, had injured his knee ending his chance to play college football, and was taking up boxing for the first time in his life. They mentioned his powerful right hand and encouraged the fans to witness his first boxing tournament.

The story ended by building up the grand finale of the evening, promising the fans a lot of leather thrown between Dickie Wills and his hard-punching opponent, Jorge Ortega.

Terry was the last to get changed and wrapped. As he sat down in front of Tony, he heard the bell at the judge's table ring several times, then the announcer's voice boomed a welcome to the fans. Tony sensed the nervousness and said, "It's okay, Ter, your opponent is just as nervous as you are. It's natural. Learn to accept it and use it to start a fire in your belly. I'll get the hand pads before you get your gloves on and we'll repeat what we did yesterday in the gym. You're gonna do just fine."

Hearing those words from an experienced and confident coach like Tony made all the difference to Terry. He had psyched himself up for many sporting events in his lifetime, but nothing came close to what he was about to do in front of 5,000 people.

"Okay, Terry, let's you and me work a little with the mitts, and Dickie, stay loose," Tony said as they proceeded out of the main floor and down the hallway.

When they got to their private area, Tony took the stance of a southpaw with his right out front and his left held back.

"The best way to fight a southpaw is to stay aggressive with him, throwing straight rights, hard and often, to keep him off balance. You can still lead with your left, but don't count on that scorin' much, just keep followin' up with your right," Tony said.

By the time Terry and Dickie were called to the gloving table they were primed like bulls in the pen of a Texas rodeo. Mike led them down the aisle, and as they were walking, Terry glanced at the trophy table. They were shiny and colorful, with the Open division a shade taller than the Novice trophies, along with two separate larger ones: Most Improved Boxer and Outstanding Boxer of the Tournament.

Randy's fight ended the same way it started – with each fighter standing toe-to-toe each minute of every round. The crowd roared with approval at the ending bell and both fighters touched gloves acknowledging the gameness of each other.

When it was announced that big Murphy Von Hutchins was the winner, no one from the crowd objected. Randy was disappointed, but knew he had given it his all. As the crowd continued to applaud, Terry could see Randy's dad standing next to the ring applauding and shouting in support of his boy. He wondered if *his* dad would have done the same. Only time would tell.

When it was Terry's turn to step into the ring, he said to himself, "Okay, it's showtime. Take no prisoners!"

The Dallas Athletic Club sponsored the boxers from Glovers Gym, in downtown Dallas, run by a coach named Doug Lord. Doug was a retired colonel from the National Guard and a successful businessman. His amateur boxers were always competitive in the Golden Gloves, and Danny Bosworth was no exception.

Doug was grooming his boxer well. Danny was 5' 10", weighed 175 pounds, and had a stocky build. He reminded Terry of his first opponent, and got him thinking about heavy body shots as part of his strategy.

As the fighters climbed into the ring, the announcer started his introductions from the judges' table to the crowd. He announced Danny's name and record first, and the crowd gave a generous applause. But when he said, "And in the blue corner..." Terry's fans stood and led the audience into a wave of whistles and cheers before the man could say his name.

The ref stood in the center of the ring, ordered the corner men down, and then said, "Box!"

Terry's left glove touched Danny's right and both boys followed with the jab to try to score first. Terry's grazed Danny's head while Danny connected his right to Terry's jaw. Whistles and cheers came for both fighters.

Terry was glad he worked with Tony on the southpaw stance, but he still felt awkward and apprehensive in following up with his combinations. Danny sensed that, like so many southpaw boxers do in the first minute, and unleashed a solid right-left-right to Terry's head scoring with all three punches.

A roar came from the seats, obviously in support of the DAC's up and coming light-heavyweight, while the SMU crowd led the audience with shouts of support for Terry.

Terry felt the burn in his stomach and bit down tightly on his mouthpiece as he tried timing his rhythm and responded with a left-right combination of his own, but fell just short of his target.

Danny was circling to his right while Terry was trying to get his opponent to circle to his left. He had to adjust to his right, otherwise, he would continue into a trade-off of punches with his opponent. He wasn't comfortable with that yet. This gave Danny the control he was looking for and he finished the first round a clear winner.

Terry went back to his corner and said, "Damn it! I let that fucker hit me way too many times!"

"Take it easy, boy," Tony said as he wiped Terry with a towel.

"I figured he'd frustrate you in the first round, but you've got a lot more power in your punches than he does," he said. "I want ya' to keep your hands up tight, and when he pops that right hand of his, I want ya' to slip off of it and hit him with a left hook to his ribs. Take a little piss-and-vinegar out of him early in the round and then start to bull into him."

"Seconds down," the referee said, and the bell sounded.

Terry came out with his hands held tight while Danny led with a double right jab. Terry dipped his torso to let the second jab slide off the top of his head and landed a solid left to Danny's ribs.

The crowd responded in favor of Terry, and Tony said to Al, "That's what I like about this kid, he does what ya' tell him."

Terry was feeling the anger and was following up with a variety of punches, determined to take control. And he did, scoring two punches to his opponent's one in both the second and third rounds, almost knocking Doug Lord's protege out in the last 30 seconds of the fight.

The bell sounded and the Mustangs cheered the loudest. The ref separated Terry from his beaten opponent and Terry turned to the audience and shook his right hand in the air.

The ref gathered the two fighters back to the center of the ring as the announcer read the results, "The winner, by unanimous decision, in the blue corner, Terr-ree Daniels!"

The crowd turned up the applause as the ref raised Terry's hand and he once again acknowledged his friends first, and then the rest of the crowd.

That night, Terry had done something no one on either his father's or mother's side of the family had done before – he won a Golden Gloves boxing tournament!

CHAPTER 12

The Tuesday morning edition of the *Dallas Morning News* had the Golden Gloves tournament in the headlines of its sports section. Ed Fincher ran into Terry in between classes and showed him the story in the paper. "Man that was a tough fight between Wills and that Mexican boy. I actually thought it coulda gone either way. I guess he was really lookin' for revenge after what you did to his little brother," he said.

"Yeah, Dickie was pretty pissed off too," Terry said. "He'd never been cut before and I think the judges were just a little swayed towards the other guy as a result. Our coach was pissed too, but what are ya' gonna do?"

"Yeah, I know. Hey, did you see your picture on page four?" Ed quickly flipped to it and showed Terry. The whole page was covered with snapshots of the evening's fights with captions underneath, and Terry's was in the upper right corner.

"Hey, that's pretty neat," Terry said.

"I'll say," Ed said. "Here, keep it. Maybe start a scrapbook. You're a real trailblazer alright. I've got the coolest roommate on campus."

Terry smiled and said, "Thanks. Hey, I'll catch up with you later,"

On the way to class, Terry was reliving what happened in the locker room after the tournament: He was admiring his new boxing trophy when he felt a slap on the back. He turned and was greeted by a smiling Doug Lord.

"It's not often when one of my boxers loses a fight, and I just wanna congratulate you on a job well done, boy," Doug said in his Texas drawl while extending his hand.

Terry reciprocated and said, "Thank you, sir," but before he could say any more, a loud pounding came from around the corner - it was Dickie Wills.

"Damn it!" Dickie screamed as he punched his fist into the locker.

Coach Tony put his hand on Dickie's shoulder and said, "Take it easy, boy. You got nothin' to be ashamed of. I know it, you know it, and the fans know it. These things happen. You'll get your chance to prove yourself again real soon, don't worry."

Doug walked over to them and said, "He's right son, every fighter loses a close one now and then, but it's the toughest ones that get right back in the ring and go on winnin'."

Terry felt bad for Dickie. The closest he had seen to a similar loss was in high school when boy a year behind him lost in his final match in the district wrestling tournament his senior year. It was devastating to the boy because he had an amazing season with only one loss going into the districts. But it paled in comparison to losing a boxing match in front of thousands of people. Dickie was pissed.

The whole evening was still spinning in Terry's head, even the late-night phone call home. It was close to 11:30 p.m. when he finally made it back to the dorm and made the call. His parents and Tom were still up, but the rest of the kids were deep in dreamland.

His father answered the phone on the third ring, and within seconds Terry could hear the joy in his voice. It seemed that his dad had made the decision not to be critical this time, and said, "You did!? Well, way to go, Ace!" A term his brother Peps used on the road crew.

Tom was next and got the blow-by-blow description of the evening. When it was June's turn she was mostly interested in hearing if he got hurt or if he was okay. By the end of the conversation, they were all relieved over the fantastic news. Terry was making a name for himself just like he promised.

At lunchtime, he walked into the cafeteria and was greeted by whistles and cheers from a table of students who were coaxing him to sit with them. Several guys from a fraternity and the football team had the sports section spread out on the table. They were all smiling as Terry approached them.

A blond-haired boy stood up and said, "Hi Terry, I'm Eddie Joe Davis and my friends call me Dedo. These are a couple buddies of mine, Mike McCann, and, of course, you know Jim and Larry. And the lovely ladies here are Lori Simmons and I believe you already know Tracie Dixon. We all saw you take the title last night, and man, was that cool!"

"Thanks," Terry said while shaking hands with everybody.

"A few more seconds and you woulda knocked that guy out," Dedo said.

"Yeah, that son of a, I mean, *guy* was tougher than I thought," Terry said while checking his language for the girls.

Dedo said, "Well, I'm from Naperville, Illinois, and I started out last year at Alabama, but I got a little homesick when a couple of my buddies from high school were here at SMU. So, I transferred to play football and baseball here. How did you come to pick SMU from growing up in Cleveland?"

"I talked with my minister at our Methodist church and he encouraged me to take theology in addition to history as a dual major. He said the college had the best theology school in the nation, but I wanted to play in the Southwest Conference."

"I know Coach Fry spoke highly of you the first week of practice, and it's a shame you had that knee injury, but if it heals good are you thinking of trying out again next year?" Dedo asked.

"No. The football trainer said I am out for good, but I'm thinking about trying out for the baseball team this spring if my knee holds up. I lettered all three years in high school as a pitcher and first baseman. When are tryouts?"

"Usually the third week in February; I'll talk with Coach Finley and see about setting up a time to stop by his office. He just took over the head coaching job and he's giving every player a chance to be part of a winning team," Dedo said.

"That would be great," Terry said, and they spent the rest of the lunch hour exchanging stories from home.

The next two weeks were filled with class time, homework assignments, basketball games, and tests. The students were even given a little extra fun outside when an unexpected snowstorm covered the campus with six inches. The art students had a blast building some unique snow sculptures in the center of campus after class.

By the weekend, most students were looking forward to the showdown with the Texas A&M basketball team. A win for either team would put them in first place in the SWC.

Terry, however, was looking forward to the Golden Gloves award banquet at the prestigious Dallas Athletic Club. The winners and runners-up from the city and state championships were invited along with their coaches to attend a dinner in their honor.

He took the bus downtown and met up with Tony and the rest of the PAL team in the lobby of the DAC.

"Okay, Daniels," Tony said, "late as usual. Well, now that we're all here, let's head on up to the banquet room upstairs."

"Where's Dickie?" Terry asked.

"I tried callin' him three times but he never answered. He's mad, and I'm sure he didn't wanna' see Ortega get what he thinks should be *his* award," Tony said, and they walked down the marble-covered hallway to the banquet room.

The walls were covered with large framed photos and paintings of past and present members of the club. Terry recognized several names and faces and was given a quick history of some of the best athletes to come out of Texas.

Lots of sports writers were there along with reporters from the local radio and television stations. The room held up to 400 people.

Each table was set up for eight, but no one was taking their seat yet. The place was buzzing with loud talking and laughter, and the air was filled with a cloud of cigar and cigarette smoke.

Terry noticed Doug Lord talking with three gentlemen and appeared to be introducing them to a well-dressed boxer. He later learned that the boxer was 24-year-old Curtis Cokes, a well-groomed, up-and-coming professional welterweight from Doug's gym.

A tall, dark-haired gentleman stood at the podium in the front of the room. He tapped the microphone a few times and welcomed everyone. "Before we sit down, I've asked Dr. Joseph Quillan, Dean of the Perkins School of Theology at SMU, to lead us in prayer before dinner. So, would you all please bow your heads? Dr. Quillan, if you please."

As Terry bowed his head and listened to the prayer, he allowed the words to sink in. A feeling of peace came over him; a feeling he always got when saying a prayer that filled his heart with warmth. It was a perfect way to set the tone for the evening, and his nerves melted away.

The main course was a combination of a 14-ounce Texas strip steak, baked potatoes and fresh asparagus. Everyone ate while the speakers traded off with entertaining stories and tributes to both amateur and pro boxers attending the event.

The evening ended with a very special moment for the winning champions – a personalized letter jacket from the Dallas Golden Gloves organization.

Al and Tony approached the podium together and Tony stepped up to the microphone to tell the audience the story of his new boxer from SMU who almost slept through his first fight in the dressing room of the auditorium. The crowd laughed and applauded when Tony announced Terry's name.

Al held a dark blue letter jacket out for Terry to slip into while Tony told the audience, "And I'm sure you would agree with me when I say that if this young man, who has the heart and strength of a lion, will be a definite contender for the Open Division next year in Dallas!"

Terry was admiring his new letter jacket while being applauded. He was excited and said to his coaches, "After tonight, more people will know who I am in Dallas than they do in Cleveland – and I lived there my whole life!"

The banquet ended around 10 p.m. and Terry caught the next bus back to his dorm. It dropped him off at Lovers Lane, and he quickly jogged back to his room to change. He had a party to go to at Jim and Larry's apartment.

He changed into gray slacks and a black t-shirt, then zipped up his new letter jacket and headed out. But first, a quick stop at the Seven Eleven on Mockingbird Lane to buy a few six- packs of beer.

Even though the drinking age was 21, his buddies had showed him how to make a copy of his driver's license and fudge his birth date. The fake ones looked like the real ones, but Terry felt that the owners of the campus store probably knew who was lying and who wasn't.

Before entering the store, he stopped to admire his reflection in the window, while sporting his new jacket. It was a dark blue cotton and wool blend with navy blue leather sleeves, and a blue and white striped expandable bottom. Looking at the window again he mussed up his hair a bit and tried not to look like the clean-cut college boy that he was.

He asked the elderly gent behind the counter for a couple of six-packs and a bag of pretzels. The man smiled as he looked at the Police Athletic League emblem on Terry's sleeve while bagging the beers. It also had *'65 Dallas Golden Gloves* on the front patch in the shape of a boxing glove and *Novice Light-Heavyweight Champ* written underneath it.

He looked down at the white patch that read *Terry* in blue script on the bottom left side and said, "You get that jacket at the awards banquet tonight?"

"Yes sir, how'd you know?" Terry said as he pulled out his wallet.

"I read about it in the paper this morning," the man said. "Keep your money in your wallet. These beers are on me tonight, Terry."

With a look of surprise, Terry smiled and said, "Well, thank you, sir."

"The name's Gus," he said as they shook hands. "And you behave yourself tonight. I don't want to hear from the local cops that I sold beer to a minor."

There was snow on the ground and a chill in the air as Terry made his way to Jim and Larry's. He said hello to a few guys in the parking lot next door, and walked up the steps to the front door. He didn't bother knocking because the music was blaring so loud that nobody would have heard him. So, he opened the door and let himself in.

The Diamonds were singing *Little Darlin'* on the stereo and the room was packed with guys and girls dancing to rock 'n' roll. Terry felt right at home with the choice of music. SMU students were mostly from Texas, but they were not really into the country-western sounds that commanded most of the Dallas radio stations in the early '60s, and many were still mixed about the British Invasion. They, like Terry, still hung on to their doo-wops.

"Hey, Terry! You made it!" yelled a glassy-eyed Dedo. He approached Terry and pulled Jim along with him.

"Hey, Kid," Jim said, "'bout time you showed up. Whatcha' got in the bag? Beer? Oh man, you're a lifesaver!"

"You gonna' need one of these?" Dedo said as he produced a can opener from his pocket.

"Nah, they're the new Miller High Life cans with the pull-tabs," Terry said.

"Boy, you sure do talk like a Yankee. Just like me," Dedo said with a sheepish grin on his face. He turned to Jim who was in the process of helping himself to a beer and said, "And why do you keep callin' him *Kid?*"

Jim went on to tell him about the night they watched *Kid Galahad* together and then watched Terry win his first boxing match a few weeks later.

"Hah! Don't that beat all," Dedo said.

Terry asked, "How did you come to be called Dedo?"

"Well, when I was growing up, my friends all called me Eddie Joe, and one of 'em had a little 3-year-old brother that couldn't pronounce my name and called me 'Dedo'. We all got a laugh from it, and they called me that ever since.

"Well, Kid, let's you and me have a beer and celebrate that new jacket you got on!"

Terry tipped his beer with Dedo and took a big swig of his ice cold brew. It had a smooth barley taste and he was ready for the buzz he knew he'd get after finishing it quickly. The boys wasted no time in draining their Millers, but before he could pop another one, Terry heard his name from across the room. Tracie Dixon was flagging him down.

He shuffled through the crowd and just as he approached her she took his hand and said, "Come on, let's dance!"

The next 45 flopped down and the stereo blasted out *Da Doo Ron Ron*, by the Crystals. Terry smiled and they both started the twist as the song played:

I met him on a Monday and my heart stood still,
Da Doo Ron Ron, Da Doo Ron Ron
Somebody told me that his name was Bill,
Da Doo Ron Ron, Da Doo Ron Ronnnn!

Halfway through the song, Terry began to sweat and took his new jacket off. He held it while they continued to twist and the music seemed to kick up a notch.

Tracie smiled and admired Terry's muscular body as he was twisting his torso in his black t-shirt and gray slacks.

"I came right from an awards banquet and didn't have much time to change," he said loudly in her ear.

"You look just fine to me!" she replied, and the two of them continued to twist right into the next song. It turned out to be a slow one by The Everly Brothers.

"Here Kid, let me hang that up for ya' in my private closet," Jim said as he grabbed Terry's jacket.

Tracie put her arms around Terry's neck as they began to slow dance and she asked, "How come he calls you *Kid*?"

Terry told her the story and she replied, "Well, in the movie he gets the girl in the end doesn't he?"

"I don't know, does he?" They both smiled and continued to slow dance to the harmony of the song.

When it ended Terry said, "Let's see if we can scrounge up a couple of beers before they're all gone."

The kitchen had an old white Frigidaire from the '50s with a couple of dents in the door, and Terry grabbed the last two cans of Coors.

"Hey, we're in luck," Terry said. They tipped their beers and began to take a swig when two guys came stumbling in.

They were both freshmen and Terry recognized the first one. The other he knew from freshman football. "Bill, isn't it?" Terry said.

"Yeah, Bill Rainer, I went to school with your roommate Ed Fincher in El Dorado, Arkansas," he said. "This is Pinky Clements, I think you know him from the freshman football team."

"Oh yeah, how are ya'?" Terry said.

"Hey, we don't mean to interrupt, but Dedo tells us you're thinking of trying out for the baseball team – is that right? We're both gonna' be playin' on the freshman team. I'm an outfielder and Pinky here's a catcher," Bill said.

"Yeah, sure, I'd love to," Terry said.

Tracie peered at Terry with a devilish smile and said, "Wow, you're just an all-around athlete aren't you - football, boxing and baseball?"

Pinky realized he and Bill were cutting in on time between Terry and Tracie and said, "Well, we don't mean to bug y'all about it right now Terry, but we'll talk more soon."

Terry asked Tracie if she'd like to finish their beers outside to get some fresh air. She smiled and accepted, and the two of them stepped out the kitchen door to a small backyard porch.

The smell of the crisp winter air gave a welcome relief from the musty smell of the apartment as they sat down on a padded wooden bench. Tracie immediately wanted to know everything about Terry, and he gave her the "Cliffs Notes" version then turned it back to her by asking, "What about you?"

She told him about growing up in Houston with her parents and two older brothers. She talked for about 10 minutes and then ended by saying, "I came to SMU to get a degree in English, and I'd like to be a teacher like my dad."

"That sounds great. Wow, it's chilly out here," Terry said as he took the opportunity to put his arm around Tracie's shoulder. She smiled and scooted close to him, and just before he could take a swig of beer, she leaned closer and they connected with a long romantic kiss.

Terry slowly swung his other arm around her, careful not to spill his beer.

Suddenly, the back door opened and several couples came outside. The music was blaring behind them and one of the boys said, "Oh, I guess we're not the only ones lookin' for some fresh air."

Terry and Tracie smiled and stood up. Terry said, "There's plenty of that out here, but it's gettin' to be a bit too chilly without a jacket."

The boys smiled as they starred at Tracie's breasts which had perked right up, and were poking through her bra and thin white cotton v-necked sweater.

"Y'all don't have to leave on our account," one of the boys said as his girlfriend caught what he was looking at and gave him a strong pinch on his arm. Terry smiled and led Tracie by the hand back into the house.

The kids danced, laughed and drank until the party finally started to break up around 1:30 a.m. Terry walked Tracie back to her dormitory and they enjoyed one last kiss on the doorstep.

She wrapped her arms around his neck and he placed his right hand on the base of her spine. They enjoyed the taste of each others lips one more time. It was a wonderful way for The Kid to end a memorable evening.

CHAPTER 13

Terry sent the family a three-page letter with pictures of him holding his boxing trophy and wearing his new Golden Gloves letter jacket. He told them about the awards banquet and how proud he was to be the only guy on campus wearing such a cool jacket. He also said he treated himself to a gift – a motorcycle.

It's a Triumph T21, he wrote. *I bought it off a guy who needed the money, so I got a great deal. It's great to ride around campus and town. I plan on riding it home!*

He ended by telling them he wanted to letter in a sport at school, and he would have that opportunity by trying out for the freshman baseball team in a few weeks.

Terry met with Coach Bob Finley after class on Monday, February 15. He was told workouts were currently underway and practice would officially start on Thursday. "Freshmen are not allowed to play varsity, but they play their games in the conference and qualify for letters," the coach said.

"That sounds good to me," Terry said.

"Now, I know you hurt your leg in football, but you're in good physical condition. I'll have the trainer look at you and see if you'll be able to run around those bases without gettin' hurt."

Terry shook his hand and said he was looking forward to it. He knew he could hold his own on the pitcher's mound.

The following week, Terry's 11-year-old brother, Jeff, had some news of his own to share with his big brother. He took first place in his division in the Ohio State Accordion Contest. It was held in downtown Cleveland, "The Polka Capital of the World," as Paul Wilcox used to say on the local TV show, *Polka Varieties*.

Jeff recalled the story to Terry telling him their mother drove him there in a snowstorm. He wrote: *"Oh, doesn't it figure?" she said. "The few times I have to go to downtown Cleveland and we've got a blizzard to drive through!"*

Luckily, Dad still had the chains on the tires of the station wagon, but Mom was white- knuckled on the steering wheel all the way there.

Jeff included a picture of him with his accordion, and holding the first place trophy. He told him that the following Monday, the principal of his school had him bring his accordion to his office to play the song over the P.A. system for the whole school.

He wrote: *When I was strapping on the accordion, I could hear his announcement echo throughout the hallways, and the palms of my hands started to sweat. I was more nervous than when I was on stage in front of the judges and audience. Then I panicked more when I looked into my accordion case for the music and saw it was empty!*

I had to do it by memory, like I did in front of the judges, but by the grace of God, I pulled it off without a mistake. My friends told me that it sounded great, but I told them if the principal ever asks me to play again, I'd only do it in my classroom!

Terry got the letter in the afternoon, but didn't have time to finish it because he was off to his first baseball practice and didn't want to be late.

When he arrived at the locker room he heard a couple of seniors harmonizing one of the Beach Boys' latest hits:

I'm gettin' bugged drivin' up and down the same ol' strip,
I gotta finda new place where the kids are hip!

I get around (Get around, round, round, I get around)
Up outa town (Get around, round, round, I get around)

Several more joined in with the harmonies and others grabbed baseball bats and used them like guitars. Terry clapped his hands together once, and said laughingly, "Alright!"

Pinky Clements shuffled his way up to Terry and said, "Hey, Terry, grab a locker down there and join the rest of us freshmen!"

Terry smiled and waded his way through the locker room and was greeted by Bill Rainer and a few other freshmen.

"My glove's at home, so I'll need to borrow one until my dad sends it to me," Terry said.

"That's okay, we got a couple spares for ya'," Bill said.

Terry quickly changed into his practice uniform. He could hardly wait to get out to the field and show the rest of the team what he could do on the mound.

When he walked out he was greeted by one of the coaches. "Hi Terry, I'm Coach Alex Hooks. Coach Finley and I would like you to start warming up with some pitches. He'd like to see what you can do for the team."

Terry started his stretching exercises and then heard the coach yell, "Carpenter, Kaufman, Hamm! Start loosenin' up! I'm gonna have Daniels throw some pitches to y'all!"

Terry's heart started pounding as he walked on the pitcher's mound. He reached down for a little dirt to grind in his right hand and then grabbed a baseball. It felt like a nice spring practice day at South High, only it was February in Dallas.

The catcher, a junior named J.W. Davis, put on his mask and squatted down behind home plate. He gave Terry a nod indicating he could start warming up.

Terry nodded back and went into a leisurely motion for his wind-up. He threw the ball at about half speed, nothing special, but right on target. He slowly worked his way up to the speed he was comfortable with and nodded over to the coaches that he was ready.

The first batter was Ralph Hamm, an outfielder in his junior year who had a decent batting average last year. Terry threw three pitches to him – one fouled, one short grounder that came straight back to Terry who quickly threw it to first base, and one strike.

Coach Finley stood there with his arms crossed, then he yelled, "Carpenter!"

Bobby Carpenter was a shortstop in his senior year with a batting average of .305. Terry turned up the heat a little and threw five pitches to him – two fast balls, a slider, and two curve balls. Bobby only got a piece of one that went foul.

Coach Finley's eyebrows went up a little on the last pitch, then yelled, "Kaufman!"

Sandy Kaufman was a varsity pitcher with a batting average of .295. He seemed confident when he stepped into the batter's box. Terry sent him two sliders, a change-up, a fast ball, and a curve. Sandy got one hit between second and third base and one pop-up. The rest were strikes.

The coach smiled and said, "Alright, Daniels. Let's see what you can do with the bat. Foster, I want you to warm up and give him some pitches!"

A thin, sandy blond-haired boy took the pitcher's mound and started warming up. Terry put a batter's helmet on and grabbed a bat; he put a weighted ring on the bat and started practice swinging.

"He bats left-handed?" Coach Finley said to Coach Hooks.

Terry took his stance in the batter's box and dug his high-top tennis shoes into the dirt to ground himself. He had not yet received his cleats, but was looking forward to getting them along with his glove.

The first pitch came low and outside, and he didn't swing. The next pitch came in fast and he swung, but didn't time it right and it cleared hard into the catcher's mitt. The next pitch was a curve ball and Terry timed it right and smacked one over the right fielder's head. The next pitch was a slider and he caught it on the meat of the bat – CRACK! The ball went high over the center fielder's head.

The coach smiled and said, "Alright, Daniels. Good job! You have officially made the freshman team!"

Terry started playing college baseball and was excited about the opportunity of putting his athletic ability to work again, in hopes of winning a letter in a sport at SMU.

He called Tony at the PAL gym a few days later to touch base with him and give him the news that he would not be able to do any boxing during baseball season. Tony said, "Hey, that's okay Terry, but if ya' have any intention of going into the Open Division next year, you're gonna have to work hard in the ring over the summer when ya' go back to Cleveland.

"I just got back from the National Golden Gloves Tournament in Kansas City and saw one of the best heavyweights I've seen in a long time. He won all of his five fights over the three-day tournament – *and all by knockout.*

"He's a white boy too, on the Los Angeles team, and kinda reminds me of you," he said. "His name is Quarry, Jerry Quarry. And if ya' have any intention of ever gettin' in the ring with a guy like that, you're gonna hafta really work your balls off!"

"Quarry? What nationality is that?" Terry asked.

"He's Irish Hillbilly," he jokingly said, "and ya' don't get tougher than that!"

The oldest boy of the Daniels family told his friends he had a lot more to prove to the people in the city of "Big D," but he was determined to be a winner who stayed on top.

* * *

Coach Finley's first season of baseball at SMU was challenging at best. Like Terry, most of his players were "walk-ons" and several, like Dedo and Pinky Clements, played for Hayden Fry's football team. When spring practice for football started, they were allowed a shortened workout at football, then went directly over to baseball practice.

"Ah, the life of the collegiate athlete," Dedo later said to Terry.

The varsity team struggled to keep up with the dominating baseball teams of the SWC – Texas and Texas A&M – but, still managed to stay out of last place. Terry's freshman team fared better, winning half of its games. Terry also scored a big victory in one of the games, creating a name for himself amongst the coaches and his teammates.

Hugh Hackney, a varsity player, told Terry the next day when he saw him at lunch that Coach Finley came into their locker room after hearing the results of the game and said, "Boys, we're starting to rebuild our team with a sound base of pitchers. One of our freshmen pitched a one-hitter against Rice today!"

The game also got Terry what he was *really* after by the end of the season – a letter in a collegiate sport. Even though it was a freshman "Colt" letter, he had the blue "M" stitched on a red sweater along with his name in a white patch on the bottom. He proudly wore it around campus.

He still had Coach Tony's words in his head about staying in shape for boxing if he wanted to compete next year in the Golden Gloves, and he had every intention of doing so.

The Texas spring had proven to be a bit rainier than previous years and the baseball team had several practices and games called off. Terry used every opportunity to train at the PAL.

He also kept up on all the news in the world of professional boxing, and on May 25, Cassius Clay claimed headlines again by knocking out Sonny Liston in the first round, retaining his heavyweight championship belt. The fight got national attention, but was called "very controversial" by a new reporter named Howard Cosell on ABC's *Wide World of Sports*.

The year was filled with all kinds of excitement, and with two weeks of school left, Terry felt he had accomplished a lot for his first year in college. He won a first-time ever Golden Gloves trophy, lettered in baseball, and maintained his grade point average above 3.0. He took a moment to say a silent prayer. He was humble enough to know where his blessing came from.

CHAPTER 14

Finals went well for Terry and he finished with a 3.5 in his first year. Looking forward to the summer break back home, he made arrangements to have his belongings shipped home so he could ride his motorcycle on the open road. The heat from the bright Texas sunshine and beautiful scenery were the deciding factors in that decision.

Saying goodbye to his new friends over his last week, Terry confirmed he would be rooming next fall with another freshman, now sophomore, whom he had gotten to know better in the second semester – Mike McCann.

Mike was from Coffeeville, Kansas, a small town similar to Willoughby. He chose SMU based on the swim team's winning record in the SWC. He was 6' 0" tall, weighed 165 pounds; had thin, sandy blond hair and a friendly smile for everyone.

Terry met Mike for the first time at lunch after his Golden Gloves victory, but really got to know him after a poker game at the Phi Delta house. Dedo invited them, and they were the only two freshmen to attend. He smiled as he remembered that night.

There were several tables for poker set up in the dining hall, with six boys at each table. The room was filled with cigarette smoke, laughter, and lots of chatter.

Dedo walked up to Terry and Mike and said, "Hey, don't be shy, boys. Help yourselves to a beer from the fridge. The campus police give us a little break towards the end of the year as long as we are discreet about it. And be ready for a seat to open up for the poker games."

"Thanks, Dedo," they said.

As they poured each other a beer, one of the frat brothers approached and said, "Hey, if you guys want to get in on a game, a couple of seats just opened up at a table over there."

Dedo waved his hand for Terry and Mike to take the seats and said, "Be my guest boys, I'm just here for the beer!"

They each introduced themselves as they sat down at a table and were instructed to buy $10 worth of chips to join the game. They played five-card poker with a three card draw, and seven-card stud, with an occasional "deuces wild."

After an hour, Mike had gone through $15 worth of chips, while Terry had doubled his original $10.

"Looks like you got the lucky seat between us two, Daniels," Mike said while shuffling the deck as the new dealer. "I get a pair of kings and you get the aces; I pull a straight and you get the flush!"

Terry smiled and said, "Just keep 'em coming my way, McCann!"

Mike smiled back, shook his head, and said, "Seven-card stud; 50-cent ante; deuces wild with the last card down."

The other boys at the table were a sophomore and two juniors that Terry didn't know, and a senior, named Doug, who sat right across from him. They both had a good amount of chips.

Terry could sense the older boys in the fraternity were sizing him up; not because he was a potential pledge, but because he was "The Golden Gloves Boxer," the "Kid Galahad" they'd heard so much about. He felt tension building in the air.

With two cards down and two up, no one in the game seemed to have much showing except Terry who had a pair of sevens. Doug was eyeballing him pretty good with just a four and a nine showing.

Mike passed the next card out to each player and called each one at a time, "Jack of clubs to Terry; three of diamonds to Teddy Boy with no help; eight of clubs to Tom with no help; jack of hearts to

Bobby which could have helped Terry; a nine of hearts to Doug; and a five of diamonds to me – no help. Doug takes the lead with a pair of nines."

Doug put the bet at $2 and Mike said, "I'm down to my last two bucks and I'd like to leave here with at least a little in my pocket, so I'll fold."

Terry and Ted called the bet while Tom also folded.

Mike flipped the next card and said, "Last card up is a seven of diamonds giving Terry trip sevens; Ted no help with a ten of hearts; and Doug gets a deuce which gives him three nines and still the lead bet."

Doug threw down three $1 chips in the pot, which was the one-time limit, and said, "Three dollars to you, Daniels," while holding a smirk on his face.

Terry thought that Doug might have a pair as his two down cards by the way he had been betting, which would give him a full house while he had just an ace and a six for his. He wasn't quite convinced though and said, "Call."

Ted said, "I fold," leaving Terry and Doug to face off.

"Okay, the last card is down and dirty," Mike said as he passed the first card to Terry and the next to Doug.

Doug picked up a king of hearts and added it to his other two down cards - the king of diamonds and three of clubs. He smiled and said, "Three dollars more to stay in to the freshman."

Terry looked at his last card, then looked at his chip count which had dwindled down to $5. He looked into the eyes of the senior across from him, and the crowd of frat brothers that stood watching behind him; smiled and said, "Crap, I can't beat your nines, let alone your full house. I'm with you McCann." He turned all his cards face down and passed them to Mike.

"Wise move, Daniels," Doug said as he raked in a pile of chips, "and you were right, I did have the full boat."

Mike took a peek at Terry's last card, which only the dealer was allowed to do, and tried hard not to show any emotion. He looked into Terry's eyes and Terry smiled while the rest of the boys slapped Doug on the back in congratulations.

Terry stood up and said, "Well, it's been fun boys. So if you excuse us, we're going to see if Dedo left us any beers."

They all shook hands, and he and Mike headed to the group of boys who were huddled in a circle singing a frat song.

As they left the table, Mike grabbed Terry's arm and said, "What the hell did you do that for, Terry? I saw that last card, the deuce of clubs, you had *four sevens*! You could have cleaned his clock! Why'd you drop out?"

"Are you kidding me?" Terry said. "Have you been watching the way these guys have been looking at me all night? They're like a bunch of sharks in the water bumping into their prey just waiting for an opportunity to chomp.

"If I'd of called his hand and took that big pot away from him, *a senior* no less, he would have been the first to escort us both to the door and tell us don't bother coming back!"

Mike glanced over Terry's shoulder and caught a glimpse of the boys leaving the table. He noticed that one of them had turned Terry's hand over. He watched as they looked back at each other in disbelief.

He smiled, shook his head and said, "Daniels, you're not Kid Galahad, you're more like Gentlemen Jim Corbett! Come on, let's you and me grab a cold one," and the two of them proceeded to join Dedo and his buddies.

Terry chuckled to himself as he thought of that evening. But before he kicked his motorcycle into gear for the long ride home, he saved his last goodbye to that special girl from Houston, Tracie Dixon.

It was a little after 8 on Thursday night, and the dorms were filled with parents and students carrying clothing and furniture out to the cars. Tracie was waiting for Terry on the front steps. She smiled and waved as he approached the steady stream of people coming and going.

"Hi Terry," she said. "Come up to my room; you can help me move a table."

She grabbed his hand and led the way up the steps to her room on the second floor. Terry admired the cute little swivel in her hips that fit nicely in the blue and white flowered summer dress she was wearing.

Tracie was 5' 5", had light brown hair that was teased into that '60s "Glamour Girl" look, weighed about 120 pounds and had hazel-green eyes. The natural beauty of her face required little make-up, and Terry liked it that way.

"So I guess the hall monitors are busy tonight, otherwise I couldn't get past the front door with you holding my hand," he said.

"You guessed it, Sherlock," she replied as she opened the door to her room.

Terry walked into the 10 x 12 dorm room and said, "Wow, this is a pretty cool-looking room for a girl's dorm."

Two twin beds were opposite each other with a nice throw rug between them on the floor. A large study desk was on the wall facing the street with a mirrored table on the other end, separated by a well-draped window. A large closet took up the remaining space.

The room looked very neat, and most everything was packed or removed except for a large color poster of The Beatles on the wall.

Tracie closed the door and said, "My roommate left yesterday and my folks are coming up from Houston tomorrow morning. I thought we could say goodbye to one another the right way."

"You mean before or after we move the table?" Terry said, smiling.

Tracie smiled back and walked up to him, putting her arms around his neck to give him a slow, seductive kiss.

"Wow, that was nice," Terry said when they finished.

She reached behind her neck, unlatched the top of her dress, and unzipped the back of it. Terry smiled and began unbuttoning his plaid shirt; he didn't need any more signals to know what to do next. They spent the next hour exploring each other's bodies and making love to one another, on her roommate's bed.

They exchanged home phone numbers and addresses before they parted and Terry said he would try to stay in touch, but didn't want to make any promises he couldn't keep. He knew they had an understanding. They weren't exactly a "couple" but instead, enjoyed each other's company and would respect each other's feelings.

As he gunned his motorcycle, he decided to ride by his dorm one more time before heading on to the highway. He saw two boys loading a car out front and pulled up next to them.

"Hey, Terry! All saddled up and ready for the long ride back to Ohio?" one of the boys asked.

"Yeah, I've got my rest stops all mapped out," he said. "I thought I'd stop by and say, 'Adios!'"

They smiled and the other boy said, "Daniels, you're somethin' else. Whaddaya got in mind for us next year – win another boxin' tournament?"

Terry smiled back and said, "You never know boys, but I got all summer to get in shape for next year!"

He turned his motorcycle to the street and popped a wheelie for them while speeding away. He was satisfied with all he'd accomplished his first year at SMU.

CHAPTER 15

Tom and Jeff were playing catch in their front yard around 7:30 Sunday evening in anticipation of Terry's arrival. It was the first week in June and the air kept a pleasant warmth to it as the sun went down. They were throwing high pop-ups and fast grounders to one another to stay busy until their brother rolled in.

They played for over an hour before calling it quits. Terry called home on Friday morning before he got on the road and said all systems were "go." He said they could expect him late Saturday or early Sunday, depending on the weather. Traffic wouldn't be a problem because he could just zip in and out of any line of cars or construction on his motorcycle.

He called them collect from a phone booth just outside of Kentucky on Sunday morning before they went to church. He told them he got stuck in a thunderstorm Saturday night and they could expect him home by evening.

The boys put the ball and gloves in the hall closet and plopped down on the couch with the rest of the family to watch the end of *The Ed Sullivan Show*. A half-hour later, they heard the engine of Terry's motorcycle as he lowered it into second gear before turning into the driveway. They all jumped up and headed out the front door.

His lone headlight shone brightly as they watched him coast the motorcycle to a stop. Jeff ran ahead of the family and was the first to greet him.

My Brother the Boxer

Terry was wearing his new Golden Gloves jacket, but Jeff was too excited to even notice. Terry said, "Hi, Jeff! Hey, everybody! Man, is it great to be home!"

He gingerly stepped off his motorcycle and swung his arms around everyone as Denny and Jeff unhooked the large duffle bag that was strapped to the back seat.

Bill noticed his slow exit off the bike and said, "Riding that motorcycle was probably like riding a horse the whole way home!"

Terry cupped his hands to the base of his back, stretched it a little and said, "I'll say…Woo!"

They spent the rest of the evening laughing and talking, but June reminded the younger ones they had school the next day, so they gave their big brother a "welcome home" hug and made their way to bed.

Before Jeff went into his room, he heard Terry talking in a low voice to Tom and pushed the door of their room open to hear what he was talking about. Tom told him to stay out, but Terry said it was okay for him to come in and listen to one of his traveling stories.

Jeff quietly closed the door behind him and Terry told them that he finished supper on Saturday night around 6:30 in Kentucky and wanted to make it to Dayton to check in for the night. He was making good time for the first half-hour when suddenly the sky turned dark blue and a few loud claps of thunder made him look for a nearby exit. He was on a long stretch of highway, however, with no exits in sight, so he pulled under a bridge just before the clouds let loose with a giant thunderstorm of rain.

"I chained my Triumph to the guard rail, took my duffle bag off and climbed up the embankment to the top of the underpass," he said.

"I just made it in time too, because the rain came down in buckets and it poured all night. I spread the duffle bag out with my stuff in it and kind of made a bed on a level spot. I ended up sleeping there for the rest of the night."

"Wow," Tom said. "You mean you slept under the bridge like some bum on the street? Weren't you scared?"

"Yeah, a little, but I had a big Bowie knife with me that I bought off a guy at school, and ended up sleeping with it close to my chest all night. It rained till about five in the morning and I got right back on the road around six. I still had stop-and-go weather, so I had to make more stops than I wanted. It turned out to be a good thing because that ride was hard on my ass!"

They all laughed and June yelled up the stairs, "Alright boys, you can talk all you want tomorrow. You've got school first thing in the morning, so let's call it a night!"

* * *

The rest of the week Terry spent catching up with his buddies in Willoughby, while the rest of his siblings finished their finals. Jeff told Terry that it felt good to look out the window in his fifth-grade class knowing that when the bell rang, it would be the last time he would hear it for the next three months.

The following Monday at 6 a.m., their dad yelled up the stairs for Terry and Tom to get up. It was time to go to work!

Both of the boys were dressed and out the door by 6:45 a.m. Tom walked out their back door and up to the golf-course garage to join the rest of the maintenance crew while Terry kick-started his motorcycle and followed his dad to the fuel-oil company yard. A new summer of road construction had begun.

Terry was well received by the rest of the guys who were standing by the trucks awaiting their orders for the week. Bill told Terry that he would be working with the crew that was redeveloping the berm on Ohio Route 2. The stretch ran from Willoughby all the way to Cleveland and they would be working on that job for the next two months.

The job was overseen by the State of Ohio, which meant Terry and the rest of the guys would be working at the hourly union pay scale. And that added an extra $2 to their normal wages from Northeastern Road. It also meant Terry would be on the job by 7 a.m. each morning and done by 4 in the afternoon. This allowed him to plan his workouts at Wagner's gym in Collinwood from 4:30 p.m. to 6 p.m. each day.

In addition, Danny Iafelice informed Terry that his dad would be coaching a baseball team in the American Legion League this summer and wanted him to be on it. Mr. Iafelice had recruited some of the best high school graduate baseball players in Lake County, and Terry said, "Of course!" That meant, however, that he also had to allow time for practice which started at 7 p.m.

Terry could hear the words of Coach Tony in his head: *You're gonna' have to work your balls off to stay in shape for the Open Heavyweight Division!* So he stayed focused on his goals.

Before they left the fuel-oil yard, his dad came out of the office and approached Terry with a letter in his hand. "Hey, before we take off, this came in our mail last week," he said. "It's addressed to you."

Terry looked down at the hand printed address on a letter which read, *To: Terry Daniels, Daniels Bros. Fuel Co., Willoughby, Ohio.* There was no return address and the date was stamped June 8, 1965 from the Dallas, Texas, post office.

He opened it and read a letter from Coach Tony:

Dear Terry,

I hope this letter finds you well. Dickie Wills told me the name of your dad's company and I trust it made it to you. I wanted you to know that I've decided to take an early retirement from the police force and join a buddy of mine in Santa Fe, New Mexico. He's got a private detective agency and can't keep up with the business. I'm going in as a partner.

> *I wish you a lot of luck in school and in boxing. Like I've told you before, if you keep working hard like I know you can, you will bring home a championship trophy.*
> *Best of luck,*
> *Tony M.*

Terry smiled and put the letter into his pocket.

"Let's go, Ace!" Peps yelled. "We're not paying you to stand there reading letters all morning! We got work to do!"

"Jump in, Terry," Danny yelled from the back of Bill's station wagon. Terry climbed in with the rest of the grunts for the start of summer road work.

Over the next three weeks, Terry would throw his gym bag in the back of his dad's car and ride his motorcycle to the work site on Route 2. He would leave directly from work each day to meet up with Tommy Morris at Wagner's gym.

Tommy was glad to see that Terry was still interested in getting into the ring. Both he and Larry Wagner noted that his boxing skills were improving, but he still had a long way to go. They focused more on improving his rhythm and speed when he threw combination punches. The workouts were intense, but Terry did everything he was told week after week.

Tommy told Terry they were putting together a boxing show at the gym at Eastlake North High School at the end of July and wanted to know if he would be interested in a heavyweight match. Terry said, "Sure, as long as it doesn't interfere with baseball."

When the boxing workouts ended, he would take a shower at the gym and then jump on his motorcycle to head home for a healthy supper. From there he was off to baseball practice at Todd Field in Willoughby every night by 7 p.m. On Friday and Saturday nights, he reserved time to go on dates with girls he knew were home from college.

By the time the Fourth of July came and the family was gathered at his Aunt Bev's pool for the family picnic, everyone noticed how Terry looked like a Greek Olympian. He disagreed though, and kept raising the bar on himself saying, "Have you seen the way Cassius Clay is built? He's not only ripped from top to bottom, but he is faster than a speeding bullet and more powerful than a locomotive. That's the way I want to be!"

While Terry was getting the notoriety for his boxing and baseball skills, his brother, Tom, was perfecting his skills in the game of golf.

Tom's work day ended between 3 and 3:30 in the afternoon at Sequoia, and he would usually shag balls in the open field behind their house for an hour or two, or play the number six and five holes on the course when play was slow, for practice.

Jeff told Terry that he watched the pro at Sequoia, Mr. Dunt, give Tom a lesson on chipping and putting recently. Terry chuckled as Jeff imitated the elderly British gentleman's voice, "Grip the club lightly when you're chipping Tommy," and Tom did exactly as he was told – over and over.

Jeff said, "He looked over at me winking and said, 'You have improved immensely in just a year Tommy; you'll be challenging *me* for my job before long.'"

Terry would play golf with Tom whenever he could, but never had the time to get good at it like Tom. He got frustrated with the game one day and said he didn't think he could ever get the swing of it, literally. Tom suggested he try hitting the golf balls left-handed.

"You bat better left-handed than you do right," he said. "So why not try hitting a few drives with a left-handed club?"

Mr. Dunt had a used pair of left-handed clubs in the pro shop that he kept as rentals. He let Terry play a few holes with them. Sure enough, Terry hit the ball straighter and longer than ever before.

"You're a natural lefty, Ace," Tom said.

From that point on, Terry would borrow clubs from his Uncle Peps, who was a true lefty himself, whenever he played a round of golf. Although he could never beat Tom, he enjoyed the competition.

* * *

By mid-July, their mother was eager to take a trip to New York to visit her side of the family. She entertained the idea of taking Debbie, but leaving the boys to hold down the fort.

She told them of her plans at the dinner table and Bill said, "That sounds okay to me. The boys and I can't leave work at this time anyhow. Jeff and Denny are old enough to watch over the house till we get home, so that should work out fine."

"I'd also like to take the drive in something different this time instead of the Buick," June said.

"Oh, yeah? Like what?" Bill asked.

"Well, have you seen those commercials for the new Ford Mustang?"

"A Mustang!?" Tom said. "Oh, Dad, that car is *cool!*"

"Yeah Dad, and did you know they got the name from SMU?" Terry added.

"They did?" Bill replied.

"Yeah, a couple friends of mine who play on the football team told me after they played Michigan in '63 some guys from Ford came into the locker room to talk with Coach Fry and the rest of the team. They told them that after coming back from being held scoreless in the first half, and battling all the way down to the final minute of the game, they decided to name a new car after them – *The Mustang.*"

"I'd just like to drive something that is a little easier to park, and isn't so big like the Buick," June added.

Bill smiled and said, "Well, I suppose I can call Stan over at Marshall Ford and see if he can get us one to look at."

By the end of the week, June got her wish. Bill pulled into the Daniels' driveway Saturday afternoon in the Buick, and June pulled in right behind him in a brand new, candy-apple red Ford Mustang.

Denny was mowing the lawn and Jeff was trimming the hedges in the front yard when they drove in. June had a big smile on her face when she pulled up and parked next to Bill. The boys stopped what they were doing and ran over to admire her new set of wheels.

"Isn't it beautiful?" she asked excitedly, stroking the shiny red top.

"Wow, Tom was right – this car is cool," Jeff said as he slipped into the driver's seat. Denny immediately went to the passenger's seat and the two of them ran their hands over the new buttons and upholstery.

Bill came up behind June and gripped her shoulders. She responded by putting her hand on his and gave him a kiss.

"Oh, I'm so excited," she said. "I'm going to pack our things tonight. Debbie and I will leave first thing in the morning!"

They all got up early Sunday morning to say goodbye to June and Debbie. June smiled and started to put her new car in reverse, but ended up grabbing air because the automatic shift was on the floor console instead of the steering wheel.

"Whoops! I guess I'll have to start getting used to that," she said.

The boys chuckled and waved as she backed out of the driveway and on to the start of their trip.

* * *

The following Monday morning as Terry and Tom dressed for work, their father gave Jeff and Denny specific instructions for the week.

"Alright you two, I want you to stay outside as much as possible. You can play with your friends in the backyard or go to their house, but if you leave, make sure you tell Aunt Sal next door. She's going to keep an eye on you until Tom gets home. So, don't do any foolish tricks or fight with each other or you'll be going to bed early with red marks on your butts from my belt!" Bill said with a scowl on his face.

It was always hard to keep a straight face when their father got serious with them, or "laid down the law," because he didn't have to do it often.

When one of the boys did or said something that needed immediate disciplinary action, their mother didn't hesitate to get the job done. None of this, "Wait till your father gets home, Buster!" No sir. It was quick spanks on the butt with her hand; a swat of a broom; wooden spoon, or whatever else she happened to have on hand. And if the punishment needed more severe action, a quick visit to the closet to get a belt did the trick.

When Bill ended his remarks, Denny and Jeff looked down at their feet and said, "Will do, Dad." All the while trying hard not to snicker and give themselves away. They both knew how much fun they would have this week and didn't want to blow it.

Keeping busy outside was never hard for the Daniels boys. Their cousins were right next door and several of their good friends were just down the road or on nearby Gardenside Drive. Everything else was just a bike ride away.

The week moved along quickly, and by Saturday night, Bill and the boys drove to Eastlake North High School to watch Terry's heavyweight debut in the ring. His opponent was last year's Cleveland Golden Gloves Novice Heavyweight Champion, Harold Carter.

The Cleveland Golden Gloves tournament was held each year at Navy Park, with the Regional Championship in Public Hall. They got a nice crowd each year, but nowhere near the amount they got in Dallas.

The gymnasium was filled with boxing fans from all over Lake County, and Terry had a crowd of fans there just to see him. They included lots of guys from his high school, and even his football/baseball coach, Neal Nelson.

Terry was last up on the eight-bout card and did not disappoint his fans. He knocked the lanky 6' 1", 195-pound Carter down twice in Round Two and won by technical knockout.

Tommy Morris entered the ring to wipe Terry off with a towel and take out his mouthpiece. Terry took a swig of water and turned to walk over to his opponent's corner to make sure he was all right and acknowledge that it was a good fight.

Carter was taking a whiff of smelling salts from one of his corner men when he felt Terry tap him on the back and say to him, "Hey, you're a good fighter."

Carter shook his head after feeling the effect of the ammonia and said, "Thanks, man. I got careless here tonight. We'll meet again though, you can count on it!"

Terry tapped gloves and they both went back to the center of the ring where the referee grabbed each of their arms and awaited the announcer. The P.A. gym speakers boomed, "The winner by technical knockout in two minutes and forty seconds of the second round, from Willoughby - Terry Daniels!"

The referee raised Terry's arm and the gymnasium filled with more whistles and cheers. The Daniels boys and their friends watched as their brother exited the ring and was mobbed by his friends patting him on the back and shaking his wrapped hands.

Suddenly, the gym echoed with *Twist and Shout* by The Beatles. Management had hooked up a record player by the microphone and was providing music as the people made their way out of the gymnasium.

Jeff and Denny looked at Terry from the stands, and in the middle of all those people, their brother looked like a real rock star. Jeff turned to Denny and said, "I can only imagine what the line at the Methodist Church will look like after tomorrow's service."

CHAPTER 16

June and Debbie got home from New York the following Tuesday afternoon, and the whole family shared stories that stretched from the dinner table well into the evening. Bill sat back and let Tom, Denny and Jeff do most of the talking about Terry's boxing victory, while their mom just shook her head and smiled.

They covered just about everything that went on while she was away, and at the end of the story, she insisted they go camping at Moffitt Beach before the end of summer.

"I really didn't get time to stop by the lake," she said. "Warren says it's just beautiful and suggested we give him a call soon to reserve a camp site."

"Well, I was considering taking time off a couple weeks before Labor Day and driving through Canada to see a horse show. So, maybe we could drive two cars and meet at Warren's," Bill said.

The plan sounded good, and by dinner the next night, June announced the details she had worked out. Denny and Debbie would ride with her in the station wagon while Bill would drive Terry, Tom and Jeff in the Buick. She would meet with Uncle Warren and his family at the lake and set up the camp, while Bill and the boys would stop overnight in Toronto to see the horse show.

Bill didn't elaborate on the details of the location in Toronto and chose not to tell the boys until the day before they left. He told them: "The horse show is being held at the Canadian National Exhibition in Toronto, and it's kind of like the World's Fair. I thought Mom and the little ones would take away the time I wanted to look at the draft horses, but you guys could keep busy while I mingle with the horse crowd - right?"

"Sure we can, Dad," Terry said.

When Monday morning arrived, June, Denny and Debbie were ready to hit the road a little after 7 a.m. The station wagon was packed with suitcases, the tent, and all the camping gear. Terry knew the routine and folded down the seats in the back of the car leaving enough space between the gear for the kids to take turns napping for an hour or two.

Within a half-hour of their mother's departure, Terry, Tom and Jeff plowed into their Buick Skylark while their dad drained the last of his second cup of coffee and closed the front door.

"Okay, you guys got everything?" Bill asked.

"Yeah, let's go," Tom said while reaching over the front seat and turning the key to start the car. Summer Vacation for '65 was underway.

They drove for about two hours on Interstate 90 before Bill took an exit for a break near Erie, Pa. They got out at a little diner and Bill went in to get them a few donuts and a fresh cup of coffee while the boys stretched their legs.

Terry tapped Jeff on the back and said, "Tag you're it!" and he and Tom took off running around the parked cars. They laughed as Jeff made a futile attempt to tag him back.

"No fair," he said, "You know I can't catch you guys! Why didn't you tap Tom first, Terry?" They just laughed and kept zigzagging around the cars.

Bill came out with a bag of donuts, a couple of small cartons of milk, and a large coffee and said, "Okay, you hooligans, let's get back on the road."

They drove another 45 minutes, then Terry told his dad to pull over at the bridge underpass ahead of them.

"If you have to pee, I'm going to get gas at the next exit," Bill said.

"No, I just want to get out and jog a little bit."

Bill pulled over and Terry got out and started to stretch. "Just drive up the road a mile or so and I'll catch up," he told him.

Bill chuckled and said, "Okay, son."

He proceeded to coast up the interstate on the berm of the road at a slow crawl. Tom and Jeff watched as Terry started out with a slow jog right behind the car, then Bill slowly picked up the pace and so did Terry.

Tom rolled down the back window and said, "Come on Ace, you're doggin' it!"

Jeff looked at the speedometer and saw that his dad was coasting around 10 mph while applying a little more pressure on the gas pedal. Terry moved into a very fast trot, and then worked into a full-blown sprint. They all started cheering for Terry to keep up, and he did for almost a mile.

Bill started to slow down as Jeff and Tom watched their big brother drift farther behind, but they were fascinated by how long Terry kept his full pace. Bill finally came to a stop when Terry caught up. Tom and Jeff opened the passenger's side of the car and got out to meet him as the cars and trucks sped by on the interstate.

"You looked like an Indian running from the Red Coats," Tom said as Terry bent over with his hands on his knees taking in as much oxygen as he could.

"Aahh…I needed that," said Terry in between breaths, "Okay, now let's head up to that next exit, I gotta pee."

They drove through the custom entrances to Canada by mid-afternoon and were in Toronto less than two hours later. Bill checked them in at the Holiday Inn just off the freeway and got directions and tickets for the fair at the front desk. Jeff was the first to look at the pamphlet on the daily events and did a double take when reading the entertainment scheduled for the evening: *At 7:00 PM – The comedy of The Three Stooges, Live and In Person!*

"Holy cow! Hey, you guys, it says The Three Stooges will be on stage tonight, live and in person!" he blurted out to Terry and Tom.

They both smiled and said, "Are you kidding me?"

Bill rolled his eyes and said, "Oh brother."

On weekdays, most of the kids in the Cleveland area watched a local variety show called The Captain Penny Show at 5 p.m. on Channel 5. A middle-aged man with a nice smile dressed in a railroad conductor's outfit welcomed kids of all ages with an hour of fun-filled entertainment. Ron Penfound, or Captain Penny, started off with a cartoon, followed by a special guest, who was usually from the Humane Society with a dog or cat for someone to adopt.

The kids especially liked it when he brought in Jungle Larry as a guest. He dressed in an African Safari suit and would bring an animal from the Cleveland Zoo.

Captain Penny would introduce a few more cartoons in between commercials to fill the show. But one day, he introduced the enormous 18 and under crowd to a short comedy film of The Three Stooges.

It was such a hit the producers of Captain Penny made the Stooges a regular part of the show. But while the kids in the Cleveland area loved the Stooges, the parents had a different view of them – especially their mothers.

The scene across Cleveland neighborhoods looked something like this: Dad comes home from a long day at work around 5:30 p.m.; he gets cleaned up and looks forward to a great home-cooked meal. Mom tells the rest of the family to get ready for dinner around 5:30 or 5:45 – right in the middle of The Three Stooges. All hell breaks loose when the kids beg to watch the end of the pie-throwing antics of Larry, Curly, and Moe.

Parents hated the disruption at the dinner table, especially when one of the boys started imitating the comedy routines they'd just witnessed.

But now Terry, Tom and Jeff were able to see their comedy heroes live and in person.

Later while they were eating, the loudspeakers from the midway announced, "Don't forget folks, The Three Stooges will be at the grandstands in the Exhibition Stadium tonight, and tonight only, at 7 o'clock. Don't miss the show!" They didn't have to tell the boys twice. Jeff was so excited, he wanted to grab his dinner and finish it in the front row of the grandstand to get the best seat possible.

Bill kept them in line, however, and said they had plenty of time to finish their dinner and check out the sights of the fair before heading over to the stadium.

Jeff said to his brothers, "He's right. We're in the middle of a gigantic fair filled with more rides and buildings than we've ever seen, and I'm going back to school and say I saw The Three Stooges *live*. How cool is that?"

The Horse Palace was not far from the stadium, and to his sons surprise, Bill walked into the grandstand and joined them to see the show. He decided he could use a good laugh, and wasn't disappointed.

There was a small orchestra playing close to the stage, and when the music got softer, the P.A. speakers started booming, "Okay folks, let's hear a big Toronto welcome for The Three Stooges!" A green flat-bed truck came out from a nearby tent with the Stooges standing on it waving to the crowd. The fans stood and cheered wildly for the famous Hollywood threesome. Jeff pushed his way through to get a closer glimpse as they drove by waving and throwing kisses to the crowd.

The show was filled with slapstick routines, corny jokes, and a few musical numbers. Larry even did a little fiddling on the violin. Bill seemed to enjoy the first 30 minutes and smiled as he watched his sons have a good time. Then he excused himself and told the boys to meet him at the horse show around 11 p.m. He gave Terry some money and told him he was in charge of Tom and Jeff for the rest of the evening.

When the show came to an end, Moe announced they would be in a booth off stage to sign autographs, but Terry made up his mind. "We're not going to spend the whole night waiting in line for their autographs when we only got a few more hours for the rides," he said.

They beat the rush for the exit and set off for the biggest ride in the fair - The Mighty Flyer rollercoaster.

They packed in as much fun as they possibly could in their remaining time at the fair. Jeff's favorite part was watching his brothers take turns throwing baseballs to dunk a clown in a glass tank. A heavy-set guy in a clown suit with big suspenders was sitting on a plank above 6 feet of water, making mocking remarks to everyone paying to throw baseballs at him. They paid 50 cents for three tries to hit the red target on the end of a lever, attached to the plank.

There were three men in line in front of Terry and Tom. They all cracked up at the cutting remarks the clown would make at each thrower, and none of them dunked him. Jeff was starting to think the lever was rigged because one of the throwers nicked the target pretty good and the lever quivered, but didn't dunk the clown.

"High and dry," the clown said after every loser walked away, and then touted the guy to buy another ticket and try again. They watched all three give up with no luck. Then it was Terry's turn.

Terry handed his ticket to the man at the stand and readied himself for the first pitch. Tom snickered as Terry took a few steps back, went into his pitching wind-up and threw a fast ball just nicking the outside mark of the target. The lever moved a bit, causing the clown to quickly grab the bottom of the plank for leverage, but the plank didn't move.

"Wow! Look out folks! I think the Dodgers are in town! We got Sandy Koufax on the mound," the clown laughingly said into a microphone above the tank. "High and dry!"

Terry and his brothers laughed with some other folks in the crowd. It was especially funny to Tom because he knew how much Terry idolized Sanford "Sandy" Koufax of the Los Angeles Dodgers. Koufax was a left-handed pitcher who batted with his right, whereas Terry was a right-handed pitcher and batted with his left.

When Terry threw the next ball, it hit right on the target - PING! The lever went all the way back and the clown hit the water with a big splash. The crowd cheered as they watched the clown re-set the plank and climb back up on his seat. Terry went on to dunk him again. Then he paid for three more balls, and dunked him two more times.

"Okay, next!" the ticket attendant said. "Two's your limit son."

Jeff and Terry laughed and cheered Tom on as he dunked the clown three more times. The poor guy never had a chance to finish his mocking remarks; he was too busy getting the water out of his ears. They all clapped when Tom left the booth – and the clown was replaced by a new one.

They made their way to the horse arena around 11:30 p.m. and had no problem finding their dad among the hundreds of horses and patrons. All they did was ask where the draft horses were showing. They found him talking with a large bearded man who was wearing blue-jean overalls and holding the reins of a big gray dappled mare. She was a Percheron, and according to the bio of the horse stapled to the stall, "Dolly" stood about 17.2 hands tall (about 71 inches) and weighed close to 2100 pounds. She looked similar to two of Bill's horses back home, so the boys were sure he and his new acquaintance had quite a few stories to share.

When the show came to an end, the horses were led back to their stalls for the night, and Bill and the boys headed to the car. There were several bursts of laughter after they started sharing stories with their dad about how much fun they had.

After getting back to their room, they took turns taking showers, and sometime after 1 a.m., their heads finally hit their pillows. Terry and Tom were in one double bed, and Bill and Jeff in the other.

Jeff chuckled before climbing into bed and said, "Moe grabbed that fat cigar Curly was smoking, and hit him over the head with it. And the drummer in the orchestra timed a rim shot perfectly!"

The boys laughed as Bill smiled and shook his head. Jeff added, "This was a great idea to stop at the horse show, Dad. My friends are never gonna believe I got to see the Three Stooges Live!"

CHAPTER 17

Camping at the lake was a relaxing, but short vacation for the Daniels family. Bill and the boys didn't join up with June, the kids, and her brother Warren's family until Wednesday evening, and by Saturday, Bill announced they would be heading home first thing in the morning to beat the rush.

They still made it a memorable trip. Jeff and his cousin, Dave, came up with some new ways to use the firecrackers Bill purchased in Niagara Falls. They made sure they were far into the woods from their campsite so they wouldn't get yelled at by their parents, and built an elaborate jungle setting and war zone with their army men.

They kept entertained for hours, but had to call it quits when the last firecracker was a cherry bomb that blew up an old tree trunk and scattered their army men everywhere. Warren found them shortly after and warned them, "The park ranger is in the neighborhood and you better quit and head back to camp, or risk being fined and thrown out of the park."

They agreed and made a quick exit back to their camp, leaving half of the army men for Dave to find another time.

By early Sunday morning, they bid farewell and headed back to Willoughby. The drive home went smoothly mainly because Bill, June and Terry did all the driving while the rest of the kids slept most of the way. They rolled into their old homestead around 3 p.m., and June had already made a list of things she wanted the boys to get started on around the house after they unpacked.

"I thought Labor Day gave workers a rest," Jeff said comically.

June kept a straight face and said, "You've had your rest, and you can start by mowing the lawn. The rest of you don't run off!"

*   *   *

Terry stretched his summer out to the end of August, when he pitched his last baseball game in the American Legion League. He gave up six hits and his team won the game, finishing first in the league with a record of 16-1.

Mr. Iafelice got each of the boys a nice trophy and named Terry and two other boys the team's most valuable players the following week at the awards banquet. Bill and June attended along with the rest of the parents. Bill was proud of the fact that Daniels Fuel sponsored the team's uniforms, which sported a big D on their green caps.

Terry rode with his parents on the way home and had them stop by the Honda dealership in Wickliffe. "I've got something I want to show you," Terry said.

He led them through an aisle of smaller mopeds and scooters to a row of larger bikes and June said, "Another motorcycle?"

"Isn't it a beauty?" Terry said enthusiastically. "It's their new CB160 and it's quicker than the Triumph I've got now – I absolutely love it!"

The salesman sensed the tension with Terry's parents and quickly added, "This is Honda's largest motorcycle and was built to compete with Harley and Triumph here in the states. It's got a lot more power and is very sturdy on the open road."

Bill was rubbing his whiskers listening to what the salesman had to say, while June still had a look of disbelief on her face.

Terry felt that his dad was the path of least resistance so he kept his eye contact on him and said, "With my trade-in, I'm able to pay the difference off in cash and still have plenty of spending money for college."

June was hoping Bill would talk Terry out of it, but he said, "Well, you're old enough to make your own decisions and spend your own money, Ter."

He turned to June and said, "You gotta admit, he has shown responsibility with the Triumph and this one looks a lot sturdier for that long trip. So, I think it's entirely up to him."

He looked back at Terry and said, "After all, it's your butt that's going to be making that fifteen-hundred mile trip this fall!"

Terry smiled and the salesman said, "Well, if you got the cash we can sign the papers tonight and let you drive her home."

Terry said, "I'd sure like to take a ride on it to show my buddies tonight. Dad, do you think you could write a check for me tonight? I could go to the bank first thing in the morning and pay you back."

Bill said, "Well…sure. June, you've got the checkbook in your purse, don't you?"

June shook her head and said, "I suppose I do. But I hope you wear a helmet with this one, Terry. It may be a lot faster and smoother, but you know I worry every time you get on one of these things."

Terry smiled and the salesman said, "Great then! Let's step inside my office and finish the paperwork so you folks can get on your way. Hey, I even have a few helmets for you to choose from, and I'll give you half off."

The following week, Terry's duffle bag was strapped down securely to his new motorcycle, while Bill and Tom were loaded in the station wagon, and the rest of the family found themselves saying goodbye to their big brother again. He was off to start his '65-'66 sophomore year.

Terry had made plans to room with Mike McCann and had to leave a few days early because both of them were late getting their paperwork back to the Admissions Office. The clerk in the office sent them a letter and told them to be there early to work out the details.

Terry called home to say they made it down in record time, and his new motorcycle handled like a dream. He said, "The only disappointing thing was that they assigned us to a room in the theology dormitory – not the most exciting dorm on campus. The clerk told us, 'That's what happens when you sign up late.'"

He also told them of the latest news about his football team – for the first time in the school's history, a Negro was on the team.

Jerry LeVias was a highly touted athlete from Hebert High School in Beaumont, Texas, and had scholarship offers from nearly 100 institutions across the country. Coach Fry was the only one from the Southwest Conference to pursue him, and in the spring of 1965, the students were spreading a rumor that the head football coach was recruiting a "colored boy." The rumor proved to be true.

Over the summer, LeVias contacted Coach Fry and told him that he chose to attend SMU over the other finalists, UCLA and Colorado.

Terry said the Dallas newspapers noted that until now, no Negro athlete had ever received a football scholarship in the Southwest Conference, and Coach Fry told the *Daily Campus* newspaper that was going to change.

Terry was in agreement with the coach. After all, this was the '60s and the world was changing in every way, right before their eyes.

The campus was bustling with students and faculty, and over the first couple of weeks Terry had met up with several of his friends from the previous year. But he was sad to learn that Tracie Dixon was not returning to school. He talked with her roommate who told him that her parents could not afford to send her to SMU. She elected to stay home to work and build up her savings account. He said he felt bad that he didn't respond to a letter that he received from her over the summer, but made a point to call her later.

Terry and Mike McCann were trying their best to adapt to the "quiet life" in the theology dorm, but found themselves missing the daily antics of their buddies in the other dorms.

"Hey, you gotta admit, Terry, we get our homework done a lot faster here than we ever did in our rooms last year," Mike said.

One evening after supper, they decided to take a walk around the building to look at its architectural design. It was one of the original buildings on campus. Being the inquisitive college boys they were, they weren't as interested in the history of the building as they were in finding a secret door or passageway.

"What are these, Mike? I see them on the side of some of the buildings around campus," Terry said while pointing to a steel grate in the ground in the back of the building.

"I don't know exactly. They're too big for water drainage. Maybe it's a way into the plumbing for these old buildings."

"Well, let's check it out," Terry said as he knelt down to take a closer look.

"I think they're bolted, Terry."

"I don't see a lock on this one," Terry said, and he wiggled his fingers through the steel bars of the grate to get a grip. The bars were about an inch thick and an inch apart on the grate, which was four feet long by three feet wide.

He started to pull up and could feel resistance, so he got to his feet and squatted down to get both hands on the bar. With one massive jerk he pulled the grate up and open.

"I forget I'm with Clark Kent during the day and Superman by night," Mike laughed.

Terry found some metal steps and the two of them climbed down into a tunnel big enough for them to stand up.

"I was right. It looks like a bunch of underground plumbing and electrical for the building," said Mike.

"Let's see if there's a light switch somewhere," Terry said.

"Hell, I can barely see my hand in front of my face," Mike said.

"Well then, let's go back and grab some flashlights. It's only 7:30. What do ya' say, Sherlock?"

Mike smiled and said, "Why not? I'm game if you are." And the two of them climbed out and headed back to the main floor of their dormitory.

They were able to convince the hall monitor to lend them a couple of flashlights from the janitor's closet while they attempted to work on Terry's motorcycle for a few hours.

They climbed back down into the tunnel and turned on their flashlights. "There ought to be an electrical box that leads off with a switch somewhere," Terry said. "We can then get a better idea of where we're headed."

"Oh sure, so we light up the tunnels and everybody sees them glowing; then some security guard decides to investigate and the next thing we find our asses in a sling. I don't think so," said Mike.

"Oh…you're right…didn't think of that."

"Alright chief, you can lead the way. I'll be right behind you," Mike said.

They were careful to turn their flashlights out when approaching a grate because they could hear nearby voices.

Mike said, "Hey, it kinda' feels like we're in the movie *The Great Escape* doesn't it?"

Terry smiled and said, "Yeah. You know my favorite part is when Steve McQueen is on that motorcycle, and tries to outrun the Germans by flying over that barbed wire."

"Yeah, that was cool," Mike said.

"I actually tried something similar to that last summer with my motorcycle. My buddy Danny and I took our bikes out on the golf course behind our house one evening around dusk. We took turns hitting the front of the number six tee and flew up in the air about five feet or so off the ground. It was a blast!"

"Wow, sounds like fun. No barbed wire though," Mike said.

"No barbed wire…wise guy."

The boys approached another grate where they heard girls talking and giggling in the distance. They turned off their lights, and Mike climbed up to take a peek.

"Hey, I think we've found one of the girls dormitories," he said in a whisper.

Terry chuckled and said, "Let's take one of these side tunnels and see if we can get closer."

They stood next to a ventilation opening with a wired cover and could hear faint sounds of laughter and conversations coming from a group of girls.

"Sounds like they're in some special room together," Mike whispered to Terry.

Then they heard the rush of water going through one of the pipes above them and the two of them shined the light in each others eyes and laughingly said, "The bathroom!"

They both laughed, and Mike held his hand up and whispered, "Cool it, cool it...Listen."

A girl said, "Hey, wait a minute! Did you hear that? Sounded like men laughing inside the walls."

Another girl said she didn't hear anything. Mike stood closer to the vent, and in his best Boris Karloff voice said, "Mother? I've missed you, mother, but I'll be home to see you. I'm coming home mother..."

Terry was holding his hand to his mouth to keep from bursting out laughing, while Mike was holding his index finger up keeping perfectly still to hear a response.

They heard one of the girls say, "Did you hear that!? Oh my God, let's get Miss Wimberley!"

Mike backed off and whispered, "That ought to give 'em something to talk about tonight. Let's head on back just in case their house mother gets wise and starts snooping around."

Over the next two weeks, the boys had pulled their ghoulish prank three times in several buildings. And in the Friday addition of the *Daily Campus*, the headline of an article on page three was titled, "Are Some Buildings on Campus Haunted?"

Terry and Mike took the paper over to see Dedo at the frat house and shared their story with him and a few of his Phi Delta buddies. After several minutes of hysterical laughter one of the boys said,

"Damn, you guys got the kind of spirit we're lookin' for. You're both gonna have to think about pledging soon."

Mike said it would be an honor and he would seriously consider it, but Terry said he would have to postpone any pledge duties until he accomplished his new goal – winning the Heavyweight Open Division of the Dallas Golden Gloves.

CHAPTER 18

Terry called Dickie Wills on the phone the third week of school. He wanted to know where Dickie was working out.

"Well, the Police Athletic League has some new coaches since Tony left but I've been workin' out at Doug Lord's gym. It's called Glover's Gym, over on Elm Street downtown, not far from where the PAL was," Dickie said.

Terry climbed on his motorcycle that afternoon and took a drive downtown to check out the gym. He chained his Honda to a parking meter on Elm Street and crossed the street to look for the address Dickie had given him.

After walking up and down two blocks he finally narrowed the address to a pool hall. An elderly man with a newspaper in his hands was sitting on a chair in front of the entrance.

"Excuse me," Terry said, "I'm looking for a boxing gym called—"

"Glover's," the man said. He pointed his left thumb to the corner of the building and said, "Go to the door around the corner in the alley, it's unlocked this time 'a day. Take the stairs to the second flo'."

"Thanks," said Terry. He could hear the fast thumping of a speed bag as he got closer to the top of the stairs and his mind was already preparing him for that feeling most boxers from other gyms expect when they enter a different gym for the first time.

It reminded him of the old western movies where a cowboy opens the swinging doors of a saloon, takes two steps in, the piano quits playing and the people stop what they're doing and stare at the cowboy. Terry opened the door and felt just like that cowboy.

Doug Lord was holding the heavy bag for a young middleweight who was pounding the bag with both fists and dripping with sweat. He heard the gym die down and looked over to see Terry standing in the doorway. Doug told his boxer to take a break while he went over to greet him.

"Terry, good to see you," Doug said while giving him a hearty handshake. Doug was 37 years old, stood 5' 9" and weighed 160 pounds. He had thin dark brown hair which he kept neatly combed, and his ears stuck out just a little – giving him his own distinct look.

"Dickie Wills told me you'd be stoppin' by sometime this week. I'm glad you made it. Any trouble findin' the place?"

"No. Well, actually the old guy sitting in the chair out front of the pool hall told me where the entrance was," Terry said.

"His name's Wheezer. He's a good ol' boy; sits there for most of the afternoon just watchin' life comin' and goin'. He usually tells guys how to find me if they haven't been here before, so I figured you'd come walkin' through that door sooner or later."

Terry took a look around, and other than looking a little dirtier than the gyms he was used to, it appeared to have everything he needed. A standard-sized ring took up a third of the space and was elevated about six inches off the tiled floor. Three heavy bags swung from the ceiling in the center of the room, and two speed bags were opposite one another on each side in the corners.

There were eight boxers working out and Doug said he would get anywhere between 15 to 20 guys in there between 4:30 and 6:30 in the evening.

"I'm an insurance salesman, and sell life and health insurance full-time," he said.

"And I make most of my appointments after seven, when the daddies of the families are home. So, I ask that everybody be done and out the door by quarter to seven. But durin' the Golden Gloves,

I'll have upwards of 20 to 30 guys in here and have to keep the place open till around eight.

"We got a changin' area in the back, but we only got a couple lockers, and those are reserved for my pros. So don't leave your wallet or any loose change in your pockets. You give 'em to me or my assistant trainer over there and we'll keep 'em locked in my office till you leave. And make sure you bring your own mouthpiece, hand wraps, and head gear. We've got everythin' else you'll need."

He looked over at his assistant and yelled, "Cornbread! Come on over here a minute, I want you to meet somebody."

The elderly man put the towel he was holding around a young boxer's neck and shuffled slowly over to them.

"Terry, this is my assistant trainer, Eli Smith, but everybody calls him Cornbread," Doug said.

"He was born and raised in the ghettos of New Orleans, and back in the '20s and the '30s he made his livin' boxin' as a middleweight in the carnivals throughout the South. He's pushin' 65 now, but he's still got a lot of fight in him and helps me with my boxers every day. That is, when he's not shootin' the shit out front of the pool hall with ol' Wheezer."

Terry shook hands with Cornbread and said, "Boxing in the carnivals in the old days? Wow, that must have been a tough life."

"Folks would pay good money to see a good fight," Cornbread said. "But they didn't like it when a Negro like me would win all the time. So, my manager would say I'd have to take a dive now and then if I wanted to get paid at the end of the night. I didn't mind though, I made a pretty good livin' at it."

Terry could see some of the old scars that Cornbread carried on his weathered face and could only imagine the stories that came with each one.

"How come they call you Cornbread?" Terry asked.

"Where I come from, they used to make cornbread in a skillet and cook it so that the outer part was hard and the inner part was hot and soft – you could carry it in your pocket or satchel for days. And when folks saw me fight they'd say, 'That boy is hard as cornbread'," he said with a grin that exposed several missing teeth.

Terry laughed and Doug slapped him on the back and said, "Well, listen Terry, I'm glad you stopped by, and you are more than welcome to join my gym. We've got to get back to our boys now, so feel free to start whenever you want. But if you're lookin' to compete in the Open Division this year, you better start workin' *hard* now."

"Thanks, Doug," Terry said while shaking his hand, "I've got my schedule at school arranged so I can be here between 4:30 and 6:30 every day. So, I guess I'll see you tomorrow. Oh and how much are your monthly dues?"

"I don't charge any money here. All I ask is that if a man wants to train here and really learn how to box, just do what he's told and don't waste our time."

Terry thanked him again and exited down the stairs. On the way out the door he thought about getting back in the groove of working toward another boxing championship, and Glover's Gym would be his new home away from home.

When he got back to campus, he joined Mike McCann and Dedo for dinner at the cafeteria and told them all about Doug's gym.

"You really got your mind set on winning another boxing title don't you, Daniels?" said Dedo.

"Yep," Terry replied. "And I'm going into the Open Heavyweight Division."

"Man, the heavyweight division is anything over 175 pounds. Aren't you worried about giving up so much weight to your opponents, Terry?" asked Dedo.

"You've seen these amateur fights. Everyone likes to watch a good fight, but they *love* a good heavyweight match. That's why people stay to the end of the night. I've decided I'm either going to beat the toughest son of a bitch in the tournament or get out all together.

And who knows, maybe I'll step in the ring with Cassius Clay some day," Terry said with a smile.

Mike McCann said, "Hey, not to change the subject, but are you guys planning on taking anyone to the homecoming dance this weekend after the Texas game?"

The boys all nodded and muttered, "Yeah, sure – you?"

Mike nodded and said, "Yeah, Judy Hazelwood and I are going. Terry, did you find a date yet?"

"As a matter of fact, I got a beautiful little blonde in mind that I met last week. I plan on calling her tonight. Her name's Sally Farmer, and she's a junior."

The boys at the table all let out a little "Oooo" in unison.

Sally was an attractive, blue-eyed girl from Des Moines, Iowa. She had asked a girl Terry knew from his economics class to introduce her to him and he wasted no time in striking up a conversation with her.

Within a few days of meeting after classes, Sally gave Terry her phone number and the date was set for Homecoming weekend.

All the students were gearing up for a good game against Texas. The Mustang football team was showing Coach Fry that they were forming into a contender for the SWC and gave him confidence that they would give the Longhorns a good game on Saturday. They beat the Miami Hurricanes in Florida in their season opener 7-3, but then got trounced 42-0 by Illinois of the Big 10 the following week.

Their momentum was strong going into the Texas Tech game on October 23. Tech brought their All-American running back Donnie Anderson into Dallas that day, and the hard-working Mustang defense held him to fewer than 80 yards. Dennis Partee missed a 33-yard field goal in the closing minutes of the game, however, and the Mustangs lost 26-24 to the Red Raiders.

Dedo shared that during practice for the Tech game, their new freshman wide receiver Jerry LeVias had run back two kickoffs for touchdowns against the varsity defense. After he scored the second touchdown, a defensive player put a late hit on him and ended up sending him to the hospital with three busted ribs.

Coach Fry told the players in the locker room after practice that he would not tolerate any player taking a cheap shot like that against a teammate, and benched that player for the rest of the season. He also said that he expected all his players to respect one another and to stand up for each other regardless of their color.

Dedo said the players heard him loud and clear, and his only fear was that LeVias would take his wide receiver position from him next year.

Terry and Sally joined Mike and Judy at the Cotton Bowl on that sunny Saturday afternoon and watched the Mustangs thrash Darrell Royal's Longhorns 31-14. Hayden Fry was pleased, and was proving to everyone in Dallas that he was building a team that would be a solid contender in the SWC.

Sally and Terry officially became a "couple" after the Homecoming weekend and their friends said they really looked good together. Terry even mentioned her name to his family in one of his letters. Jeff thought she really must be something special because he hadn't heard him mention a girl's name since he went to college.

Sally not only found Terry attractive, but was fascinated by his stories. She loved his charm and wit when they were amongst friends, and the genuine affection he showed toward her. The only thing she expressed concern about was his interest in being a Golden Gloves boxing champion.

Terry assured her that he was being trained by excellent people. "In fact, I will be boxing in a few weeks on an amateur card that my coach recently set up for me along with a couple of other boxers from our gym. You can come and see for yourself," he said.

"Oh, I'm not sure I could stand seeing someone hit your face and cut you or something," she said while softly brushing his chin with the palm of her hand.

In his best Rocky Graziano imitation he said, "Ah shucks, Doll, I promised myself that if I ever really got hoit in da' ring, dat I would leave the sport for good...definitely."

She laughed, kissed him on the cheek and said, "Okay, but I'm going to hold you to that promise, tough guy!"

* * *

On Saturday evening, in November, the Dallas Athletic Club sponsored an amateur boxing show at a nearby high school gymnasium. There were eight bouts scheduled on the card and Doug Lord had six of his boxers in the lineup, with Terry and Dickie scheduled for the final two bouts of the evening.

The day before, the *Dallas Times Herald* had a nice write-up promoting the card and Doug was expecting a good turnout. He was not disappointed. The stands were filled to capacity in the gym before the bell rang to announce the first match.

Sitting in the middle on one side of the stands was a group of Terry's friends from school. Sally was also there with a couple of her girlfriends whom she had coaxed into coming.

A few of the football players were there to let off some steam from their disappointing loss to Arkansas earlier in the afternoon. The Razorbacks beat the Mustangs 24-3 before a crowd of 67,000. It was the largest crowd to watch an SMU football game in over a decade. Coach Fry told his players after the game not to be discouraged; that *they* would be the team to beat in the SWC, and the boys believed him. But for now, they just wanted to see one of their buddies pound the living crap out of somebody.

Terry was in the 7th bout of what proved to be a very exciting boxing card for the Dallas crowd. His opponent was from Farmers Branch and had a 20-pound advantage over him.

Dedo was concerned about the weight differential at the start of the fight, but after Terry almost knocked his opponent out of the ring in the third and final round, his confidence was renewed: His friend had what it takes to be a heavyweight contender.

The entire crowd stood and let out a roar that rattled the walls of the old gymnasium. The SMU fans were cheering the loudest, and they continued their cheers when the referee raised Terry's hand for a unanimous decision.

Doug had a smile from ear to ear when he and Cornbread escorted Terry out of the ring. "I think we got ourselves a real crowd-pleaser here, don't you, Cornbread?" he said.

Sally and her girlfriends quickly made their way down the stands to greet Terry before he had a chance to go back to the locker room. Mike and Dedo watched as their good friend from "Woolabee, Ohio" got hugs and kisses from the girls. "Lucky dog!" they said in unison.

News of Terry's victory spread quickly around campus the following week, and it did not take long for his popularity to pick up where he left off from last year's Golden Gloves tournament.

The SMU football team still had the students attention, however, and ended its season tied for fourth in the SWC with a 3-4 record. The talent on the team was what the fans were most impressed with. Outstanding players on defense for the season were John LaGrone, Jerry Griffin, Lynn Thornhill, Doug January and Billy Bob Stewart, while the offense was lead by Mac White, John Roderick, Mike Tabor and Wayne Rape.

The attraction toward Jerry LeVias had been kept to a minimum during the season, but the racial tensions on campus made his first year at SMU challenging.

In the fall of 1965, the entire country was on edge with race riots and negative news about the war escalating in Vietnam, and in the boxing world Cassius Clay drew world attention when he changed his name to Muhammad Ali.

Ali defended his title in Las Vegas on November 22, and stopped two-time heavyweight champion Floyd Patterson in the 12th round.

ABC played the fight a week later and Terry watched it in the dorm living room with Mike McCann.

After the fight, Ali demanded that the interviewer from ABC Sports call him by his new name in honor of the Nation of Islam. That did not go over well with the massive television audience.

"Man, he's a cocky nigger isn't he?" Mike said to Terry at the end of the fight.

"Yeah, well he can call himself whatever he wants as long as he keeps fighting like that. And he'll keep getting big paydays until someone knocks him on his ass," Terry said.

"Now I would pay big money to see that!"

"You and the rest of the world. And think about it – if he was white and talked like that, there is no way TV would give him that much press. Say what you want, but the guy is a hell of an athlete, and an absolute marketing genius," Terry added.

Either way, Cassius Clay had made professional boxing popular again with audiences of all ages, and the popularity carried over to the amateur fighters.

* * *

The 1966 Regional Championship Golden Gloves Tournament was scheduled the first week in February at the Memorial Auditorium in Dallas.

Larry Wagner and Tommy Morris had kept Terry active in the gym during his Christmas break back home, and he returned to Glover's Gym in top shape.

"We've got a good team of boys goin' into the tournament, mostly lightweights and middleweights, but you and Dickie will be who everybody's gonna come to see," Doug said to Terry.

Terry and Dickie had been training hard at the gym every day. Doug had them spar a few rounds with each other, then trade off with other heavyweights in the gym. He made sure they both put in at least six rounds of sparring each day, and when the first round of the tournament came up on Thursday evening, he knew he had the best heavyweight contenders in Texas.

Opening night at the tournament had the usual attendance of over 4,000 spectators. There were 42 scheduled bouts, with Terry and Dickie scheduled to go on in bouts 41 and 42 respectively.

Terry went up against a boy from Fort Worth, and won by a knockout in 30 seconds of the second round. The crowd got what they were waiting for all night and let out a thunderous roar. Doug and Cornbread put a towel around Terry's neck and told him he could take a seat with his friends while they stayed in the corner for Dickie's fight. Dickie touched gloves with Terry as he exited the ring and said, "I'll see if I can beat your time on knockin' my guy out Daniels."

Terry smiled and said, "I'll be right up there in the crowd watchin' you buddy."

Dickie's opponent had a little more boxing experience than Terry's opponent, according to Doug. He also weighed in at 195 compared to Dickie's wired body of 185 pounds. That didn't seem to matter much to Dickie, however, because he smothered his opponent with a barrage of punches in the last minute of the first round and scored a TKO himself.

Dedo was sitting next to Terry in the crowd and said, "Holy cow, can that boy fight! That's the guy you said you workout with? Man, if you guys go down to the finals, would you two have to square off against each other?"

"I guess so," Terry said, "but I'm not going to think that far ahead."

The ring announcer entered the center of the ring as Dickie exited, and thanked everybody for attending. He reminded them that the action would continue Friday and Saturday with the finals on Monday.

The next day at the SMU cafeteria, Terry found himself the topic of discussion amongst his friends at lunch.

"The paper says you and Wills will be going up against the winners of tonight's fights on Saturday," Mike McCann said to Terry.

"Yeah, we'll be doing a little homework of our own tonight at the auditorium," Terry said.

Sally was sitting next to Terry at the table and said, "Does that mean no date night for me then?"

The rest of the kids laughed and said, "Uh oh…"

Terry looked at her, smiled and said, "I'll be sure to pick you up right after the last heavyweight fight and treat you to a late-night chicken fried steak at Roscoe White's."

Dedo chimed in and said, "Hey, me and Sherri will join you, but you better watch your greasy foods at those late hours, Terry. We don't want you slipping out of shape!"

They all laughed as the bell went off indicating the change of classes, and the students were reminded of what was really important – their studies.

Terry called home late Saturday afternoon to tell his family of the results of his first bout in the Golden Gloves, and Jeff was fortunate enough to take the call.

"Oh, man, you won your first fight by a technical knockout! That's awesome," he said. "All my friends at school have been asking about you in the tournament. So you have another fight tonight? Are you going to call us back?"

"Yeah, tell Mom and Dad I'll give you guys a call late tonight when it's over," he said.

Bill had made plans to take June out to LaVelle's for dinner Saturday night because his cousin, Frank, was providing the music and entertainment. In addition to running Daniels Fuel, along with Bill and Peps, Frank was a piano player with a jazz band that played in the Lake County and Cleveland area bars and restaurants on weekends.

Whenever the billboard out front read, "Frankie Daniels and his Band Tonight," they expected a crowd to stay into the late hours of the evening. But June insisted that they leave after Frank's first set, so they could be home in time for Terry's phone call.

The call came into the Daniels' household at 11:05 p.m. Terry called collect from a pay phone at the auditorium, and June was ready nearby, while the rest of his siblings scrambled in line to talk.

"Hello? Oh, I knew it was you, Honey! Now, please tell me you didn't get hurt," she said. "You won on a split decision? Oh, I hope you're all right, I know I shouldn't worry, but I do!"

Tom rolled his eyes and put his hand out first to talk with Terry and tried to speed his mom along, but he got nudged out by his dad. June politely cut Terry off and handed the phone to Bill.

The kids all got a chance to talk with their boxing brother, and he ended by telling them that the other heavyweight from his gym, Dickie Wills, won his fight too.

Jeff asked, "Does that mean you'll be fighting Dickie for the championship?"

"Yes is does little brother. I'm not sure how our coach is going to work the corners because we're from the same gym and fighting for the championship, but I guess I'll let you all know Monday night," he said.

After he hung up, Terry went outside to meet with Doug, Dickie and a couple other boxers from the gym.

"C'mon Terry, I'm gonna' treat y'all to a good steak dinner at Sammy's Steakhouse," Doug said.

"Well, I kinda' promised my girlfriend I would take her out for a bite, so I guess I'll take a rain check," Terry responded.

"Nah, you're comin' with us, and she is invited too," Doug said with a Texas-sized smile on his face. "You've earned it. *All* my boys earned it!"

CHAPTER 19

On Monday night a banner at the entrance of the Memorial Auditorium read, "Metzger's Milk proudly presents The 30th Regional Championship Golden Gloves Tournament." The fans had been streaming into the building since 6 p.m. and the seats filled quickly for the opening bout scheduled at 7:30.

In the locker room, Doug held the program of the night's lineup as he addressed the five finalists from the Dallas Athletic Club.

"They got two rings goin' at once and there are 24 championship bouts scheduled tonight. Jack Franklin's goin' first from our gym in bout number seven for the High School Featherweight Championship, so pay attention when you're up. Terry, you and Dickie are scheduled last," he said.

Both of the Dallas newspapers had front page articles in the sports section covering the big event that day, and of course, the bulk of the articles centered on the Open Heavyweight Championship fight.

When asked how he would handle the two popular heavyweights that were both from his gym, Doug was quoted as saying, "These boys are the hardest working boxers I have in the gym, and maybe in the state. I plan on watching them from the crowd like you; there is no way I could work the corner for one or the other. I've arranged to have good coaches from one of the other gyms in their corners. It's going to be a good fight!"

After reading the article Mike McCann asked Terry how he felt competing against his teammate and Terry said, "I'm sure he feels a little awkward about it, just like I do, but hey, neither one of us holds anything back when we spar in the gym. So, we certainly aren't going to hold anything back for the title that both of us want."

Normally, Terry would warm up with Dickie before the fight, but in this case they both found their own space to get ready. Terry chose to get his workout done early while the lightweight fights got underway; then he relaxed after the break and watched the 19th bout open the second half.

The match was for the High School Middleweight Championship and pitted David Turner from Doug's gym against a tough blond-haired football player from Bryan Adams High School named James Helwig.

Terry had seen Helwig fight one other time and he reminded him of himself. He fought like a tiger and rarely backed down, and that's exactly how Helwig carried himself in the match tonight.

Turner was new to Doug's gym this year and handled himself well for a beginner, but Helwig's tenacity and toughness proved too much for the boy and he won by a unanimous decision.

The Novice Heavyweight Championship bout got the fans on their feet several times while Terry and Dickie got laced up. The bell rang ending the fight and the announcer's voice boomed out the winner, "The bruising Murphy Von Hutchins!" Terry's heart started beating harder in anticipation of the action to come.

He didn't think he would get this nervous, but he noticed Dickie wasn't making eye contact with him and had a look on his face that would get an angry pit bull to stop growling. Terry knew this was going to be his toughest fight yet, and all he could think of was Coach Tony's advice, which was the same thing Doug told him the night before: "For every punch you take, you try your best to give him two back and you'll come out a winner."

The gentleman in the bow tie approached Terry and Dickie, and said, "It's time boys," while pointing to the center ring.

Terry was focused on his opponent and didn't hear the crowd, mostly led by SMU fans, when his name was announced. The ref called the boys to the center of the ring, gave them the usual instructions, ordered them back to their corners and then signaled for the bell to start the first round.

They touched gloves and each immediately fired off left jabs to score early and get the butterflies out. Each connected and the crowd let out a quick roar followed by whistles and hollers. Both had a look of determination on their faces, and sensed the other's will to win.

Each punch of Dickie's seemed to have a little more zip on it than Terry was used to in the sparring sessions they'd had together, and by the end of the first round, he knew he was a few punches behind. His corner men were giving him pointers during the minute rest, but he knew exactly what he had to do.

He came out the second round with his hands held closer to his face and bobbed side to side with his shoulders, careful not to give Dickie a clear shot. Wills kept his traditional stance and moved in with a double jab, but Terry slipped off the second jab and followed up with a quick right-left-right combination, drumming Dickie's mid-section.

The flurry of punches connected and Terry heard a grunt from his opponent after the last punch thumped his rib cage. He immediately felt stronger and chose to make up for lost punches by throwing a flurry to Dickie's head and shoulders, causing him to go into a defensive mode.

The two of them were toe-to-toe in the center of the ring; slugging it out. The crowd cheered their approval. The ref had to jump in between to separate them and instructed them back to their corners ending the second round.

"Terry took that round for sure," McCann said to Dedo.

"Yeah, Wills looked good in the first and Terry evened the score. This round's gonna be the one – that's for sure."

Sally was sitting behind them with the rest of the SMU students and yelled, "C'mon Terry! You can do it!"

Terry didn't hear a word from the crowd. He blocked everything out, focusing strictly on his opponent. He was going for a knockout this round. He stood up from his stool – he gave up standing like the champ ever since he entered the open division – "Second's down," the ref ordered as the cornermen shouted last-minute instructions and pulled the stool out of his corner. The bell rang and the speakers echoed, "Third and final round!"

The spectators stood on their feet clapping and cheering while the two fighters touched gloves in the center of the ring. Dickie led with a flurry of punches most of which were blocked by Terry.

Dickie knew he had scored because he saw a small bruise under Terry's right eye. Terry knew he had scored because a little blood was showing in Dickie's nostrils.

The two of them were determined to out-punch the other, but Dickie was careful not to give Terry a clear shot with his powerful right hand. He never dropped his left from his cheekbone.

Terry was frustrated and kept hitting Dickie with body shots, hoping he could get him to drop his guard for just a second, but the bell rang ending the fight. The ref separated them again, telling them the fight was over. He knew if he hadn't pulled them apart they would have continued till one of them dropped. The houselights rose and the crowd cheered for one of the best fights of the tournament. Terry and Dickie were exhausted.

A man sitting behind Doug in the crowd patted him on the back and asked him who he thought won the fight. Doug said, "Man, that's a close one. It could go either way, but I'd have to give the edge to Daniels."

The SMU crowd started singing their fight song, but cut it short so they could hear the announcer give the result of the fight.

"Judge Skip Cherry scores the fight 28 to 26 in favor of Wills. Judge Chuck Cravotta scores the fight 27 to 26 in favor of Daniels. And Judge

Bob Maloney scores the fight 28 to 26, with the winner of the Open Heavyweight Division, in the red corner – Dickie Wills!"

The crowd let out a mixture of cheers and boos. Terry and Dickie were too spent to acknowledge the crowd; instead, they touched gloves and patted each other on the shoulder. They each knew they gave it their best and the decision could have gone either way.

The flash cubes were popping as the announcer entered the ring with both fighters. "How 'bout another round of applause for these two fine young men folks?" he said. "I swear, both of these guys deserve a championship trophy!"

Dedo put his fingers to his lips and let out an ear-piercing whistle while Mike and the SMU alumni joined in with cheers and applause.

The next day, on the front page of the sports section, there was a photograph of Doug standing between Terry and Dickie holding both their arms in the air. The headline above read, "Heavyweights Top Exciting Evening at Golden Gloves." McCann was reading the article out loud to Terry and the rest of the guys and gals sitting in the cafeteria.

"The fight was as good as any classic heavyweight amateur fight I have seen for some time," he read. He looked at Terry and said, "He's got that right! I still think you had the edge in the final round though, Terry. How did you feel you did?"

"I knew I was still a little behind Dickie in total punches landed, and I was trying hard to land a solid right to his chin, but his defense was better than he'd ever shown me before. And the three-minute round went so fast," Terry said.

Dedo said, "Maybe ol' Dickie wasn't giving all he had in the sparring sessions with you at the gym. Who did your coach think won the fight?"

"He said we both fought a good fight; good enough to beat any heavyweight in Texas."

Sally was sitting next to Terry at the table and said, "Tell them what your dad said to you when you called home from your dorm."

"Oh, well, it was late, of course, and my brothers and sister were in bed because it was a school night, but my mom and dad were still up waiting for my call. I talked to my mom first and told her the results and then my dad got on the phone. He said he was sorry to hear I didn't win, but he made it clear that I ought to be focused on academics anyway. He reminded me again that he was helping pay the bills for college, not boxing!"

Hugh Hackney was listening and said, "Well, I'm kinda glad you didn't win because that means you can be on the baseball team again, and we need all the good pitchers we can get."

"Hey, that's right, Terry," Dedo added, "and practice starts next week. Maybe you get a no-hitter this year like you almost did last year, and get back on the good side of your old man."

Terry smiled and said, "Maybe I will buddy, maybe I will."

* * *

Coach Finley struggled to make his baseball team competitive in the Southwest Conference. He confessed to his assistant coaches, "If we weren't dealing with injuries and players changing schools, we'd be a lot better off this season – horseshit!" That was a word the players would hear him use often, so much so, they eventually nicknamed him Bob "Horseshit" Finley.

Although he had higher expectations for his team than his critics, Coach Finley's players always gave it their best effort. After a 3-5 start and being shutout in one game by Texas A&M, the boys came back to beat Loyola in a double-header 13-2 and 14-1, and got to .500.

It wasn't as if they disappointed a lot of fans though. Most of the people in the stands were relatives of the players who lived nearby. The students had spent most of their money on tickets watching the SMU basketball team win the SWC championship, and a baseball team that struggled getting to 50-50 just didn't get the same backing.

The players didn't seem to mind. They came prepared to win each game and still enjoyed the opportunity to play college baseball in Texas.

It frustrated Terry, however, especially after playing on the winning team last summer in the American Legion League and being voted one of the team's MVPs. He also had to hear it from his roommate, Mike, who was on the championship swim team, and from his friends on the track team.

By midseason the baseball team had seven wins and seven losses and they were headed up to Austin to play the Texas Longhorns in a doubleheader on a Saturday afternoon. Coach Finley and the players traveled in a bus, while the assistant coaches followed in a van with the equipment. This trip, Terry's teammate, Wil Bennett, got permission from the coach to drive separately, because he told the coach he wanted to stay and see family after the game.

"A buddy of mine from high school plays for Texas," Wil told Dedo and Terry. "He's invited me and whoever else wants to go for a few beers after the game. You guys want to go?"

"Sounds good to me," Dedo said while Terry nodded in agreement.

"Count me in too," Bobby Collins added. "It'd be nice to beat 'em in their backyard, but if we come up short again, well, I'd just as soon have 'em buy us a couple pitchers of beer to soothe the pain."

Terry pitched the first half of the opening game and gave up four hits to the Longhorns before he was relieved in the top of the sixth inning. The Mustangs were up 5-2 when he left, but the Longhorns figured out the next two pitchers and went on to win 7-5. The second game ended with the Mustangs on the losing end again 8-1.

As the players lined up to shake hands at the end of the game, Wil took his buddy aside.

"Guys, I want you to meet my friend from high school I told you about, Lootie Carlyle from Dallas. Lootie, this is Bobby Collins, Terry Daniels, and Eddie Davis," Wil said.

"Pleased to meet y'all," Lootie said as he shook each boy's hand.

"Hey, when you get done in the locker room, me and a few other guys will meet y'all in the parkin' lot. We're gonna' go to a place not far from here called Scholz beer garden," he said.

"Okay, sounds good. We'll get cleaned up and meet y'all in a bit," Wil said.

Scholz Garten was a few blocks away from the university and a favorite hangout for the Texas students and players after sporting events. August Scholz, a German immigrant, purchased the place, which was originally a boarding house, shortly after the Civil War. By the early 1900s he and his family had converted it to a tavern, which had become popular among other German immigrants in the surrounding Texas counties.

Upon entering the establishment, the boys paused to read a plaque by the door. It stated: *The 1966 Texas Legislature honors Scholz Garten in House Resolution #68 as a gathering place for Texans of discernment, taste, culture, erudition, epitomizing the finest tradition of magnificent German heritage in our State.*

"C'mon, we're gonna' go to the back of the building where they got a patio with picnic tables," Lootie said.

Terry looked at the sign above the door that led to the outdoor tables: *The Biergarten.* Dedo slapped Terry on the back said, "I don't speak any German but I sure know how to drink German beer!"

The patio had about 20 picnic tables spread out in a fenced area. Looking around they saw a mixture of adults with their families and college students, eating and enjoying the German music from the outside speakers.

Lootie directed the boys to one of the last tables in the back corner and told them to grab a seat while he informed his favorite waitress they were there.

"The food here is incredible," said one of the boys from the Longhorn team. "It's homemade German recipes – even if you don't like German food, you'll love this stuff."

"It smells so good it's making my stomach growl. I got my mind set on a big brat with plenty of sauerkraut," said Terry.

"I'll second that," Dedo added.

Lootie came back to the table escorting a blonde dressed in a German Alps outfit, complete with suspenders, top hat and a short skirt.

"Boys, I want you to meet Shelly, she's a junior here at Texas and she'll be takin' care of us," he said.

"Guter Abend die Herren. Was kann ich fur Sie erhalten?" she asked.

The boys smiled, but looked a bit puzzled, and then Wil said, "Ach, no sprechen Sie Deutsch heir fraulein, but it is a pleasure to meet you."

Shelly laughed and said, "I'm majoring in German and accounting, and I work here part-time to help pay for school. I'll get you a couple pitchers of 'fine stout' to start you out, and I'll be back in a sec to take your food order."

Lootie looked at Wil and said, "She's a doll, isn't she? Whenever she's workin' I make sure she takes care of us. She's got a great personality and a cute little body don't ya' think?"

Wil replied, "Yeah, she's a doll all right! I only took one course in Spanish, but now I wish I had taken a couple courses in German. We'll make sure she gets a good tip before we leave."

Two tables over, Terry noticed several beefy-looking guys watching them closely as the waitress took their order. He thought for a moment that maybe a few of his teammates were out of place with their SMU t-shirts on. But he decided to concentrate more on his table and spent the next hour drinking beer, laughing, sharing stories and indulging on German cuisine.

The music from the outdoor speakers died down around 9:30 p.m. while the music inside turned up, and the boys could hear a live band playing German songs to a crowd on the dance floor.

Terry and Bobby excused themselves to go to the men's room and stopped along the way to listen to the live band play a polka while a few couples danced to it. The band consisted of a tuba player, a trombone player, an accordion player, and a drummer.

"Hey, listen to the 'Oom-pah-pah' from that guy on the accordion," Terry said to Bobby. "My little brother plays the accordion. He's pretty good too. I bet he could keep up with that guy."

Bobby smiled and said, "Yeah, well how 'bout we keep doin' the polka to the john – I really gotta take a leak!"

The two of them shuffled their way through the crowd while the boys back at the table tried to get a little party of their own going with Shelly and some of the other cute waitresses.

Wil tapped Lootie on the shoulder and asked, "Who is that big guy a couple tables over?"

Lootie turned to look and said, "Oh, that's Billy Joe Collier. We call him 'Killer Collier,' he's a junior and played defensive tackle on the football team. Why?"

"Because he's been eye-ballin' me for the past half-hour and I'm wonderin' if I should go over there and ask him if he's got somethin' to say to me."

"Nah, I wouldn't go doin' that! He's meaner than his older brother Carl, and Carl was all-conference last year."

"Well, it looks like I'll find out in a second, he's headed our way."

At 6' 2" 250 pounds, "Killer" sported a sandy blond crew-cut and an attitude. As he made his way toward Wil's table, he was followed by a couple of other guys. He stopped within a foot of Wil and said, "Hey boys, this place caters to Longhorns, not *Mustangs*, and I think it's 'bout time y'all just mosey on outta this corral and get on home. I've seen about enough of your flurtin' with our waitresses for one evenin.'"

"Wait a minute, Killer," Lootie said. "He's a friend of mine; we went to high school together. Now, give 'em a break, we just beat 'em in a doubleheader and thought we'd spend a little social time with 'em."

"Yeah, it figures we beat 'cha in a double header, but social hour with *my* waitress is over boys. Y'all can just head on out, I'm tired o' lookin' at your sorry asses," Killer growled.

All of them had consumed a generous amount of beer, which helped fuel the situation, and it didn't help matters when Dedo stood up and said, "Yeah, we lost today, but who beat your asses on the *football* field this year?"

Killer's eyes widened, but before he could respond, a voice from behind him said, "Hey guys, what's goin' on?"

Killer turned to face Terry and said, "What's goin' on is I want your Pony asses outta here, *that's what's goin' on!*" As he said it he pushed Terry back with both hands.

"Oh, bad idea," Wil said under his breath.

Terry instinctively put his right foot back and got his fists up in a boxing stance. Killer's eyes widened even more and he said, "Why you sorry son of a—"

But before he could complete his obscenity, Terry hit him with a left-right combination and the tower of 'Grade A' beef feel backward onto the ground.

Wil and the rest of the boys looked on with astonishment, and before anyone could say, "Whoa mule!" Terry hit one of Killer's teammates as he was advancing with a solid right to the stomach and a quick left hook to the head. The boy bent over from the blow to the stomach, and twisted 180 degrees from the hook before twirling to the floor.

Wil and Lootie intercepted the third Longhorn and got him to back off. The whole incident was over in less than 30 seconds, but it caused quite a ruckus among the rest of the patrons. One of the waitresses screamed, and the boys knew that it was time to leave.

Lootie and his teammates held the third football player while the other two Longhorns lay on the floor with their eyes rolling around in their heads.

"Well boys, I guess it's time we say goodbye! Let's throw some money on the table to cover our bill and be on our way," Wil said.

He turned to Lootie, who still had a look of disbelief on his face and said, "Guten tag Lootie, my friend. I'll call ya' and maybe we can do it again sometime!"

Lootie blinked his eyes several times and said, "Yeah, sure, only next time I think it'll be in Dallas!"

Dedo grabbed a quick kiss from one of the waitresses before she could get away with the others, gulped down the rest of his beer, and joined his buddies who were headed back to the main hall.

Two large men from management met them at the entrance and asked what happened. Wil pointed back to the table and said, "I don't know, I think some guys fainted over there. They look like they're pretty loaded."

"Okay, we'll take it from here," the man said and the two of them proceeded to the table of Texas players. The guys continued to the door leading into the parking lot.

Terry spotted Shelly at the corner of the bar and approached her before heading out with the others. "Hey, I'm really sorry that happened, Shelly. We weren't looking for any trouble."

"Oh, that's all right," she said, "Billy Joe has been known to throw his weight around once in a while, but I've never seen anyone knock him down like that before. I mean, wow, are you some kind of Marine or something?"

Terry smiled and said, "No, I'm just a sophomore at SMU. But a guy's gotta know how to defend himself, right?"

She smiled back and said, "You better get goin' with your friends stud, before the manager figures it out and bans y'all from this place. I sure wouldn't want that to happen."

"Okay, well –"

"Hey Terry, let's go!" Bobby yelled from the doorway before Terry could get her phone number. The boys piled into the car and sped off.

Dedo yelled out the window, "The beer garden has now had the pleasure of meeting Kid Galahad! Good night and good riddance! Yee haw!"

CHAPTER 20

May 1966 – The SMU baseball team finished its season just under .500 and fell short of making the playoffs. "We'll get 'em next year," Coach Finley told his players.

Spring semester was coming to an end and finals were just a week away. The Texas heat was sweltering, and most of the students were studying in the air-conditioned buildings on Sunday when a thunderstorm broke from the skies and drenched the campus with two inches of rain.

Terry and Mike were studying in their dorm room when the storm finally stopped. Mike looked out the window and said, "Man, there are some *lakes* out there. Let's take a break and get our swim trunks on, I know a few places we can get waist high and cool off a bit."

Terry laughed and said, "That sounds good to me. We can take a football with us and maybe get a game going."

They quickly changed and headed out the door. Terry knocked on a couple of doors in the dormitory, but got no takers. As they left, they met a guy on a bicycle who was completely drenched.

"Looks like you got caught in that downpour," Terry said.

"Yeah, I came across the Mockingbird overpass on my way back from town and there's a big ol' bunch of water sittin' under the bridge on the Central Expressway. The drains must be clogged and there are no cars able to get through," he said.

"Looks like we got our lake, Terry," Mike said.

Terry smiled and said, "Go deep; we'll have to score our way there," and motioned Mike to run a pattern while he cocked his arm back and threw the football.

They traded passes until they arrived at the bridge. "Wow, check it out!" Mike said. "It must be 8 or 10 feet deep!"

They climbed over the guardrail and went down the embankment to the edge of the highway. Mike carefully waded into the water which quickly got up to his waist. Then he dove under and came up in the middle of the road. His head was bobbing up and down, and he said, "It's a little over my head. Come on in, the water's fine!"

Terry made his way in and felt immediate refreshment. The thunderstorm had done its damage, but the Texas sun wasted no time heating up the landscape again. Small vapors of steam were wafting up to the sky around them, but the water felt perfect.

Terry swam back to the edge, climbed out and said, "Come here, Mike! I'm gonna jump off the bridge into the water and I want you to pass me the football!"

Mike swam toward him and said, "Daniels, you're crazy! Just make sure you keep your legs out straight and go in butt first, you don't wanna break that leg of yours again!"

Terry made it up to the middle of the bridge while Mike stood in a throwing position from the water below. "On three," Terry yelled, "one…two…three!"

He jumped off and McCann hit him right in the hands with the football. He hit the water with a big splash, and came up with the ball held above his head.

Mike laughed and said, "SMU scores first in the 'Rain Bowl!'"

Terry headed for the edge while Mike took his turn jumping off the bridge. Both took turns catching passes and doing different twists off the bridge; carrying on like typical college hooligans, when Mike suddenly stopped and looked down the highway. "What's this guy think he's gonna do?"

Terry turned to see a white Volkswagen Beetle coming towards them. Until now, there had been no cars on the highway. When they could see that the driver wasn't slowing down, they figured the guy couldn't see the large body of water that had collected under the bridge.

They quickly made their way to the edge and stood in the shallow water while waving their hands and yelling for the guy to stop. They could see the driver's face light up when he realized what he had come upon as he hit the brakes, but it was too late.

A wave of water sprayed up in the air on both sides of the car and the little Beetle turned into a bobbing buoy when it hit the water. Terry and Mike made their way toward the car and could see the terrified looks on the passenger's faces. He noticed they were foreigners.

The driver in the car attempted to open his door as the car was bobbing up and down and side to side. Mike yelled for him to stop and stay in the car, but it was too late. When the man opened the door, water rushed in. He realized he made a mistake, but the damage was done. The woman next to him attempted to do the same, but Terry held the door and said, "Keep the door shut and climb out the window. I'll help you. The water is not that deep."

The boys learned that the woman in the car was 22 years old. She and her husband were from Pakistan and they were foreign exchange students majoring in psychology at SMU. The couple was grateful to them for helping to push their car back to the dry part of the road, and to their astonishment, the car fired right up after it drained for a few minutes. They were able to drive back to the exit, leaving behind a mess of papers and gum wrappers floating in the water.

Mike and Terry shook their heads and laughed as they made their way out of the water. Mike said, "We should call the police and tell them to put a barricade up or something."

Terry laughed and said, "Yeah, let's get outta here before something bigger comes down the road."

* * *

Spring finals ended with Terry keeping his grade point average above 3.0 for the second year in a row. And once again, he rode home to Willoughby on his motorcycle.

For his brother Jeff, the summer of '66 started out with a phone call from his cousin Skip, who said he needed another worker on his golf course crew and told him to be at the work shed by 7 a.m. sharp Monday morning.

"Sure thing, Skip," Jeff said. "And thanks for calling."

At age 12, Jeff felt like he was finally moving up the ladder of teenage-hood. A full-time paying job! He would be right up there with his big brothers, being able to buy what he wanted, whenever he felt like it.

When Monday morning arrived, Jeff was dressed before his dad yelled for Terry and Tom to get up. After breakfast, Tom and Jeff walked out the back door together while their dad and Terry drove off to the road construction company.

"Any idea of what kind of money I'll get?" Jeff asked.

"Dad said they'd start you off at a dollar an hour this year, and I'm up to a buck seventy-five," Tom said.

Skip told Jeff that he'd be working till 2 or 3 each day, and put in 25-30 hours a week Monday through Saturday. Jeff later shared with Tom his feeling on his pay, "Twenty-five to thirty bucks a week – that's a king's ransom!"

On Friday, Jeff wrote in his hours on the company timecard, clocking out exactly at 2:45 p.m. He left the Sequoia pro shop, jumped on his bike, and went a half-mile down the road to the Daniels Brothers Fuel Company to turn it in and collect his first paycheck. One of the secretaries called his dad on the company radio to ask him how she should pay him, since it was less than $25. Bill said to just pay him in cash for now until he started to build up enough hours to take taxes out.

She walked over to the cash register, punched in the numbers, pulled the lever down and "cha-ching" the drawer opened. She counted out $22 for him. The company service manager was sitting at his desk in the adjacent room and saw the look on his face as he stuffed the "wad" of bills into his pocket.

He smiled and asked, "Wow, what are you gonna do with all that money, Jeff?"

Jeff looked wide-eyed and said, "Boy, oh boy, I'm not sure yet, Jack." But he knew exactly where he was going next – straight to the Great Lakes Mall.

At the time the "Secret Agent" shows were the craze on TV, in the movies, and in the book stores. It all started with the movie, *Goldfinger*, and the popularity grew from there. Some of Jeff's favorite shows were: *I Spy, Secret Agent Man,* and his favorite, *The Man from U.N.C.L.E.*

He had seen a *James Bond Attaché Case* in Newberry's a month earlier, and didn't have the $15.95 to pay for it, but was determined to get one before one of his friends did. And he knew his parents weren't going to give him the money for something like that.

"You boys, with all your violent movies about spies and killing, that's not the kind of stuff I want you filling your head with," his mother would say. But now he could buy it with his own money.

He bought the last attaché case in the store and proudly held the bag under his left arm while riding his bike home on Route 84. He immediately went to his room and opened his new purchase: The *James Bond Attaché Case* came complete with a semi-automatic cap pistol, not Bond's signature Walther PPK, but it did have a silencer. It also came with a code book and a plastic knife hidden on the outside of the case – just like the one Bond used against the villain in *From Russia with Love*. It even had a cap explosion if a person didn't open the brief case the proper way, something his mom found out the hard way. He could hardly wait to show his buddies his new purchase.

Jeff and his friends were at the age when they loved to act out scenes from movies or TV shows they had viewed using plastic guns, firecrackers, smoke bombs, etc., in their backyards on Saturday afternoons. They practiced judo moves on one another and even started their own secret agent club – which included passing "coded messages" in class at school when the teacher wasn't looking.

They knew, however, this would be the last year they would do such things before starting junior high and graduating up to being a teenager. Twelve was the last age of just being a kid.

Having money in his wallet also prompted Jeff to think of other things he wanted to do, like taking up a new sport. He and his friend Cliff bought tennis rackets and entertained themselves for hours before and after dinner at courts nearby.

By the end of their first week, Cliff suggested they sign up for lessons at the park to learn how to play the game right. Jeff agreed, and by mid-summer they were keeping the balls on the court and enjoying the game a lot more. Jeff also felt good about excelling in a sport that none of his brothers or cousins participated in.

Tom was back to shagging balls after work; practicing his chipping and putting, while Terry was off to play baseball in the evenings. The Daniels boys had plenty of things to keep themselves busy this summer.

Terry managed to work out at Tommy Morris' gym in Wickliffe three days a week, and in mid-July, Tommy told Terry he was putting together an amateur boxing show in Eastlake in August. He asked him if he would be interested in being in the premier heavyweight bout on the card. Terry agreed and the date was set. This was going to be an action-packed summer.

One Friday night, Bill and June went to dinner by themselves while Terry drove Tom, Denny, Debbie and Jeff over to Manners Big Boy on Mentor Avenue, next to Sequoia golf course. They always enjoyed eating there because their double burgers and fries were the best, and it was one of the last places nearby where you could still park outside with a speaker and order your food, car-hop style.

On the way home Tom had the radio dialed into their favorite radio station, WIXY.

"Hey, I thought you guys were all WHK'ers," Terry said.

"Not anymore," Jeff said. "WIXY 1260 plays the most Beatle songs, and KYW is now WKYC. Jerry G does a show on WKYC called, *The Beatle Beat*. He's been touring with them all summer and plays recorded interviews with them on his show."

Terry smiled because he knew Jeff and Denny were the biggest Beatles fans in the car. "What's their latest hit called again?" he asked.

"Day Tripper!" Denny and Jeff yelled in unison.

The WIXY disc jockey came on the air and said, "Hey, Beatle fans, as you know, tickets for The Beatles show in Cleveland were sold out a day after they went on sale, but comin' up in the next hour we've got a pair of tickets available to the lucky caller. So, be listening for your chance to win a pair of tickets to see the Fab Four at Municipal Stadium, Sunday, August 14th only on (tune comes on with a melody of singers) *WIXY Twelve Sixty – Su-per Ray-deeoo!*"

Tom said, "They're lucky they're even playing in Cleveland this year. Remember what the mayor said after that riot during their '64 concert? He said they would never play in Cleveland again."

"And with John Lennon saying they were more popular than Jesus a couple of months ago, I know the folks down in Dallas, heck the whole South for that matter, didn't want to have anything to do with them," Terry added.

"Are you kiddin' me?" Denny said. "They're the biggest band in the world! No one will ever stop The Beatles!"

Terry pulled into their driveway, and Denny and Jeff made a mad dash to the basement. They both knew what they'd be doing for the next hour – listening to the radio on their stereo and hoping to get a chance to call in for tickets to the concert.

June had a new "Trim-Line" phone installed in the basement a couple months earlier for the kids, mainly because Tom and Terry both complained about not being able to talk to girls without everyone eavesdropping on their calls. It came with push button numbers, so it made it easy to dial the radio station.

When the DJ came on and said he would take the 10th caller, Jeff dialed as fast as he could, got a busy signal, held the disconnect button for a second, and dialed again and again. Denny insisted he try a few times but got the same results.

The DJ got back on the air after a song and a string of commercials and said he had a winner. They turned off the stereo when they heard some girl screaming for joy, realizing she was the lucky one, and they called it quits for the evening.

* * *

With the Beatles concert just three days away, Cliff and Jeff had given up hope that they could score tickets to see the Fab Four.

They were hitting balls back and forth at the tennis courts with two of their friends from school when Jeff asked, "Do you guys know anyone who got tickets to see the Beatles this weekend?"

"Are you kidding me?" one boy answered. "There are over two million people in the Cleveland area, and half of them are Beatles fans."

By the time Jeff got home and ate dinner, he was beat from working on the golf course and playing tennis. He watched a little TV, and hit the hay after 10 p.m. because he could hardly keep his eyes open.

At 11:10 p.m., his mom came into his room. "Jeff, wake up, I have some news for you," she said while nudging him several times.

He awoke out of a deep slumber and said, "Wha – what is it Mom?"

"I couldn't wait till morning to tell you. Cliff's dad was able to get you four tickets to The Beatles' concert!"

Jeff had a hard time making sure he wasn't dreaming, sat up in bed and said, "What? Are you kidding me?"

She was smiling and laughing, knowing it was the best news her son could possibly hear, "No, it's not a joke! You're going to the concert!"

From the look on her face and the enthusiasm in her voice, he knew this was no dream. His adrenaline started pumping like greased lightning, but he kept his voice to a whisper so he wouldn't wake Denny who was fast asleep in the bed next to him.

"Four tickets to see The Beatles. Wow!" he said.

"Well, I know how excited you are sweetheart, but try and get some sleep. See you in the morning," she said and then closed his door, leaving him sitting up in bed, totally bewildered.

"I get woken up from a deep sleep with unbelievable news, and I'm supposed to lay back down and *try to go back to sleep?*" he whispered to himself. After he actually fell back to sleep, it seemed like only minutes later when his father was yelling up the stairs for the boys to get up for work.

When he told Terry and Tom the news at breakfast, they were nowhere near as excited as he was, and Denny was still asleep. "I hope he isn't going to be too mad when hears that I had already figured who Cliff and I would ask to go along with us to the concert," he said, "and it isn't going to be him."

After working at the golf course, Jeff met up with Cliff at his house. "So, what have you been doing all this time, holding out on me?" he asked.

"No, my dad told me earlier in the week that he knew a guy that worked at the station," Cliff said. "And he was going to ask him if he had any spare tickets he could buy. He never said any more about it, so I thought it was a dead issue.

"But then the phone rang late last night while I was upstairs in my room, my mom answered it and I thought she was talking to my aunt, because she kept saying, 'Really? You're kidding me,' just like she talks to my aunt.

"Then the next thing I know, she comes into my room with the news! I told her to call your house and tell you the good news too," he said.

"Cliff, ol' buddy, ol' pal, you came through again!" Jeff said while slapping him on the back. "Man, is this going to be fun!"

They hit balls back and forth to each other at the courts while trying to decide which of their friends would make up their own Fab Four for the concert.

Jeff made the topic the discussion at the dinner table with the family that evening. Before he could continue, however, his mom interrupted, "And how do you expect to get there and back?"

"Oh, well, we were wondering if maybe you and Cliff's mom could drive us," he replied.

"And then what? Sit in the parking lot of the Municipal Stadium on a Sunday night surrounded by thousands of screaming teenagers? I don't think so," she said. "And I know neither your father nor Cliff's dad would be willing to do the same. No, I think your oldest brother should be in charge of taking you there, sitting with you in the crowd, and making sure you boys get home safely."

Terry choked on the milk he just drank and said, "What? Me? Ah, come on Mom, you know I really don't care for The Beatles!"

"*And* you're taking your little brother with you," she said to Jeff.

"Denny? He's only 10 years old!" Jeff said in protest as Denny raised his hands above his head and looked like he just scored the winning field goal.

"This concert is for *teenagers!*" he added.

"You're not a teenager yet, Jeff," Denny said.

"I will be in December," and then he turned back to his mom and said, "Cliff will be 13 soon too, and in his religion he'll be considered a man!"

June chuckled and said, "You and Cliff will have just as much fun with your brothers there, and if you don't like it, well, I can always call Mrs. Spiro back and tell her to give the tickets to Cliff's sister, Jan. I'm sure she'd make good use of them."

His protest had been cut short, and that was that. He called Cliff after dinner and Cliff said, "My mom told me that she agreed in advance with your mom on who all would be going, as well as the alternative if we didn't like it.

"Anyway," Cliff added, "you know the stadium will be filled with screaming kids going crazy. We'll be too excited seeing the Beatles perform to think about anything else!"

Jeff agreed, and after hanging up, he went to the stereo in the basement and put on "The Beatles Second Album." He turned up the volume as high as he could get away with, and pretended to sing on stage while holding his tennis racket like a guitar. He wanted to "live in the moment" right then.

* * *

When the family got in their car to go to church Sunday morning, black clouds were gathering in the sky, and while Jeff was sitting in Sunday school thunder and rain poured from the clouds.

The teacher asked them to bow their heads in prayer at the end of class, and after saying The Lord's Prayer in unison with the rest of the kids; Jeff continued to pray in a whisper, "Please let the clouds clear in time for the concert to start, Dear Lord."

The rest of the day seemed to drag on slowly with the rain not showing any sign of letting up. Finally, at 5:45 p.m., Terry said to Jeff and Denny, "Well, let's get going guys, we've got to pick Cliff up and get on the freeway." The rain was reduced to a light drizzle.

It took almost an hour to reach the municipal parking lot because of the traffic, and when they exited the car and started the long walk to the stadium, the rain stopped. Jeff looked up to see the thick gray clouds were still not letting any sunshine through, but it felt like the rain was done for the day.

The stadium lights were shining in full force, intensifying the vision of everything the closer they got to the entrances. They were walking with people of all ages but most of them were teenagers. Denny was walking next to Terry, and Jeff could tell he loved every minute. He smiled and reminded himself how good it felt whenever his big brothers included him in things they would do with their friends. Instantly, he felt bad about putting up a fuss about not wanting his little brother to go, and gave him a smile and pat on the back.

They stood in line for 20 minutes before they got to the entrance. Terry gave them each their own ticket and Jeff looked at it – still in disbelief. It was light green and stated: *Super Radio for Northern Ohio… WIXY 1260…Proudly Presents the Fabulous, BEATLES …In Concert, In Person.*

Each of their tickets was $4; the poster next to a guard taking tickets read $3.00, $4.00, $5.00, and $5.50 underneath the pictures of each Beatle.

"Man, these tickets are a little pricey, but worth it – huh, Cliff?" Jeff asked.

"Yeah, and they got a couple other groups that play before them, including The Cyrcle," he replied. They chimed into a verse from the group's current hit on the radio:

And I think it's gonna be alright,
Yeah, the worst is over now
The mornin' sun is shining
Like a Red Rubber Ball!

The other groups in the lineup included The Remains, and one of Terry's favorites, The Ronettes.

They were escorted to their seats, which wouldn't have been bad if it was an actual Indians game at Cleveland Stadium, because they were between home plate and first base, three rows up from the railing. But this was a rock concert not a baseball game, and the stage was set up on second base of the infield.

It was close to 7 p.m., with the concert scheduled to start at 7:30, when all of a sudden, the crowd started screaming. Jeff and the boys turned their heads to see a black limousine heading their way and saw Paul McCartney's smiling face in the window, waving to the crowd as they passed by.

My Brother the Boxer

The screams intensified and the limo kept going until it had made a complete trip around the infield stopping in front of them on first base.

The front doors opened and two men wearing dark blue sport coats with the WIXY1260 emblem on the breast pocket opened the back doors. Out popped John, Paul, George and Ringo.

The lower and upper decks were packed with over 25,000 screaming fans and flash bulbs were popping off by the thousands. The whole stadium was shaking from the vibration of the excitement as The Beatles made their way to a trailer set up behind the stage.

Terry looked at the astonished faces of his brothers, laughed while giving one big clap with his hands and said, "Alright!"

The Remains performed first and the crowd showed the band some respect, and then again to the Motown singer named Bobby Hebb, whom none of the boys knew until they heard him perform his hit song, *Sunny*. The restlessness started to show when they heard, "We want The Beatles! We want The Beatles!" while the WIXY DJs introduced the next act.

The chanting for The Beatles was replaced by screams again when The Cyrcle took stage, and turned up a notch when they did their hit, *Red Rubber Ball*.

By the time The Ronettes were introduced, the crowd was frustrated in anticipation of The Beatles and started chanting for them again. It was rude, but the singers on stage never missed a beat.

Jeff turned to look behind him and saw two girls in tight skirts with bee-hive hair-dos stand up and start dancing when The Ronettes went into their last song, *Da Doo Ron Ron*. He leaned over and tapped Terry on the shoulder and pointed to the girls. Terry looked them up and down, smiled, and turned back to watch one of his favorite bands perform live.

There was a short break while the stagehands transported instruments to and from the stage. The fans got ever more restless, and then a couple of the WIXY DJs got on stage. One of them grabbed the microphone stand and said, "Hi everybody! I'm Jack Armstrong!" He leaned the microphone over to the man next to him who said, "And I'm Johnny Canton!" Together they got the crowd to spell W-I-X-Y.

They carried on for a few minutes more and then said, "Here they are – The Beatles!"

The crowd roared again and a row of police and bodyguards lined up from the door of the trailer to the steps leading to the stage. The door opened and spotlights shined down on the heroes of the evening as they ran up the steps and on to the stage.

Jeff had to cover his ears in fear of becoming deaf from the crowd. He wanted to hear the group play. But the fans kept screaming as John, Paul and George harmonized in their microphones the opening number, *Twist and Shout.*

Jeff looked over at Cliff and Denny and saw them beaming with smiles from ear to ear. Terry was even smiling saying, "Holy cow!"

The place was rocking, and when George Harrison opened with his guitar solo for their fourth song, *Day Tripper,* the fans went ballistic. They watched as a man jumped out from the center stands, hurdled the snow fence, then got wrestled to the ground by a couple of stadium cops right around the pitcher's mound. He was followed by a girl who zigzagged along the same route with the same result, and then a thousand kids flowed from their seats and on to the field.

The crowd mobbed the stage in hopes of getting a better look at their idols from England, and a few even got up on stage. Jeff's adrenaline was pumping heavily when he looked at Terry and said, "Come on, let's go, Ter!"

Jeff was caught up in all the excitement, but Terry instantly brought him back down to earth by saying, "Sit down," in a voice that sounded like their dad. "You're not going out there with those assholes!"

The WIXY DJs stopped the show while The Beatles were escorted off stage and back to their trailer. They told the crowd that The Beatles wanted to perform for them, but they could not allow them to do so unless everyone returned to their seats. This was similar to what the DJs for WHK did when the group performed at Public Hall in downtown Cleveland in '64, and exactly what the mayor feared would happen at this concert.

The show resumed about a half-hour later and the best rock band in the world went right into another hit like nothing ever happened. After their 10th song, Paul grabbed the microphone and said it would be their last number. He said they really enjoyed playing their songs for all their fans, and went right into, *Long Tall Sally*.

The crowd continued to scream and take pictures, and when the song ended, The Beatles unplugged their guitars and ran offstage into a waiting limo. Thousands of fans stormed the field toward the limousine and were determined to block the nearest exit. Terry said, "Wow, it looks like when the Browns won the NFL championship in '64."

Several hundred crazy fans were forming a human wall to block the exit, and without slowing down, the limo took a hard left and headed for the snow fence. Some cops grabbed the fence and ripped an opening in it while the limo sped through and continued out a different tunnel. The boys watched from their seats as the cops outsmarted the crowd.

Terry motioned for them to leave and they all slowly made their way down the aisle to the exit ramp. Jeff turned to see the crowd disperse from the field and took one last look at the stage to remember the concert forever. He recognized another personality and nudged Cliff, "Hey, Cliff look, it's Jerry G!"

They yelled his name in unison and the famous Cleveland DJ smiled and waved back. Jeff said, "What a cool evening, aye buddy?"

By the time they dropped Cliff off and parked in their driveway, it was past midnight. Their mother was still up to greet them at the door. She had seen the coverage of the concert on Channel 8 news and knew about the riot. "I knew you'd be okay with Terry. That's why I wanted him to go with you boys," she said.

Terry smiled and said, "Ah, they were good boys, Mom. We had a blast didn't we guys?" and never once mentioned Jeff's request to join the riot.

Denny and Jeff smiled and each gave their big brother a hug. "Thanks again, Ter," Jeff said, "I think you may have been converted into a Beatles fan tonight."

They all said goodnight and went to bed. Terry was humming *Da Doo Ron Ron* as he brushed his teeth before bed. He looked in the mirror and had a flashback of the last time he saw Tracie Dixon at SMU. He smiled and continued the tune in his head.

Tom had just laid down in his bed, and before Terry turned out the light he said, "I've got to get up early for work tomorrow, I've got a baseball game Tuesday night, and oh yeah, I've got to work out hard for that boxing match Friday night!"

Before slipping under the covers, he quietly sang: *And when he walked me home, Da Doo Ron Ron, Da Doo Ron Ron...*

CHAPTER 21

With the wild Beatle weekend over, Terry drove to Tommy Morris' gym in Wickliffe on Monday after work to get in a good workout. Tommy told him who his opponent would be in the Friday night amateur card at the Eastlake community fair.

"Harold Carter?" Terry responded. "Isn't that the colored boy I knocked out last year?"

"Yeah, but he should be a little tougher to handle this time around," Tommy said. "He won the Open Heavyweight Division in the Cleveland Golden Gloves this year. I called his gym last week and the coach said he would like another shot at the only white boy to TKO his fighter."

Tommy convinced the city council to let him develop an amateur boxing show that would showcase local boxers from surrounding gyms. He told them he would provide the ring and the equipment, and all he would need was a couple of city workers to help him install the ring. They agreed and the show was set.

Bill and June didn't want to go, and let Tom drive his brothers and their friends to the fair. Tom told Denny and Jeff to meet back at the car around 11 p.m., and reminded them that the boxing show started at 6:30.

Jeff and his friend, Steve "Scooter" Francis, decided to grab an early dinner at a pizza stand before standing in line for the rides. Sitting down on a nearby bench, Scooter asked, "So, your brother's gonna fight some boxer from Cleveland tonight? Did he tell you anything about him?"

"Yeah, he said he's the same guy we saw last year at the Eastlake High School gym. He TKO'd him in the second round. Remember me telling you about it at baseball?"

"Oh yeah, this ought to be cool!"

"Terry told us the guy won the Cleveland Golden Gloves this year, and that he may have his hands full. He said he's been working a lot on the road crew this summer and didn't get to the gym as often as he wanted, so he may be a little rusty on his timing."

"Well, the paper said your brother almost won the heavyweight title in Dallas, so he can't be *that much* out of shape," Scooter said.

After several rides on their favorite rollercoaster, The Wild Mouse, they heard the P.A. system announce that the boxing show was going to start in 15 minutes, "And folks had better hurry, seats are filling up fast."

When Jeff and Scooter got to the ring at the end of the first match all the seats were filled, but they didn't mind – the excitement of watching Terry in the ring was enough to keep them standing to the end.

The sun was starting its descent, but there was still enough natural light to last until 8:30. The hot August air had subsided, which made for ideal conditions for the boxers in the ring.

The first five bouts got the crowd eager for the last one of the evening – their hometown hero, Terry Daniels, against the tough, lanky heavyweight from Cleveland.

When the bell rang for Round One, Carter was quick to get the first punch off, and he kept command of the fight right up to the end of the round. The carnival music was blaring and the crowd was buzzing with chatter, so Terry's brothers couldn't hear him shouting to Tommy Morris in the corner.

"That motherfucker is hitting me whenever he wants! I can't seem to get my timing together. I can't get a good shot at him," Terry shouted.

Tommy smeared a little more Vaseline on Terry's reddened face and said, "Don't worry about that! When he starts to shuffle to his left, you step in hard and cut him off, he'll shift to his right and you step in to keep throwing him off. He'll stop all that show-boatin' and be forced to trade punches with you – and that's when you take his head off!"

Jeff didn't know what Tommy was saying to his big brother. But he could see by Terry's face that he was getting madder by the minute, a look he and his brothers had seen before – and the results were never pretty.

The bell rang for the second round and the crowd was cheering for Terry to take it to his opponent. Terry cut Carter off just like Tommy told him, and continued to bob and weave while stepping into him. He dug his right shoulder into Carter's chest, like a linebacker, and pushed him into a corner.

Terry fired a left hook into Carter's mid-section, and followed with his right. Jeff could see the intensity of his punches and the crowd got on their feet. They were yelling at the top of their lungs for Terry to take his head off.

Carter kept his fists close to his face while bending over to try to deflect Terry's powerful hooks, and that allowed Terry to straighten up and start swinging more shots to the head.

The look in Terry's eyes was that of fury and anger. Jeff could actually hear the thumping of his punches above the roar of the crowd. Carter made a desperate move to push Terry back, trying to shuffle out of the corner and circle into the center of the ring, but Terry cut him off.

He hit him with a quick left hook to the head that buckled Carter's knees. The referee stepped in between them and ordered Terry to a neutral corner while he gave Carter a standing eight-count.

Scooter and Jeff were screaming along with the rest of the crowd at the tremendous turnaround Terry had made from the disastrous first round. They could see Tommy yelling instructions to Terry from the corner, but neither Terry nor anyone else could hear him.

The ref motioned the fighters to the center of the ring and yelled, "Box!"

Terry moved in quickly for the kill, while Carter shuffled backward and sideways, trying his best to avoid the bombs Terry was trying to land. But it was useless. Terry caught him with an uppercut, then followed up with a barrage of punches to his head and stomach. The ref jumped between them waving his arms and said, "That's it, that's it! The fight is over!"

Scooter and Jeff were screaming at the top of their lungs as they watched a reporter from the *News-Herald* take pictures of the action in the ring. Scooter said, "Wow! I've never seen anything like that in my whole life! Your brother is somethin' else!"

* * *

Prior to leaving for his junior year at SMU, Terry made a major purchase with some of his summer earnings – a '64 Pontiac LeMans – to make the long trip down to Dallas a smoother ride.

"That was a good decision, Honey," his Mom said. "Your dad and I are planning to follow you down this year – I hate to see you make that long drive by yourself."

"That would be great, Mom," Terry said. "I'm rooming with Mike McCann again, only this time we are in a dorm that's near the rest of our buddies on campus. Hey, why don't you and dad stay down for our home opener, and maybe go out to dinner afterwards?"

"I'm sure you're father would love that. He's also arranged to have your motorcycle shipped down, so you should have everything you need to start your school year off right."

The leaves were still green in Ohio when they left, and showed slight colors of autumn the farther south they drove. Terry's sophomore year, his parents had made the trip by plane, and they wanted to experience the fall foliage.

His folks helped him get settled into his dorm and then checked into the Adolphus Hotel in downtown Dallas.

On Saturday, Terry's parents accompanied him with his girlfriend, Sally, to a tailgate party at the Phi Delta house. They were entertained by Mike McCann, a recent Phi Delta Theta member, and his fraternity brothers singing frat songs. They even indulged in the hotdogs and Cokes before the home opener with the University of Illinois.

Bill was curious to see how Hayden Fry's Mustangs would do against a Big 10 team from up north, and his curiosity was answered when SMU scored the first time it had possession on a 20-yard run by quarterback Mac White. Both teams' defenses stiffened and kept the score at 6-0 until the fourth quarter when Jerry LeVias turned a 10-yard reception into a 60-yard touchdown. The exciting fourth quarter ended with the Mustangs getting revenge from last year's defeat by beating the Fighting Illini 26-7.

Before the game, June informed Terry that she and his father would be leaving early to get on the road for the long ride home.

"Well, it was very nice to meet you folks," Sally said. "Terry's told me so much about his family – I feel like I've known you forever."

"It was very nice to meet you too, Sally," June said. "You're everything Terry described. I hope you both have a good year."

Bill shook Terry's hand and said, "Just promise you'll keep your grades up and graduate from college before you go looking for any more boxing championships. Okay, Ter?"

"Sure, Dad," Terry replied, but he, and his brothers at home, knew he wouldn't quit until he went all the way to the top.

Terry was in his counselor's office on Monday to see about dropping a class for the semester. "This engineering major is making me question whether I really have what it takes to get a degree, Mrs. Stevenson," he said.

"Well, you certainly have chosen a dangerous sport to dedicate your time to," she said. "I think it would be wise to make a decision as to what is more important – getting a college education or stepping in the ring with Cassius Clay someday."

Terry appreciated the advice, but elected to reduce his heavy course load for the fall semester. He couldn't resist the accolades he received from his peers. He told them, "I continue to get better in the ring and it's no different than if I was able to play football – I can do this!"

* * *

By the last week in October, Terry was struggling to keep his grade point average above 3.0, but was determined to meet the daily challenges he faced academically. Saturdays, however, brought welcome relief from his studies when he sat in the stands of the Cotton Bowl with his friends for home games.

The Mustangs were 4-1 overall and 2-0 in the SWC. Terry, Sally and their friends were looking forward to driving to Austin to see their team battle the mighty Longhorns. The papers said Texas coach Darrell Royal wanted revenge for the beating they took in Dallas the previous year, and the students were up for a real knock-down fight on the gridiron.

Texas scored first with a 74-yard touchdown run on its third play from scrimmage, but missed the extra point. The Mustangs countered with a touchdown and extra point and left the field at halftime with the score 7-6.

Bobby Collins, sitting behind Terry, watched a defensive tackle from Texas trot off the field with his teammates. He tapped Terry on the shoulder in front of him and said, "Hey, Terry, isn't that number 71 there the meat-wagon you laid out at Scholz's beer garden last spring?"

Terry looked at the player Bobby was pointing to then down to his program and said, "71, B. Collier. Yeah, I guess that's 'Killer.'"

They both chuckled, and Terry turned to see Sally squinting her blue eyes at him. She said, "What did he mean by that?"

"Nothing, Sweetie," he said while putting his arm around her and giving her a kiss. She smiled and kissed him back.

"Oh boy, this game's gonna' heat up now," Bobby said as they laughed.

With less than three minutes showing on the clock in the fourth quarter, and SMU down 12-10, linebacker Billy Bob Stewart stuffed the Longhorn running back and forced a fumble on the Texas 43-yard-line. The Mustangs recovered and pushed all the way down to the 15, where Dennis Partee kicked a field goal in the last few seconds to win the game 13-12.

The excitement continued each weekend and by the end of the season, Hayden Fry's Mustangs were 10-2 overall and 6-1 in the conference, giving them the honor of Southwest Conference Champions – their first conference championship in 18 years.

Terry sent a late Thanksgiving card to the family with a clipping of the news about the Mustangs after they beat TCU at home, 21-0, on November 26.

When football season was over, it was time to study for finals, just two weeks away. Terry felt confident he would score well on all his exams. His focus got sidetracked, however, when he received a phone call on Tuesday evening.

"Terry? This is Dickie Wills."

"Dickie, how are you buddy? I haven't seen you since you moved to Fort Worth. Still planning on turning pro?"

"I'm doin' okay, and yeah, I do plan on turnin' pro sometime next year. Listen, I hope you don't mind me callin' you at school – I got your number from Doug Lord."

"No, not at all. What's up?"

"Well, I got a favor to ask of you. A friend of mine got beat up at a bar last week. Now, he's a big ol' boy and can take care of himself, but it was three against him – and two of 'em used pool sticks on him when his back was to 'em."

"Oh, man. Is he all right?"

"Yeah, he'll live, but they fractured his skull and he's gonna miss a couple weeks of work. Now, he's tough, but I plan on gettin' revenge for him – he's got a wife and two kids at home, and it's gonna be some time before he can do *anything*.

"I'm sure I can handle those fat ol' drunks myself, but just in case, I may need someone to watch my back and you came to mind first."

"Sure, Dickie. What do you want me to do?"

"Well, the bar is a little hole in the wall called Joey's Place. It's a few blocks down from Glover's Gym. Do you think you could meet me there this Friday night around 7:30?"

"This Friday?" Terry said, while taking a breath to think for a moment. "Yeah, I guess I could meet you."

Then Dickie told him of his plan: He knew the three guys would be in the bar around 8:00 p.m. to play pool and drink beers for their night out. Dickie would arrive around 7:20 and act like he had been drinking all afternoon, then nurse a shot and a beer until the three thugs arrived. Terry would come in around 7:30, sit at the end of the bar, and nurse a beer as well, acting totally oblivious to Dickie and his surroundings.

"I'll take it from there. You just make sure none of those bastards takes a pool stick to my backside," Dickie said.

Terry hung up the phone after the conversation and mumbled, "How the hell do I let myself get into these situations?"

Friday's last class ended at 3:50 p.m. and Terry walked back to his dorm to take a nap. He placed his books on the desk in his room before falling onto his bed, and lay there, spread-eagle, slowly drifting off to sleep.

He awoke when Mike came in whistling a tune. He looked over at his alarm clock and it read 8:17. *What the* - He then realized he forgot to wind it yesterday.

"Ah, shit. Mike, I took my watch off. What time is it?" Terry asked while wiping his eyes.

"Oh, sorry, Terry, I didn't know you were taking a nap – it's about 6:30."

"Ah, thank God. I dozed off for what I thought was an hour and it turned into two and a half!"

He got up and washed his face with lots of cold water, then changed into one of his black t-shirts and blue jeans. He wanted to look like a guy from a gas station, not a clean-cut college boy.

Before going out the door, he turned and said, "Ah, I forgot to call Sally—"

Just then, the phone rang. "That's probably her. Tell her I had to go back to the library and I'll pick her up around 8:30 to take her to Adair's."

Mike picked up the phone and nodded to him that it was Sally. Terry gave him the OK and slowly closed the door on the way out.

He drove to a parking lot near Joey's Place and arrived at 7:15. There were several cars in the lot, but he didn't have a clue what Dickie was driving, so he just sat there for the next 15 minutes thinking about what to expect.

His training in boxing always had him thinking of offense. He repeated the words of his Coach Al from the PAL about self-defense and street-fighting: "Know your surroundings; hit 'em fast and hit 'em hard – you don't want a bar fight lasting longer than a minute."

He took a look at his watch – 7:29. He took it off and laid it on the passenger's seat. He could feel the butterflies stirring in his stomach. He took a big breath through his nose and exhaled hard through his mouth. Then he looked up at the stars and said aloud, "Okay, let's get this over with. I got a date tonight."

He closed the car door and turned the collar up on his jacket to block out the cold chill in the air, and walked across the street to the door of the bar. There was still no sign of Dickie. He took another deep breath to brace himself, then opened the door and went in.

Two middle-aged couples were sitting at the bar talking with the bartender and sipping on their drinks. A few feet over was a pool table with a man playing a game by himself in the smoke-filled room. The little dance floor was vacant while a Hank Williams record played on the juke box.

Terry sat at the first stool of the bar as the bartender approached and asked what he'd like. "I'll take a Miller High Life," he said in a Texas twang.

He looked at the clock on the wall – 7:33 and no sign of his buddy. Then the door to the men's room opened and out walked Dickie, with a little swale in his step as he smoothed back his greasy hair and adjusted his dark-rimmed glasses. Terry watched him in the large mirror behind the bar as he pulled out a cigarette from the pack he kept on his sleeve. He lit it before straddling his bar stool.

The bartender returned with a tall glass of ice-cold beer and placed it with the bottle in front of Terry. Terry put a few dollars on the bar, acknowledged the bartender, and took a large swig.

After five minutes, Dickie said, in a loud slurring voice, "Is that all we got on that juke box – Hank Williams?"

He stepped off his bar stool and shuffled slowly to the juke box and "accidently" nudged the guy's pool stick, just before he hit the cue ball.

"Oh, sorry buddy, I'll be more careful…sorry," he said with a little smile on his face.

The guy shook his head, put his pool stick down, and walked over to his glass of beer on the nearby table. He took his burning cigarette out of his ash tray and took a long drag off it as he eyeballed Dickie.

The front door opened and two pot-bellied men walked in. The guy at the pool table smiled at them as they smiled back.

The bartender said, "You men want the usual?"

"You bet, Joey," one of them replied.

Terry sized them up: Both looked to be in their early 40s, each weighing between 180 and 200 pounds, and the guy at the pool table looked to be 6'1", maybe 20 years old with a slender build. "Nothing we can't handle," he whispered under his breath.

The three men joked around after taking their jackets off, while the bartender brought over a pitcher of beer with glasses and three shots of whiskey. Terry figured they were related because he heard the slender guy refer to them as "uncle" and "cousin."

He watched in the mirror as the men drank their shots and racked up the balls for a game of pool. All the while, Dickie stood over the jukebox pretending to be looking through the choices of records to play.

The next song played was *Flowers on the Wall* by the Statler Brothers. Dickie stepped back, took the cigarette out of his mouth, and chimed in with the record while doing a little dance.

He sang off key while shuffling back and forth, "Countin' flowers on the wall, that don't bother me at all...Smokin' cigarettes and watchin' Captain Kang-Kangaroo. Now don't tell me...I've nothin' to doo."

Terry smiled, gulped down his beer, and waved the bartender over for another – to help settle his nerves. He watched in the mirror as his buddy walked toward his seat and nudged the slender guy's pool stick again, causing him to miss the cue ball.

"Damn it! That's the second time you've done that," the guy said while pushing Dickie in the back and knocking the glasses off his face.

Dickie slowly picked up his glasses and stood face-to-face with the guy and said, "No need to get pushy pal. I ain't lookin' for no trouble."

"I ain't your pal, you drunken redneck! Now, sit down before I knock you down!"

Dickie put his glasses on the bar next to his ash tray, turned back to the guy and said, "Watch who you're callin' redneck – *peckerhead!*"

Terry took a gulp of beer and tried not to laugh out loud.

The guy smiled, put his left hand on Dickie's right shoulder, and hit him with a right fist in his stomach.

Dickie knew it was coming and tightened his stomach muscles while exhaling a quick burst of air as he doubled over.

The other men stood there and laughed, and the bartender said, "Come on, guys, if you're gonna start that stuff again – take it outside!"

"Take it easy Joey, he's just gonna rough him up a little," one of the men said.

The couples moved away from the bar and Terry turned his knees towards the men while remaining seated on his stool.

Dickie straightened up and threw a round-house left hook that was easily blocked by the guy, who countered with another punch to his stomach.

"Ugh!" Dickie yelled while grabbing his stomach again in an animated fashion.

The men continued to laugh, and one of them said, "Come on, Jimmy, you showed him who's boss. Let's play some pool."

Dickie straightened up and looked at the guy, who had a little smirk on his face, and said, "Now Jimmy…you need to know how to throw a proper combination to take a man out…like this!"

Dickie immediately hit the guy in the stomach with a short left punch and followed it up with a powerful right cross to his left temple. The guy spun around and went face-first onto the pool table. The smiles left the faces of the other men, and they made their way around the table to help their cousin.

Dickie swayed as if he was still intoxicated as the first man approached him. The man said, "Boy, you shoulda quit while you had the chance. Now, I'm gonna hafta throw your ass outta here!"

Dickie feigned a drunken smile, but inside, his veins were on fire. He targeted the man's chubby-whiskered face and hit him with a solid left-right-left combination. The man's head jarred back with each punch and he flew backward into a table, then onto the floor.

The taller thug, Jimmy, stood up from the pool table and Dickie turned back to let him have it with a powerful left hook, sending him reeling backward and onto his back near Terry.

The other man left standing grabbed a pool stick and came around the opposite side of the table with his back to Terry. He swung the stick back like a baseball bat at Dickie, but felt resistance when he tried to swing – Terry had grabbed it with his left hand, then threw a solid right punch to the man's face. He hit him *hard*, right between the eyes.

The man gasped, and it looked as if a shockwave ran from his head down to his toes. His entire body seemed to turn to jelly as he fell onto the floor, out cold.

The bartender was holding a shotgun in his hands and yelled, "That's enough, boys!"

He looked at Terry and Dickie and said, "Y'all get on outta here now! These men are regulars, and I'll take care of *them*. They ain't gonna do this shit again in my bar. Now, get!"

The boys looked at each other, nodded in agreement, then collected their belongings and headed out the door.

They crossed the street and Dickie slapped Terry on the back and said, "Hot damn, Daniels! You took that hillbilly out with one punch, and I was just gettin' warmed up!"

Terry's heart was beating so fast he had to catch his breath before he said, "Hit 'em fast and hit 'em hard. Keep your barroom fights under a minute!"

"The street fightin' motto of the PAL gym – got it!" Dickie said.

"Well, buddy, I've got a hot date to pick up tonight. Don't think it hasn't been fun, though. Let's meet again sometime, only let *me* pick the place next time," Terry said.

"You got it, Daniels," he said as they smiled and shook hands.

When Terry arrived at Sally's apartment, his heart was still pounding from the excitement. "Wow, that must have been some serious studying you did at the library," she said.

"Just getting pumped up for finals week," he said. "Come on, I'm ready to tie one on tonight!"

CHAPTER 22

Finals for the fall semester seemed tough for everyone on campus, and Terry's grade-point average dropped below 3.0 when he pulled a C- on his physics exam.

"Heck, a 2.8 is almost a B average. If I could sell that to my folks, you could too," one of his buddies told him at lunch.

He convinced his parents over Christmas break that his engineering classes were frustrating him. He assured them that by changing his major to political science, he could raise his grade-point average.

Upon returning to SMU, Terry treated himself to another Christmas present with money he earned over the summer. He traded his Honda in for a 1965 Triumph Bonneville 650 motorcycle. This one was bigger, had more horsepower, and handled more smoothly on the open roads. The happiness was short-lived, however, when he received a letter in the mail that was forwarded to him from Willoughby – it was from Sally.

In the letter she stated that she would not be returning to SMU because she'd decided to take a job offer with Pan American Airlines. Being a stewardess was something she had always dreamed of. She ended by saying she loved him and wanted him to keep in touch, so they could meet whenever she was nearby.

He called her that evening and they talked for over an hour. They knew they were too young to think about a permanent relationship, but Terry felt hurt inside. He wished her the best.

My Brother the Boxer

The following week, Doug called him wanting to know his schedule at the boxing gym. Terry informed him that he had a lot on his plate with classes and studies, and a part-time job, but said he'd workout at least an hour and a half twice a week.

Terry's roommate, Mike, had landed a good paying job with the Texas Pacific Railroad over the holiday break and convinced his boss to hire Terry when they needed an extra hand during peak seasons. Their job was to unload new automobiles off the railway cars and reload them on to semi trucks for delivery to car dealerships in the Dallas/Fort Worth area.

"The pay's good at five bucks an hour, with a raise after 30 days if the management likes you," Mike said. "And a fringe benefit is driving some hot cars around the rail yards when we unload 'em!"

Terry's favorite was climbing behind the wheel of a new '67 Camaro. It was Chevy's answer to Ford's popular Mustang.

Mike warned Terry of an issue he was dealing with on the job. It seemed that some of the union members were not keen on the new "college boys" that were working under non-union contracts. They made it clear that if they wanted to work side-by-side with union workers, they had to pay dues, even though they were part-time.

Mike let Terry know that management would bug him about joining the union and paying dues, but he was under no obligation to do so.

Terry said, "Well, let's make sure we stick together around the rail cars just in case one of these 'Texas Gumbas' decides to use a little muscle in their next pitch."

Terry learned about union strong-arm tactics when he worked out at Billy Wagner's gym. Billy's brother, Larry, came into the gym one night with a black eye and a small butterfly bandage covering a cut on his eyebrow.

"Rough night at the bar last night, Larry?" Terry asked.

Larry smiled and said, "Nah, we still got a couple of wise guys at work who think they can work there as scabs. I had to remind 'em that their time was up on gettin' a union card.

"It took me a little longer than usual to convince 'em, but when it was over, they had no problem signin' the papers," he chuckled.

A couple of weeks later, Mike and Terry found themselves put to the test during a lunch break. Three men approached them and one was carrying a steel coiled spring that was taken from the inside of a truck shock absorber. He had straightened out the ends of the spring by about six inches, and had bicycle grips attached on each end.

"Hey, boys, you ever seen a contraption like this?" one of the men asked in a stern voice.

"Yeah, it looks like a piece of equipment that will help build your chest muscles," Terry said. "I've seen them in a gym, but never one that big."

The man was medium height, about 180 pounds, and was wearing a white shirt with scuff marks on it. His sleeves were rolled up past his biceps to expose his Popeye-size forearms.

"Show 'em how it works, Odie," one of the other men said. "Show 'em what it takes to be a union man here at the yard."

Odie smiled with a cigarette hanging in his mouth and swung the steel spring into his grips, proceeding to bend it to a point where the grips were eight inches away from one another. His face reddened while he held the spring in his flexed arms for about six seconds before slowly working it back to its original position.

"Now, you try it, boy," he said as he handed it to Mike.

Mike was a competitive swimmer on the championship swim team at SMU, but he didn't spend much time lifting weights in the off-season. Nonetheless, he gave it the "good ol' college try." He grabbed one end and swung the heavy spring into both his grips, then tried with all his might to get it to bend.

My Brother the Boxer

"Ugghhh," he groaned as his face reddened and the veins on his neck bulged. After 30 seconds of grunting and trying with all his strength, the spring barely moved an inch.

The men laughed, then Odie took it out of Mike's hands and pushed it into Terry's chest. "Here ya' go, college boy. Let's see if you can do a little better than your partner. Show me if you got what it takes to work here with us *men*," he said as the inch-long ash on his cigarette fell to the ground.

Terry had a bored look on his face. He grabbed the spring at both ends, and without hesitation, bent the spring into a pretzel. He held it for 10 seconds before slowly releasing it to the astonishment of the men, whose smiles quickly disappeared from their faces.

He pushed it back into Odie's chest and said, "Hey, that's not a bad workout!"

From that point on, the union men never asked Mike or Terry about joining, and their part-time job became much more enjoyable.

* * *

In the professional boxing world, Cassius Clay, now demanding to be called Muhammad Ali, continued to get the attention of the worldwide press. The animated heavyweight champion had boxing matches in Europe and the United States. He had built a huge fan base, and was always featured on ABC's *Wide World of Sports*. Whether it was a taped delay of his fights or live interviews with Howard Cosell, he was a real attention-getter.

A year earlier, the newspapers and television reported that Ali had been called by the draft board and was ordered to report for examination of his status for the war in Vietnam. He went, but told the board that his religion and Islamic beliefs prohibited him from killing anyone. Then, a news reporter wrote down the statement Ali made that would cause controversy for years to come: "I ain't got no quarrel with them Viet Cong."

His lawyers challenged the draft board to accept Ali as a conscientious objector and that bought him time to defend his title in '66, but most of the public expressed distaste for his actions. They didn't feel religion and personal beliefs should be displayed on a regular basis from a heavyweight champion.

Tom, Denny and Jeff watched Ali's fight with the British heavyweight champion, Henry Cooper, on ABC the following week at home. Cooper was cut badly above his left eye from the third round, but hung on with solid punches of his own until the ref stopped the fight in Round Six.

Ali kept his composure during the interview with Howard Cosell after the fight. He gave praise to the London slugger and didn't discuss religion at the end, which the Daniels boys thought was good. But the papers would continue to report what Ali said in interviews, like: "The Nation of Islam was for segregation." He branded the white race as "White Devils." These statements stirred the pot of racial tensions in the U.S.

In Dallas, Doug kept the boxing fans entertained with amateur and pro fights featuring fighters from his gym. He got Terry in an amateur show a month before the Golden Gloves at one of the high schools and he won his bout with a hard-earned split decision. After the fight, Doug told him that he thought he was the best heavyweight in Texas, and said if he would continue to work with him, he could be a national contender.

On January 27th, a week before the '67 Dallas Regional Golden Gloves, Doug invited Terry to his house for dinner. The Lords lived in a two-story colonial on a quaint street in Dallas. Terry looked forward to it and arrived on time.

The door opened and he was greeted by an attractive woman with sandy brown hair, wearing a colorful flowered dress and a pearl necklace. She extended her hand and said, "Hi Terry, I'm Opal Lord, come on in.

I'm just now fixin' the potato salad. Douglas is out on the back patio and is about to put the steaks on. Would you like a Coke or some iced tea to drink? I'd offer you a beer, but I know you're in training."

"Iced tea would be fine ma'am," Terry replied.

She smiled and said, "My, I've seen your picture in the paper a few times, and you are even more handsome in person! You can go on through the livin' room to the screen door that leads to the patio. I'll bring your iced tea in a minute."

Doug was stoking the coals in the barbeque and turned when he heard the screen door open. "Hey, ya' made it! Pull up a chair!"

There were two folding chairs with a round metal table between them about 10 feet from the barbeque. Terry took a seat while Opal set his iced tea down next to him. "Honey, would you bring me another Coke please?" Doug asked as he wiped the sweat off his forehead.

"Sure. Did you want me to bring the burgers out for the kids so you can get them fed first?" she asked.

"That's a good idea, the fire will be ready in a few minutes."

Doug sat down and said, "So, tell me about yourself, Terry. What brings a good student from up north all the way down here to Dallas?"

Terry told Doug about his roots in Lake County, the family corporations that his grandpa, dad and uncle built, and how he came to make SMU his choice of colleges. He ended by asking, "And what's your story?"

Doug smiled and said, "Well, Terry, we couldn't be more alike than an apple and an orange. My daddy died when I was 9 years old. He worked at a company in Dallas that made feed and flour sacks. He was the head pressman that printed the labels on the sacks.

"I'll never forget the time my momma took me in to visit him at work one day. He couldn't give me a hug or nothin' because he was covered in all kinds of ink from the presses, and that's what got him sick – his kidneys got infected from all the lead in the ink. And before he died, he made me promise him that I would live at the Masonic Home for Orphans in Fort Worth."

Opal approached with a plate of hamburger patties and said, "If the fire's hot Honey, you can start the burgers for the kids. They're gettin' kinda' restless and need some food in their tummies!"

"All right then," Doug replied as he started the hamburgers.

"Wow, I'm sorry to hear that about your dad, Doug," Terry said.

"Well, those things happened to families back in the '30s, with the Depression and all, but I honored his request and moved in a month after his funeral. I was fortunate enough that daddy was a 33-degree Mason. I got a good education, learned all about farmin' because we raised everything right there on the 200 acres the Home owned, and I met my wife Opal there," he said.

"Now there's a plus," Terry said. "What about sports? Did you get interested in boxing then?"

Doug chuckled and said, "Heck, every boy in there knew how to fight, and if you didn't, you sure did learn quick. But the headmaster and teachers wouldn't tolerate any fightin' or wrestlin' on school grounds. If they caught you, oh boy, they'd paddle you so hard, you couldn't sit for days!

"Now the Home did have a small football team when I got there, and when I say small, I mean like 12 boys on the entire team."

Terry listened intently as Doug told him about how a man named Rusty Russell started a football team there in 1927. He taught the boys how to run plays from set formations, proper methods of blocking and tackling, and did it all with the most primitive equipment one could imagine.

"Heck, we weren't allowed to wear shoes on our feet for six months outta the year 'cause we didn't have any money to buy new ones when they wore out," Doug said.

Opal came out again carrying a large plate with buns and said, "If those burgers are done, I'm gonna serve the kids so they can eat and go back to playin' their game of kickball with the neighbors across the street. Then we can enjoy our steaks with a nice peaceful dinner out here by ourselves."

Doug said, "That sounds good, Honey," and transferred the burgers to the plate.

"Terry, take the foil off that bowl on the picnic table there and hand it over to me if you would, please. These steaks have been marinatin' all afternoon, and it's time to get 'em fired up," he said as he picked each thick rib eye out of the marinade with a two-pronged fork.

The steaks sizzled when they hit the grill and the smoke and fire intensified from the hot charcoals. Doug grabbed a plastic mustard bottle with water in it and squirted some on the fire, then continued.

"Like I said, we only had 12 or 13 boys make up a team each year, but when I got there they had built up a pretty good reputation in the Dallas/Fort Worth area. Folks around used to call us 'The Mighty Mites' 'cause we played with such intensity and whipped some of the best high schools in the state."

"Wow, you had just 12 boys on the team?" Terry asked. "That meant that everyone played both ways, well, 11 did with one replacement. But what if somebody got hurt, I mean, would the coach just make do with one or two less players on the field?"

Doug smiled; shook his head and said, "If someone got hurt, you just sucked it up and continued the best you could. There was no givin' up by an orphan. And keep in mind, we all wore leather helmets with no face masks back then. Heck, half the team didn't have the pads to put underneath their uniforms until the locals took up collections to buy us equipment after we proved we could beat the tar outta the other teams.

"We beat Doak Walker's alma mater, Highland Park, two years in a row in the state playoffs," he added, "and they had the money to buy the best equipment and playing facilities in the area – and still do!"

"That's incredible, Doug," Terry said. "So, did you ever box in the Golden Gloves when you were young?"

"That's another story," Doug said as he turned each steak over.

"I was kinda gangly as a young teenager, you know a late bloomer, so to speak, and I really didn't start fillin' out till I was 16 years old. Football helped me with that. Anyway, a couple of us used to caddie at a nearby country club. I was 15 at the time. There was a colored boy there, five years older than me, that shined golfer's shoes and helped in the caddie shack. He really didn't like me for some reason.

"He yelled at me one day to get my 'white-trash ass' back to that orphanage I was from and not to come back or he'd give me a whoopin' I'd never forget. I told him that I was done for the year anyhow, but I'd be back next year and that he could *count on it.*

"Well, I went back the following summer at the age of 16 with more weight and muscle on my body from football, and sure enough he was there. He saw me and said, 'I thought I told you last year that I didn't want to see your honkey-ass around here. Now, am I gonna have to kick your ass out?'

"I said, 'I'd like to see you try, nigger!'"

"He jumped over the counter of the shack and I stood up to him with my fists in a fightin' position. All the other boys surrounded us, and one said we had better go behind the shack so the manager wouldn't see us. So, we did, and when we got back there he came at me like he wanted to tear my head off! I took one step back and hit him right on the jaw with the hardest haymaker I ever threw in my life!

"I knew I stunned him, and then I just hit him with punch after punch until he fell down. I wanted to kick his head like I was tryin' for a field goal, but one of my friends pulled me back and said that was enough."

Doug smiled and said, "He didn't show his ugly face around there for two weeks after that, and when he finally did, he never shot his mouth off to me again. That was my start to gainin' respect amongst the boys I hung out with, and that same year, we snuck out to go to downtown Fort Worth to see if some of us could enter the Golden Gloves tournament."

Opal came out carrying potato salad in a bowl with one hand and a bowl of steamed broccoli in the other and said, "I hope those steaks are done boys, 'cause the kids are fed and I am starvin'!"

Doug asked that they bow their heads while he led them in prayer. Terry could hardly wait to hear the word "Amen" because his stomach was growling, and the smell of that charred Texas black angus was driving him crazy.

"Honey, I was just tellin' Terry about my time in the Golden Gloves when I was 16," Doug said in between bites.

Opal shook her head and said, "Oh my gosh, those boys just couldn't stay put after dinner at the Home. If they weren't off to the swimmin' hole for a dip in the evenin', they'd be sneakin' off to downtown Fort Worth lookin' for somethin' to keep 'em busy!"

"And buddy, let me tell ya'," Doug said with a chunk of steak bulging out of his left cheek, "we couldn't wait to get into that tournament and show each other who was the toughest."

Terry smiled as Doug continued, "There were four of us signed up when they had the weigh-ins. We had to fudge some signatures on the entrance forms, which included the OK that we were fit to fight."

He chuckled and said, "Heck, we only had two pairs of tennis shoes between us, so we had to share them. And I stole a mouthpiece off a trainin' table when no one was lookin' and we all shared that too."

Opal shook her head again and said, "It's a wonder y'all didn't get sick with all those germs in that place."

He continued, "Anyway, my first fight was against a guy who was in the Navy. He was bigger and stronger than me, but I fought him all three rounds. I was in way over my head, but my buddies rooted me on and the crowd gave me a nice round of applause at the end even though I lost on a unanimous decision. The crowd was as big as it is today at our tournament in Dallas.

"And one of our boys made it to the finals," he said.

"Oh, you gotta hear this Terry," Opal said with a smile.

"A big ol' boy from our football team named Ray Musslewhite. He was only 14, but big for his age. He fought like a tiger and really surprised the rest of us. He won his first four fights and made it into the finals. And get this – he only had one good eye!"

"One eye? How'd the ref let him continue?" Terry asked.

"Well, he told the ref that he had a glass eye, and asked him if it would be okay if he took it out and just kept his eye shut while fightin'. But the ref said he had to keep it in, otherwise he would disqualify him from the championship bout."

"So he did," Doug said, "and the other boy landed a punch in the first round that knocked his eye outta' the socket!"

Terry laughed and said, "Holy cow!"

"And when that boy looked down to see Ray's eye rollin' around on the canvas, Ray hauled off with a couple haymakers and knocked that boy silly. The ref raised his hand with a knockout win in the first round!"

They all laughed and enjoyed the rest of their dinner while the calm Texas evening slowly came to an end.

Terry and Doug helped Opal clean off the picnic table. Opal excused herself by saying, "I'm going to bring the kids home. They'd stay out all night playin' if I didn't. So, Terry it was very nice to finally meet you. We'll have to do it again, maybe when the tournament's over."

"That would be nice, Mrs. Lord," Terry replied.

"No, it's Opal, Doug and Opal," she said with a big smile.

Doug lightly slapped Terry on the back and said, "Come on, I'll walk ya' out to your wheels."

Terry got in his car and rolled down the window as Doug said, "I almost forgot to tell you that I changed the name of my gym this year to Associate Bookings Corporation, to accommodate both my pros and amateurs, and I wanna see ya' in the gym tomorrow afternoon for some heavy sparring.

"There were quite a few boxers at the weigh-ins the other night, but you know how that goes – about half won't show up once they get a good look at the competition. But you can count on one boy in your division who moved into Dallas about six months ago. Bob Taylor, from the East Side Gym, told me about him – he was last year's National AAU Runner-up; an experienced fighter by the name of Cookie Wallace."

CHAPTER 23

The cover of the *Dallas Times Herald* sports section featured the 31st Regional Golden Gloves Tournament in Monday's edition. Mike McCann was quoting excerpts while reading it to his friends.

"They're saying that the Open Heavyweight Division should be as action-packed as ever with Terry Daniels, last year's finalist who lost a narrow decision to Dickie Wills, and a new man who moved into Dallas last year by the name of Cookie Wallace. Both are picked as favorites to watch. Wallace brings to the ring more experience than Daniels with over 35 amateur fights and was last year's runner-up in the National Amateur Athletic Union tournament."

"Cookie?" Dedo asked. "What kinda' guy calls himself Cookie?"

"The paper says he's a hard puncher with moves like Cassius Clay, I mean Ali," Mike replied.

"Oh, another 'Ali-wannabe,'" Dedo said. "What's Terry say about him?"

"To tell you the truth, I think he's more worried about a big exam he's got coming up on Friday than he is this tournament," Mike replied. "He said he promised his dad he wouldn't let boxing interfere with his grades, because last semester he was below a 3.0 average."

The news traveled quickly around the SMU campus, and by Thursday, opening night, Terry's classmates learned that he had drawn last year's Novice Heavyweight Champion, Murphy Von Hutchins for his first bout.

My Brother the Boxer

"That Von Hutchins is that big boy that won last year," Dedo said to Terry at lunch. "He must have three inches in height and 20 more pounds on you. Aren't you a little nervous stepping into the ring in this heavyweight division, Terry?"

"Who wouldn't be?" Terry replied. "But I came here to play football, and would have to get used to running into 260-pound tackles and beefy linebackers too."

"That's true. But I had a friend in high school that wrestled at 142 pounds, up from 136, and he said he always had a tough time with guys weighing 4 or 5 pounds more than him. And then you got this Cookie Wallace that's way more experienced than you."

"I know," Terry said. "But like I told you guys before – people come to see the heavyweights, because *they* get the headlines. And the first time I get my ass whipped in the ring, it'll be my last."

There were 56 bouts scheduled in front of the 3,000 fans and Terry went into the ring, weighing 192 pounds, to face his 215-pound opponent just before midnight. The front page of the Sports Section of the *Dallas Morning News* the next day said: "Boxers in Fast Start – 11 TKOs, 4 KOs in Gloves Matches" – *Leather-pounding, from start to finish, was the work Thursday night as the tournament got off to one of its finest openers ever at Dallas Memorial Auditorium.*

If this, the opening night, set a precedent for the three upcoming nights, this should be one of the greatest Golden Gloves events in Dallas history. Action was so fast and furious it even had such veteran ring observers as referee Pat Riley awed by such first-night battling.

And, there wasn't any end to it until the 56th and final battle, when SMU student-athlete Terry Daniels bombed 1966 Novice champ Murphy Von Hutchins to the floor twice shortly before midnight to claim a mild upset in the Open Heavyweight division.

Daniels, last year's Open runner-up, gave away 23 pounds to the burly Negro battler, but survived a flurry of punches on the ropes in the initial round to come back strong and grab the victory.

Terry tagged Von Hutchins with a solid left in the second round and the ex-Novice king started backing and lunging. In the third, the SMU puncher caught Hutchins with a wicked left to the body that put him on the floor for the mandatory eight-count. Seconds after Hutchins got up, Terry sent him to his knees with a right to the head and it was all over.

Hutchins remained on one knee while referee Dickie Cole raised Daniels hand much to the pleasure of the late crowd.

Terry was up early the next morning studying for an exam that he took later in the day, and ended up doing well on it. When he got back to his room, he noticed a drawing on a 5 x 8 inch piece of paper taped to his door, titled: "The Massacre." It had a boxer standing over another on his knees face down, with an arrow pointing to the downed boxer and the name: Murphy Von Hutchins.

He opened the door and found Mike lying on his bed reading a *Playboy* magazine. "Hey, did you draw this?" Terry said while pointing to the picture.

"Yeah, I was in a lecture hall today and had to listen to that ol' windbag, Dr. Guttenberg go on and on about the Renaissance period, and drew *that* instead of taking notes."

Terry laughed and said, "Not bad, McCann. Hey, Cookie Wallace is fighting tonight in the tournament, but he's not due to go on till last. Do you, Dedo and some of the guys want to go to the El Toro Room for a while and then on over to the fights around 10?"

"Sure. I'm going to be eating dinner at the frat house with the guys. Why don't you join me and we'll see who all wants to go?"

The boys watched the flamboyant Wallace, with a record of 31 wins and 4 losses, pick his opponent apart and win a unanimous decision in the last bout of the evening.

"He's got the moves, I'll give 'em that," Dedo said.

"Yeah, and he does mimic Ali in between rounds, but I don't see anything you can't handle, Terry. Do you?" Mike said.

"He's quick alright, but his opponent never got in a clean shot. I'd like to see someone hit him with a few solid shots to his head."

My Brother the Boxer

"Yeah, and I'd like to see that *someone* be you! Come on, let's get you home, champ. You got the semifinals to get through tomorrow night before you start concentrating on this Wallace character," Dedo said.

* * *

The SMU crowd at the tournament Saturday night consisted of 20 guys and gals, and they formed their circle in the stands amongst the rest of the crowd in the auditorium. They watched some of the best amateur boxers in the state, and just as an exciting movie builds to a climatic ending, Terry stepped into the ring for his match. Cookie Wallace was scheduled to follow for the final bout of the evening.

Mike was sitting with Dedo and 12 other guys from the Phi Delta Theta fraternity and was proud to say to all his new fraternity brothers, "It's showtime! Wait till you see what my buddy can do in the ring!"

"What do you mean *your* buddy? You mean *our* buddy," Dedo quickly added.

Cornbread put a stool and a bucket in the corner as the announcer turned the P.A. system up a notch and said, "In the red corner, representing the Police Athletic League with a record of 7 wins and 2 losses; standing 6' 2" and weighing 292 pounds, Charlie Sites!"

The announcer continued, "And in the blue corner, representing the Associate Bookings Corporation with a record of 13 wins and 1 loss; standing 5' 11" and weighing 192 pounds, Terry Daniels!"

His friends led the chorus of cheers from the audience as Doug lightly touched up his boxer's face with Vaseline. "Go to work on that fat belly of his," Doug said, "then move up to his head with short left hooks and uppercuts. But take your time, and watch for his haymakers, he telegraphs 'em every time!"

The referee called the two fighters to the center of the ring and Terry was rolling his head to try to stay loose, but his heart was pounding so hard he was afraid Sites could hear it.

The ref ordered them back to their corners and said, "Box."

The bell rang and Sites came out holding his left arm fully extended at eye level with his right hand cocked back close to his jaw, while Terry held both hands close to his head and moved from a slightly crouched position. Both fighters moved cautiously toward one another to the center of the ring.

"Look at that guy," Dedo said, "he reminds me of that boxer they made that movie about, you know, the one Anthony Quinn played... what's his name?"

"Primo Carnera," one of the frat brothers said.

"Yeah, that's right, only a little heavier though." He looked up and said, "C'mon Terry, pick your shots!"

Terry *was* picking his shots, but Sites kept sticking his long arm on the top of Terry's head keeping him a good distance from his body. Terry bobbed left and right while slowly wading into his opponent an inch at a time.

Suddenly, Sites unleashed a straight right to Terry's head, but Terry slipped the punch and it grazed his right ear. "Oooo," the crowd said in unison, then Sites poked a few jabs that lightly touched the top of Terry's head.

Each fighter took the first minute of the round to get in the groove, then Terry unleashed a right hand that landed solidly on Sites' nose. The big hulk stumbled backward and fell down on his back. The crowd erupted with whistles and cheers.

The ref ordered Terry to a neutral corner and started counting as Sites got to his feet after five. The ref dusted off his gloves and ordered the boxers to continue.

Sites kept his gloves close to his face as Terry came into him with three jabs in a row, followed by right and left hooks. The SMU crowd stood, along with the rest of the fans, and cheered wildly – they wanted to see "Kid Galahad" finish him off.

After 20 unanswered punches, the referee stepped between the fighters and waved the match over in 1:58 minutes of the first round.

Mike, Dedo and several other boys met Terry as he left the ring.

"Wow, Terry! You thumped that guy hard. I thought he was out when he went down the first time!" Mike said.

"I thought he was too, that's why I hit him with everything I had. Then the ref told us to keep fighting!" Terry said. "I don't know what I would have done if he lasted the round, because, *man* I was spent."

Doug approached them and said, "Go have a seat with your friends, Terry, and pay attention to the winner of the next match – it's who you'll be fightin' Monday night."

The next morning, a boy in the dorm knocked on Terry and Mike's door. "Hey, Terry, I thought I'd bring ya' the Sunday paper. You're on the cover of the sports section again!"

Terry opened the door; smiled and said, "Hey, thanks. Come on in, let's see what they had to say."

The headline read: "Daniels Steals Gloves Show; Wallace Wins" – *Daniels spoiled the anticipated show from Cookie Wallace at the Golden Gloves last night by stealing the admiration of some 4,000 fans in the Dallas Memorial Auditorium a bout earlier.*

While Wallace, the reigning National AAU runner-up, sat smiling in the gloves-box outside the ring, Daniels spotted his 292-pound challenger, Charles Sites, an even 100 pounds and quickly registered a first-round TKO.

The audience loved Daniels' performance, but they were waiting for the Cookie-Emmit Banks production, last of a 34-bout semifinals program. It didn't take them long to discover that most of the Open Heavyweight action was recorded in the 1:58 it took Daniels to dispose of his burly opponent.

"Yeah, they said Banks was the 1957 New Mexico champion, and he looked like he was 30 years old. All he did was tie Wallace up and neither one got off any solid shots. The crowd started booing by the second round and Cookie wasn't used to that. He won a unanimous decision, but the crowd still booed at the end," Terry said.

"Well, I'm sure your name's gonna be brought up a lot on campus Monday," the boy said.

Terry called the family after church to share the exciting news and assured them he was ready for the fight.

"I know this Cookie Wallace is going to let it all out in our fight, to try and win back the fans," he said, "but I've really improved the power and timing of my combinations. My coach said for me to take it to him early, and that's what I plan on doing."

They wished him well and told him to call them with the news right after his fight the following night.

CHAPTER 24

It was 62 degrees on Monday, February 6, 1967, when Terry arrived at the Memorial Auditorium in Dallas. He took a deep breath of the crisp, clean Texas air as he stepped off the bus, and tried to convince himself to stay loose. But the dreaded butterflies were churning more than ever.

The guard at the entrance motioned that he didn't need his ID. "Your coach is in the first set of rooms down the hall on the left. Good luck tonight, Terry," he said.

Doug and Cornbread were wrapping the hands of three boxers of the ABC gym who made it to the finals when Terry arrived.

"Hey, Terry, put your bag down and we'll be with you in a few minutes," Doug said.

The evening moved quickly in the two rings, and the boxing fans of the Dallas/Fort Worth area got the best sports entertainment in the state. There were split decisions that were booed, unanimous decisions that were cheered, and knockouts that brought the house down. And of course, there were even a few fights in the crowd among disgruntled fathers of the boxers.

James Helwig, now with Doug's ABC gym, ignited the crowd when he came from behind in the third round and won his fight by unanimous decision. Helwig was the previous year's High School Middleweight Champion and packed a wallop with both hands.

But the tension in the air was building from the rowdy Texas crowd in anticipation of the big heavyweight showdown – Terry Daniels versus Cookie Wallace.

The management of the auditorium wanted to give the concession stands one last opportunity to collect money from the patrons by having a 10-minute break before the main event. Doug was in the locker room with Terry, giving his fighter a few last-minute pointers. "This guy likes to mix it up early, so be ready to go toe-to-toe and show him who's boss. You're in the best shape of any of these guys, includin' him, so take it to him early and take it to him *hard*!"

The locker room door opened as the lights in the main auditorium went dark, and Terry's heart started to beat rapidly when he heard the roar of the crowd. He could hear Mike and Dedo leading the cheers as he made his way into the ring.

On the opposite side of the ring, Cookie removed his robe and shuffled around while lightly throwing punches.

"I hope these people don't get too comfortable sittin' down, 'cause this fight ain't gonna last long," Cookie said to his corner man with a cocky smile on his face.

The ring announcer got the crowd worked up with his charismatic introductions of the fighters. Then the ref signaled for the opening bell and Terry waded into the center of the ring. Cookie came right at him and led off with two quick jabs. The first fell short; the other found its target.

Terry was quick to respond with a solid left jab, tagging Wallace on the lower jaw. The crowd responded even though the punch had little effect on him, and just as Doug predicted, neither fighter backed down.

Cookie shuffled to his left while throwing quick jabs to Terry's head and short right hands to his body. Terry kept his arms in tight and responded with short uppercuts, followed by left and right hooks.

After a minute of non-stop action, the fans were on their feet with Terry's classmates leading the cheers.

"C'mon Terry, stick it to him!" Mike yelled.

"Don't back off Terry, make him quit first!" screamed Dedo.

Both fighters were still in the center of the ring, and now were throwing everything they had. Then Terry dropped his right foot back and hit Cookie with a powerful left-right combination. Cookie's knees gave out, and for the first time in has amateur carrier Cookie Wallace fell to the canvas.

The ref ordered Terry to a neutral corner. By the time the count got to seven, Cookie was on his feet and nodded to the ref to continue the fight.

Terry followed the same battle plan he did on Saturday night against Sites – he stepped in close to Wallace and hit him with several hard, unanswered punches. The ref separated them and ended the fight.

The bell rang several times while the referee was waving his arms and the crowd continued the roar of cheers and applause. Terry went to his corner and was greeted by Doug, who had a Texas-sized grin on his face. Cornbread said, "You showed him who was boss tonight, Daniels!"

Several minutes went by before Cookie was able to gain his composure and join Terry in the center of the ring. The announcer boomed over the P.A. system while the ref raised Terry's hand, "And winner by TKO in 1:35 of the first round – in the red corner, Terr-ree Dann-yells!"

When he stepped out of the ring, Terry was mobbed by Mike, Dedo, and several other classmates.

"Man, Terry, I bet that guy's never been hit like that before!" Dedo said.

"Yeah, Terry, I think you made a tattoo on Cookie's head!" Mike added.

He stood in his trunks and robe and joined his friends to hear the results of the final trophies awarded to the best boxers of the show: Greenville's Alan Wallace won the J. B. Nichols Trophy as the outstanding Novice high school fighter, Open Bantamweight champ Noah Ramirez won the Mike Rodriguez award for most improved fighter, and Terry was awarded the Scotty McLaughlin trophy for best boxer in the tournament.

He was beaming from ear to ear as he accepted the trophy and waved to the crowd. He stepped down from the ring and said to his friends, "And now, it's official – I'm an experienced Open Division Heavyweight champ!"

* * *

The next day, Terry met up with his small fan club at lunch in the cafeteria on campus. Although Sally was not there to greet him with a kiss and a smile anymore, Mike McCann introduced him to an attractive girl with sandy blond hair named Carol.

"Hi, Terry. Mike told me you're unattached now, and I've just been dyin' to meet you," she said. "I was in the stands cheerin' you on with my girlfriends last night!"

"You were at the auditorium? Cool," Terry said.

Mike said, "Take a gander at today's sports section."

He held the *Dallas Times Herald* out for all to see – the headline on top of the page was titled, "Talking Continues, Clay Clobbers Ernie Terrell" followed underneath with three pictures of Ali landing a solid right to Terrell's face.

While the Golden Gloves finals were happening in Dallas on Monday evening, the Houston Astrodome was hosting the Heavyweight Championship of the World with Muhammad Ali, the WBC Champion, pitted against Ernie Terrell, the WBA Champion. The winner would be crowned, *Undisputed* Heavyweight Champion of the World.

Clay, as he was referred to in the article, won a 15-round unanimous decision to a crowd of over 37,000 spectators. The staff writer, Blackie Sherrod, wrote that after pummeling his opponent the first seven rounds: *He began to taunt Terrell by saying, "What's my name?" over and over again. Referring to Terrell's refusal to address Clay's preferred Black Muslim name of Muhammad Ali.*

Beneath the pictures of Ali on the cover page was a second headline: "Daniels Winner, His Cookie Crumbles."

Mike went on to read a paragraph from the article out loud to the rest of the group, "Wallace, the man of a few million words, a national AAU runner-up last year, was TKO'd by Terry Daniels, the Cinderella heavyweight from SMU."

"How about that, Terry, you're as popular in Dallas as Cassius Clay, I mean, Muhammad Ali!" he said.

After lunch, Mike and Terry walked back to their dorm, and Terry confided to Mike about his dad's inability to accept him as a boxer. Mike could hear the frustration in his friend's voice and said, "Well, ya' gotta admit, Terry, you *are* in uncharted territory. He's just thinking logically, like everybody else's dad, and wants what's best for his number one son."

Terry looked down and said, "Yeah, but if he was there and came up to pat me on the back like you guys did, it would've meant the world to me. I just wish he could've seen the biggest thing that ever happened to me. I wish he could be in *my* corner."

Two weeks later, Terry found himself in the finals for the Texas State Golden Gloves Heavyweight Championship. He lost on a split decision to a boy from Houston, but was informed that the boy had broken his hand, and Terry would be going as the heavyweight on the Texas National Golden Gloves team.

His classmates congratulated Terry at the cafeteria, and by the end of the week, most everyone on campus knew of his new achievement when an article appeared in the *Daily Campus* titled: "Another TD for Mustangs," by Tommy Thomas.

It stated: *You could say there are some pretty rough characters, of sorts, at SMU.*

There's the guy who tries to run you down in front of the Student Center with his GT. And there's occasionally some jock who has a few drinks and suddenly turns street-fighter. Then there's the genuine thing.

His name is Terry Daniels. His title: Dallas Golden Gloves Champion of the Open Heavyweight Division.

The article highlighted how Terry went from playing football for SMU to boxing, his latest accomplishments in the ring, and how he would be participating in the National Golden Gloves Tournament in Milwaukee.

On February 24th, the day before the national tournament was to start, another article appeared on page 3 of the sports section in the *Dallas Times Herald.* It had a picture of Terry in the ring with his hands in the air after beating Cookie Wallace, with the headline: "Terry Steps Up – Suddenly Champ."

In the article, it stated: *A few weeks ago, he entered the Dallas Regional Golden Gloves Tournament a nervous heavyweight.*

Now, three fabulous knockouts later, he has been named on the Texas team for the National Golden Gloves Tournament and on the USA's team for a string of international matches.

Virtually every jock on campus knew Terry by sight, especially when he wore the new "boxing" letter jacket he received at the awards banquet at the Dallas Athletic Club.

His fame increased back home as well when he sent a letter that included the first news clippings of the tournament from the Dallas newspapers to the *News-Herald.* The article appeared in the Saturday edition with the headline reading: "A Fighting Rebel: Former South Star Texas Ring Champ." It was dated two weeks after his championship fight with Cookie Wallace.

His class picture from college was in the middle of the article. He had no idea how much attention it got from the locals back home, or how it would affect his younger brother.

Jeff was in 7th grade and attended Willoughby Junior High School when the story came out. He was at a sensitive time in his life – he was officially 13 and a teenager. He was starting to discover girls, and was very self-conscious about his weight. He was 10 pounds over the normal weight for a boy his age, and all of it seemed to sit right at his waistline.

Tom and Terry would tease him about it, and he would shout back at them that he knew what he had to do, but would do it when he was good and ready. After reading the article, he was ready. Tom told him the best way to lose as much weight as he wanted was to join the wrestling team. "You'll build muscle too," he said.

Both Terry and Tom wrestled their sophomore and junior years at South High under Head Coach Don Rositano, and they received their basic training from Coach Ken Roskos at Willoughby Junior High School.

"Mr. Roskos," as he demanded the boys call him, was a disciplinarian, but a fair one. He seemed to know just how far to push a boy in gym class before embarrassing him in front of the rest of the students.

He stood 6' 0", had a rounded chest with a small waist, wore steel-rimmed athletic glasses, and headed up the football, wrestling, and track teams throughout the year.

In gym class, Jeff stood in line with the other boys for roll call. His name was to be called after Curt Cook. The coach yelled for Cook, and he responded, then he hesitated a moment before calling, "Daniels!"

The acoustics rang out whenever Mr. Roskos had something important to share with the class, or the rest of the school if one of the gymnasium doors were open.

"Here!" Jeff yelled.

"Daniels, I read about your big brother in the paper over the weekend. That was very impressive," he said in his deep booming voice.

"Jeff's brother is the heavyweight Golden Gloves Champion of Dallas, and going on to the national tournament," he said to the class. "I guess I'm going to have to start working you a little harder in wrestling from now on, so you can grow up to be more like him."

Not everyone in class read the paper over the weekend, but whoever didn't certainly knew about it now. Jeff stood there at attention, turned bright red and said, "Yeah, I guess so, Coach," while the rest of the boys chuckled.

His buddies came up to him after school and said how cool it was to know someone who had a brother like his. Most had big brothers and some were outstanding athletes, but no one had ever gotten headlines like Terry.

His big brother had set the bar, which seemed sky high to Jeff, but whether he was ready or not he had new goals in his life, thanks to Terry.

CHAPTER 25

On Friday evening, February 24th, the first half of the Texas team of champions arrived in the Milwaukee airport. The tournament was scheduled to start on Saturday and finish the following Wednesday.

The boys wore light blue sport coats with a white and gold emblem on the pocket that stated, *Texas Golden Gloves*. They were also required to wear ties and dress slacks – the tournament directors had an image they wanted their boxers to maintain in public.

Terry sat next to Ronnie Wright, the middleweight champion from Fort Worth, on the flight over. He beat James Helwig in the state finals. They struck up a conversation about their fights while waiting in the terminal and took an immediate liking to one another.

Ronnie was 20 years old and had a stocky 5' 9" build for a middleweight. He was active in the Air Force Reserve and worked in the Fort Worth offices as a medical typist. The job required him to travel to Tokyo several times a year, which kept him out of Vietnam.

"I sure hope those two stewardesses make their way down to us durin' the flight," Ronnie said with a smile. "The blonde was checkin' you out when we boarded, so I guess I'll try and make time with the little redhead."

Terry smiled and said, "Okay, let's be on our best behavior; maybe they'll ask for our autograph or something."

"Yeah, well I hope it is some *thing*," Ronnie said with a chuckle.

Coach Jack Robertson, from Farmers Branch, was in charge of the Texas state champions and gave the boys the agenda for the tournament.

"The weigh-ins will be at the auditorium tomorrow mornin' at nine, so don't eat too much tonight and nothin' in the mornin' if you got a problem makin' your weight class," he said.

"The fights will start at one o'clock in the afternoon, and then again at seven in the evenin'. We've got three boys make it to the quarterfinals on Tuesday, where y'all will fight your matches from one o'clock on. Then the semifinals will be on Wednesday afternoon, with the finals starting at seven Wednesday night."

Unlike the other boys, Terry had the advantage of not having to make weight and planned to eat two plates of spaghetti and meatballs for dinner. He wanted to load up on carbohydrates for tomorrow's opening bout.

The next morning, the boys took the hotel shuttle to the auditorium for the weigh-ins. Upon arriving, they were escorted to the center of the auditorium where they joined hundreds of other fighters in colored jackets and sweats.

Three rings were surrounded with lines of guys stripping down to their shorts and stepping onto the nearby scales. The place was filled with chatter, laughter, and cigarette smoke from the nearby Golden Gloves officials, trainers, and reporters.

Terry occupied himself by casually picking out the heaviest fighters and sizing them up. He knew at this point that everyone who made it this far was in good physical shape and the winners would be the ones who had mastered the *mental* part of the sport.

Ronnie slapped Terry on the back and said, "Some pretty tough lookin' hombres, huh, Daniels? Donnie Jones, our light welterweight, lost a split decision to a tough colored boy from Detroit, Saturday night. He told me that he thought Detroit and Los Angeles had the best lookin' teams."

"Well, they haven't seen the second half of our team yet, have they?" Terry said.

Ronnie let out a nervous laugh, then was interrupted by Coach Robertson who said, "Ronnie, the middleweights are at the scale over there. Get down to your shorts and get in line. What'd the hotel scale say you were before you left?"

"It read 162 Coach, and I skipped breakfast," Ronnie replied.

"Good, it looks like all our boys are gonna make weight today. Now, I want y'all to meet me at the south exit where we'll get the shuttle back to the hotel; then you can get somethin' to eat. And after a little rest, they have a few seminar rooms available for the teams to warm up.

"First bouts start at one o'clock sharp, starting with the welterweights. I'll have a list of your opponents in a few hours," Jack said.

The winter made Milwaukee too chilly for the team to jog outside, so most of them used the hotel stairways to run up and down to get a sweat going, then went to the seminar rooms to shadow box and skip rope.

Jack got the team together in the corner of one of the rooms to give them a list of their opponents along with any information he knew about them. When he got to Terry he said, "Daniels, I believe you will have the toughest opponent in your first bout – it's last year's national champion from the Los Angeles team, a fella' named Clay Hodges."

Jack tried a little coaching pitch by saying, "I tell ya' what Terry, I'd rather see ya' take a guy like Hodges in your first fight while you're fresh, rather than have ya' all wore out and takin' him on for the title.

"Besides, if you take it to him the way you took it to Cookie Wallace for the regional championship, you could win yourself a national title!"

The other boys acknowledged what Jack said, and it made Terry feel even more confident. He needed the support, since he didn't have family or his college buddies there to support him. There was a little lift to his spirits when he returned to his hotel, however, when the desk clerk said he had two telegrams for him. They were forwarded from his dorm. One was from Carol and the other was from her friend Barbara, both wishing him "Good Luck." They had the mark of a red rose on the top of each page.

After reading them Terry smiled and said, "What a couple of sweethearts!"

The team arrived at the auditorium a little after noon and they were told where to set up. The crowd of several thousand was filing in from the entrances, quickly taking the best seats up front, while many of the boxing teams took the seats in the back.

The coaches gave the boys a few programs to share and told them to be ready to get their hands wrapped a half-hour before their fight. Freddie Caram, the welterweight, was number 12 on the fight card and was due in ring 3 when called.

The elimination bouts were similar to the Texas Golden Gloves with three rings going at once, but the participation of the states having a team there made it much bigger. This tournament was guaranteed non-stop action all day and night.

Terry and Ronnie sat next to each other and figured the middleweights would not be up for at least an hour, but decided not to wander off because the fights were fast and furious.

"Man, these welterweights are throwin' some leather," Ronnie said.

"You're not kidding," Terry said. "Who's Freddie's opponent?"

Ronnie looked at the program and said, "Louis Sanchez from New Mexico. I read in *The Ring* magazine a while back that a tough kid outta Detroit won this division in last year's tournament – Hedgemon Lewis. They said he's in the pros now and would be a definite contender."

Terry watched the fights from one ring to the other and wondered how many names in the program would actually make it to fame and fortune in professional boxing some day.

The seats filled throughout the day, and by 4 p.m. the crowd had grown to about 2,500. Ronnie won his middleweight bout earlier with a unanimous decision over a guy from Chicago, and now the light-heavyweights were starting into the rings.

Coach Robertson approached Terry and said, "C'mon over to the bench in the back there and let's get you wrapped up Daniels, you should be up within the next 45 minutes."

Terry felt overpowered with energy, and after watching continuous action in the rings for the past couple of hours, he could hardly wait to get the gloves on.

"You'll be in the center ring," Jack said as he started wrapping Terry's hands. "I saw your opponent in the corner a few minutes ago skippin' rope."

Just then, Terry felt the warmth of a heat rub cream being worked into his shoulders and neck from one of the trainers. It felt good, and took some tension out of his muscles.

"He's not much bigger than you, so it doesn't look like he'll have any reach advantage. Just remember, he puts his pants on one leg at a time – just like you."

Terry smiled to himself because he'd heard Coach Nelson at South High say that same thing to his team before a big football game. He jokingly said, "It's not his legs I'm worried about – it's his fists!"

The air in the auditorium had the familiar smell of cigar smoke and buttered popcorn. Beer and mixed drinks were allowed at the tournament, and by the time the heavyweights started entering the rings, the crowd whistled and applauded louder than they had all day.

Terry was directed to the seating area for the boxers and met his opponent for the first time. Clay Hodges was seated and wore a bright yellow robe with green trim and matching green trunks. On his back was printed: *Heavyweight Golden Gloves Champ* in green with *Los Angeles, Ca.* underneath.

Terry made a quick scan of him: he had dark hair and brown eyes, like Terry, with a slightly bent nose and chiseled chin. He weighed in at 210 pounds, and looked about the same height.

The Texas team had red robes and trunks with white striped trim. The words, *Texas Golden Gloves* appeared in bold white lettering on the back of the robe and on the trunks.

Terry was feeling the tension building, and to keep his mind at ease, he kept a song going in his head – Brian Wilson's new smash hit, *Good Vibrations,* by the Beach Boys.

When Terry and Hodges entered the ring, the crowd applauded and cheered with the anticipation of a good heavyweight fight. Terry got a round of applause when his name and record was announced, but it did not compare to the whistles and cheers that last year's champ received.

"Don't worry about the crowd Terry, you just get the first punch off," Coach Robertson said emphatically.

The bell rang and the ref yelled, "Box!" Terry met Hodges at the center of the ring and touched gloves. The crowd cheered louder, and both fighters bounced back a step before Terry shot out the first jab.

They mixed it up early and the crowd cheered the aggressiveness by "the kid from Texas."

"That's it, Terry," Jack yelled from the corner.

Hodges was bobbing his head, careful not to be a standing target, while Terry kept throwing punches and landing one and two at a time. He pushed Terry back to throw him off and started into him with two quick left jabs followed by a short left hook.

Half the spectators were now on their feet while the two warriors battled it out in the center ring. Terry connected with a solid uppercut to Hodges' jaw and the rest of the crowd stood up as they watched the favorite from Los Angeles go down.

Terry was directed to a neutral corner before the referee started his count. He looked over to see his coach standing and motioning with his hands to take the fight to his opponent, and he nodded back.

Hodges took his time getting up because the ref seemed to delay his count by a few seconds. Once the ref got to six, Hodges quickly got to his feet and nodded to the ref that he was good to go. The ref said, "Box."

Terry came right back after him, intending to end the fight in the first round, but Hodges proved his experience and protected himself well enough to end the round.

"That was beautiful, Terry," Jack yelled as the other corner man poured several gulps of water down Terry's throat.

"Do the same thing to him this round and make him quit first!"

The bell rang for Round Two and Ronnie Wright and the rest of the Texas team were screaming at the top of their lungs for Terry to keep up the combinations, but he didn't need to be reminded.

Hodges kept moving, side-to-side, and countered many of Terry's punches while scoring with solid punches of his own. And when the bell rang to end the second round, Terry felt that his opponent had out-boxed him and feared he might be slipping on points.

He came back to the corner feeling gassed. He had thrown everything he had that round and Hodges was throwing everything right back at him. Jack told him to keep the pressure on, but Terry knew he only had about a quarter of a tank left in him.

The bell rang for Round Three; both fighters met at the center of the ring and continued where they left off. Terry was looking to land that one big right-hand to end it all like he did to Cookie Wallace, but it never happened. Hodges continued to prove his experience and boxing skills in the ring, and scored two punches to Terry's one.

The crowd cheered with approval after the bell rang ending the fight, and Terry was completely exhausted. It was everything he could do to get the words, "Nice fight" out to his opponent. His lungs were sucking in what little oxygen there was in the smoke-filled air. He wasn't sure how the fight ended, he was just glad he finished standing up.

A few minutes went by and then the P.A. system announced, "In ring number two, the winner by unanimous decision, the blue corner – Clay Hodges!"

The ref raised Clay's arm as Terry smiled and tapped gloves with him. Jack put Terry's robe around his shoulders and said, "You have nothin' to be ashamed of, son. That was a helluva fight!"

They exited the ring as a new pair of boxers entered. Terry's first national boxing tournament had come to an end in his first fight. On the bus ride back to the hotel, Ronnie kept telling Terry how his fight will probably make the papers tomorrow.

"It was a big fight to get the crowd comin' back for more," Ronnie said.

Terry smiled in appreciation. He looked at Ronnie and said, "I almost made it to the top tonight. The question is: Do I quit for good or just give it a rest?"

* * *

Terry and Ronnie sat together with the Texas team to watch the final *Night of Champions*. Ronnie had lost his fight in the quarterfinals to a boxer from the Los Angeles team who was in the finals. Terry didn't feel so bad because Clay Hodges made it to the heavyweight final as well, and both fighters won their matches decisively.

"It would have been nice to come home in the top 10 of our division, but if you gotta lose, you might as well lose to the champion," Ronnie said.

Hodges was awarded a special trophy for Best Boxer in the Tournament along with the national title. His victory also clinched the Team Trophy for the tournament with Los Angeles claiming three champions, while Detroit and Minneapolis finished second and third respectively.

Jesse Valdez gave the Texas team something to cheer about by being crowned Junior Middleweight Champion of the tournament.

Terry had called his family with the news of his fight Tuesday evening, and they were enthusiastic and supportive of his now famous amateur boxing career. His dad was not home to hear the news and Terry said, "That's okay. It's not something he wants to hear anyway. I'll be busy with school when I get back in the classrooms Friday, so I'll write soon."

The team arrived at the Dallas airport early Thursday evening and he was in his dorm room by 7 p.m. Mike had left him a note and told him to meet him at the Phi Delta Theta house when he got home.

Terry entered the living room of the frat house and was greeted by Mike, Dedo, and several others.

"We read about your first bout in the *Dallas Morning News*," Mike said. "Man, that's too bad you had to start out with the toughest heavyweight in the tournament right out of the gate. What was it like when you knocked him down in the first round?"

"I hit him hard and he went down. I went to the neutral corner and I kept thinking, 'Don't get up! Don't get up!' but the son of a bitch did, and made me pay for it the rest of the fight!"

They laughed over the next hour trading stories, then Terry excused himself. "I've gotta get back to my room and get some sleep. I've missed four days of studies and I'm sure there's gonna be hell to pay from some of my profs tomorrow."

Getting caught up on a week's worth of assignments was not going to be an easy task. Most of the professors were enthusiastic to hear about Terry's results and indicated that his assignments would be manageable, but not so with the professors in his engineering classes.

He was back in his counselor's office the following Monday, and again, convinced her to reduce his credit hours so he could manage his grade-point average. He knew he was setting himself back from graduating next year, but his newfound popularity in Dallas was winning him over.

The following week, he received a letter addressed to him directly to his dorm room – the return address read *The Fort Worth Star-Telegram*. It was dated March 9, 1967 and read:

Dear Terry:

Please accept my personal thanks for representing the Texas Golden Gloves in the Tournament of Champions in Milwaukee last month.

I have never been more proud than when you decked Clay Hodges of Los Angeles in the first round or more furious at the referee's bumbling manner of handling that knockdown.

You might well have won the fight under normal circumstances. As you know, Hodges went on to win the championship.

We're very proud of you and are looking forward to seeing you in the State AAU Tournament here March 23, 24, 25 and 27. If you win here, you get a trip to the National AAU Tournament in San Diego April 6, 7, 8 – and maybe another crack at Hodges.

Sincerely,
George Kellam
State AAU Director

Terry was surprised and pleased with the comments Mr. Kellam made in the letter, and it motivated him to stay in the sport. He made the decision then not to give up. Not until he got to the top.

'67 SMU Class Picture

'66 Terry with Mom (notice size of his hand)

'66 Bill, Terry, and June leaving for SMU

Bill with horse team & kids '66 Memorial Day Parade
Willoughby, Ohio

'67 AAU Team USA vs Mexico

'71 Hotel near Astrodome

Smokin' Joe ready for exhibition

Terry & James Helwig after fights

Autographed card given to JD at Houston fight

My Brother the Boxer

'72 Terry Daniels, Heavyweight Contender
For more pictures and articles visit www.mybrothertheboxer.com
ID: JD
Password: smuboxer

CHAPTER 26

Muhammad Ali continued to command the attention of the press and kept every heavyweight inspired to focus on winning his crown – which was now Terry's pipe dream.

On April 28, 1967, Ali stirred the pot even more when the media reported that he refused to be drafted into the army. Immediately after that was an announcement from the New York Athletic Commission (NYAC) stating that, "Cassius Clay, also known as Muhammad Ali, has been stripped of his heavyweight title and would be banned from professional boxing until further notice."

Sportscasters around the country announced that the boxing world would be busy trying to fill the void in the heavyweight ranks, but had a lot of talent to choose from. Promoters from all over the world petitioned the NYAC to commission a professional elimination tournament to determine the next heavyweight champion. The sport had now received an even bigger shot in the arm.

Days later, Terry's life became more interesting when he got a call from Doug informing him that he had been nominated to a team by the Amateur Athletic Union. The Texas team would represent the U.S. against a team from Mexico in the third week of May and the event would be held at the Memorial Auditorium in Houston.

The AAU was scouting for potential champions eligible for the '68 Summer Olympics. Doug said he would be coaching the team and Dickie Wills had volunteered to help.

"That's cutting it close to my final exams, which will be the first week in June," Terry said.

"They're puttin' together a total of 10 bouts starting on a Saturday afternoon," Doug said. "So we'll spend the night and have ya' back by Sunday afternoon. You'll get some nice exposure, too."

Terry couldn't resist the opportunity so he agreed to do it, but he did not want his folks to know. Doug assured him that the coverage would be limited to the southern states and Mexico only.

The next day, Terry spent all morning and afternoon in the library, catching up on his studies. As he exited the building, he heard his name. "Hey, Terry," a guy yelled while pulling up in a black '66 Pontiac GTO.

There were two Phi Delts that he'd met by the names of Jack and Toby. "We're goin' over to the grocery store to stock up our refrigerator at the frat house. Hop in, you can give us a hand and then we'll drop you off."

"Thanks, guys," Terry said as he stepped into the back seat.

"Man, this car is sweet. What do you have under the hood?" Terry asked.

"I got a 400 cubic inch 6.6 liter V-8 workin' for me," Jack said as he made his way to Yale Boulevard. When he merged on to the North Central Expressway, he gunned it and everyone's head jerked back.

"Yeee-haaww!" they yelled as they thrust their speed up to 100 miles per hour before Jack let the engine wind down to 75.

Terry laughed and said, "All right! I forgot how much power these babies have."

He glanced down and reached for a magazine he thought he recognized under the passenger's seat. "Hey, it's a *Mad* magazine," he said.

"Oh, I think my little brother left that in my car last week," Jack said.

"Yeah, my little brothers love this magazine too," Terry said as he opened it.

Within seconds he started laughing at the stories and drawings in it. "Hey, they got a bunch of stickers in this issue," he said.

He read some of them out loud as the boys laughed and exited the expressway. They entered the parking lot of the Piggly Wiggly and drove around to look for a spot.

They finally found a space, but it was too small to park the Pontiac. "Look at this motherfucker," Jack said. "He double-parked that stupid Fairlane."

He started to back up when Terry said, "Hey, wait a minute."

The boys looked at Terry in the back seat while he reached into the magazine and carefully tore out one of the 2 x 3 inch stickers. "Let me stick this on that guy's window," he said.

The boys laughed hysterically when Terry showed them the sticker: YOU TOOK TWO PARKING SPACES – YOU HOG!!

When they left the store, they found the Fairlane was gone, and two cars were parked in the spaces.

"I guess he got the message," Terry said.

The boys laughed and invited him and a date to join their party at the frat house.

"Why not? It's Saturday night and I've got just the girl to have fun with," he said.

* * *

With the pressure of the boxing tournaments over, Terry allowed himself to relax on campus. He missed a few classes by sleeping in, but felt confident he would finish each course with a decent grade.

He ran 3-5 miles each day with his football buddies in spring training, and sparred at the gym with Dickie Wills in preparation for the AAU match with Mexico in a few days.

A letter arrived at his dorm room that Friday; it was from his brother Tom. It included an article from the *Painesville Telegraph* and the headline read: "South Scores Upset Victory in Golf Event."

The article reported how the Willoughby South Golf Team upset favored Wickliffe and Eastlake North for the district championship. There was also a big picture of Coach Ro Pallante holding the district trophy and squatting down with the winning foursome of Tom, Jerry Czir, Dave Petterson and Ken Kary who posed with their drivers surrounding their coach.

Tom wanted his big brother to know about *his* latest accomplishment and ended by wishing him luck in the upcoming boxing match that weekend. Terry pinned the article to the bulletin board in his room, next to the rest of his clippings.

The Texas team dominated the Mexican team over the weekend, with Terry winning a unanimous decision. The exposure he received gave him more notoriety throughout Dallas, as Doug predicted. This made it even more difficult for him to focus on his studies, and by the time finals were over, he knew his grade average of 2.5 wouldn't cut it with his dad.

* * *

The drive home to Willoughby didn't seem as adventuresome as it had in the past for Terry. The school year was over and packing his belongings into his car and shipping his motorcycle back made him feel like he was doing it for the last time. He knew his dad wouldn't tolerate his falling grades and without his father's support, he knew it would be difficult to cover all the expenses of SMU. He had a lot to think about.

Saying goodbye to Mike, Dedo and the rest of his frat buddies was tough – he wasn't sure if it would be for the last time. They promised to keep in touch, but he knew they were just being polite.

He sat in his car for a few minutes before turning the key in the ignition. He looked at the students that were loading their cars and vans with their parents, some for the last time. He smiled when he thought about the first time he visited the campus and the feeling of adventure he had about starting a new life. *Well, it's not over yet.*

He found his way onto Interstate 30. As he looked into his rearview mirror to see the skyline of Dallas, he turned down his radio and said boldly, "I'll do whatever I can to get back here, Big D!"

CHAPTER 27

The weather in Ohio was extra hot and dry for the month of June. It had not rained in three weeks, and the grass on the fairways on Sequoia Golf Course was turning brown. When Terry arrived home, he told the family it felt warmer in Ohio than it did in Texas.

A few nights after he arrived home, his father pulled him into the den to have the serious talk he knew was coming.

"I called the campus to speak with your counselor and find out when we could expect your grade card. She said they just went out in the mail. I asked her what your final grade-point average was and she said—"

"It was below the three-point average we agreed upon," Terry said with a sigh.

"God damn it, Terry, you knew you were letting your studies slip all along yet you told me you were working hard. You let boxing take up all your spare time, as I knew it would! You've let your studies take second place. And now, you've let *me* down!

"Well, you can be damn sure that I'm not spending any more money on an expensive school like SMU! Not if you insist on getting in a ring and getting your brains knocked out! What are you thinking?

"You need to save as much money as you can on the road crew this summer," he said, "and start looking at schools that aren't so far away. From now on, *if* you want to graduate with a degree, you're going to have to pay your own way."

The ultimatum came as no surprise to Terry. He thought about what his dad would say all the way home. Now he was faced with the reality of showing everyone what he was capable of doing – graduating from college, and continuing to excel in a sport that was making him more famous every time he stepped into the ring.

* * *

One night Terry brought the latest copy of *The Ring* magazine home to show his brothers the story of Curtis Cokes' victory in Dallas. He successfully defended his WBA/WBC Welterweight title with a technical knockout of Francois Pavilla in the 10th round.

"Wow, and this guy works out at your gym?" Jeff asked.

"Yeah, and his brother Joe went to the nationals with me. They can both hit like a ton of bricks," Terry said, laughing.

The boys read another article that went into detail about a professional tournament being discussed to crown a new heavyweight champion. The WBA had its version of where and when a tournament would be held, and the WBC, of course, countered with its own plan. The sports writers continued to share the frustration of having two professional boxing organizations instead of one, but the public knew the politics involved would never allow the two to merge.

Working, playing sports and weekend activities seemed to make the summer of '67 move quickly, and by mid-August Terry announced his decision to return to SMU and finish his junior year of college.

"I've made arrangements to move into a house, not far from campus, with a few other guys, and I will be taking fewer courses so I can work part-time to cover my living expenses," he said.

"Sounds like a good plan to me," his dad said with a straight face.

The rest of the kids knew not to mention anything about boxing, or even the possibility of having him stay closer to home, because they knew he had his heart set on the Lone Star State.

Terry's drive down went smoothly, and he spent the weekend with a few of his frat buddies at the Phi Delta house before moving into his rental. He told them that he would be making his affiliation with the fraternity official this semester.

On Saturday, he paid a visit to his friend Bobby White, who owned a big car dealership downtown and sponsored several amateur boxing shows. Bobby had become an avid fan of Terry's and gave him a nice deal on a navy blue '66 LeMans.

Terry was proud to drive his new set of wheels into the rental house off campus. His new roommates were waiting for him with a barbeque party in the backyard, and he was ready to start a new adventure for himself with the promise of a new school year.

* * *

In the fall of 1967, he decided to change his major from engineering to political science in hopes of getting into law or politics some day. He also limited himself to 8 credit hours that semester to have time to train at Doug's gym three days a week.

The counselor warned Terry that he would not be keeping an academic minimum to remain in SMU, however, he assured her he would work with her the next semester.

Doug, meanwhile, had notified him that he moved into a newer gym in the warehouse district near downtown Dallas.

"My boxers were knockin' too much plaster off the ceilin's of the pool hall below and we were asked to leave. I was plannin' on it anyway 'cause I needed more space," he said.

In October, the WBA took the headlines of professional boxing by announcing an eight-man elimination tournament for the vacant heavyweight title. The tournament would be spread out over a six-month period with the winner to be crowned "Undisputed Heavyweight Champion of the World." Every time he read about the title, Terry's pulse quickened and he asked Doug, "Could that be me some day?"

Doug made sure the Dallas papers kept his heavyweights in the news by letting them know that Terry would headline an amateur boxing show over the Thanksgiving holiday at Denton High School.

When Terry arrived home for Christmas break he told Jeff about his plans for returning to campus. "Don't tell mom or dad, but I will only be taking a few classes over the winter semester at school – I got a job and I'm going to focus on the '68 Golden Gloves tournament," he said.

Jeff assured him that he'd intercept any letters postmarked from Texas. Jeff also showed him that he and Denny had started a scrapbook to organize Terry's newspaper articles. He smiled and said, "All right! I'll make sure you get the ones I've kept at school too."

Christmas break was topped off with a New Year's Eve party at their house with all of Terry's friends from Willoughby. His parents attended a party at Hellreigel's Inn in Painesville, while Tom took his date to a special dance at the Willoughby Methodist Church. Terry let Jeff, Denny and Debbie serve snacks and refreshments to all of his guests, as long as they stayed out of the way.

Their dad had purchased a large color TV as the family's Christmas present and Terry had the kids entertain themselves in the living room while he and his friends danced to the music in the basement. His only request was to be reminded when *The Tonight Show* was on, so they could gather round and watch Johnnie Carson and his guests count down to the New Year of 1968.

He felt good about making the decision to return to SMU and to be with his fraternity buddies. His bank account was filled with earnings from driving a fuel-oil truck during break, and he felt no pressure about carrying a light load of classes for winter semester. He was focused like a laser on one goal for 1968 – to be the Golden Gloves Heavyweight Champion of Texas, and get another shot at a national championship.

CHAPTER 28

Since Terry was paying his own way through school, his father was no longer giving him grief about his boxing matches. So, he had no reservations sending a letter to the family that included an article from the *Dallas Times Herald* dated January 25, 1968 titled: "Daniels Likes Hard Knocks" with a picture of him in his boxing shorts holding a speed bag steady.

It stated how he got into the Dallas Golden Gloves and was hoping to win the state title that eluded him the year before.

The following week, on Saturday night, February 3rd, Terry called to tell his family that he won his semifinal match by unanimous decision and would be in the finals Monday night.

When asked who he thought he would be up against, he said, "No one special. Dickie Wills and Cookie Wallace both turned pro, and I haven't seen anybody that I can't handle."

Monday evening seemed to be a re-run of last year, as Terry called around 10 p.m. to tell everyone that he won his championship match with a second-round knockout. He was the Dallas Regional Golden Gloves Open Heavyweight Division champion for the second year in a row.

Two weeks later, he called to tell them he won all three of his fights and was now the Golden Gloves Heavyweight Champion of Texas. Jeff couldn't believe it – Terry was guaranteed another shot at the national championship.

His dad wouldn't admit it, but the kids saw a smile on his face when he finished his conversation with Terry. It's hard for a father to hide his emotions when he's beaming with pride.

The news spread quickly around Lake County and Terry's brothers gave all the "behind the scenes" details to their friends. Tom was a senior and had his own notoriety at South High. He was able to garner some extra attention from both the boys and girls in school because of his big brother's news.

But for Jeff, it was a different story. Shedding pounds and building some muscle in 7th grade football and wrestling was a start, but he struggled with being second string on both teams during the '68 school year. Some of the 9th-graders made rude comments stating that they thought he should have been tougher since his brother was a boxing champion, and their taunting made him work harder in practice.

Jeff came to realize that telling someone your brother was a boxing champion got a different response than telling them he was a football standout or a state wrestling champ.

Guys were always asking him if his brother was a bully or in trouble with the law. He always gave the same answer. "No, he's a good student and a great athlete!"

"At times, it's tough living up to the likes of Terry," Jeff confessed to Tom.

* * *

Without his family or his father there to congratulate him on winning the Texas State Golden Gloves Championship, Terry began to depend on the attention and camaraderie he received from his friends at school and his coach, Doug.

Doug cared about all of his boxers, but took a special interest in Terry. He could not only see Terry's potential as a money-making headliner at professional boxing matches someday, but he also liked the fact that he was a gentleman and a dedicated athlete.

The night before Terry left for the national tournament in Salt Lake City, Doug called to wish him luck.

"I'd love to see you and Joe Cokes (Curtis Cokes brother) win national titles for my gym, but Curtis and I just got back from Oakland a few days ago and I got a lot of work to catch up on.

"Opal and I wish you a lot of luck, and I'll make sure to check with the newspaper to see where the standings are each day," he said.

After the first two days of the tournament, an article in the *Salt Lake Tribune* reported: *The crowd of over 3,500 were treated to many action packed fights from some of the best amateur boxers in the nation... The top heavyweights moving on to the quarterfinals, and from what this reporter has seen will probably face each other in the finals, are Terry Daniels from the Dallas/Ft. Worth team, and a hard puncher from the Akron, Ohio, team named Earnie Shavers – both had impressive knockouts in their first two matches.*

Unfortunately, neither Terry nor Shavers made it past the quarterfinals. Terry was pitted against a 6' 2", 230-pound beast of a man from Chicago named Frank Steele. The fight got the biggest round of applause from the crowd that evening, with both fighters scoring a record *four* knockdowns – two by Terry and two by Steele.

Although Terry hung on to the last second of the fight, the judges gave the nod to his opponent. At the awards ceremony, Terry was surprised to learn that he was awarded a special trophy – The Joe Louis Sportsmanship award. It wasn't the national championship trophy he had hoped for, but it still got his picture in the papers.

Joe Cokes lost in the semifinals to the eventual lightweight champion from Cleveland, Ronnie Harris, but Rudy Barrientes and Lorenzo Trujillo from the Texas team, former PAL proteges, won the Flyweight and Featherweight divisions respectively.

On the plane ride back to Dallas, a stewardess approached Terry and said, "A gentleman in first class asked me to give you this message."

He opened the note and read: *Please come and join me for a drink – Odd Job.*

Terry walked through the curtains and immediately recognized the big man in the middle row of the luxury seats. The man looked up, gave that unmistakable smile of his and said, "Ah, Daniels, glad you could join me," while extending his thick, meaty hand.

The man was Harold Sakata, who played Odd Job in the James Bond movie, *Goldfinger.* He said he was in town on business and saw Terry's fight. He was impressed with his ability to take a punch and his unwillingness to quit, and wanted him to spend the rest of the ride with him in first class.

Terry called home to tell his family about the trophy he won, and his surprising plane ride home. Jeff said, "I can't believe he actually got to meet a guy who starred in a Bond movie!" But then, nothing seemed to surprise him with the stories he heard from his famous brother.

The news of the WBA's boxing tournament was taking headlines in the sports sections of newspapers, and two weeks after Terry returned from Salt Lake City, the final match of the professional elimination tournament took place in the Coliseum Arena in Oakland, California. The match was between Jimmy Ellis and Jerry Quarry.

Ellis was from Louisville, Kentucky, and was the friend and former sparring partner of Muhammad Ali. He received the "Progress of the Year" award in 1967 from *The Ring* magazine and had defeated Leotis Martin and Oscar Bonavena to get to the final match with the hard-hitting "Irish" Jerry Quarry.

Terry watched the televised match live with some of his frat and football buddies. At the end of 15 brutal rounds, Jimmy Ellis was crowned the new heavyweight champion by way of a majority decision.

Most of the frat boys thought Quarry won the fight and wanted to know what Terry thought. Although he agreed that Quarry had gotten in some solid punches, he said he had to go along with the judges who counted more scored punches for Ellis.

"Man, wouldn't it be cool to see you in the ring with one of those guys, Terry?" asked one of his frat brothers.

"Yeah, and I'd sure take advantage of the money they cleared tonight," he answered. "But my manager said I've still got to work on gaining a little more weight to contend with the pros. And the heavyweight division is bigger than we saw tonight."

Terry was referring to a month earlier, on March 4, in Madison Square Garden, when Joe Frazier beat his former amateur nemesis, Buster Mathis, by a knockout in the 11th round. Other boxing organizations were recognizing *Frazier* as the Heavyweight Champion of the World.

* * *

By the end of winter quarter, Terry was told by his counselor that unless he took more credit hours and brought up his grade average, he could not stay at SMU. It came as no surprise; in fact, he had already made plans to move into a house with a couple of buddies who transferred to North Texas State University (NTSU).

NTSU was 40 miles north of Dallas in Denton, and he enrolled with two courses in the evenings three nights a week. He needed his days open because he had a new daytime job with a local beer distributing company, driving a delivery truck.

His dad had him obtain his chauffeur's license – Ohio's requirement to drive commercial trucks – while he was home on Christmas break, so he could drive the fuel oil trucks.

Bill said to Terry, "You learn how to drive and park one of these big trucks carrying a full load of fuel oil, and you'll be able to drive anything."

Terry noted it on his application, plus the fact that he was a Golden Gloves champion and did not drink during daytime hours. Management was keenly interested in the last part because they had a devil of a time keeping their drivers sober when making their drop-offs at the bars and carry-outs throughout Dallas and Fort Worth.

The pay was good, and every payday management gave Terry a keg of beer for the weekend as a bonus. The keg helped ramp up his popularity with his new friends at school and his classmates knew whose house to visit on Friday night to get the weekend started.

At a party, one of Terry's buddies, Mike Walthal, introduced him to a girl he was dating. "Terry, I'd like you to meet Karen Allison. Karen, this is my boxing buddy I was telling you about."

Terry smiled and shook her hand; as he did, a bell went off in his head – only this one wasn't caused by a punch. He was immediately taken aback by her long blond hair and attractive figure, and for the first time in his life he was speechless in front of a girl.

Karen felt the slight delay and said, in a sweet Texas drawl, "I'm pleased to meet you. Mike has said so many good things about you; he showed me some of the boxing articles from the paper – you're quite a celebrity!"

Terry cleared his head and said, "Oh, well it's just something I've gotten good at over the past couple of years."

Mike took his opportunity to join the conversation and said, "Don't be so modest. He's the best amateur heavyweight in Texas, and one of the best in the whole country. Hey, I heard the Olympic trials are coming up. Are you going to compete?"

Still smiling at Karen, Terry blinked a few times and said, "The Olympic boxing tournament? Compete? No, you had to have won a national AAU or Golden Gloves National Championship in the past four years to be invited. Besides, they're having them start in less than two weeks in Detroit and I wouldn't be able to take off from school or my job."

"What about turning pro? You could probably make some good money with all the fans you've got here in Denton, and the Dallas area," Mike said.

"A professional boxer?" Karen asked. "I would think y'all would take up acting or modeling with your good looks."

Terry could see that Mike was feeling a little out of place so he said, "Hey, how would you and Mike like to stop down at my gym tomorrow?

You could see what it's like and meet some of the other pros that work out there. I'll get a date and the four of us can go out someplace afterwards – whaddaya say?"

Karen laughed and said, "Boy, you sure talk like a Yankee."

Mike sounded relieved and said, "Sure, that sounds great!"

Terry mingled with the rest of the guests that filled the house that evening, but couldn't help making eye contact with Karen as the night progressed.

The next day, Mike, Karen, Terry and his date, Sue Ann, all drove down to Doug's gym in Terry's car. Terry had met Sue Ann a week earlier at a dance at NTSU. This was their first date and she seemed a little apprehensive when Terry asked her to visit a boxing gym, but relaxed once she learned it was a double date.

They arrived in the parking lot across from the building and the heat was a sweltering 92 degrees. It was generally pleasant in the last week of March in that part of Texas, but that day was well above average. It got even hotter when they walked into the ABC gym.

"I apologize for the heat in here, folks," Doug said as he greeted Terry and his friends, "but I can't afford for my boxers to get a cold from the air conditioning.

"We're just about finishin' up for the day, Terry. Why don't you introduce your friends to the Welterweight Champion of the World over there – he just got done skippin' rope."

Mike and Karen were impressed meeting Curtis Cokes, but Sue Ann quickly reached into her purse to pull out a tissue after shaking the champ's sweaty hand. Terry could tell that she was uncomfortable in his environment.

Mike was busy admiring the life-size pictures of Muhammad Ali, Sonny Liston and Rocky Marciano on the walls. Doug had accumulated posters of past championship matches from all over the world and proudly displayed them in the gym.

"Wow, that little guy is really hitting that small bag above his head. What does that do for a boxer Terry?" Karen asked.

"That's called a speed bag, and it helps a boxer time his punches with speed and accuracy."

The girls were trying their best to be polite, but Terry could see his tour should be cut short. He whispered to Mike, "I'm used to the smell and heat of this place, but I should have known they'd be uncomfortable."

"Well, I'm starting to work up a sweat myself," Terry said to the girls. "Whaddaya say we mosey on over to Stan's Blue Note for cocktail hour and order something to eat?"

"Sounds good," they all responded in unison.

The rest of the evening was spent with laughter, good food and drinks – all in the comfort of air conditioning.

Later, when they arrived back at Terry's house, he offered to make them a nightcap. Mike and Karen said, "Sure," but Sue Ann declined. She said she didn't have that far to drive, but didn't need any more alcohol. She told Terry she had a wonderful evening and gave him a little peck on the cheek before getting in her car.

"Yikes," said Mike, "I guess 'Miss Prude' is glad to be going home."

"Yeah, I should have known it wasn't exactly the place to take a girl on a first date," Terry said.

They finished their gin and tonics, and Terry walked them out to Mike's convertible. Terry opened the passenger side for Karen, leaving Mike to awkwardly walk behind them and around to the driver's side.

As Mike started the car, Terry, feeling the effects of having "one too many," said to Karen, "So, if you're not doing anything next weekend with Mike, how 'bout I give you a call?"

Mike said to Karen, "He does *realize* I'm sitting right here, doesn't he?"

Karen just giggled and said to Terry, "I'll think about it, champ."

CHAPTER 29

Spring semester came to an end and Terry decided to take his time going home for summer break. The manager at the beer company told him he could stay and drive his beer truck as long as he wanted. It also meant he could spend another week or so seeing Karen.

Karen lived near NTSU in Denton with her aunt. She was 19 years old and worked as a teller for a local bank. She confided in Terry that Mike was just a friend and she'd been eager to go out with Terry since they'd met.

Any new relationship had to continue by mail however, because his dad called him the second week in June and said, "You'd better get your ass up here. We've got two crews working overtime everyday and you'll be making close to six bucks an hour plus OT pay. And there's no beer company that's going to pay you those kind of wages!"

He headed out on the road at 6 sharp the next morning with his car fully loaded. He hit the first dial on his radio and heard Gary Puckett and the Union Gap singing their new single, *Young Girl:*

Young girl get outta my mind!
My love for you is way outta line.
Better run girl! You're much too young girl!

He switched to another station, because it wasn't the tune he wanted to hear at the moment, and heard Simon and Garfunkel's latest hit:

And here's to you, Mrs. Robinson,
Jesus loves you more than you will know.

When Terry got off the Willoughby exit he realized his dad wasn't kidding about the road construction in the Cleveland area. There were detour signs and traffic jams everywhere. Big housing developments were continuing to pop up in Willoughby and Mentor, with roads bringing in large crews and heavy equipment. New families were moving in, which meant more tax dollars for improvements because Lake County was growing quickly.

The companies the Daniels families owned were flourishing from the community growth, and Bill and Peps rarely took time off. Tom moved from the crew on the golf course to the road crew and worked along with Terry, while Jeff worked with the crew of Sequoia and got a nice pay raise.

Tom graduated from South High and was looking forward to the pay raise because he was accepted to Ohio University, and needed extra money to play on their golf team. He knew his father would expect him to pay his own living expenses while going to college, and he wanted to build up his savings because he didn't want to work part-time his first year of school.

The long hours on the road crew left Terry with little time to workout at Tommy Morris' boxing gym in Wickliffe. At age 22, he was too old to participate in any of the baseball leagues in the area, but it didn't seem to bother him. Most evenings he would lie down after dinner and take a short nap before going out with some of his buddies or girls who still lived in the area.

Tommy told Terry that he and Larry Wagner were putting together a boxing show the week before school started and wanted Terry and Billy Wagner to be the headliners. Billy had turned pro earlier in the year and they booked the show at Billy's alma mater, St. Joseph High School in Cleveland. They were sure to have a big Cleveland crowd.

Terry said he would do it because it was two months away, giving him enough time to train. Tommy knew that might be a challenge because he didn't have that many heavyweights in the area, and certainly none that could compete with Terry's power.

"I'll make sure I got someone for you to spar with," Tommy said. "You know Joe Topoly, your assistant football coach from South? He's been helping me at the gym and he used to be a good boxer. I'm sure he'll go a few rounds with you if need be."

Jeff overheard Terry on the phone the next night talking with Karen. He heard him tell her he was planning to stay home after his boxing match in September and would be back in Texas sometime after Christmas. She must have been crying because he heard him add that he hadn't gone out with anyone that could hold a candle to her.

Jeff knew he meant it because Terry had several pictures of the two of them together on his mirror in his bedroom, and he and his brothers knew that honor only belonged to the girl he cared most about. Terry was challenged the following week however, when he received a phone call from one of his old flames – Sally Farmer.

Sally called their house on Sunday evening and talked with Terry for about 45 minutes. When his mother inquired about the call he said, "That was an old girlfriend of mine from SMU. She works as a stewardess for the airlines and said she's going to be in Cleveland this week. She asked to see me."

Jeff was within earshot and said, "Hey, that's pretty cool to have out of town girlfriends Terry!"

Their mother frowned and said, "There's nothing wrong with having girls as friends and having *one girlfriend*, as long as you keep it that way, Jeff."

It seemed to be her way of educating her sons on the proper way to have relationships with the opposite sex. Their father looked up from his newspaper when June raised her voice.

Terry seemed irritated with his mom's comment and said, "Oh, for cryin' out loud, I'm going to take her out for dinner with Danny and his girlfriend. Then she'll be flying out the next day. Who knows when I'll see her again?"

Jeff knew he shouldn't have said anything and scurried out the back door. He hopped on his bike and took it for a ride.

At the dinner table Thursday night, Terry said how wonderful it was to see Sally. "And I told her I had met a girl that I've been seeing on a regular basis – and Sally said she was seeing someone too," he said pointedly while looking in his mom's direction.

June acknowledged him with a smile, and then his father changed the subject by saying, "Well, here's some news for you – I've decided to trade your mother's Mustang in for a newer model. You boys want to go with me this weekend when I make the deal?"

They all said, "Sure!" in unison with Terry adding, "Yeah, Dad, I read an article recently about the new Shelby Cobra Ford has out. It's a souped-up Mustang named after the guy who designed it, and comes with a lot more horsepower than what Mom drives now."

Tom noticed Terry left out the part about how they both read about it in *Playboy* magazine.

Bill drove Terry, Tom and Jeff to Marshall Ford in Mayfield to look at one of the new models. The salesman had three Shelbys on his lot – two GT 350s and one GT 500.

"The 350 has a 302, cubic inch, V8 engine, whereas the 500 has the 428 for about $600 more, otherwise, they're the same car, Bill," the salesman said.

Both cars looked awesome to the boys. They had scoops in the hood and on the sides of the car, and the trunk had a spoiler. The one that really caught Bill's eye was the dark green GT 350 with the tan-colored convertible roof. Terry and Tom were trying to get him to test drive the red GT 500 because it had so much more horsepower.

"I'll get a temporary plate on the convertible and you guys can take it for a ride," the salesman said.

The plush interior was black with dark wood paneling and an automatic transmission stick on the floor. Bill did the driving while Terry sat in the passenger seat, and Tom and Jeff sat in the back.

Jeff took a deep breath of new-car smell as his dad turned the key and revved the engine. "What's this for?" he asked Tom while pointing to a thick black bar above his head.

"Oh, cool – that's a roll bar, in case you flip over; all the race cars got 'em. Man, with those white racing stripes on the side of the car, this is hotter looking than a Corvette!"

The salesman was standing next to Bill's window and said, "Now take a left out of here and go about a mile down Mayfield Road; look for a restaurant on your right – you'll see a cop there. He's there every Saturday night looking for drag racers. Once you get past him, you can punch it to see the kind of power this baby has!"

They all smiled with anticipation, and when Bill got about a mile past the cop he punched the accelerator. Jeff watched the speedometer go from 35 to 65 in a second, and then 75 before his dad applied the brakes to bring the car back to the speed limit.

Bill let out a chuckle while the rest of the boys acted like they were on a new ride at the county fair. Jeff and his brothers could feel the excitement as Jeff said, "Could we possibly own a hot car like this?"

A few minutes later, Terry said, "Hey, Dad, pull over at that gas station there and let me drive it back to the lot."

It was a balmy 80 degrees on an August night and Bill said, "Let's put the top down and see how it feels."

When Terry drove by the cop in the restaurant parking lot, Jeff saw a man and woman stop and stare at them until they got out of sight. When they parked back at the dealership they stood and admired the gorgeous emerald green car, and understood why people couldn't take their eyes off it.

Bill went into the salesman's office to talk about a deal, while the boys looked at the car in more detail. They knew this was going to be a challenge, because next to the GT 500, the car had the highest price tag of any Ford in the lot – over $4,500.

Tom said to Terry and Jeff, "If Dad doesn't make a deal on this car, let's have him drive us down to Lombardo Pontiac in Wickliffe and talk him into buying a new GTO."

After half an hour, they saw their father shake hands with the salesman and they knew they were going to drive the beautiful convertible home.

June and Denny came out to greet them as they pulled into the garage. The Buick was parked on the right, outside of the garage, so June could see what Bill had purchased under the garage lights. Terry, Tom and Jeff got out of the Shelby and excitedly told her, "Dad got a deal of a lifetime!"

"My gosh, Bill," she said. "I knew you wanted a better model car, but isn't this overdoing it a little?"

"Well, I thought it was about time I splurged a little," he said. The boys looked puzzled at their mother because this was a dream come true, and a welcomed addition to the Daniels family.

But June kept her eye on her husband. Her intuition was taking over and she was just a little suspicious.

CHAPTER 30

Several hundred fans attended the fights at St. Joseph High School and were pleased with the two pro and four amateur fights. Billy Wagner had come down with the flu two nights before and had to cancel his bout, but Terry made up for it by winning his. He took command at the beginning of the first round and never let up, scoring a TKO in 1:59 of the second round.

Sitting in the crowd in a ringside seat was a new Cleveland professional boxing promoter, Don Elbaum. Don stood 5' 8", and had a stocky build that he earned in his younger days as an amateur and pro welterweight/middleweight in Erie, Pennsylvania. Tom, Denny and Jeff were in the locker room when they saw Don approach Terry after the fight.

He introduced himself to Terry and said, "It's time you consider turning pro and earning money for the show you put on for the fans here in Cleveland.

"Hell, you're over 21 now," he said. "And from what I've seen, you could easily work your way up to a top contender – and that's where *the money* is."

Terry's brothers looked wide-eyed, waiting to hear his response. He said, "I'm considering that Mr. Elbaum, but I'm planning to go back to Dallas after Christmas to finish my senior year in college before I do anything else."

"A college boy no less," Don said with a smile on his face.

"Well, here's my card. If you feel like makin' money as a pro boxer, be sure to give me a call."

Tom drove Denny, Jeff and their friends home from the boxing show, and they couldn't stop talking about the possibility of seeing Terry climb into the ring some day with a pro like Jerry Quarry. Of course, they all pledged not to tell their parents about it.

A few days later, the Daniels family was saying goodbye to Tom as he started his freshman year at Ohio University in Athens. His parents drove him down in the station wagon.

Since Terry was carrying the full responsibility of paying all his expenses for college, he elected to sit out the fall semester and was in charge of the household whenever his parents went out of town. He was earning good money on the road crew and wanted to build up his bank account with an extra few months of work before heading south. He was also enjoying his freedom from studying every night.

On Friday, he asked Jeff if he would like to go to a football game with him when he got home from work.

Jeff said, "Sure! Who does South play tonight?"

"I think I'd rather see the Mentor Cardinals play tonight instead," Terry replied.

"*The Cardinals?* They're our archrivals! If my friends find out they'll accuse me of being a Communist!"

"Nah, they shut-out Massillon High, 19 to nothing in their opener, and they shutout Cleveland John Adams last week 40 to nothing. The papers say they could be one of the best teams in the school's history. I just want to see if they've really got what it takes to beat Painesville Harvey tonight," he said.

In 1963, Dick Crum took over as head coach of Mentor High School, and from '65 through '67; his teams only lost twice. Players like Galbos, Ryczek, Derrick and Viher on the '68 team were on the sports pages of the local papers every week.

The Cardinals played their home games at the stadium at Mentor Memorial Jr. High, which used to be the old Mentor Senior High, located at Mentor Avenue and Route 615. The traffic was miserable and they had to park in the grassy lots down the road.

"We're going to sit on the visitor's side so we are sure to get a seat. Let's go down behind the fence line this way," said Terry as he motioned to Jeff.

"Yeah, but the ticket booth is way over there," Jeff said.

Once they were far enough away from the other pedestrians, Terry kneeled down and pulled apart a section of the fence. He said, "I told you I wanted to see the Cardinals play tonight, I didn't say I would *pay* to see them play!"

They sat down in time to hear the announcer bellow, "Let's hear it for our Fighting Mentor Cardinals!"

The home team crowd let out deafening cheers as the team burst onto the field. They were wearing white uniforms with red stripes and numbers, sporting the Cardinal emblem on their helmets.

"Wow, they look like a bunch of swarming bees!" Terry said loudly in Jeff's ear.

They watched as the Cardinals trounced the Red Raiders for their third straight shutout 46-0. The next day, the *News-Herald* stated that the Mentor Cardinals should rank in the top 10 best teams in the state, and by the morning edition of Wednesday's Cleveland *Plain Dealer*, Mentor had earned the ranking of fourth in the state. "Finally, a team from Lake County is back on the map!" Terry said.

Jeff always marveled at how his brother could think of things to do that most other people would raise their eyebrows and wonder about. But Jeff looked up to his older brother and found himself saying, "Sure" to just about anything he asked of him.

On Saturday, October 12th, the Summer Olympics started. Terry told his brothers that the U.S. heavyweight was George Foreman, whom he had met at the boxing match against Mexico in Houston last May.

"Oh, that's cool. You know the guy that's fighting for an Olympic medal?" asked Jeff.

"Well, I don't *know* him. He came up to me and introduced himself while I was loosening up for my match. He said he heard that I lost to Clay Hodges in the Golden Gloves tournament and he had lost to him too, in an AAU tournament."

"Wow, Terry, you're getting to know some of the best boxers in the world," Jeff said.

"Yeah, and speaking of World Champions, I got tickets for a pro boxing match in Akron Monday night. You wanna go?"

"You bet! Who's the main event?"

"The Middleweight Champion of the World, Nino Benvenuti, is in a non-title fight against a tough guy from Akron named Doyle Baird. Baird is managed by the fight promoter I met in the locker room after my match in Cleveland, Don Elbaum."

"Oh yeah, I remember that guy."

"It's being held in the Akron Rubber Bowl and starts around five o'clock. I'm taking off work early so we can get on the road by three."

"I'll be ready Ter, thanks!"

On Monday, they arrived at the Akron stadium parking lot, but were directed to a grassy lot nearby. They walked through the entrance minutes before the first preliminary fight started.

Jeff was beaming with pride as he accompanied his big brother to a professional boxing match and got to sit next to the Texas State Golden Gloves Heavyweight Champ.

The ring was set in the middle of the football field with seats around it 30 rows deep. The rest of the crowd of 6,000 sat in the cement stands of the stadium. Terry and Jeff sat six rows back from the ring.

The weather was unusually warm for the second week in October, and it was the perfect temperature for a match outdoors. The crowd was cheering wildly in the first four bouts of the five-bout evening. When intermission came, Terry and Jeff beat the crowd to the concession stands.

They each got a Coke and hotdog when they heard someone shout, "Hey, Terry, over here!"

Terry saw Tommy Morris and Larry Wagner having a smoke outside one of the entrances leading to the field. Terry introduced them to his brother, Jeff.

"Glad to meet you, Jeff," Tommy said as they shook hands. "You gonna take up boxing like your brother? I got a nice gym in Wickliffe."

"Well, I'm on the football team at Willoughby Junior High right now, and after the season ends, I'll be on the wrestling team. So, I won't have much time, but we're all excited whenever we get a chance to see my big brother box," Jeff said.

"Yeah, Jeff's gotta get through all the school sports like Terry did," Larry added with a smile.

"So Tommy, tell me about this Benvenuti," Terry said. "What kind of a champion is he? I haven't read much about him in *The Ring* magazine."

"Nah, *The Ring* doesn't carry much coverage outside the U.S. and Mexico, but this Benvenuti is a tough fighter, and there hasn't been too many that come outta Italy," Tommy said.

"He defended his title in Madison Square Garden in April last year to Emile Griffith," Larry added, "and then lost to him in a close rematch in September in Shea Stadium. He won it back in a 15-round decision last March and has had three non-title wins since then."

"Wow, I actually get to see a real world champion box tonight," Jeff said.

"Yeah, he's a good lookin' guy like your brother, too," Tommy said. "And this Doyle Baird he's fightin' is from Akron. He's had most of his bouts around here and Pennsylvania. His record is 24 wins and 2 losses, and he's on a winning streak with 13 in a row leading into tonight's fight – a tough son of a bitch!"

Terry and Jeff found their seats in front of the well-lit ring in the middle of the football field. Jeff could feel the tension in the air in anticipation of seeing what a world champion middleweight could do with a tough local fighter.

The boxers made their way into the ring. The fans gave loud cheers and whistles for their hometown hero and boos for the foreign champion. Baird stood 6' 0", had a trim, but iron-like physique, and combed his thin sandy brown hair straight back from his receding hairline. His nose was crooked and both eyes showed tissue build-up from all the punches he'd taken over the years.

Jeff leaned over and whispered in Terry's ear, "Baird looks like one of those thugs you see in the old *Dick Tracy* comics."

Terry chuckled at his little brother's ability to pick the perfect way to describe someone in a funny, but right-on sort of way.

Nino Benvenuti wore a white and red striped robe with Italian words and symbols on it. His brown eyes and brown hair, tan complexion and his muscular 5' 10" frame resembled Terry's. His face showed little signs of trauma, but his nose was naturally dented from his 30-plus professional fights.

Jeff noticed that the fighters had a look of confidence on their faces – not intimidating, or like they were trying to win a "stare down" contest. He could see the determination in their eyes when the referee was giving them instructions in the middle of the ring.

The fight was intense from the first round to the last. Both boxers showed world-class skill, scoring punches at the right moment so neither seemed to dominate the other.

The crowd stood and cheered when the bell ended the fight. Terry put his fingers to his mouth and gave several ear-piercing whistles, while Jeff hooped and hollered with the rest of the Rubber Bowl crowd.

"How's that for your first world-class boxing match?" Terry yelled into his brother's ear.

They watched Don Elbaum, in the challenger's corner, dip a sponge into his water bucket and douse his fighter while yelling, "That was beautiful Doyle! You did good kid, *real good!*"

The ring announcer gathered the judges' cards, and went back to one of them to confer. When the bell rang several times, the crowd came to a hush, and the announcer read each of the score cards. He ended by saying, "The fight is a draw!"

The stadium was filled with boos and obscenities. Popcorn boxes, cups of beer and Coke went flying into the ring. Benvenuti and his cornermen quickly exited the ring while Baird and his men stood there taunting the Italian champion to "Get back in the ring and let's finish this fight!"

Don Elbaum pulled his boxer out when a chair from the crowd went flying over the ropes and into the ring. Terry pulled Jeff by the arm and said, "Let's go," while more broken pieces of folding chairs went sailing into the ring.

Jeff realized then that his brother would soon be entering a dangerous new world.

* * *

On the following Wednesday evening, October 16th, 1968, Terry watched the Olympic Games at home with Jeff, Denny and a football buddy of his from high school, Jerry Toth. ABC Sports was covering the Games with live and taped events throughout the day. They were eagerly waiting for George Foreman's debut.

"This guy, Foreman, is a hard puncher huh, Terry?" Jerry asked.

"Yeah, that's what I heard. He's like a big bear, pawing at his opponent with jabs and follows up with a solid right hand. I think he's six-two and weighs over 200 pounds."

The announcer, Jim McKay, was on TV saying, "We now bring you a taped delay of the heavyweight boxing match of U.S. versus Poland."

The boys watched Foreman out-box his opponent for three full rounds and win the match by unanimous decision.

"He's big and packs a wallop, like you said Terry, but he looks kinda sloppy," Jerry said.

The boys continued to chat about the match and decided to watch some of the medal awards before calling it a night. An award ceremony came on for a track and field event recorded earlier– a ceremony that would keep them, and the whole world, talking for days.

Three athletes stood on the podium for the 200 meter race. The U.S. had won the gold and bronze, and Australia won the silver. When the national anthem started, the two Americans, wearing black gloves, raised their fists in the air and bowed their heads.

"What the hell are those guys doing?" Jerry blurted out.

The whole room got quiet as they watched and listened to the crowd start to boo as the national anthem continued. John McKay announced that the ceremony had taken place earlier, and the two athletes, Tommie Smith and John Carlos, were showing their solidarity to their "Black-American Race."

"They look like they belong to that gang outta California – The Black Panthers. Did you read about them in *Life* magazine a few months ago?" Terry asked.

"Yeah," Jerry replied, "they said the Negroes in America were being united after Martin Luther King Jr.'s assassination, and would no longer be called, 'Negro' or 'Colored.' They now demanded to be called, 'Black.'"

"That's just great," Terry said. "We got riots on the college campuses and at the Democratic convention in Chicago against the war in Vietnam, race riots after MLK Jr. was shot, Bobby Kennedy assassinated, and now this. Get ready for another round of riots in the streets tomorrow."

✱ ✱ ✱

The race riots did not continue as Terry predicted. Actually, those who were upset by what Smith and Carlos did got some relief later in the Summer Olympics when George Foreman won the gold medal in his heavyweight match on October 26th.

After having his hand raised by the referee in his match, Foreman went to one of his cornermen and got a small U.S. flag. He went back to the center of the ring waving the flag, and bowed to the judges. It was well received by the crowd and the television audiences around the world.

The Vietnam War, however, was trying the patience of every American. It was always the number one news story on TV and in the newspapers, reminding people daily of the rising death toll of young American soldiers.

Richard Nixon was the elected president in November, and won the election by vowing to end the war in Vietnam. The Daniels family always voted Republican, even though Bill didn't care for Nixon. He told his boys, "If they'd elected Barry Goldwater instead of that dumbass Johnson in '64, we wouldn't be in this war with Vietnam."

Nonetheless, the war was affecting many families across America, even the Daniels family.

Terry was delivering fuel oil in December, building his bank account for his long awaited move back to Texas in January. His plans were to move into an apartment with a friend in Denton and take his time deciding about school, work, and even professional boxing. But his plans were put on hold when he received a letter from the U.S. Defense Department.

The letter was dated December 15, 1968, and addressed to Terry at his permanent address in Willoughby. He opened the letter when he got home from work on Thursday night and read it to the family at the dinner table.

It had his full name and social security number on it and read, "Due to the lack of maintaining full-time status in a recognized secondary educational institution by the United States Government, you are hereby ordered to report to your nearest draft board within 30 days from the date of this letter."

His dad had not yet arrived home from work, and was not present to hear the devastating news. But everyone else was. June dropped her fork and put both her hands to her face. She tried to remain calm in front of the kids, but couldn't hold back the tears.

Tom was at Ohio University and was due back the following week for Christmas break, so he was spared the news for a few more days.

Jeff sat with his mouth open, staring at Terry in silence, while Denny and Debbie, who were 12 and 10 years old, sat with frowns on their faces.

"What does that mean, Ter?" Debbie asked.

"It means I have to join the Army or the Marines to fight in Vietnam," Terry said.

June got up from the table and walked out of the room, while the rest of the kids darted their eyes back and forth at one another.

Their big brother broke the awkward silence by saying, "Look guys, this doesn't necessarily mean I'll get thrown in some jungle and have to do hand-to-hand combat. We've got a new president now that says we're going to end this war soon. Besides, they've got to send me to some camp for testing and training, which takes about a year or so, before they can send me anywhere overseas.

"Let's not let this letter ruin our Christmas, okay? You know I can win at just about anything I set my mind to, and this is going to be another test for me to see if I can meet the challenge. That's all."

A hush fell over the family. After dinner everyone quietly went to their rooms to do some reading and go to bed. June stayed up to wait for Bill, who got home around 10 p.m.

The kids heard a car door slam, then their dad came in the front door. They heard their mom ask him where he'd been and he replied, "I stopped off at LaVelle's to have some drinks with my friends."

June said, "Well, you could have called…come into the bedroom so we can talk. The kids are in bed."

Terry, Jeff and Denny were awake listening intently to the muffled discussion coming through the walls between their parents. After a few minutes they heard their father say loudly, "God damn it! I knew him fooling around with boxing would lead to something like this!"

June told him to keep his voice down, and the rest of the conversation became difficult for the kids to hear. They talked for about a half-hour before they heard their parents' voices die down, and silence filled the house.

Jeff found himself praying for his brother's safety, asking the angels to stay beside his brother when he faced the draft board. Tears rolled down his face and onto the pillow. He vowed to pray for his brother, and his family, every night.

Terry lay in his bed with the lights out and his eyes wide open. The winter moon cast a reflection of light through the side bedroom window, and he looked down at the colored checkered squares of the rug. He too prayed, and that allowed him to relax.

In the stillness of his dark room he mumbled to himself, "I can't believe it, a draft notice… *Well, Merry Fucking Christmas.*"

CHAPTER 31

In spite of Terry's draft letter, Christmas for the Daniels family was filled with joy. Terry's confident demeanor kept the family positive, and they were reminded on Christmas Eve, at the Willoughby United Methodist Church, to remember what they were truly thankful for – health, family, and their community. It wasn't about the presents under the tree.

On Christmas morning, Jeff and Denny were woken by Debbie, and the three were the first to enter the living room at the crack of dawn. The biggest present in the room, unwrapped and brand new, was a three-piece drum set – and Jeff knew who it was for.

When Jeff was 12, he took drum lessons, and played in the Willoughby Junior High symphonic band. By the time he reached 15, he was the number one drummer out of four in the percussion section. All he had to practice on at home, however, were two drum-pads and a snare drum.

But there it was – a white pearled set of *Rogers!* He was totally surprised. Especially because when he told his father that's what he wanted for Christmas, his father said, "Maybe next year when you're 16."

Denny said, "Hey, Jeff, why don't you do a little drum solo to wake the rest of the family?"

Debbie said, "No! You don't want to get Mom and Dad all grumpy this early. Let's open our stockings and wait for Terry and Tom, then we'll get Mom and Dad in a while."

Little sister's comment made sense, but Jeff went to get his drum sticks and started practicing on the drum pads to be ready for the right moment.

The moment came at 7:35 a.m. when the kids could wait no longer, and Terry and Tom were upstairs taking turns in the bathroom. Jeff did a quick solo and ended with a smash on the cymbal.

"Alright, alright," June said from behind the closed bedroom door. "Don't wake the neighbors too! We're getting up!"

The family cherished their '68 Christmas together, and appreciated all they had. Terry showed a positive attitude throughout the day and into the next, but shared his frustration and confusion to Jeff a few days later.

He pulled into the driveway, walked into the house and noticed Jeff was the only one home. Jeff was watching a pre-game show of the AFL Championship Game between the Oakland Raiders and the New York Jets when Terry asked, "Where is everybody?"

"Mom took Denny and Debbie to the new Disney movie at the Vine Theater," Jeff said. "Tom went over to his girlfriend's house, and I'm not sure where Dad went."

"Oh. Well, my car is packed and I've decided to get on the road tonight. I've got some friends in Columbus that I want to see and I should have left an hour ago. But I had to say goodbye to some of my friends here, and it took a bit longer than I thought."

Jeff turned off the TV and said, "Jeez, Ter, everybody's gonna be kind of hurt that they weren't here to say goodbye. Can't you wait until tomorrow?"

"I wish I could, but I've made some commitments to my friends. Besides, I gave a lot of hugs and kisses to everybody over the last couple of days and they know how I feel."

He hesitated and then continued, "Jeff, I need to tell you something. I think out of everyone in the family, I feel closest to you, even though we're eight years apart. It seems like every time I've had something exciting happen to me, you've always been there for me.

"I want you to know that I've thought a lot about this draft notice and I've decided that if they enlist me, I'll tell them I'd like to join the Green Berets. I'd rather go to battle with them than be teamed up with a bunch of stupid shits that'll probably get us all killed."

Jeff chuckled while trying to hold back the tears.

"I want to get to my apartment in Texas, with plenty of time to see all my friends before I report to the draft board. Anyway, give everybody my love, little brother," he said while opening his arms up wide.

Terry gave Jeff a bear hug as they realized they weren't sure when they'd see each other again. Looking up to the big brother who had taught him so much, Jeff had a tough time saying, "Good luck to you, Ter. You know we love you."

* * *

Monday, the 30th, Terry arrived at the house that his buddy Dave Roberts, rented in Denton, Texas. He made arrangements to stay with him until he found out the results of his draft notice. He looked forward to the New Year's Eve party the next night with friends, neighbors, and of course, Karen. They planned to watch the SMU Mustangs take on the Oklahoma Sooners in the Astro-Bluebonnet Bowl. Terry was feeling melancholy realizing this could be his final hurrah for some time to come.

He purchased a discounted keg of beer from his friends at the distributing company, and he and Dave provided plenty of cold cuts, potato salad, and barbequed chicken for their guests. They all enjoyed themselves by dancing to records, eating and drinking, and watching one of the most exciting college bowl games of the season.

The 20th- ranked Mustangs were underdogs to the 10th- ranked Sooners, and were down 14-6 by the end of the third quarter. Each team seemed to make an adjustment on offense in the fourth quarter, however, and SMU's quarterback, Chuck Hixson, ignited his team with a touchdown pass to his favorite receiver – Jerry LeVias.

Terry was proud of the fact that he knew several players on the Mustang team and had the whole party in the living room rooting for them. The SMU defense stiffened on the goal line when the Sooners attempted a two-point conversion in the last three minutes of the game and the Mustangs held on to upset Oklahoma, 28-27.

The party carried over to New Year's Day when the Ohio State Buckeyes came from behind to beat Southern California 27-16 to claim the National Championship. At the end of the game, Terry felt like he'd watched two heavyweight championship fights.

* * *

Terry met up with Doug at the gym in downtown Dallas a couple days later. He told him he was scheduled to report to the draft offices in Dallas on Friday, and they agreed he should work hard in the gym to keep his stress level to a minimum.

"I know what you're goin' through, son," Doug said to Terry. "I spent time in the Navy in World War II, and some time in Korea. I saw lots of guys drafted who really didn't know where they belonged, and all I can tell you is – to go in with a positive attitude, and know that God has a plan for us all."

Terry didn't call home before he walked into the Federal building in downtown Dallas that Friday morning. He thought it would only bring more stress to his family. He reported to several offices for paperwork and exams along with many other young men from the area. In the last office, a doctor examined the x-ray of his left knee.

He asked Terry why he had pins in his knee and wrote his findings on a form. Then he folded the form, and told him to get dressed and report to the nurse's station down the hall.

Terry felt like he was living in a "Purple Haze" all day. He did as he was told and went through the two-hour ordeal like a robot. He gave the nurse the form and she told him to take a seat while she typed out the final document. When she finished, she called him to her desk, gave him the envelope and told him he could wait on the bus.

He boarded the bus and stared out the window at the cold, rainy day. He was interrupted when a guy about his age got on, wiped his dripping hair and sat next to him.

"You mind if I sit here?" the young man asked.

"No, go right ahead," Terry said.

"I guess this is our lucky day, huh?" he asked Terry.

"What do you mean?"

"The letter – you got one too. Didn't you read it?"

Terry looked in his hand and opened the unsealed envelope. He blinked his eyes a few times and stared at the big bold letters stamped across the form – *REJECTED*.

The pins in his knees that had kept him out of college football, but steered him towards boxing, now kept him out of the war. He shook his head in disbelief; closed his eyes and said a silent prayer.

* * *

The following Monday, Terry went to the admissions office at North Texas State and met with his counselor to schedule courses for winter semester. He kept his hours to a minimum again, to focus his energy on his new part-time job – as a professional boxer.

He discussed the opportunity with Doug, who agreed to be his manager with one condition. "I will bring you about slowly, which means the money won't be there until you're a world-class contender. Curtis Cokes took the same route, and now he's a champion. We're gonna do the same for you."

Terry agreed, but before signing the contract he asked, "25 percent for all fights under a $2,000 purse? Isn't that a bit steep?"

"I normally charge 30 percent. I'm gonna' keep you motivated to stay on top of this sport, and the best way I know how to keep a boxer interested is to raise the bar a little at a time. Once you get past that $2,000 mark, my percentage will drop as the purse checks go up.

"Curtis is drawin' in the Texas crowds, and I think you'll be a good addition to my stable. I've got Curtis' brothers, Joe and Ernest, signed on too. People like to see a good mix of lightweights and heavyweights at a boxin' match."

Doug encouraged him to take the contract home and consider what he was getting into. Terry agreed.

Later, he took Karen out to dinner and told her about the decision he was considering. She expressed mixed emotions about the news.

"Believe me," Terry said, "I'm not getting into this for the money. The first time I lose badly to some other fighter, I'm going to think long and hard about staying in the sport. But I gotta tell you, Karen, with Muhammad Ali out of the picture, I think I can work my way up to a world-class fight in a year or so – and that's where the money and fame comes in."

"What do your folks think about this? I'm sure your brothers are excited, but your mom and dad aren't going to like hearing that you're going to be a professional boxer," she said.

"Yeah, I know. I'm going to call them this weekend and let my brothers know first. Then I'll think about how I want to tell my parents."

The following Saturday, Jeff answered the phone and Terry shared his news with him.

"Mom's out shopping, and I'm home with Denny and Deb," Jeff said. "Man, we were so happy to hear you weren't drafted last week, Ter!"

"I know, and now I've got some more news for you little brother— I've decided to turn pro and start getting paid for knocking guys out in the ring."

"Oh, that's cool! Denny and I just read an article about Jerry Quarry in *Boxing Illustrated*, and we agree that you could be just as good as him."

"Well, it certainly is a goal of mine. Look, tell Tom and Denny, but don't say anything to Mom or Dad yet. I still have to find a way to tell them."

"Okay, but Ter, I got some bad news – Mom kicked Dad out of the house a few days ago."

"*What?* Why? How did that happen?"

"Well, we heard them yelling at each other downstairs late at night last week, and we heard Mom say something like, 'If you're going to continue seeing some other woman, then you can do it while living somewhere else!'

"Then Dad yelled something about him paying all the bills around here, and he doesn't see anything wrong with seeing another woman now and then. I think he was drunk too. It was awful."

"Oh man, that's terrible," Terry said. "I noticed a difference in Dad over the past year though, I mean, getting a hot car and staying out late with his buddies, drinking at the restaurant. It *is* bad news Jeff, but it really doesn't surprise me."

"Well, Dad's moved in with Grandma Daniels for now. Do you think they'll get a divorce?" Jeff asked in a cracked voice.

Terry sensed his brother's concern and said, "Oh, it's too early to start thinking like that."

They talked for a few minutes and Terry felt as if he needed to be the one to provide guidance and support for his family. During this difficult situation he wished he was closer to home. He told Jeff he could call him whenever he wanted to talk.

He spent the rest of the evening talking to Karen. "Now it all makes sense, Dad's sudden care-free lifestyle and Mom giving me those lectures about dating more than one girl. I guess I'll have to put off the news about turning pro for now."

"Oh, how embarrassed and humiliated your mom must feel right now," Karen said.

"I want to pick up the phone and call Dad and tell him what a mistake he's making," he said. "But I know he'll tell me that I wouldn't understand, and turn the conversation around regarding my plans after graduation – and that would lead into another shit storm."

When he went to bed, Terry recited a long and meaningful prayer. He asked God to bless him in the choices he was making in his life, and to bless his mother, brothers and sister. He wanted the power of The Holy Spirit to always be in their household. He ended by asking God to guide his father, Bill, in making better decisions that would affect his family.

Terry always felt at ease after praying. At the age of 22, he was headed down a new path and wanted to be the best he could – physically, mentally and spiritually.

* * *

By the end of January 1969, Terry was becoming well-known among his new collegiate friends on the campus of North Texas State. He set up his schedule so he only had two classes to report to – one on Tuesday and Thursday afternoons, and one on Wednesday evening.

His popularity skyrocketed when a lengthy article appeared in the sports section of the *Denton Record-Chronicle* announcing his professional debut, February 10th, in Beaumont, Texas. The first paragraph read:

> *He's like many college seniors today – except Terry Daniels is becoming a professional boxer. He's a heavyweight, and he's about to join a hardened group of gladiators who demand toughness and determination and who get banged up as easily as they knock other boxers around.*

The article gave a brief history of his amateur career while attending SMU, which included 40 wins in 44 fights with 31 knockouts. In the article, the writer noted his striking good looks and confidence.

Terry read in *The Ring* magazine that the WBC champ, Joe Frazier, had defended his title twice in 1968 – against the heavyweight champion from Mexico, Manuel Ramos, with a second-round TKO, and a unanimous decision in a 15-round slugfest against the Argentinean, Oscar Bonavena.

The WBA champ, Jimmy Ellis, had meanwhile defended his title with a 15-round close decision against the former two-time heavyweight champion, Floyd Patterson, in Stockholm, Sweden.

Doug was determined to get his new heavyweight protege all the publicity he could in 1969. And after Terry made his debut in February by knocking out Charles Barnett in the first round, Doug knew the Dallas and Fort Worth papers would have a hometown heavyweight of their own to follow.

Terry called home and broke the news to his mom, who encouraged him. He assured her he knew what he was getting into and asked her to pass the news on to his father.

"I haven't seen or spoken to him since he left, and I don't think I want to talk to him for a while," she said. "He'll learn soon enough. I'm sure your brothers will tell him when they think the time is right."

Terry could hear the anger in her voice and said, "I want you to know that I think what Dad is doing is wrong. You've been a good wife and a good mother, and you *don't* deserve this, Mom."

"Well, thank you, Honey," she said. "It seems like the whole country is getting into this free love movement. It's in the movies, on television, and even in the magazines at the grocery store checkout. Call me old fashioned, but people still need to have good morals and principles to live by."

"You know Dad always has to be in charge, even when he's wrong," Terry said. "Once he gets something in his head, it's hard to change his mind, even his attitude with me in boxing."

"But you know your father loves you. Right?" she said.

"Yeah, I guess I would just like to hear him say it more often – like he used to. Anyway, I sent a couple articles about me that were in the paper recently to you guys yesterday. One of them is pretty amusing too," he said, hoping to end the call on a positive note.

"I'll keep in touch. Love you, Mom. Give my love to the kids."

When the letter arrived, the family had a good laugh. One of the clippings had a small headline that read, "Daniels Managed by Lord." It talked about Terry's decision to turn pro and being managed by Doug Lord, who also managed Curtis Cokes.

He said in his letter that he attended church that Sunday, and several people had obviously not read past the headline because they came up to him and said, "Bless you, son. The Lord will always be in your corner!"

His popularity continued with stories in the Dallas papers, the NTSU paper, and a story on the local TV station about "A college student working part-time in a rugged professional sport – no, not football – professional boxing!"

By the end of June, Terry had racked up five wins, all knockouts in the first and second rounds. He knew he had to climb the ladder slowly, however, and kept tabs on the current champions of the heavyweight division, Joe Frazier and Jimmy Ellis.

Frazier defended his title twice in 1969: In April, he defeated Dave Zyglewicz in the Houston Astrodome with a first-round knockout, and in June he beat Jerry Quarry six out of seven rounds in Madison Square Garden. The fight was stopped by way of a bad cut under Quarry's right eye, and the record books would record it as a KO 7. Ellis, meanwhile, limited himself to exhibitions.

With classes over for summer break, Terry decided to move into the Phi Delta Theta fraternity house at SMU and be closer to the ABC gym in downtown Dallas. There was plenty of room at the frat house, with only a few boys attending summer classes.

When he got settled in his room, he looked out the window and said to his roommate, "For the first time in my life, I won't be spending my summer living and working in Willoughby."

He told his roommate that he began to feel a little homesick and wrote to see if his brother Jeff could take a week off from work and fly down to stay with him for a few days. Jeff jumped at the chance, and spent his own money to buy a round-trip ticket to hang out with college fraternity guys eight years his senior.

Terry picked him up at the Love Field Municipal Airport on Friday, July 18th. He met him as he came in from the gate and said, "Hey, Jeff, over here!"

Jeff almost tackled him when his brother opened his arms to greet him. On the way to the baggage claim, Jeff said, "Hey, isn't this a switch – *you* picking *me* up at the airport!"

They laughed and talked all the way home. Terry couldn't get over how much his little brother had filled out.

"I'm 5' 9" and weigh 157 pounds," Jeff said. "I've been working out with your old weights at home and football practice starts in a few weeks at South High. Can you believe I'll be a sophomore and play on the same field you did?"

As they drove down Lovers Lane Ave., Terry turned onto Hillcrest and said, "I'll give you a little tour of SMU before we get something to eat. Tomorrow, I'll take you by the Cotton Bowl then we'll go to my gym to workout, and I'll introduce you to the guys." He felt good that someone from home was there to support him.

After dinner, he got Jeff settled in his room at the frat house and said, "If it gets too damn hot, we can move to my buddy Derek's room on the first floor. It's the one Don Meredith lived in when he went here, *and* it's the only one that has a window air conditioner!"

By 7 p.m. Saturday evening, Jeff heard that Terry and his buddies were going on dates and asked if he could stay in the air-conditioned room while they were out. Derek said, "Sure, little brother, make yourself at home. I've got a TV mounted on the wall facin' the beds, and you can watch the special of the astronauts landin' on the moon tonight. Hey, did you know that Neil Armstrong was a Phi Delt?"

The top story in the Dallas newspapers was about the U.S. landing on the moon for the first time in history. The television stations were carrying coverage, and the astronauts were expected to land sometime late Saturday evening. Jeff was 15 years old and was being treated like "one of the guys" on this prestigious campus. He sat back in a chair and soaked it all in.

Derek and his buddy, Rudy, were discussing the dating situation before they went out. Derek was trying to hook Rudy up with a blind double date and Rudy was not showing any interest.

After 15 minutes of haggling, Rudy asked, "What does she look like? Is she gonna wanna have sex?"

Derek said, "She was here yesterday with Cheryl. Jeff here saw her. She was a dish, wasn't she Jeff?"

Jeff was flipping through a *Playboy* magazine. He looked up and tried his best to remain neutral by saying, "Uh, all I saw was her walking out the door. I didn't get a good look at her face, but she seemed to have a nice figure."

Derek winked at him, then looked back at Rudy and said, "Well, there ya' have it. Come on, just work with me. She's a friend of my girl. You'll have fun – I promise."

"I'm not lookin' to have fun, I just wanna get laid," Rudy said.

Terry and the guys came back from their night out around 1:00 in the morning, and woke Jeff up with the noise of chatter and laughter. While they watched the coverage of the moon landing, Jeff heard someone ask Derek, "So, how was Rudy's date?"

Derek was lying on the lower bunk with his feet up, and said, "Oh man, she turned out to be a librarian! She was about as excitin' as watchin' paint dry. I don't think Rudy's gonna be talkin' to me for a while!"

Jeff laughed along with the rest of the boys and fell back to sleep in a matter of minutes. He woke up a few hours later to the sound of snoring, and found all the guys sprawled out in the only air-conditioned room in the house.

He got out of bed and nudged Terry, who was sleeping underneath the air conditioner. Terry opened his eyes with a bewildered look on his face and Jeff whispered, "Hey, Ter, you want to get dressed and go jogging before it starts getting hot?"

Terry rubbed his eyes, then rolled over and got up. "Yeah, good idea," he said.

Large shadows from the buildings surrounded them as the sun started its ascent into the clear blue morning sky. They started stretching, and Terry said, "I'm glad you woke me up. I like to jog this time of day, and I would've slept in if you hadn't been here."

"I need it too," Jeff said. "Practice starts in a few weeks and I've got to be ready."

"So, you got a girlfriend at home?" Terry asked as they started jogging at a slow pace.

"Well, I did up until school let out."

"Oh yeah? What happened?" Terry asked.

"I took a girl I got to know to the ninth-grade dance last April. We double-dated with a buddy of mine and his girlfriend, and he drove. We had a blast and went out for pizza afterwards.

"When I dropped her off, she had me walk her to their backdoor, and when we finally said goodnight, I put my arms around her and we kissed."

Terry smiled and said, "Jeffro's first kiss?"

Jeff smiled back and said, "No…well, I guess you could say this was my first *real* kiss. Then we kissed again, only with more passion, and I felt my blood starting to boil."

Terry chuckled and said, "Now, don't leave out any juicy details."

"Nah, the outdoor light came on and her mom opened the door to greet us. We did sneak another quick one in, however, before her mom could get a clear view of us.

"Anyway, I started seeing her more often, going out to the movies and stuff, and just before the last day of school she gave me a note. She said she started to feel like we were 'going steady' and she wasn't ready for that.

"She wanted to slow down, and just be friends – that kinda stuff," Jeff added in a disappointed tone.

Terry saw his opportunity to give his little brother some advice and said, "Hey, I know it's not easy to fall in-and-outta love, but it happens to all of us. Heck, at least you got to experience a little romance at your age. I didn't get to kiss a girl like that until the end of my sophomore year in high school."

"You? Mister Studly?"

"That's right. But looking back, I guess I can say that dating girls became an adventure all in itself. Don't feel discouraged when things don't go your way. Girls will let you know when the time is right to take it to the next step. And don't try and rush into a relationship either.

"The best time of your life is just now starting, Jeff. Keep active in sports and stay healthy. You won't have any problems with dating girls."

Jeff smiled and said, "So, what's the story with you and Karen? Is she *your* steady girl?"

"Well, she *is* special," he said. "We're not talking about living together any time soon because she knows I like my freedom, but I could see myself possibly settling down with her eventually.

"Now, let's stop talking and pick up the pace. You're gonna be timed for the mile before practice starts, and Doug's got a six-rounder lined up for me next month. So, stay close behind me, boy!"

CHAPTER 32

Jeff stood at the airport saying goodbye to his brother. "Wow, it was great to see all the people and places you've talked about over the years, Ter. And I loved hanging out with you guys on campus."

"Yeah, it was great having you here, Jeffro. Hey, don't forget, I've got a boxing match in Los Angeles in a few weeks. I'm gonna give Danny Iafelice a call to let him know I'll be there for a few days. He lives there now."

"Oh, hey, that's cool. Tell Danny I said hi! And keep those KOs going, I want to read in the papers that you'll be fighting Jimmy Ellis soon," Jeff said.

Terry smiled, "Who knows? I'll be giving 'em my best shot. Good luck to you in football. Just keep working hard and show the coaches you're willing to do whatever it takes to earn a starting position. I really didn't start to develop until my junior year, so keep the faith. "

They gave each other a hug and Terry waited until his brother walked up the steps to the plane. Jeff turned back toward the terminal window, and gave him one last wave goodbye.

That weekend, Terry told Danny the match would be at the Valley Music Theatre in Woodland Hills, near L.A. on Tuesday, August 12th. He would arrive Friday and wanted to know if he could stay with him for a few days.

"Sure! I rent a split-level off Vine in Hollywood. I've got an extra room, so that would be great, Ter." Danny said. "Who's the guy you're up against?"

"His name's Floyd Casey; nothin' I can't handle. My manager said the promoter in L.A. has made money off Quarry, and wants other 'white hopes' to keep bringing in the crowds."

"Well, that sounds good. I got a full-time job now at a graphic design company downtown and I go to night school three days a week, but I'm sure we'll have a good time while you're here."

"Okay, Ife! I will see you Friday."

After thinking about being cooped up in a van with several other boxers for 1,400 miles, Terry chose not to drive with them. Instead, he asked Doug's permission to fly there.

"I got enough to cover our expenses there and back. You wanna go your own way, you pay your own way," Doug said.

Terry decided to save a few dollars by purchasing a one-way ticket to get there, and then riding home with the guys. He landed at L.A. International on Friday afternoon and made arrangements for Danny to meet him at the baggage claim.

Terry waited for 45 minutes before he saw a guy in dark sunglasses come through a sliding glass door and flash that familiar Italian grin. He smiled back and greeted him with a handshake and bear hug.

"Ife, it's good to see you!"

"Good to see you too, Ter!" Danny said. "Hey, sorry I'm late, but I couldn't get out of work until after two, and traffic in this town is unbelievable."

"No problem, buddy, I'm glad we get to spend a little time together."

"Oh man, it is so great to see a familiar face from home – *especially yours!* Well, I had to park about a half-mile away, but you could probably use the exercise after that plane ride, so let's get goin'. Hopefully, we'll beat rush hour."

When they got to Danny's they barbequed a couple of steaks on the grill in his small backyard patio. They spent the rest of the evening getting caught up on everything that had happened to them over the past year.

Early the next morning, they drove to a nearby park and jogged for a few miles. Then Terry gave him directions to a boxing gym where he would meet with Doug and the rest of his amigos.

Terry sparred six rounds with two local boxers who traded off between rounds, and worked up a good sweat before finishing with three more rounds on the heavy bag and skipping rope. He was scheduled for a six-round fight with the local L.A. heavyweight, and it was one of six professional matches for the evening.

"Wow, Daniels, you certainly have bulked up since I saw you fight last. I think it was in Eastlake when you beat that heavyweight from Cleveland," Danny said.

Doug approached Terry and told him that the promoter wanted to see what he had to offer. "The pay day is $200," he said, "but if he thinks you can bring in a crowd like Quarry, then you could stand to make a bunch more in the future."

The guys joined Doug and the other boxers for a nice dinner out, and afterward, Danny showed Terry around town.

"I know you can't drink, but we can try and get into a place called, 'Whiskey a Go-Go.' It's where The Doors started out, and bands like Buffalo Springfield and The Turtles played there. The chicks that go in there are outta sight!"

"Sounds good to me Ife. I'll just nurse a glass of orange juice, dance and have fun!"

They waited in line for over a half-hour before they got in and the music from the band was one psychedelic song after another. The management finally switched to top records on the charts and they enjoyed watching the "go-go" dancers in their mini-skirts get up in the cages. But when midnight hit, they called it an evening and went home.

On Sunday night, Danny told Terry he had a class he couldn't miss on Tuesday evening, and wouldn't be able to go to his fight.

"My cousin, Robert, would love to go, and he said he could drive you there. Also, I've been seeing this girl for a couple of weeks now, and she's got a roommate that's a doll," he said. "If you'd like, I could give her a call and see if the two of them would like to join us for dinner Monday. I'd really like to do something special before you leave."

"A blind date, huh? She's not a librarian, is she?"

Danny looked confused and said, "What? No, they both have part-time jobs and work as extras in the movies. They're trying to make it as actresses, and they've sure got the looks to go with it."

Terry laughed and said, "I'm just kidding. Sure, let's go. Hey, but what if I hit it off with this chick? Would there be any problem if we sacked out in your spare room?"

Danny smiled and said, "What are you talkin' about? I thought boxers weren't allowed to have sex before a fight!"

"Nah, you've seen too many movies – that's an old wives' tale. Make the date and let's have fun."

On early Monday evening, the boys prepared for their night out. "I told the girls we'd pick 'em up around 6:30, and go to dinner by 7," Danny said.

"Sounds good, Ife. Where are we going?"

"A place called Dino's Lodge. It's Dean Martin's old place and it's right next door to 77 Sunset Strip, you know, where they filmed the show."

"No way! *Cool!*" Terry replied.

The TV show *77 Sunset Strip* was a popular detective/mystery show that ran from 1958 to 1964, starring Efrem Zimbalist Jr., Roger Smith, and the favorite of teenagers, Edd Byrnes. It was about two ex-government agents with a private detective agency on the strip, and Edd Byrnes played Kookie – a cool young man who worked as a valet, and occasionally got involved with the cases.

Terry chuckled and started clicking his fingers to the theme song of the show as he started his shower:

Seventy-seven Sunset Strip (Click-Click).
Seventy-seven Sunset Strip (Click-Click).

As they traveled down the road, Danny pointed out several landmarks. He came to the intersection of Hollywood and Vine and said, "The famous Grauman's Chinese Theatre is down that way – it's where all the stars put their hands in the cement."

He drove to the intersection of Vine and Santa Monica Boulevard, turned left and said, "There's a Hollywood cemetery over on the right where a lot of stars are buried."

Terry looked over and said, "Probably along with a lot of movie scripts that never made it, too."

Danny chuckled and said, "Man, you have no idea how big the movie business is here, Ter. My cousin works in the lighting crew for several studios, including Johnny Carson's, and he sees movie stars every day. But there are so many one-hit-wonders, it's a cutthroat business. You know?"

"Yeah, I'll bet," Terry said. "But it's really no different than anywhere else if you think about it. I mean, if a person wants to do something with their life, and does whatever it takes to be good at it, things go their way. And if they don't, then they have choices to make. My motto is: Always keep striving to be good at something. Don't just sit around and piss away your life."

Danny pulled into a parking lot of a two-story apartment complex and said, "That's the Terry Daniels I know!"

When they got out of the car, Terry said, "Hey, what's this chick's name again?"

"Suzette. She's a brunette, and my girl's name is Candy. She's a blonde."

"Suzette the brunette, and Blonde Candy – got it. Hey, maybe we shouldn't tell her I'm a boxer. I don't want to scare her off or anything."

"Okay, I didn't tell Candy anything about you. I just said you were a good friend of mine from high school in town for a visit."

Danny knocked on the door and was greeted by his date. She had straight, shoulder-length blond hair and wore a yellow-colored headband with a yellow mini-skirt and white high-heeled boots.

Danny introduced Candy to Terry, they shook hands, and Candy introduced Terry to Suzette. She was 5'4" with a slender build like Candy's; wore her dark hair in a flip, and had a light-blue headband, matching her mini-skirt.

In the car, Terry said, "So, Danny tells me you girls are actresses. That sounds exciting. How long have you been doing that?"

They chatted about their backgrounds, growing up in California, and how they decided to make the motion picture industry their goal. The boys didn't get a word in until they were seated in the restaurant.

"And what do you do, Terry?" Suzette asked.

Before Terry could answer, Danny said, "Terry's taking some time off from football practice with the Dallas Cowboys. He had to get a knee operation last year from a nasty hit he took in practice his rookie season. But you're almost ready to go back to playin' – aren't ya' Ter?"

Terry looked over at Danny – who had his "grin" on – smiled back and said, "Uh, yeah. Doctor says I will be back to practice soon, but no full contact for a month or two."

Suzette touched Terry's forearm on the table and said, "A pro football player? What position do you play?"

"Well, I was a running back, but after the injury, I'm not sure where the coach will play me next," Terry said.

Danny smiled as the girls continued their conversations centered on fashion and people in the industry, throughout their dinner. He felt good about where the evening was headed.

When the girls excused themselves to go to the powder room Danny said, "Okay, I'll order us another round of mixed drinks for dessert, except for Terry. He's gotta stick with iced tea."

They watched the girls' hips sway in motion as they made their way down the aisle to the restrooms.

Danny nudged Terry's arm and whistled. He said, "Hey, way to go, Ace! You played along nicely with my intro. I think Suzette is warming up to you."

He ordered the drinks, then turned to Terry and said, "Candy hasn't been over to my place yet, so this might be an opportunity to ask them if they'd like to see it. Maybe they'll feel more at ease going together."

The girls arrived back at the table just as the waiter brought their drinks. Danny passed one to each of them and said, "A toast! Here's to my buddy Terry's success, and a good time while he's here in L.A.!"

They clinked their glasses together and Danny told a joke. When he finished, Terry laughed and boldly reached under the table to run his hand up Suzette's thigh, gently rubbing her panties.

Suzette laughed along with him at Danny's joke, and put her drink down. Terry slowly slid his hand back to her knee, hoping he would get a positive reaction from her.

Suzette rested her hand under her chin while putting her other hand down under the table across Terry's forearm and said, "So, Danny. What kind of graphic designer are you exactly?"

When Danny answered, she slowly slid her hand up to Terry's crotch and started to message the totem pole in his pants. Terry let out a little chuckle, even though his friend was talking serious about work.

Danny stopped for a second, glanced over at Terry and said, "But, hey, we didn't come here to talk about work. Let's finish our drinks and go for a drive. I wanna show my buddy some of the sights while he's here."

They walked out to the car with each couple holding hands. Danny pulled out of the parking lot and headed west on Sunset Boulevard.

"Hey, Terry, look at the sign on the street over there," Danny said.

"Welcome to Beverly Hills," Terry said. He added, "Home of the Beverly Hillbillies," as the girls laughed.

Danny drove a few miles farther and said, "Down the hill is a famous curve, and I don't mean Ann-Margret's." Without saying any more, he started to sing: *"I was crusin' in my Stingray late one night, when an X-K-E pulled up on my right."*

"Dead Man's Curve!" Terry said. Then he chimed in to try and harmonize like Jan and Dean, the recording artists that made the number one single: *"He rolled down the window of the shiny new Jag, and challenged me then and there to a drag."*

The girls laughed and clapped to create a beat while the boys increased their voices: *"Let's race all the way – to Dead Man's Curve!"*

Terry and Danny both sang in the choir back in high school, and never missed an opportunity to turn the radio down and sing along with one of their favorite tunes while riding in cars together. The girls loved it.

The couples spent time at Pacific Ocean Park, and had started their way back when Danny suggested stopping by his place for a nightcap before taking the girls home. They enthusiastically said yes.

By 10:30 p.m., both bedroom doors were closed, and thumping and moaning noises could be heard throughout the apartment. The noises "peaked" about 11 when the doors opened and each took turns in the bathroom. Then they drove the girls home.

Suzette gave Terry her number and told him to call her next time the Cowboys were in town, or if he visits with his friend again. He said he would, but knew he wouldn't.

The next night, Robert picked up Terry for the boxing show at 6:15 p.m., and along the way, Terry told him that he slept most of the day and felt ready for tonight's fight. They spent the rest of the time talking about life in Hollywood and Dallas, and how both cities have grown over the years. The conversation helped keep Terry's butterflies to a minimum.

He met with Doug and the other boxers from his gym and Doug said, "I always get a little nervous when you're outta my sight before a boxin' match, Terry. Now get into your trunks and robe, and Al will get you wrapped. I'll be back in about 20 minutes – I got a guy who wants to meet you."

Doug's new corner man was a 6'0" 220-pound, 32-year-old man named Al Banks. Al had biceps the size of grapefruits and had experience in the amateur and pro ranks of boxing before working in the road department for the state of Texas. He liked Terry, and helped by sparring with him whenever he needed someone extra for ring work.

Doug came back to the locker room at 7:35 and was accompanied by a large man in a black pinstriped suit. He stood 6' 1" and weighed 275 pounds, had black bushy salt-and-pepper hair with a well-trimmed beard to match.

Terry had just finished lacing up his boxing shoes when Doug approached him and said, "Terry, I want you to meet the promoter of tonight's boxin' matches – Karl Wolfstein."

The man extended his meaty hand and said, "Terry, I've read some good things about you in the articles Doug sent me. I'm looking forward to seeing what the fans think of you tonight."

"Thank you, Mr. Wolfstein. I always come to win," Terry said.

He glanced at the thick hair on the back of Karl's hands, and the hair that poked out around his watchband. Karl noticed and said, "I used to wrestle around these parts as a professional. I went by the name of 'Wolf Man,' now I promote professional wrestling and boxing here in the L.A. area."

Doug said, "Well, let's get you back out there, so you can get your welcoming speech ready for the audience, Karl. The place is startin' to fill up."

Terry could hear the occasional roars from the crowd for the fights before him. He hoped Curtis Cokes' brothers were the ones the fans were rooting for.

Al and Doug came into the locker room later with a sweaty Ernest Cokes and said, "Okay, Terry, they're ready for you."

Terry followed his manager and corner man to the ring through the crowd of roughly 3,000. At the time, the top 10 heavyweight fighters in the U.S. were generating crowds of 6,000-8,000, and that is what "Wolf Man" was trying to crack on a monthly basis.

Terry's opponent entered the ring wearing a white robe with red trim, and dark red colored trunks. Floyd Casey had the look of Sonny Liston, and even stared at Terry with an "Ugly Bear" scowl on his face.

The announcer read off the stats of each boxer, and the crowd applauded louder when Terry's professional record of 5 wins with 5 KOs boomed through the speakers.

Doug was rubbing his boxer's neck while giving him last-minute instructions, "Take your time with this guy in the first minute, there's no need to extend yourself early unless he appears 'gun-shy.' Stick him with your jab as often as you can, then slowly lead into him with combinations."

The referee waved the men to the center of the ring and gave them instructions. The only thing new to Terry was, "When a fighter is down, I want the one standing to go immediately to a neutral corner – I will *not* start my count until that is done!"

The bell rang to start Round One, and the crowd cheered for the heavyweights to start throwing leather. They had become restless from the first two lightweight matches and wanted to see bigger men slamming punches in the first round.

Terry worked his double jabs as instructed and Casey kept his right glove close to his chin, while returning jabs to stay even. After two minutes, the crowd gave shouts for action. Terry heard them and turned up the heat.

The crowd responded. Terry's adrenaline pumped through his body as he followed his jab with a solid left hook to Casey's head. BOOM! His torso twisted along with his head, and down he went.

Most of the fans were on their feet and the ref turned to Terry and said, "Get to a neutral corner," and pushed him back.

Terry turned and walked to his corner. The ref came from behind and grabbed his right arm, "I said a *neutral* corner," while pointing to the other corner.

Several seconds had elapsed before the ref started his count, and Casey was on his hands and knees shaking his head, trying to clear it. When the ref got to seven, Casey pushed himself up, gave the OK to continue, then put his hands up as Terry came in for the kill. Three seconds later, the bell rang ending the round.

Terry came back to his corner and Doug said, "That was beautiful Terry, you did just what I told you to do."

"I don't know what I was thinking, though. I feel like I'm kind of mixed up tonight," he replied as Al rinsed his mouthpiece out and gave him a slug of water.

"You focus on leading with your jab and follow with the combinations this round, and we'll get outta here early!"

The bell rang and Terry stormed into the center of the ring. The crowd cheered his gamesmanship. Casey met him with a stiff jab, and didn't show any sign of backing down. He protected himself well as Terry threw as many combinations as he could. The punches came in from all angles, and Casey crouched down while holding his gloves tightly to his cheeks.

"Take your time!" Doug yelled. "Step back and gather yourself!" But Terry couldn't hear a word above the crowd.

Two minutes had gone by and Terry felt like it was five. His arms felt thick and he was running out of gas. Suddenly, Casey unleashed a quick left hook to Terry's temple that he didn't see coming. BOOM! Terry felt the hard thump on the right side of his brain and all he could see were the lights above spinning in slow motion.

He lost his balance and went down, and when his back hit the canvas, his head snapped backward and everything went black.

The next thing he knew, he smelled the heavy scent of ammonia from the tablet that Doug was waving under his nose. He looked around and realized he was in the locker room.

Doug applied a cold towel packed with ice on the back of Terry's neck and said, "You with us now, Terry? I bet you don't even remember us helpin' you walk back to the locker room."

"Ah, shit. The fight is over?" he asked.

"Yeah, he caught you with a 'Bolo' punch – the one you never saw. I don't think the punch did you in though, I think it's when your head hit the canvas.

"We were screamin' for you to back off a bit and regroup, but you couldn't hear us above the crowd."

"Son of a bitch, I'm sorry Doug. I got careless, but I thought the motherfucker would back down and quit the second round."

"I'm sorry too. Karl was really countin' on you to win his crowd over. It's bad luck, I know, because a good win tonight might have paved the way for more money. Don't worry though, you're a strong young man – it's all part of the sport."

Terry met up with Robert, who was watching the end of the fifth fight. "I already called my cousin at home and told him the result," Robert said. "Man, I feel bad for you, Terry. Everyone thought you were gonna knock that guy out for sure."

"Yeah, he got me with a lucky punch. I got greedy, and should have taken my time."

"I know. Well, Danny said to call him when you get back to your hotel. I'm not going to stick around for the last fight, so, it was nice meeting you."

Terry called his buddy from the hotel before he went to bed. Danny got him laughing immediately when he answered his phone, "Old wives' tale, huh?"

CHAPTER 33

October 1969 – Terry moved into a two-bedroom apartment in Denton and continued to take a few courses at NTSU. He had recently racked up two more knockouts at shows in Fort Worth and Houston and was feeling strong. Karen joined him at his last fight and they enjoyed the weekend at the Hilton in downtown Houston.

Two weeks later, they were having dinner at his apartment when Karen said, "Honey, I need to talk to you about something."

Terry finished his last piece of steak and said, "Sure, Babe. What is it?"

"I'm pregnant," she said hesitantly.

He wiped his mouth with a napkin, looked her in the eye and said, "Wow. Are you positive? I mean, have you been to the doctor?"

"No, I haven't been to the doctor yet. The past two mornings I've had to run to the bathroom and vomit, and I'm feelin' all the symptoms I've read about that a girl goes through when she's pregnant."

Terry could see that she was getting jittery, and tears were starting to well in her eyes. He gently held her hand and said, "Oh, Sweetie, I love you. I've been thinking about what it would be like to marry you. That's one of the reasons why I moved into this apartment. Now, you've just confirmed what I know we should do."

She started to cry and said, "I love you too. I just feel so bad that I've put you in such an awkward position."

He embraced her. She sobbed quietly into his chest and he said, "Honey, don't think that for a second. I would love to marry you."

"You would?" she asked with her face still buried in his chest.

He lifted her chin and said, "Karen, I've stopped trying to figure out why things happen to me the way they do. I truly believe that God has a plan for us all, and I don't question anything in my life anymore."

He grabbed a napkin from the table and wiped her eyes. "We love each other, and this just confirms it. I wouldn't hesitate for a second to say – Will you marry me?"

Between sobs she laughed and said, "Yes, I will. I'd love to marry you!"

* * *

Terry and Karen were married in the Denton United Methodist Church. A small reception was held afterwards at Karen's parents' house with close family and friends.

The Daniels family was thrilled with the news. The *News-Herald* ran a short story stating the newlyweds were planning a wedding reception in Willoughby over the Christmas holiday.

The following week, Terry had a match in Corpus Christi, Texas, with a tough heavyweight from New Orleans named Leroy Caldwell. The fight was scheduled for six rounds, and Terry struggled for the first four, but ended the bout by knocking Caldwell out in the first minute of Round Five.

He and Karen stayed an extra two days and enjoyed the sun and sand on the beautiful beach at their oceanfront hotel.

"Keep joggin' in that sand. It's a good workout," Doug said to Terry. "You make sure you're back in the gym by Monday. You got a fight scheduled in two weeks with your ol' buddy, Dickie Wills."

Dickie had a professional record of 16-3 and fought mostly in Texas and Oklahoma. He and Terry had lost touch since he moved to Tulsa, but Terry knew his former teammate would be ready to fight. And no friendship would be shared in the ring.

Doug had the Dallas/Fort Worth papers write a story about the two boxers meeting in 1966 in the Golden Gloves tournament, and how Daniels was looking forward to the rematch. The *Dallas Morning News* stated: *Terry was recently married and hopes to begin a belated honeymoon with his first main event victory.*

The fight was held at the Northside Coliseum in Fort Worth, and Terry's buddies from the Golden Gloves tourneys, Ronnie Wright and Jesse Avalos, were also on the card. The attendance was close to 4,000 people and all of them were ready for action that Saturday night.

Ronnie got the crowd cheering with a knockout of his opponent in the first round, and Jesse kept the energy alive when he scored a second-round knockout in the semi-final bout of the evening. The fans were ready for the two popular heavyweights when they returned to their seats from intermission.

The fight was scheduled for 10 rounds, but Terry knew the fight wouldn't go past five. He planned to hit his old buddy with both cannons – friends or not. He knew if he hit him hard early, Dickie would retaliate with a flurry of his own, and neither one would back off.

"He hasn't changed his style," Doug said while smearing Vaseline onto his fighter's face. "He still takes his fights straight on, and keeps his left popping with his right cocked close to his jaw."

Al Banks was loosening up Terry's neck with a massage and said, "Keep that low crouch, like we've worked on, and follow up with hard combinations off your jab. You'll do just fine."

The door of the dressing room opened and they walked down the hall to the arena. A bright spotlight followed Terry to the ring while the audience applauded and cheered. This would be his *first* headline fight, and his nerves were getting the best of him.

Karen was in the crowd next to a group of friends. Her palms were sweaty and she felt slightly nauseous. "This may be the last fight I watch my husband, at least for a while," she said to a friend sitting next to her.

Terry and Dickie were in their corners when the bell rang several times and the announcer welcomed everyone to the main event of the evening. He spent the next few minutes reading the stats of each fighter, then exited while the referee called the two men to the center of the ring.

Neither one made eye contact, nor showed any emotion. They shook their arms loosely and rolled their heads around to keep calm as the ref read them the standard rules set forth by the Texas Boxing Commission. Terry felt the adrenaline when the ref said, "Touch gloves, and good luck to both of you, gentlemen."

The bell rang and they met each other in the center of the ring. It had been three years since the two of them met under similar circumstances at the '66 Golden Gloves tournament, but now they were both experienced *professional* boxers. The crowd applauded as Dickie led off with two quick jabs to get Terry's attention, and followed with a left-right combination that grazed the top of Terry's head. Not enough to do any damage, just enough to show his opponent who would lead first.

Terry did as instructed. He shuffled to his left while countering with jabs, and followed up with a right hook that caught Dickie's left temple. The crowd cheered, but Dickie smiled to let them know it wasn't enough to have any effect. He kept moving into Terry with his jabs and combinations while forcing him into a corner.

Terry and Al prepped for this fight by working hard on a move that would catch an opponent off-guard if timed correctly when up against the ropes. He instinctively used it now. He dipped his left shoulder off the oncoming jab and followed up with two quick right hooks – one to Dickie's exposed rib cage, and the other to his left ear. The last punch stunned him enough to stop his advancement.

The crowd cheered and Karen found herself screaming above them, "Come on, Terry! Take it to him!"

The adrenaline electrified his body and the butterflies were gone. A minute and a half into the first round, Terry was advancing with lefts and rights. Dickie was surprised at his tenacity and the relentless barrage of punches coming from his former teammate, and tried his best to protect himself. But as he did, his right hand slid down from his right cheek and Terry's left hook hit him like a laser-guided rocket.

The crowd got on their feet as Dickie's head twisted. He bounced back against the ropes and Terry followed with a straight right that caught him on the nose. The ref stepped in and ordered Terry to a neutral corner, then started his standing eight-count.

Terry could feel that familiar rush of heat in his veins while the crowd cheered his name.

"Ter-ree! Ter-ree!"

It was time to finish this fight. He looked to his corner and read Doug's lips, "Take – Your – Time!"

Dickie gave the ref the OK and met Terry in the center of the ring with his hands held tightly to his face. He knew what was coming next. But instead of plowing into his opponent like a reckless linebacker, Terry led with a series of left jabs. He kept pecking away looking for an opening. It was time to drop the bomb.

With 30 seconds left in the first round, Terry hit him with a double jab and followed up with a solid right. Dickie's legs gave out and he went down.

Karen screamed above the crowd, "Yeah, Terry! That's it, that's it!"

The ref was counting, and Dickie got back to his feet at the count of six, but blood was pouring out of a cut on the corner of his left eye. The ref signaled for a doctor to look at the cut while the fight clock was stopped with just 15 seconds left in the first round. Both fighters were instructed to return to their corners.

After several minutes, the ref went to the judges table and informed them that the doctor would not allow the fight to continue. The bell rang several times indicating the fight was over.

The crowd eventually died down when the ref called the fighters back to the center of the ring and allowed the announcer to say, "Doctor

Richard Singleton has ordered the fight stopped in two minutes and forty-five seconds of the first round, due to the cut on Dickie Wills' eye, and the winner, from Dallas, Texas – Terry Daniels!"

The Sunday morning paper had a story on the fights in the sports section:

Dickie Wills, the Light-heavyweight champion from Oklahoma, was surprised at the speed and power of his opponent, Terry Daniels. "We hadn't fought each other since the amateurs and I thought I'd have the upper hand with a little more experience. I was wrong, and got careless, but I know I could have recovered if my eye wasn't cut. I would like a rematch," Wills was quoted as saying.

Doug said to Terry two days later in the gym, "He was surprised at your strength and power. He wasn't careless. If the fight continued without the cut, you'd a put him away in the second round. We'll give him a rematch though. The fans will demand it."

Terry finished off his year on December 1st, with a semifinal match against a man who insisted on one more shot at him, even though "the college boy" knocked him out twice in bouts the previous year. Terry ended his third fight with Joe Sharlow early, with a first-round KO in Austin.

"That'll show him," Terry said to Doug in the locker room after the fight.

When his first year in professional boxing was finished, *The Kid* found himself with a record of 10-1 with 10 KOs. He told Doug, "I would have been undefeated if I wasn't so careless in California. Live and learn, I guess."

* * *

Terry and Karen boarded a plane a few weeks later to spend Christmas with the Daniels family in Willoughby. They also held a second wedding reception at the basement hall of the Willoughby United Methodist Church on Sunday afternoon.

Earlier in the week, Terry had stopped by his father's office to invite him to the reception. He hadn't spoken to him in several months, but was determined to stay positive throughout his parents' separation. He knew how short-tempered his dad could be at times.

His Aunt Sal was the secretary in the central office and saw him enter the side door. "Well, hello Terry!" she said enthusiastically.

Terry smiled and said, "Hi, Aunt Sal," while wiping the snow off his shoes.

Terry's father, Bill, and his Uncle Peps looked up from their desks as Terry stood in their doorway. They got up from their seats and greeted him with handshakes and congratulations.

Bill shook his son's hand and said, "Welcome home, Ace!"

Terry wanted to give him a hug back, but Uncle Peps stuck his hand out; smiled and said, "Jesus, Terry, look at you. You must have gained 10 pounds of muscle!"

They exchanged idle conversation while others in the main office took some time away from their jobs to gather round and welcome Terry home.

Terry said, "Hey, I just wanted to stop by and say hello to everyone, and see if y'all were planning on stopping by the church on Sunday for our wedding reception to meet my new bride."

"Y'all? They got you talking like a Texan now?" Peps said with a chuckle.

Terry started to feel uncomfortable. What he really wanted to do was talk with his father in private, but he could see that no one would offer him the courtesy.

"Ah, just a little slip of the tongue," he replied. "They say that so much down there, you can't help but pick it up."

He shook hands with everyone again and noticed that his dad was about to return to his desk. He said, "Hey, Dad, you're coming, right?"

Bill sat down and said, "Why sure, I'll be by, Ter," with no indication that he would walk his son back to the car.

Terry smiled and said, "Okay. Well, I guess I will see *you all* around."

As he walked back to his car, he noticed two fuel-oil delivery trucks parked in front of the mechanic's garage. The large door was up and he could see his cousin Charlie and several other friendly faces. He decided to say hello.

"Hey, look who's back! The college boy, turned boxer," Charlie said.

They all turned to greet Terry. "I see you're making a name for yourself in Texas," one of the men said. "When are we going to see you fight here in the Cleveland Arena?"

"Soon, I hope, but I don't miss this Ohio weather. I'll tell you that," Terry replied.

"What's this I hear about you settling down and getting married?" another asked. "You're only 23, Ace. You must have pussy chasing you all over Dallas when you're out on the town! How you gonna keep your schwanz in your pants with a wife at home?"

Terry smiled and replied, "No problem. I'm a 'one-woman' man now.

"Come by the Methodist church Sunday around one o'clock and you can meet my new wife – and see for yourselves how lucky I am," he added with a wink.

The group joked and laughed for several minutes, then Charlie said, "Hey, you guys, we better get back to work before Peps sticks his head out the back door and bitches us out."

Terry bid farewell to his former working buddies and headed back to his car feeling significantly better. Charlie walked with him. He was a year older than him, and they always felt at ease talking to one another.

"So, how are things going for you down there, Ter?" he asked.

"Well, it's been a helluva year, Charlie. I don't know where this sport is taking me, but it has been a wild ride. My wife, Karen, is behind me 100 percent, and I plan on getting a good steady job once I get a degree," Terry said.

"That's good to hear. But I wouldn't set your sights on coming back *here* for a career."

"No? Same old shit, different day, huh?"

"Yeah, pretty much. Peps is in charge and insists on having a say in *everything*. And your dad lets him do whatever he wants – as long as his brother doesn't give him any shit about the stuff he's pulled on your mom."

"I know. I'd like to have a heart-to-heart with my Dad sometime, but you know how weird that can be," Terry said as he looked down at the ground.

"Well, that's the way our grandpa raised *his* kids, so I guess it's something we've inherited," Charlie said. "But if you were to pack up and move back to Willoughby, I think you'd be disappointed. There is no 'top position' to shoot for as long as Peps and your dad are around. You'd end up getting a raise when they felt like giving you one, and you'd be doing manual labor like me and the rest of the guys. Things won't change around here until somebody dies – and I don't mean Bill."

It was nothing Terry hadn't known already. Charlie just reminded him again. Terry was determined to follow his own dream, and on his terms.

The reception at the church was filled with several hundred people. Pot-luck dishes were prepared by Terry's aunts, and the church supplied everything else to make it a wonderful event.

Later, when the crowd began to slowly disperse, Bill walked in. Terry saw him immediately. As he approached his father, he watched his mother glance in their direction. Then she quickly turned her back while continuing to talk with her friends at a corner table. Terry ignored the awkward feeling that came over him, and greeted his father with a welcome smile and handshake.

"Hi, Dad! I was hoping you wouldn't forget to stop by," Terry said.

"Are you kidding? I'm sorry I'm late. I had to meet a vet this afternoon at the stables. One of my horses has been sick and it took longer than I anticipated," Bill said.

Terry's brothers and sister also approached their dad. They knew he would appreciate their support. They also wanted to show their father and the people in attendance that they remained civilized regarding their parents tumultuous relationship, and hoped to put an end to the gossip.

Karen joined them a few minutes later, and Terry cordially introduced her to his father. They had discussed the circumstances in great detail beforehand, and she knew how Terry felt about his parents' breakup. As a woman, she had more empathy for her mother-in-law, but she did a good job of hiding any bias by greeting Bill with a polite, "Hello. I'm so pleased to meet you."

The rest of the people in the hall soon started to leave, and Bill followed. But not before he passed an envelope to Terry and said to his kids, "I'll stop by the house the week after Christmas, and see you young hooligans then!"

Terry took the opportunity to walk his father out to his car. When they got far enough from the crowd Terry said, "Dad, I appreciate you coming today, and I just gotta get something off my chest."

Before he could continue, Bill said, "If it has anything to do with me getting back with your mother, you can save your breath. I'm not ready to have that conversation yet."

"It's not about what you're doing to Mom; it's what you're doing to *the family*," Terry replied.

"Look," Bill said in a stern voice, "I've been married to your mother for 25 years, and she doesn't care to have the same kind of fun that I want to have. We just think differently now, that's all. I'm not going to abandon the kids. They're just going to have to give me some space right now – and *you do* also."

Terry watched as his father drove out of the parking lot and he kicked a pile of snow in anger. He was determined to stay positive, however, and not let the conversation ruin his time with his family.

He and his new wife opened their gifts at the Daniels' house later that evening. "I feel like it's Christmas two days early," Terry said. "Karen and I are going to have to spend extra time sending thank-you notes out before we head home next week."

Before they settled in for the evening he said, "Oh, I almost forgot," as he pulled out the envelope from his sport coat. In it was a Christmas card designed to hold cash, and Terry saw the familiar face of Ben Franklin in the open-holed center. Inside were ten $100 bills.

A note on the card read, *Congratulations to you and Karen! Give one of these each to Tom, Jeff, Denny and Doll for Christmas – and you keep the rest. Love, Dad*

The kids smiled as their big brother passed out the money, and Karen put her arm around Terry. She smiled seeing their excitement and added nothing more. Then she saw June watching from the kitchen and noticed a tear in her eyes.

She joined her new mother-in-law and gave her a hug. "I know this is hard for you," Karen said in a quiet voice. "But your kids love their dad just as much as they love you. It's *really* gonna be hard on the little ones, especially goin' into the holidays.

"Please know that they don't approve of your husband's actions. I know Terry and I certainly don't. Just try and stay strong through all this. We pray for you and the family every day."

June smiled and said, "Thank you, Honey. You have a good heart; I can see why Terry loves you so much."

CHAPTER 34

Terry and Karen nursed a total of two beers at a party on New Years Eve, 1969. They were both in training for January 1970 – she, now three months pregnant, and he, prepping for a rematch with Dickie Wills.

Terry and Dickie were the preliminary fight to the main event of Curtis Cokes against the Middleweight Champion of Mexico, Roberto Pena. Curtis lost his welterweight title to a solid-punching Cuban, Jose Napoles. He was tired of always working hard to maintain his weight and was making his debut a little heavier, as a middleweight at the new Convention Center in downtown Fort Worth.

Terry and Dickie seemed to continue where they left off from their last fight, with both throwing leather at the start of Round One. Dickie had not changed his style and neither had Terry. It was obvious that *both* wanted an early victory - again.

The crowd clapped and cheered as they watched "the good-lookin' kid from Dallas" whip his opponent with a barrage of punches in Round Two. With 1:48 left on the clock, the ref separated the fighters and gave Wills a standing eight-count. When he called them back to box, Terry hit Dickie with four unanswered punches and the ref waved the fight over. Terry was awarded the win by way of TKO 2.

After the announcement of his victory, Dickie said to Terry, "I'm headed back to Oklahoma, Daniels, and I think I'll leave you as 'The new sheriff in town.' I'm gonna think long and hard about stayin' in the ring. Good luck to you buddy!"

Later, Terry confided to Karen that he'd feel bad if he was responsible for ending the boxing career of his good friend.

"Oh, I know, Honey, but you told everybody that you have *no friends* when you step into that ring. It's the nature of the sport," she said with a comforting smile.

Karen kept her job at the bank while Terry continued to take a few courses at NTSU. He had not lost sight of his college degree. The papers in Denton and Dallas increased Terry's popularity with the locals, and he started having people approach him in stores and restaurants, asking him for his autograph. He got a kick out of it, but was smart enough to know that he had a long way to go before he could consider himself a celebrity. Especially after seeing Joe Frazier beat Jimmy Ellis.

He watched the fight in the Memorial Auditorium in Dallas on closed-circuit TV with several thousand people in February. The match was held in Madison Square Garden and the winner was to be crowned the undisputed Heavyweight Champion of the World.

When asked by a reporter what his strategy would be the day before the fight, Frazier replied, "I'm gonna come out smokin'." He lived up to that promise and dropped Ellis twice in Round Four, leaving him to barely beat the count of 10 each time. Frazier was awarded a KO when Ellis refused to come out of his corner in Round Five.

The next day, the news media reported that *Smokin'* Joe Frazier was now *the* Heavyweight Champion of the World.

In March, Doug raised the bar by getting Terry his first main event 10-rounder in Dallas at the Sportatorium. His opponent was Kenny Hayden from Oklahoma City. He was a two-time Golden Gloves winner and All-Navy amateur champion. His manager told the papers that he had over 100 fights with only 8 losses as an amateur, and as a pro was 15-2 with 12 knockouts.

Once again, Terry's opponent had the height and weight advantage; coming in at 6' 1" and 210 pounds at the weigh-ins the day before the fight. Hayden boasted to the reporters after stepping down from the scales, "You better have your cameras ready when the first round bell rings, 'cause this boy ain't gonna last long!"

After the weigh-ins, Doug introduced Terry to the promoter of the boxing show, but this time it was *outside* of the locker rooms.

"Terry, I'd like you to meet the person responsible for tomorrow night's show, Mrs. Sue Moses."

A petite brunette wearing a sleeveless dark blue dress and hat to match extended her hand and said, "Terry, I'm very pleased to meet you."

Terry gently took her small hand and said, "Likewise, Mrs. Moses."

She chuckled and said, "Oh, please call me Sue. My husband and I have watched you fight several times and we've decided you are the one boxer that Dallas will want to see more of. I told Doug that if you continue to grow in popularity, we may have ourselves a contender for the heavyweight title soon!"

Sue and Bern Moses were successful entrepreneurs in Dallas, owning several businesses. They had a passion for boxing since Cassius Clay won the title in '64, and it was Doug who convinced Sue and her husband to finance their endeavors in making Dallas a key city for professional boxing shows. She wanted to compete with Chicago, Las Vegas, and New York, and believed Terry could draw the crowds.

"Well, thank you, Sue. I always come prepared to win when I step into a ring. My football coach at SMU had a sign in the locker room for the players that read: 'A man can only be beaten twice – once when he dies, and once when he quits.' And I never quit a fight," Terry said.

Sue smiled and said, "That's what my husband and I thought. We look forward to having a good relationship with you and your manager, Terry."

Later that evening, he told Karen of his meeting and said, "I meant every word of it too!"

Karen, who did not attend the fight on Thursday night, smiled as she read the sports page the next morning – it confirmed what her husband told her when he came home that night: "Daniels Flies Past Hayden; Wins No. 13." Dallas – *For Terry Daniels of Denton, the "game" of professional boxing is about three-fourths confidence and another quarter of raw ability.*

He has that last quarter; he proved it for the 13th time here Thursday night by knocking out Kenny Hayden in the second round of a scheduled 10 round fight. And Daniels seems to be gaining a little ground in the confidence end of his profession.

A 6 x 6 inch photograph next to the headline showed Terry standing over Hayden with the caption underneath: "Daniels Sends Hayden Down – For the Last Time." The article ended with a quote from Hayden that got Terry's attention: *He told Daniels he thought he could "…make it in this game… You've got the power but you're easy to hit."*

In the gym the following week, Al Banks said to Terry, "You and Quarry got the same style. You both bob and weave, jab and throw good combos, but you both keep lookin' to drop that big right-hand bomb. As a result, you take your mind away from keepin' your dukes tight to your head, and in that split-second, your opponent sees an opening and pops you one."

To prepare for the next fight, Al had Terry hit the hand pads that he wore and positioned them for different combination punches. Then he'd follow with a light tap to Terry's face whenever he caught him dropping his hands.

"Now that last one I gave you coulda been the one that knocks you out, or at least leaves a bruise on your face," he said.

After several weeks, the workouts paid off. Terry notched another KO with a fight in Beaumont in April, then he was pitted against Sonny Moore from Tyler, Texas.

Sonny had the looks and the moves of another Sonny – Sonny Liston. In fact, he had fought him the previous year in Houston. He lost by way of a third-round knockout, but made it a good fight. He also fought Zora Folley in '69, and now he wanted some "fresh meat" from Dallas.

In June, Terry battled Moore in the Memorial Auditorium to a cheering crowd of 4,000. He stunned Moore with a solid right to the head in the second round, sending him to the canvas. Moore made it through the round and responded with a flurry of punches, sending Terry to the canvas in the third.

The fighters respected each other from the third round on, and Terry showed his improved boxing skills by picking his shots. More importantly, he showed Doug and Al that he was able to cover up better, and his stamina allowed him to go 10 brutal rounds – something he had never done before.

Terry was awarded the split decision by the judges, and the papers the next day showed him slamming the face of Moore with a solid right. The reporter said the fight was close, *"But Daniels was clearly the victor of the two gladiators in the ring."*

Doug was pleased with the fight, and accepted a rematch with Moore for July 13th, one month later.

Karen, in her final month of pregnancy, had taken maternity leave from the bank. By the time the rematch came she said to Terry, "Please protect yourself, Honey. I want our baby to grow up with a daddy that's kept his good looks!"

The papers in Dallas, Fort Worth and Denton had articles two weeks in advance of the match, and by fight night, the crowd of 5,000 was ready for the big showdown – thanks to Sue Moses and her talent in gaining publicity.

Doug had his amateurs, James Helwig, Joe Courrage, and Dan Horton, lead off with their AAU matches. Each came away a winner, and got the hometown crowd warmed up for the preliminaries of the pro fights which included Jesse Avalos, Jose Gabino and Ronnie Wright.

The fight with Sonny Moore, like his rematch with Dickie Wills, appeared to pick up where it left off a month earlier, except there were no knockdowns. When one fighter fell behind he'd follow up with counterpunches to catch up, and by the 10th and final round, Terry pushed himself to the limit. He hit Moore with everything he had left in the tank, but Moore protected himself well enough to weather the storm.

Both men proved to the crowd, and the reporters, that they were indeed professional heavyweight contenders. And apparently, the judges came to the same conclusion, because the fight ended in a draw.

"That's okay," Doug said to a disappointed Terry. "It was close. I thought you won it, and I'm sure a lot of fans thought you did too. You proved you can go the distance, and dish it out right up to the final bell. You just jumped over another hurdle."

Three days later, Karen gave birth to a healthy boy whom they named Bret Daniels.

* * *

By the end of September, Terry sent a large envelope home to his family in Willoughby stuffed with articles, pictures of Karen with the new baby, and a three-page letter. The articles covered Terry's fights since his rematch with Moore – two KOs in the first and second rounds and one KO in the 10th – all in Dallas and Fort Worth.

The last fight was on September 11th against a tough fighter from Cincinnati named Tiger Joe Harris. The paper said Terry was knocked down in the second round, got his head together, and showed a vast improvement by keeping his composure. He put together several clean combinations of punches in the 10th round and won a unanimous decision – bringing his record to 17-1-1 with 15 KOs.

In the letter, he told his family that he and Karen moved from Denton to a two-bedroom apartment in Dallas on McKinney Avenue across from Highland Park. He wrote that he would not be going back to North Texas State and would be putting his college degree on hold for a while.

He also said that Karen would be staying home with Bret, and that he would be picking up the slack in their budget by going back to his beer distributing company. He ended by sending his love to everybody and included their new phone number.

A few days later, on Sunday evening, Jeff called his big brother at his new home.

"Hey, Terry, we got your letter," Jeff said. "I feel like I'm talking with a real celebrity athlete, with the news clippings to prove it!"

"I know, Jeffro. I'm getting to know some of the Dallas Cowboys, and I've even been asked to do a car commercial for a buddy of mine down here," he said. "How's everybody up there? You're a junior this year, right?"

"Yeah, we're into football now, and I'm playing on the offensive line. We're good this year too. The coach has everybody on the team geared up to win the Greater Cleveland Conference – you know, the new conference we switched to from the Freeway Conference in '68."

"Oh, yeah, that's the year Mentor won it with the undefeated team. They got shafted by being placed at number two in the state polls though; they really deserved to be number one that year!"

"I know... Hey, Ter, I got something I want to tell you," Jeff said.

Terry could hear the serious tone change in his little brother's voice. "Sure Jeff. What is it?"

"Well, last Friday, Mom and her friend drove Denny and me to the Lake County Courthouse in Painesville. Mom filed for divorce, so we had to sit in front of the judge and listen to him explain how everything works."

"Oh, man, I'm sorry to hear that, buddy. I wish I was there with you guys," Terry said.

"I wish you were too. You're in Texas, Tom's at OU and is getting married in December, and I feel like I'm the oldest one carrying the sword and shield for us. Debbie was allowed to stay home with Aunt Sal after school, but Denny and I had to listen while the judge asked us who we wanted to live with."

"Oh, no..." Terry said. "That's awful. I can only imagine how hard that must have been for you."

"Well, of course we answered, 'Our mother,' but it felt weird. Ya' know? I mean, Dad moved in with another woman and the two of them live someplace in Mentor. What could we do? Leave the house we grew up in, then change schools?" Jeff said in a cracked voice.

Terry smacked his hand on the table as he realized the difficult circumstances that his family had been exposed to, but kept his composure. He said, "No, you guys did the right thing. Just because he made choices to do the things he's done to Mom and the family, doesn't mean you have to go along with him.

"Listen, I've been talking with Don Elbaum, and he's told us that he wants Billy Wagner and me to headline a few of his fight cards in Cleveland before the end of the year. He said he's going to let me know for sure in the next few days, meanwhile, you tell Denny and Deb that I said to hang in there. I'll be up to see you guys soon, and I'll make some time to have a private talk with Dad."

"Okay, Ter. We look forward to hearing from you again real soon."

Terry hung up after their goodbyes and immediately got a pen and paper. He started reciting the questions he had for his dad and wrote them down while they were fresh in his mind.

Before going to bed that evening, Jeff told his mother how he felt. "All Denny and I wanted was an opportunity to talk with some other adult about everything before we were given the final ultimatum," he said. "We were shocked that we had to choose between our parents in front of a perfect stranger."

* * *

The following week, Terry was the headline fight on another one of Sue Moses' shows. He was up against a man named Terry Sorrell, who boxed professionally in Los Angeles and had moved to Beaumont, Texas, earlier in the year.

The paper noted Sorrel was coming off a two-year tour in Vietnam. He was looking forward to his first 10-round fight. Terry cut Sorrell's goal short by knocking him out in the second round.

Muhammad Ali grabbed headlines in the sports section the next day when it was announced he was allowed to fight the WBA's number three contender, Jerry Quarry.

On October 26th Ali showed the world he was as sharp as ever and hit Quarry with several damaging blows, the worst being a straight right cross that opened a gash above Quarry's left eye. The fight was stopped and Ali was awarded a technical knockout in the 3rd round.

With Ali back in the game, heavyweight fighters across the world were now back in the spotlight. Doug called Terry the next day to tell him that Sue Moses was putting together an "All Heavyweight" show November 10th.

"She wants to raise the bar again and said she would like to see you fight another contender on 'the comeback trail' – Amos Lincoln," Doug said.

Amos "Big Train" Lincoln stood 6' 4," weighed 220 pounds and was known as a crafty fighter. He had over 200 amateur fights before turning pro in 1954 and compiled an impressive record with bouts that included Sonny Liston, Karl Mildenberger, Thad Spencer, and "Scrap Iron" Johnson.

He had taken a few years off and worked construction since late 1968, and lost a comeback match against Boone Kirkman – the 1965 National AAU Heavyweight Champion and pro contender – a few months earlier. He was now 33 years old, but ready to move back up the ladder in the professional heavyweight ranks.

The four-bout card was held at the Memorial Auditorium in Dallas and several newspapers ran stories about the show. An article in the *Morning News* had a headline, "Big Train Hopes to Derail Daniels." It stated:

> *The 10-round main event at Memorial Auditorium will match the young "white hope" against the black "old pro." But of course, this is the biggest fight of Daniels' young career. The fall guys are gone now, and Daniels will have to give up four inches in height; 20 pounds of weight and a "decade" of experience.*

The article quoted Lincoln saying, *"I don't think a heavyweight fight should go 10 rounds. I'll knock him out, or he'll knock me out. Why fight 10 rounds and get cut, etc, when you can knock him out and go home early?"*

"Big Train" got it right, but it was Terry who got to go home early – he knocked him out in Round Five. His pro boxing record stood at 19-1-1 with 18 KOs.

The following weekend, he received a call from Don Elbaum in Cleveland. "I want you and Billy Wagner to headline my fight cards at the Cleveland Arena on November 25th and December 15th. You can bring your wife and new baby and spend Thanksgiving with your family," he told Terry.

They arrived at Cleveland Hopkins Airport three days before the fight, and Terry made arrangements to stay with his mom and siblings in Willoughby. A thick layer of snow made their commute longer than expected, but all the nervousness and anticipation of coming home disappeared when they walked through the front door of the Daniels' home on Johnnycake Ridge.

June was the first to greet her daughter-in-law and new grandson with lots of hugs and kisses. "Oh, I'm so glad to see you! Let me hold that little boy and give you a break," she said to Karen while cradling Bret in her arms.

Terry placed their luggage down and he greeted Jeff, Denny and Debbie with bear hugs and laughter.

"Tom called and said to tell you he has classes at OU, but will be up in time for Thanksgiving," Jeff said. "He and Marcie are putting the final touches on their wedding plans next month."

Tom and his high school sweetheart were to be married on December 12, 1970. Her brother Darrell and Jeff were juniors at South High and played football together.

"Holy cow, I can't believe how much you guys have grown!" Terry said. "Jeff, you must have added another two inches in height and put on 20 pounds of solid weight since I saw you last. And Denny, you've grown at least a foot and beefed up too," Terry said.

"I had a good year in football," Jeff said. "We finished tied for first in the Greater Cleveland Conference with Mentor, and I got my first letter jacket!"

"I've been working out at Tommy Morris' gym in Wickliffe," Denny said. "Don Bernard has been training me in boxing, Ter. He said I will be in a boxing show in a few months too!"

Terry held his hands up and said, "Show me some moves, Kid."

Denny went into his boxing stance, but June said, "There will be enough time for that tomorrow. Let's get them settled in their room first, boys. Terry, we've pushed your double beds together in your room and I borrowed a crib from a friend for the baby."

The rest of the evening was filled with good food, stories, and laughter. The Daniels had their big brother home again, and it was a special holiday for the family.

* * *

Don Elbaum met Terry and Billy at Wagner's Shamrock Gym in Collinwood the next evening to observe their workouts. He showed the boys a poster of the fight while they warmed up.

"You are the headliners for the card," he said. "Terry, you'll be up first, then Billy will be the final fight of the evening."

"My manager said this guy from Canada has a straightforward orthodox style. So, I guess my best shots will be hooks and straight rights?" Terry asked.

"Yeah, they call him Paul 'The Investment' Nielsen," Don said. "His manager told me he draws in the crowds, so I billed him as 'Canada's Great Prospect' with seven KOs in 10 wins. But I'd say he hasn't met anybody with a right hand like yours though, Daniels. Doug Lord told me you out boxed 'Big Train' Lincoln, and he's no slouch. I think you'll do just fine.

"Billy, I tagged Roger Rouse as having two world title fights as a light-heavyweight, but he's on the way out. With the kind of power you've developed, you shouldn't have any problem either. I'm sure you'll both put on a good show."

Larry Wagner took the poster from Don and said, "I'll put this on the outside of our front door downstairs. Meanwhile, you guys get warmed up. Terry, Harold Carter should be here any minute, you can spar with him tonight. Billy, I want both you guys to get in six rounds each. So let's get movin'!"

The next day, Terry made arrangements to take his father to lunch. He drove the Shelby to pick him up at the fuel-oil office. Bill was happy to see him, but Terry could tell his dad was uncomfortable the moment he sat in the passenger's seat of the car.

"Your mother and I still haven't agreed who's keeping this car," he said in a rather stern voice.

Terry purposely drove the car to get a reaction from his father right up front. He used it as an opener by saying, "Dad, I've tried to be understanding with whatever it is you're going through and I know you and Mom have your differences, but what about the rest of us kids, especially the little ones? Have you thought about what kind of effect your actions have had on them?

"I have a family of my own now, so it doesn't really affect me. But it *is* having an effect on Jeff, Denny and Deb. They gotta go to school each day and face their gossiping friends and teachers who know they've got trouble at home. It's not fair."

Bill took his eyes off him, starred straight ahead and said, "I know it's difficult for them, but I've made my decision and they're going to have to adjust to it. I'm still supporting them, and they've made their decision who they want to live with. I know it's not going to be easy, but that's the way it's going to be."

Terry spent the rest of the drive explaining why his siblings decided to stay with their mother, but he could tell it was a sore spot with his father. He also knew there were other people in his dad's life that influenced his thinking.

After lunch, Terry dropped Bill off at the office and said, "Here are two tickets to the fights tomorrow night. I want you to come and root for me, Dad. I know it's not what you wanted me to do with my life, but I want you to see for yourself why the papers and the fans want to see me in the ring. I still plan on graduating from college, but for now, I feel like I just gotta see this thing through while I'm young enough."

Bill took the tickets, opened the car door and said, "Okay, Ter, I'll go. You're old enough to make your own decisions, and I respect that. Now, you've got to respect *mine*, no matter what you think I'm doing to our family."

Terry watched his father walk into the building while he put the car in reverse and pulled out onto the road. He punched the accelerator to the floor and let the tires squeal.

As he slowed for the stop sign, he smacked the steering wheel and turned the radio up loud to let off some steam. He didn't want to continue to fight with his dad, but he was determined to stand his ground. "Ah, this *stinks!*" he yelled.

CHAPTER 35

Jeff used the family station wagon to drive some of his football buddies and Denny to see their big brother fight professionally for the first time on November 25, 1970. Terry and Karen drove together while June and Debbie stayed home with the baby.

The snow was piled high on the side of the road, but the streets were clear, so June wasn't worried about Jeff driving into Cleveland with the carload of boys.

"Just go the speed limit and remember where you parked. It can get very confusing downtown you know," she said as they were leaving.

While on the freeway, a song by the Carpenters came on the radio: *We've Only Just Begun.* The boys in the back seat started to sing in mocking harmonic voices, and Jeff was quick to change the station to something a little more upbeat.

"My brother's wife loves the Carpenters, but I know – it's music for *lovers,*" he said.

The new station came into the middle of one of Jeff's favorite groups – The Guess Who – and the boys in the car chimed in:

No sugar tonight in my coffee,
No sugar tonight in my tea!
No sugar to stand beside me,
No sugar to run with me!

The boys were into the groove of the music, and would have missed their exit if Denny hadn't shouted out, "Hey, Jeff, the Euclid Avenue exit is coming up!"

Jeff cut over to the right lane and was fortunate no one was behind them, because Clevelanders were not tolerant to inconsiderate drivers. He turned left onto Euclid from the exit ramp and drove east for a few minutes until they saw the familiar marquee of the Cleveland Arena with the neon figure of The Barons' hockey mascot.

They marveled at the sign which read: "Pro Boxing Tonight / Wagner vs Rouse / Daniels vs Nielsen / Prelims 8 PM."

"Wow, that's cool to see Terry's name in lights, isn't it Jeff?" Denny asked.

"Yeah, it is," he replied. "Now who's gonna pay the $2 parking fee?"

"Jeez, two bucks to park and $7 a head to get in. This is more expensive than watching the Indians play," one of the boys said.

The wisecracks stopped, however, when they reached their seats and looked out at the ring in the center of the floor. Half the seats were filled and more people were coming in.

Jeff and Denny shared a program and kept score of the boxers round by round. It helped them understand the sport. After each bout, they would listen to the fans around them voice their opinions of the judges, then compared their findings.

"The ref seems to let these guys get away with a lot of cheap shots to the back of the head when they tie up," Jeff said.

A big man behind him said, "They let 'em get away with that shit in the pros, but they'd never let 'em do that in the Golden Gloves."

The third bout of the evening got underway, and Jeff could feel the butterflies building in his stomach. His brother would be up next. The bout they watched was to be a six-rounder, but ended in the third round by way of a TKO. The winner was the hometown favorite, Harold Carter.

At intermission, Jeff and Denny saw their dad standing with their cousin Frank and several other men by one of the concession stands that served alcohol. They seemed to be having a good time, so Jeff decided they'd better not interrupt the party.

Based on the few occasions he'd seen his father after he'd "had a couple," Jeff knew enough to let it go. He wasn't their old dad when he got intoxicated, and Jeff didn't care to start a conversation with him in that state of mind.

The bell rang several times and the house lights went down when they returned to their seats. The crowd started whistling and cheering as the announcer stepped into the ring to let everyone know one of the main events was about to start.

Jeff's heart started pounding and his palms started to sweat when he saw Doug separate the ropes for Terry to step into the ring. He and the boys led the hometown fans with loud whistles and cheers as they watched him move around the ring.

Terry wore a dark red silk robe with white trim and belt, with his name embroidered on the back. Nielsen entered the ring after Terry wearing a black silk robe with white trim and belt.

The announcer looked and sounded just like the one in Madison Square Garden and got the crowd excited for a good heavyweight fight. The first four rounds consisted of both fighters moving cautiously around the ring, careful not to let their guard down. Every time Terry started to work Nielsen into a corner, he would protect himself and push Terry back, shuffling his way out to the center of the ring.

The Cleveland crowd was growing restless, and at the start of the fifth, there were loud chants of, "Come on Daniels, take this guy out!" and, "Make your move Daniels, this guy ain't that tough!"

Jeff saw Karen sitting ringside, and six rows behind her he spotted his father with his friends. Terry could hear his dad shouting amongst the crowd. "Yeah, hit him like you mean it, Daniels!" he yelled in a drunken slur.

Suddenly, the crowd cheered, and Jeff shifted his eyes back to see his brother standing over his opponent while the ref was pushing him back toward a neutral corner.

"Ah shit, I missed it!" Jeff yelled. "What happened?"

"Terry hit that guy with a big right hand. Wow!" Denny said.

Jeff realized right then – when you take your eyes off a boxing match, even for a second, you can miss the best part.

Nielsen was up at the count of five and waited for the ref to ask if he wanted to keep fighting. He nodded and put his gloves close to his face to stop the furry of punches from Terry who charged like a bull out of the corner.

Most of the spectators were on their feet cheering Terry on to finish the fight, but Nielsen wasn't about to give up. He was careful to keep moving while countering Terry's punches, and was able to finish the round.

Jeff and Denny were cheering along with the rest of the crowd, "Yeah, way to go Terry! He's our brother, woo!" they yelled. Jeff could see his dad taking slaps on the back, and laughing while shaking his head like he was in disbelief of what happened. The crowd was now behind Terry and wanted to see "The KO Artist" from Dallas take this guy out.

The bell rang for Round Six and the fighters stormed into the center of the ring. It appeared that both their cornermen were encouraging them to come on strong this round. The Cleveland crowd was eating it up.

Nielsen led with double jabs and followed with straight right hand shots, but Terry did well in slipping off most of the punches and countered with hooks and uppercuts. Jeff didn't take his eyes off his brother for a second, and saw a left-right combination delivered to Nielsen's head in a split-second.

Nielsen went down and the spectators jumped to their feet. Terry immediately went to a neutral corner while the ref started his count. Nielsen showed his courage again by beating the count and wanting to continue. Terry took his time and showed his professionalism in the ring. He was determined to pick his shots, but end the fight in this round.

He saw his opening and popped a straight right hand to the top of his opponent's left eye. Nielsen fell back against the ropes from the impact of the punch. The referee had seen enough and waved the fight off. Terry was awarded a TKO in Round 6.

Jeff made his way over to sit next to his sister-in-law during the middle of Billy Wagner's fight. He walked from the back of the crowd so he could pass his dad in the process. When he got to him he put his hand on his dad's shoulder to get his attention and said, "Hey, Dad; hello, gentlemen."

Bill turned and said, "Well, hi Jeffro," then went on to introduce him to his friends. They were all glassy-eyed and smelled of alcohol, making Jeff feel uncomfortable, so he excused himself and walked over to join Karen.

Terry and Doug joined them in the last round of Billy's fight. Billy had won most of the rounds and tried desperately to put his opponent away in the last round, but the old pro was able to end the fight standing. The house lights went on and the crowd was heading for the exits, most not waiting to hear the unanimous decision of the 10-round fight that obviously belonged to Wagner.

Terry was being congratulated by many friends and fans on the way out of the arena, including Don Elbaum who said, "Well done tonight, Terry! You and your manager stop by my office, and I'll take care of your purse tonight."

"You'll see this guy again in December!" he yelled out to the remaining crowd.

Later, Jeff learned what inspired Terry to turn up the heat in the fifth round of the fight when Terry said, "I heard Dad shouting from the crowd, 'Hit him like you mean it!' and I felt insulted. I know he was drinking and he made me feel like a *punk*. When the bell rang, all I wanted to do was take that guy's head off!"

Jeff could see the frustration in Terry's face and said, "Yeah, well Dad doesn't get a chance to see you fight in Dallas and you showed him what you can do in front of a Cleveland crowd. It could have been worse – it could have been you that went down instead of Nielsen."

Terry smiled, took a boxing stance and started throwing quick punches to his brother's head and body, stopping just millimeters short of his targets.

"Never happen, kid," he said while the two of them laughed and took shots at each other.

* * *

On December 15th, Jeff and his buddies were back at the Cleveland Arena along with Denny and Tom. Don Elbaum decided to place Doyle Baird as a co-headliner for the five-bout card. He wanted to give the Cleveland fans a little mix in the action with his popular middleweight.

Baird was scheduled to go on before Terry and was paired against another tough Cleveland middleweight named Earl Johnson. Johnson was undefeated in his last nine fights since 1969 while Baird had lost two out of his last five fights. But Baird's losses were against world class contenders – former Middleweight Champion of the World, Emile Griffith on a 10- round decision and in his rematch with Nino Benvenuti in Italy, by a TKO in the 10th.

Terry was in the heavyweight bout on the card and his opponent was Joe Byrd from Grand Rapids, Michigan. Doug was not overly concerned with him. He had been knocked out two months earlier by Tiger Joe Harris, whom Terry beat last September in Fort Worth. He still reminded Terry not to get careless, though.

There was action in each of the preliminary bouts and they had the boys on the edge of their seats. Denny especially liked a light-middleweight named Frankie Kolovrat. He was originally from

Yugoslavia, but now fought out of Cleveland, and had to remind the papers and announcers at the fights that his name was pronounced, "Cola – vart."

"Man, did you see how Kolovrat kept comin' in on his opponent?" Denny said to Jeff. "I love the way he doesn't give up; he just keeps punching and moving – that's the way I want to box!"

After the intermission, the Cleveland Arena announcer introduced each fighter, and did an excellent job creating an exciting atmosphere for the Cleveland fans. They cheered the loudest when Doyle Baird was introduced.

Baird took his traditional stance at the center of the ring in the first round, and both fighters traded punches with Baird taking command early.

"He's the guy I told you about in the Rubber Bowl a few years ago," Jeff said to the boys. "Baird is tough as nails!"

The fans cheered for the Akron fighter at the start of the second round. Baird charged out of his corner and Johnson kept his hands close to his head while shuffling to his left. Baird cut him off and surrounded him in a corner with a flurry of lefts and rights.

The ref gave Johnson two standing eight-counts in the round before calling the fight off at 2:02 of the second round. The crowd roared with approval as Baird went back to his corner. And when the announcer gave the results to the fans, Baird never smiled.

"See what I mean? That guy's a *real* badass!" Jeff said.

Terry and Joe Byrd entered the ring immediately after Baird and Johnson exited, to keep the crowd primed. Jeff, Denny and Tom led the loudest cheers from the audience. They wanted to see their brother do the same to his big opponent, and so did the rest of the Cleveland fans.

They were not disappointed. Terry looked as sharp as ever, commanding the fight the second the bell rang. At the end of the round, his corner man gave him a drink of water while Doug wiped his face and chest with a towel. He wasn't breathing hard and the boys knew their brother wasn't going to let the match go the distance.

They led the Cleveland crowd by yelling, "End it now Terry, this is *your* fight!"

Terry continued to pop the big guy from Michigan with jabs and took his time with the combinations. But with two minutes gone in the second round, he cornered his opponent and clobbered him with a barrage of left hooks and right uppercuts. Byrd's head lifted on one of the uppercuts and Terry finished him with a final left hook.

The crowd stood and cheered as the referee started his count, but it was obvious that Byrd was in no condition to get up. The ref finished his count of 10 anyway and said, "You're out!"

The boys jumped up and down and were slapping each other on the backs as Terry got his hand raised in victory. It was number 21 with 19 KOs under his belt.

Later in the locker room, Don Elbaum told Terry and Doug he wanted them to come back soon. He wanted Terry matched against Floyd Patterson or Jerry Quarry in Cleveland in the coming months.

"The Cleveland fans love him, and I'll make it a good-paying gig," he said. "Besides, you know Frazier is going to have to face up to Ali after Ali beat Bonavena in the Garden a couple weeks ago, and I wanna keep the fans glued to the heavyweights this year!"

On December 7th, Muhammad Ali knocked Oscar Bonavena down three times in the 15th round and was declared the winner by way of New York's "Three Knockdown Rule." The North American Boxing Federation (NABF), declared him its heavyweight champion, and Ali demanded Frazier give him a shot at his title.

"We've got some commitments with the promoter in Dallas, and Terry's got a few more hurdles before he climbs into the ring with either of them," Doug replied. "But we'll keep in touch, that's for sure."

Terry, Karen and Bret arrived in Dallas on December 20th after an early Christmas at the Daniels' house. They spent Christmas Day with Karen's parents, and then it was back to the gym for Terry.

In the first week of 1971, professional boxing grabbed the headlines of the sports pages throughout the world when Joe Frazier announced he would fight Muhammad Ali on March 8th. The fight would be held in Madison Square Garden and each boxer was guaranteed $2.5 million. The press was already calling it "The Fight of the Century."

Sue Moses wanted to capitalize on the boxing news and raised the bar again for Terry. She paired him with a tough black light-heavyweight out of Austin, Texas named Willis Earls. The 10-round bout would be one of two main events January 11, 1971 at the Memorial Auditorium in Dallas.

The day of the fight, an article in the *Dallas Times Herald* read: "Earls Says Daniels Not Ready for Bout" and stated, *"If I was handling Terry, I wouldn't let him fight me right now," Earls said.* The article went on to state: *He is the fifth-ranked light-heavyweight in the world with kayo victories over Joe Burns and Sonny Moore. Daniels failed to knock Moore out in 20 rounds.*

The day after the fight, an article on the cover of the sports section read: "Daniels Stops Earls in Fifth" and stated, *Terry Daniels took an awesome clobbering from Willis Earls for four rounds Monday night, then came back from the dead and destroyed Earls with three knock downs in the fifth to give him his most impressive win yet.*

Al Banks told Terry that he needed to continue to focus on not dropping his right so much. "Earls picked up on that weakness of yours right away and dropped you in the first round. You're lucky you're young enough to take a punch like his, but you'd better work on your defense harder or you'll never be able to take on Quarry or Patterson," he said.

Doug told him a few days later that Sue Moses wanted him to fight a guy who was one of the few to beat Joe Frazier in the amateurs, and held a draw with Jerry Quarry. "His name is Tony Doyle, outta Salt Lake City. Some say Angelo Dundee is lookin' to put him up against Clay, but I think you've got the experience to take a guy like him on now. And you certainly got the power to stand up to any fighter in the top ten," he said.

The fight was scheduled for February 22, and on the day of the fight Al told Doug that Sue Moses might have put "the whammy" on them as he showed him the article on the cover of the *Dallas Times Herald* sports section. The headline read, "It's D-Day in Ring, Daniels Faces Doyle Tonight" and there was a picture of Terry posing in the foreground in his trunks and gloves with Sue in the background pointing to the marquee of the auditorium. The black lettering read, "DANIELS VS CLAY."

"Ah jeez, she's jumpin' the gun a bit. She had that picture taken a month ago and said she would use it for publicity. I didn't think she'd use it for *this* fight," Doug sighed.

Later that night, Terry fought Doyle and gave it all he had, but lost a unanimous decision to the 18th- ranked heavyweight in the world. He was stunned and depressed afterward. Karen gave him an ice pack for his bruised face, realizing Terry felt defeated. She said, "Ah, Sweetie, he just out-boxed you tonight, that's all. At least you're not cut…oh, I feel just awful."

Terry put the ice pack on his left cheek and said, "My heart feels worse than my face. I'm gonna be 25 years old this year, Babe, and I'm gonna take a few days off to see if I really want to keep grabbing for that 'brass ring' on this merry-go-round."

She gently kissed his other cheek and laid her head on his shoulder and said, "You know I'm in your corner no matter what you choose."

CHAPTER 36

A package from home arrived in the mail for Terry a few days after the Doyle fight. When he opened it he found letters written to him from Jeff and Denny, and a 12" X 12" lithograph picture of Terry in a boxing pose on a yellow metal plate in a frame with black wire around the corners, giving it the appearance of a boxing ring. He said, "Man, this is beautiful."

He read Denny's letter first, because the picture was dated and signed by him. Denny, who was now 14, wrote that he designed it in shop class at school with the help of his instructor, and one of Terry's former classmates, Max Schoff. *I got an A on it, and Mom said she couldn't do better herself!*

He also wrote that he won his first amateur boxing match at Eastlake North High School, by unanimous decision. Terry got a little misty-eyed at the end when he read, *Don Bernard said I reminded him of you, but I told him nobody could be as strong as you. Love you Ter, Denny.*

Then he got inspired when he read Jeff's letter. In it he wrote: *We started the big intramural wrestling tournament after Christmas break. I was in the 175-pound weight class and hadn't wrestled since Junior High, but I won all four of my matches and made it to the finals. We had them at lunch time in the gym last week and the stands were packed!*

My opponent was our senior All-Conference halfback, Paul Rieger, and man was I nervous! I was hoping he wouldn't notice how sweaty my hands were when we shook at the beginning. But I remembered you telling us how nervous you were in your first Golden Gloves tournament in front of all those people and I did what you did – focused on the basics of what I needed to do to win. And I beat him 4-2!!

Terry smiled after reading the letters, and called them that evening. He told them how proud he was of each of them, and that even though he'd lost his last match he was inspired by them to get back in the ring. He didn't want to quit boxing after that loss. He knew he had the power and determination to beat the best on any given day. He promised them that he wouldn't quit at age 24.

He went for a long run in the park the next day, and when he finished, he drove to the gym and met with Doug.

"After two years in a row of wins, I'm going to continue to work hard this year," he said. "I'll quit when I lose two or three in a row, then I'll know God has other plans for me."

"Good. I think you can compete with those guys in the top 10," Doug said. "Doyle gave you a boxing lesson, but so what – it happens to every good fighter. If I thought you should throw in the towel, I'd tell ya', but I don't think now is the time.

"Frazier and Clay – I still can't call him Ali. Anyway, they got the whole world focused on boxin' and I know the fans in Dallas like watchin' you in the ring.

"I got a call from Sue Moses yesterday and she'd like to put together a card in April if we're interested. If you're serious about workin' hard, I'll start makin' some calls and find an opponent."

"Let's do it," Terry said. "I'll work on the heavy bag until Al gets here, then we'll go five or six rounds. He'll help me correct what I did wrong in my last fight."

The next evening, Doug called Terry at home and said, "I talked to the manager of a guy who fights outta San Antonio, named Bob Scott. He's a big white boy; stands 6' 4" and weighs 215.

"He said Scott was doin' time in a penitentiary in West Virginia and learned how to box there. He beat every guy in the gym and eventually was allowed out to box professionally. He said his fighter's had 75 amateur and pro fights, and only lost four of 'em. Of course, I'll verify that with the boxin' commission.

"Sue said it was my call, so I'm thinkin' we take this guy on and see how you do. She said she'd try and put another card together later in the month."

"Sounds good to me, Doug," Terry said.

"Oh, and one more thing," Doug said, "I also got a call from Elbaum in Cleveland. He said he would like to match you against Floyd Patterson sometime in May. I told him we'll see how you handle Scott and then let him know."

"Yeah, why not?" Terry said. "I'll be 25 soon, and it's time for me to take on the top contenders."

A few days later, on Friday, March 5th, Terry got a call from a reporter at the *Dallas Times Herald*. "I'm interviewing people in Dallas for this Sunday's edition; we're running a story on the big fight Monday with Frazier and Ali. Do you have a minute to give me an answer to a question?"

The following Sunday, Terry got up early and picked up a copy of the paper. He brought it home to read before they went to church. The headline of the sports section was titled, "Frazier Goes for the Whole Heavyweight Ball of Wax."

Before he started reading, he noticed a picture beneath the headline and said to Karen, "What's this, a new white fighter getting publicity?"

The photo had a man in his 20s wearing a suit and tie, making a muscle for the camera. A gentleman who looked to be in his 40s, also in a suit, was smiling and testing the young man's bicep.

Terry read the caption underneath: *New Orleans Saints head coach J. D. Roberts checks the valuable passing arm of his prize rookie quarterback, Archie Manning.*

He smiled and said, "Ah, for a minute there, I thought someone was muscling in on my territory!"

In the Frazier article, it stated: *Neither fighter has lost as a professional, Clay running up 31 consecutive victories with 25 knockouts since turning pro after winning the light-heavyweight gold medal in the 1960 Olympics, and Frazier gaining 26 victories with 23 kayo's after taking the heavyweight gold medal in the 1964 Olympics.*

Terry noticed that the Texas news media still referred to him as Cassius Clay.

It went on to say that their momentous fight would be live in Madison Square Garden and millions more would view it at 350 closed-circuit television sites in North America. There were also millions more viewers in other countries.

A small caption in the center informed readers where they could view the fight in Dallas: *The State Fair Music Hall with tickets at $12.50 each.*

Terry whistled after reading the price per ticket, then turned to page 3 to read the article by Jim Woodruff titled, "The Witness Stand: Frazier Gets Nod."

He wrote: *Members of a Dallas group predicted a long evening for Cassius when they took The Witness stand and were asked – How do you figure the Clay-Frazier fight will come out?* A few interviewed from the article are quoted below:

LUCKY JORDAN, Dallas Golden Gloves coach – My money is on Frazier.. Maybe a few years ago Clay could have handled him, but not now. I saw Quarry get to Clay and if he can, you know Frazier can. Ellis hit Frazier with some beautiful one-twos and he just kept coming. That breaks your spirit, and he'll keep coming against Clay too.

CURTIS COKES, former world welterweight champ – I lean toward Clay if the fight goes 15. He can outbox Frazier...I don't believe he carries the punch to knockout Frazier. If it goes less than 15, I think Frazier.

JACK COLE, *referee* – Gotta go with Frazier. He's too strong. I don't believe Clay has fought anybody that's carried it to him…Frazier is perpetual motion coming at you.

TERRY DANIELS, *heavyweight boxer* – I think Clay will win. I think he has the superior height, reach and strength to keep Frazier harmless…I think Clay has the gear to win…I know Clay appears to have a big mouth, but I've met him and I think all his mouthing is for publicity. Underneath, he's a pretty good guy.

PAT RILEY, *referee and former national Golden Gloves champ* – I think Clay will win it. He's too smart. He's too quick. He's going to cut him up and win.

JACK WOODRUFF, *referee and judge* – Frazier will beat him if Clay doesn't fight a lot better than he did against Quarry. Frazier has too much offense. Because of all that bobbing and weaving, I don't think Clay can catch him. And if Clay doesn't tag him early, Frazier will wear him down.

Monday evening, March 8, 1971, Madison Square Garden hosted the historic fight to over 20,000 fans, which included movie stars, recording artists, and popular sports celebrities. The news media estimated another 300 million would view it on closed-circuit screens in auditoriums in major cities around the world. Terry drove to Music Hall to view it.

Back in Willoughby, Jeff, Denny and their mother listened to "delayed coverage" on the radio. A short synopsis of each round was described by an announcer after a two-minute delay.

"Wow, I feel like we're living in the '20s instead of the '70s listening to the fight on the radio," Jeff complained.

"Yeah, I bet it was cool to listen to those famous announcers describing the action in the ring as it happened," Denny said. "It's too bad the only place to see it is on closed-circuit in downtown Cleveland – on a school night."

June looked up from her game of solitaire on the kitchen table and said, "I can remember when my brothers, Warren and Charlie, would listen to boxing matches on the radio. I think their favorite boxer was Rocky Graziano. He had a lot of fights in Madison Square Garden too."

Even with the delay, the boys were excited to hear the results of each round change from Frazier being the aggressor, then to Ali. They couldn't believe the action in the first 10 rounds. The announcer said he viewed the fight as, "extremely close between these two gallant warriors after Round 10!"

As they listened to the results of Round 11 the boys started to cheer – Frazier had landed a solid left hook to Ali that made his legs wobble. Denny said, "Yeah!" and threw a left hook to Jeff's head in slow motion. Jeff twisted his head and pretended to take the punch on the jaw, and the two of them started to shadow box.

"Okay, you two. Wait for that foolishness till after the fight ends," June said.

At the end of the 14th round, the announcer stated that Ali hit Frazier with a flurry of head punches and seemed to be taking command of the fight. The boys could only imagine how exhausted the two fighters must have been after 14 rounds.

June put the deck of cards aside and listened intently with Jeff and Denny for the results of the 15th and final round. They couldn't believe it when the announcer said, "Ali took several punishing shots to the head and body from Frazier, and Frazier knocked Ali down with a solid left hook! Ali got up at the count of four and took the standing eight-count before continuing the fight. His jaw was swollen from the deadly hooks that Frazier had thrown all night…We'll be back with the decision in a moment."

Terry watched and listened to the result live, along with several thousand other fans at Music Hall. The place exploded with cheers when the announcer, John Addie, read off each of the judges' cards

Jeff Daniels

and concluded by saying, "Winner by way of unanimous decision, and *still* the undefeated Champion of the World – Philadelphia's Smokin' Joe Frazer!"

* * *

On April 5th, the day of Terry's fight, a column by Blackie Sherrod appeared on the first page of the sports section in the *Dallas Times Herald,* titled: "Fistic Coming out Party." It was a story about how Bob Scott came out of prison to step into a ring with Terry Daniels at the Memorial Auditorium that night. The story had a picture of Scott from the waist up sporting a well-trimmed beard, wearing a suit and tie, and showing his large fist to the camera.

The story stated: *He was paroled last year after eight years behind the walls of a penitentiary in West Virginia. Since then, he has had 11 pro fights, won them all, nine by knockouts in the first round. He could find no sparring partners in Ohio, so they sent him to San Antonio…He's ready to let his fists make money; they've already made his freedom.*

At the fight, Karen sat ringside and watched her husband cut the big man down to size each round. Terry appeared faster and stronger than he did his last fight, and by Round Four Scott was slowing down.

"You're doin' great Terry, keep it up!" she yelled before the bell rang to start Round Five.

Terry could sense that his opponent didn't train half as hard he did for this fight, and decided to throw more combinations early in the round. Scott was breathing hard and lost the snap in his punches that he'd had in the first round. Terry saw his opening and took it, firing a strong left-right combination to Scott's head.

POW! His right fist thumped the top of Scott's left eye hard, and he crumpled to the canvas. The ref finished his count of 10 with a minute and a half left in the fifth round.

Doug rubbed Terry's face with a cold wet sponge and said, "That was beautiful, Terry. I think you could a beat anybody in this ring tonight!"

Karen hugged and kissed her husband as he stepped down out of the ring. He smiled and said, "I feel great, Honey! I told Doug to get me on Sue's next card, and then up to Cleveland. I'm ready to turn up the heat!"

* * *

The next day, back in Willoughby, Jeff had made arrangements to leave school early with two buddies at lunch time. It was April 6th, the home opener for the Cleveland Indians.

"How'd you get Mr. Heglaw to give us passes for early dismissal?" asked his friend, Billy Balante.

Ed Heglaw was the assistant principal at South High, and a strict disciplinarian. He rarely let students leave early unless there was a death in the family.

"I lucked out!" Jeff said. "First of all, I stopped by his office this morning and waited until his second cup of coffee. I knocked, even though the door was open, and he said, 'Daniels, what can I do for you?' in his gruff voice. I explained that my father had made special arrangements to spend some time with me and wanted to take to me the Indians home opener.

"You know he had Terry and Tom here at South before me, and he knows my parents are divorced. He also knows my dad still donates generously to the Boosters, so I guess I wasn't surprised when he said, 'Well, I suppose that would be alright, but be discreet about it. I can't let students know they can cut school for sporting events – even if it is the Indians' opener.'

"Then I pushed the envelope by saying that my dad offered to drive me and two of my friends to the game," Jeff said.

"Uh oh, here it comes," Billy said.

"When I told him it was you and Mark, he shook his head a little and said, 'Aahh, I don't know why I'm doing this.' Then he reached back in his drawer and pulled out two more passes!"

Jeff heard a voice behind him in the hallway say, "Typical Daniels luck!" It was Mark Visnick, their third man for the trip.

Jeff smiled and said, "Vis, you made it just in time, my dad ought to be here any minute. And what do you mean luck? Mr. Heglaw likes you guys!"

Mark was one of only a handful of juniors starting on the varsity football team. Mr. Heglaw favored him because he liked Mark's sense of humor.

Billy won Mr. Heglaw's confidence by recently being voted as having "The Most Team Spirit" in the school and would become next year's "Fighting Rebel" mascot.

At 11:45 a.m., the boys saw the hot green Shelby pull into the school parking lot. It was sunny with clear skies and in the mid-50s. The fourth-period lunch crowd was in the hallways and standing outside the opened exit doors. They got a look at the car as it pulled up.

"Oh, great," Jeff said to Mark as they climbed in, "so much for being discreet!"

Jeff introduced his friends and said, "We better make a hasty exit Dad, before Mr. Heglaw sees us!"

The boys were impressed with his dad's choice of transportation to the game. They especially liked it when he told them to open the coffee thermos in the back and each share in a shot of whiskey to prep for the cold spring weather.

"Detroit's gonna have their hands full today," Billy said as he slugged down a shot and passed the cup to Mark.

"You know it," Mark said as he took the cup. "Graig Nettles, Ray Fosse and Ken 'The Hawk' Harrelson are in the starting lineup – it should be a great game!"

When Bill pulled into the Cleveland Stadium parking lot he stopped to ask the attendant how much parking was.

A big man with a fist full of dollars said, "Two dollas, suh."

Bill said, "Okay," and put the money into the man's hand, but before he could add the money to his wad, Bill snatched the dollars back out of his hand and gunned the engine!

The boys were totally caught off guard with the joke and started laughing. They could hear the parking attendant screaming as Bill sped around two open lanes before slowing down.

He parked the car, and as they all got out, two parking attendants came running up to them and said to him, "Quit yo' foolin' around!"

Bill chuckled as he paid the man and said, "Sorry, just want to keep you guys on your toes."

He paid for the tickets and treated the boys to hot dogs and Cokes, but denied Jeff's request to buy them beers. "Not while you're wearing your varsity jackets and looking like teenagers out early from school," he said.

Jeff's father made it a memorable day for the boys, even though the Indians lost to the Detroit Tigers, 8-2. On the way back to their car, Mark and Billy said, "Thanks for everything, Mr. Daniels. I don't think we'll ever forget this opener!"

Jeff caught his dad's eye and knew that he still loved his kids.

CHAPTER 37

In Dallas, Terry was back in the gym working hard and sparring with several boxers. Doug came in while Terry was cooling down. He approached him and said, "I talked with Don Elbaum this mornin' and he has a contract for us to sign with Floyd Patterson. He said he was lookin' to have the fight early May, but Patterson hurt his hand in a workout a few days ago and is lookin' to make it for the last week in May instead.

"We're also booked for Sue Moses' card at the Memorial again on April 26th. I got an opponent for you – he's a club fighter outta Brooklyn named Freddy Williams. He should be a good tune-up for Patterson."

"That sounds good to me, Doug," Terry said.

That evening, Karen and Terry went out to dinner with another couple, and Terry shared the news.

"*The* Floyd Patterson? The one who's gunning for his *third* heavyweight championship belt?" his friend Bart asked.

Bart was a general manager for a large radio station in Dallas. His father owned the station and about 15 others. He heard Terry interviewed on his radio show one day, and offered to take him to lunch to get to know him better. Bart was the same age as Terry; single, and known as quite a playboy among the Dallas elite. They enjoyed each other's wit and soon became friends.

Before Terry could answer, they were interrupted by a third couple who approached their table.

"Sorry I'm late," said a tall, well-built man with a foreign accent. He was wearing a beige suit with black stripes, and a big-collared white shirt. He left the top three buttons open to expose his hairy chest.

They all stood up and shook hands as Bart introduced his friends to Terry and Karen. "This is my friend, Colin, and I'm sorry, I'm afraid I don't know your name, Miss," Bart said while looking at Colin's date.

"Oh, this is Linda," he said.

Bart immediately interjected, "You spell that, L-I-N-D-E-R," mocking Colin's accent as they all sat down.

Terry and Karen laughed as Bart continued, "Colin played for the Dallas Cowboys, and as you can tell by the accent, he's from Australia. He owns a company with Sue Moses' husband, called Club America."

"Terry told me a little bit about that company, but what exactly does Club America do?" Karen asked.

"We're a unique entertainment organization that people join for a yearly fee, which entitles them to participate in various things," he said. "We have a monthly magazine that gives them discount deals on clothing, restaurants, golf courses and tennis clubs. We even own a 707 jet that flies people to and from special trips that we offer."

"Colin, is this restaurant included in your deals?" Terry jokingly asked.

Colin smiled and said, "Afraid not mate, but I would like to buy a round of drinks for all of you who've graciously waited on us to get 'ere."

They placed their order for drinks and dinner. Then Bart said, "Terry's in training, that's why he ordered iced tea. He was just telling Carol and me that he will be signing a contract to fight Floyd Patterson in Cleveland, Ohio, next month."

"Oh, is that right?" Colin said. "Bern and Sue think you'll be a top 10 contenda' soon. I know you lost to a good fighta' back in February, but won by a knockout a couple nights ago. You're a good lookin' bloke with a darlin' wife – what are ya' doin' in a ring with the likes of Patterson?"

"Like I told my manager, I'm not sure how much longer I've got in this game, but it's time to take on the tough competition," Terry said.

"Well, that was quite a fight Frazier and Ali had last month. Ya' think ya' could stand their punches, as hard as *they* hit?" Colin asked.

"That depends on whether I hit them harder *first*," Terry replied.

Bart chuckled and said, "You know, Colin was in the '64 Olympics in Japan, the same time Frazier was there. You were on the Australian track team, right Colin?"

"Right mate, I was a high jumpa', but I didn't take a gold medal like Frazier. I didn't even get a medal, but I did clear seven foot on the bar – not bad for a six-foot-five Aussie galoot like me."

They enjoyed the rest of the dinner with laughter and good food, and at the end of their meal Colin said, "Why don't you all follow me over to a little bar across town and join me and Linda for a nightcap? I can introduce you to some of the Dallas Cowboys who visit there on the weekends."

Upon arriving, they noticed a long line, but Colin gathered the group in the parking lot and said, "It's okay, I'll have the feller at the door let us in. We can go up to the second level; it's where the celebrities gatha'."

The big bruiser at the door smiled after Colin whispered his message in his ear, and unhooked the velvet stanchion in front of the entrance. His eyes widened when he saw Terry.

"Hey, Terry, how you doin' buddy?" he said. "When's your next fight?"

"In a few weeks at the Memorial downtown," Terry replied.

"Great, I'll tell my friends to keep an eye out for the announcement in the papers. Good luck to you, man!"

The music got louder as they made their way into the bar – *Joy to the World* by Three Dog Night was blaring out to the packed dance floor.

Joy to the world,
All the boys and girls now!
Joy to the fishes in the deep blue sea,
Joy to you and me!

Colin led them through the maze of people to a thick carpeted stairway that had another big guy standing guard. The man smiled as he stepped aside to let the group proceed upstairs.

The upper level overlooked the dance floor below. It was dark and the only light came from florescent spotlights in the ceiling above. When they got to the top, Terry tried hard not to look at the waitress' short satin "hot pants." The florescent lights made their butts stand out like neon signs every time they bent over to take a drink order.

Colin was being flagged down by a table of guys and gals that he recognized, and they waded their way over to them.

The couples stood up and Colin shook hands while introducing Karen and Terry. "I'd like you to meet Craig Morton and Charlie Waters," he said. "Craig is the backup quarterback to Roger Staubach of the Cowboys and Charlie is a defensive back."

Karen and Terry each nursed a Coors and spent the last half-hour on the dance floor. At the end of the evening, Craig Morton grabbed a microphone from the DJ and made an announcement to the crowd.

"Hey everybody, I wanna call your attention to a young man and his wife on the dance floor," he said. "His name is Terry Daniels, and he is the 'Dallas Dynamo' heavyweight boxer that I'm sure you've all read about in the papers. He's got a fight at the Memorial Auditorium on April 26th, and I'd like you to give him your support by attending it. And after that, he's got a fight in Cleveland next month with the former Heavyweight Champion of the World, Floyd Patterson!"

The crowd cheered and applauded as Terry held Karen around the waist and waved to everyone. Craig gave him a smile with a thumbs-up and wished him good luck.

On April 26th, Terry beat Freddy Williams much the same way he had with Bob Scott three weeks earlier – with a knockout in the 5th round. His record now stood at 24-2-1 with 22 KOs.

Sue Moses was pleased with the crowd and the performance. She made arrangements a few months earlier to give Terry a weekly draw to cover his living expenses, and paid him a percentage of the gate to make up the difference when he fought in Dallas. The steady income allowed Terry to trade in his '66 LeMans for a 1970 Pontiac GT 37. "It was time to look and act like a pro," he told Karen.

The GT 37 was a scaled back version of the GTO. It came with four-speed transmission, dual exhaust, and a 326 V-8 engine. It was metallic blue with a white racing stripe and mag wheels. The car gave him the same feeling as the Shelby did when he stepped on the gas.

He had to keep his purchase locked in a garage at a friend's house, however, because he and his family were booked on a flight to Cleveland, May 16th for the biggest fight of his career. It was Terry Daniels vs. Floyd Patterson.

* * *

Terry, Karen and Bret took a shuttle from the airport to the Willoughby Holiday Inn, where they met Jeff and Denny.

"Dad let me barrow the station wagon," Jeff stated. "He said to say, 'Hello,' and would like to stop by the house when we're all home together."

"How are your mom and dad doin'?" Karen asked. "Are they talkin' to one another these days?"

"Yeah, they seem to have gotten past the anger stage and are communicating better than before. But, it's still a little weird – as you can imagine," Jeff said.

"Hey," Terry said; changing the subject. "It's great to see you guys. I know Tom said he'll come up for the fight, and I'm hoping we can see everybody while we're home."

Later they got situated at the Daniels' house, and after one of June's great meatloaf dinners, they relaxed with the usual game of cards before calling it a night.

Terry got a phone call the next day from Don Elbaum. He wanted to let Terry know about the publicity for the fight.

"I talked with a couple of guys from the papers and one of them wants to do an interview with you at the gym tomorrow," Don said. "He'd like to do a story about you growin' up in Willoughby and comin' from a wealthy family. Ya' know, college boy in a boxin' ring – that kind of stuff."

Don had been working the phones since Terry won his last fight in anticipation of seeing a big Cleveland boxing crowd follow his fight card. Terry had already handled two interviews by phone the week before – one from the *News-Herald* and one from the Cleveland *Plain Dealer*.

"Yeah, okay," Terry said. "I usually get there around 4:30."

"Can you make it around two? He wants to go from there and take some photos of you with your family. Oh, and the guy said he'd also like to interview your dad. Ya' think ya' could have him meet us there too?"

Terry paused for a second, and said, "Sure, why not? We'll see you there tomorrow afternoon."

He later told Karen about the interview and said, "I'm curious to see how Dad reacts to being interviewed before one of my biggest fights."

Terry called the fuel-oil office and got right through to his father. He told his dad about the interview at the gym. He said, "The reporter would like you there too."

"Me? What does he want me there for?" Bill asked.

"I guess he wants to know how *my father* feels about his son getting in the ring with a guy like Patterson," Terry said.

"Oh," Bill said and paused for a second. "Well, I guess I could. What time are you supposed to meet?"

"Two o'clock tomorrow at the gym. I'll pick you up at the office around 1:00 and we'll go together. You don't like driving into that part of Cleveland, anyway," Terry said.

Terry met his father at the office the next day. It was a balmy 74 degrees and they both wore casual attire. Before they left Bill said, "We're not driving the Shelby to the gym in Collinwood. Kids will be getting out of school soon, and I don't want the kind that lives in that neighborhood to see *that* car. We'll take my Buick."

Bill parked the car and followed Terry to the side entrance of the old drug store on 152nd Street. Terry opened the door and said, "The gym's on the third floor; we gotta go up two flights of stairs. I like running up them one step at a time to get my blood flowing. You're welcome to try and keep up with me if you can!"

Bill chuckled and said, "Lead the way, Ace!"

Terry grabbed hold of his gym bag and quickly picked his knees up while running up the stairs. Right behind him was his Bill, letting out a chuckle.

Inside the gym were Don Elbaum, Larry Wagner, a reporter and photographer from the *Cleveland Press*, and two heavyweight boxers. They were having a conversation when they heard thumping noises getting louder from the hallway stairs. They stopped talking and turned to see Terry and his dad charging through the open door of the gym.

Don Elbaum laughed and said, "What're you guys doin', playin' a game of tag?"

Terry chuckled and said in between breaths, "I always like chuggin' up that old flight of stairs before I workout, and I wanted to see if my dad could keep up with me."

"Looks like he did a pretty good job," Don said as he extended his hand to meet Bill for the first time.

The reporter asked Bill some questions while Terry got changed, then they watched Terry go four rounds each with the boxers in the ring.

"I'll be honest with you, this is the first time I've ever been in this gym," Bill said to the reporter.

"Your boy looks great," Don said. "We should have a good-sized crowd at the Arena next week. I'm sure he'll do fine."

"What does Patterson have to say?" Bill asked.

"We talked with him a few days ago and we'll have the story out about the same time we run this one," the reporter said. "He's not much for words – polite and quiet as usual. He said he's in good shape and thinks he can get his title back."

"I'm gonna work up a fight for the winner to take on Ali here in Cleveland," Don said.

Bill smiled and said, "Jesus, my kid could go up against Muhammad Ali? *This is crazy!*"

On the way home, Terry asked his father how he thought he looked in the workout today. Bill said, "You look good, Ter. I just hope you can handle a guy with so much experience."

"I can do it, Dad. You're going to the fight, aren't you?"

"Yeah, I've got some friends going too. Tom will be up from Athens on Tuesday and he plans on driving Jeff, Denny and their friends to the arena Wednesday night."

He pulled into the parking lot of the office, and as the two of them got out of the car, Terry said, "I've gotta meet the reporter and photographer over at the house. You're welcome to join us if you can."

"No, I've screwed around enough today, I've got calls to make. Let's get together for dinner Saturday night – you, Karen and the kids – we'll go to Hellriegel's Restaurant."

"Sounds good, Dad. I'll talk to you soon," Terry said.

On Saturday morning, Terry got Denny and Jeff to join him in a three-mile jog down the nursery road behind the golf course. He kept a steady pace and was surprised to see them both leading the way.

"Hey, this isn't a race to see who wins! I just wanna get my blood pumping," he said.

When they got back to the house, June had the sports section of the *Cleveland Press* on the kitchen table. "Look who made page one," she said.

The boys smiled at the picture the photographer chose to show with the article. It was one of many taken by the fence in the Daniels' backyard. It showed Denny and Terry in the foreground, sporting boxing poses on one another, with the rest of the family in the background against the fence. The caption underneath read: *TERRY AND THE DANIELS – Terry Daniels (right) gives some boxing tips to his brother Dennis while the rest of the family watches. In the rear are sister Debbie, brother Jeff, Terry's wife Karen and his mother, Mrs. June Daniels holding her grandson, Bret.*

The article, by Jim Braham, was titled: "A rich kid makes it in a poor man's sport." The article stated: *Terry Daniels, Willoughby's K.O. king, is sparring wearing a head protector, and the punches don't hurt as they will at the Arena. But the man standing by the ring winces when Terry gets hit, even in training.*

Bill Daniels, head of Daniels Fuel Co., a big man in Willoughby, still isn't accustomed to seeing his son get belted in the face. Boxing is not the career Bill Daniels had in mind for Terry.

"I didn't try to persuade him or dissuade him," the father says. "I just told him I didn't want him walking around with his head like this," Bill Daniels says, imitating a fighter walking around with his brains half-scrambled...

Terry Daniels, 24, a heavyweight with two years of pro experience, 23 knockouts in 27 fights, steps from the ring.

"I think I'll forgo the heavy bag," he says and he gives himself away. An intelligent, rich kid in a poor man's sport...Finishing college, working in the fuel company, the "conglomerate" as Terry calls it, are in the distant future, however. Boxing is his bag now.

The article continued on page 3, with the last two paragraphs stating: *Any young man who can beat Floyd Patterson can go a long way in this boxing business. Long enough to forget all about Daniels Fuel, the conglomerate, and the golf course in the backyard.*

This is why the rich kid is working out in the dingy gym, why the fuel company president winces when his son is hit, why the mother worries and the kid brother goes on squeezing those tennis balls.

"Wow, my friends are gonna love this," Jeff said. "But, 'a big man in Willoughby; the conglomerate' – why do they have to add that stuff?"

"Yeah, I know," Terry said. "In Dallas, they eat those comments up – it's all part of the publicity."

"Hey Terry, later on, can we go over to Tommy Morris' gym?" Denny asked. "I'd love to work out with you and have you meet some of the guys."

"Sounds good, kid," Terry said, imitating an old boxing promoter. "But right now, I want to eat a big breakfast, starting with a piece of Mom's left over meatloaf with a cup of hot tea!"

* * *

On Wednesday morning, the day of the Patterson fight, Terry went out to jog a few miles. He didn't sleep well and wanted to clear his head. Words from the press and other people in the business were wearing on his psyche: *It's the young kid against the old pro. Daniels was nine when Floyd won his first heavyweight championship belt…Floyd will win by knockout in round 3, predicts Dan Coughlin of the Plain Dealer…Patterson has knocked out many young fighters on his come back trail so far, and Daniels doesn't look any different.*

At South High, Jeff heard from everybody about the odds against Terry winning Wednesday night, including comments from teachers and coaches. He was encouraged from one coach, however, who knew Terry's outstanding athletic ability in football and trained with him in the ring from time to time – Coach Joe Topoly.

Joe was 40 years old and still had a good build from staying active in sports. His bent nose and a small scar on the corner of his eye were reminders of the many amateur fights he had growing up.

"I think these guys got your brother all wrong," he said to Jeff in the gymnasium during lunch break.

"I worked out with him at Tommy Morris' gym a few times, and when he hit me with that right hand of his, it felt like he had an iron bar hidden in his glove," Joe said.

A story of the fight was on the cover of the sports pages in every newspaper in the Cleveland area. The Daniels family got a kick out of seeing a cartoon character drawing of Terry and Patterson on the *Plain Dealer* sports page. The title was: "Daniels Ready for Big Chance – Patterson 3-1 Favorite."

Another drawing appeared in the *Cleveland Press*. It had Terry and Floyd in their boxing trunks waving to Chief Wahoo, the Cleveland Indians mascot. The title above it showed them saying, "Get on the bus, and leave the fighting to us!"

"There's more publicity for this Cleveland fight than any other one I can ever remember," Tom said to Terry after reading the morning papers.

"I know. I wish I could ignore it all and just climb in the ring and get it over with," Terry said.

By the sound of his voice, Tom realized how the hype must be wearing on his mind. This was his brother who taught him the techniques he had learned to become a good baseball player at age 5, how to keep score and trade baseball cards. The one who would read him stories with a flashlight when they camped out in the backyard together. And the one who included him in football games when he was old enough to throw the ball.

Now he would be watching his brother step into a boxing ring with a true world champion.

Terry made plans to take Karen out for a light dinner, then come back and rest up before heading to the arena around 7 p.m. They would drive separately while Tom would take his siblings and friends in the station wagon. The fights were to start at 8:15 with the main event expected to start at 10:15.

June made arrangements to go with her friends, the Burrys, and before the boys went to change clothes for the event she said, "I got you all the same color shirts to match Terry's robe and trunks. Tom will show you which pants to wear."

As Jeff held up a shirt he said, "Hot pink? *This* is the color of Terry's trunks?"

"Yeah, he showed them to me this morning," Tom said. "They're velvet with white trim, and are just a shade darker than the shirts. Pretty cool looking, actually."

The shirts were short-sleeved button down, and went well with black trousers. "I *guess* so," Jeff said reluctantly.

The boys arrived at the arena with their friends at 7:30 and each paid the $12 charge for the floor seats. "Sorry, the two tickets that my brother had went to our parents," Jeff said to his buddies.

There were four preliminary fights before the main event, and a young scrapper from Cleveland named Tap Harris got the fans revved up when he out-boxed his opponent all eight rounds of his welterweight fight. He now had a record of 12-0.

Frankie Kolovrat got the crowd cheering when he brought his record up to 14-0 by knocking his opponent down three times in Round Two and winning by technical knockout.

The remaining bouts were not as exciting, and after the intermission, everyone in the arena was ready for a good heavyweight fight.

The house lights went out and the ring shined brightly on the center floor as people quickly made their way back to their seats. Jeff's heart started pounding hard when he saw his brother being led to the ring by his manager and corner man.

The crowd cheered when Doug separated the ropes and Terry stepped onto the canvas, sporting his new dark pink trunks and robe.

Tom tapped Jeff on the shoulder and said, "You see what I mean about his choice of color?"

"Yeah, you're right. It does look pretty cool – *and* certainly different," Jeff said.

The fans kept cheering as Floyd Patterson stepped into the ring 30 seconds after Terry. He wore a white robe and trunks with black trim. His name was in script on the back of his robe and Tom told Jeff and Denny he felt like he was looking at a movie star. They agreed.

Floyd took a low profile when he arrived in Cleveland the day before, and did not hold a press conference with Terry. But there was no mistaking his face or hair style – neither one had changed in 20 years. He was 36 years old, but he still had the body of a 26-year-old.

The crowd didn't know it, but Terry told Doug he was so nervous he couldn't feel his feet. He said, "Floyd Patterson, the legend I've seen on TV and in the papers since I was a kid, is standing over there."

Doug kept his fighter focused by saying, "Keep that right hand up, pick your shots, wear him down and drop the big one on him."

The ring announcer got everyone's hearts pounding when he said, "Ladies and gentlemen, welcome to the main event of the evening!"

He read off the records of both fighters and stepped out of the ring when he was finished. The ref called the two boxers to the center of the ring and gave them instructions.

Terry did not make eye contact. He rolled his neck and shoulders quickly a few times and tightened his fists when the ref said, "Touch gloves, and return to your corners. Come out to the center of the ring when I instruct you to do so. Good luck, gentlemen."

Jeff told Tom that he felt like a cherry bomb went off in his stomach when the bell rang to start the first round.

The two fighters met at the center of the ring and Patterson was first to get off two stiff jabs, which Terry picked off with his right glove held closely to his face. The crowd cheered at the early action of the "old pro" and watched as he countered Terry's every move.

By the end of the fourth round, Terry hissed to Doug, "I can't get a clean shot on that son of a bitch! It's like he's got radar, like a bat – the instant I throw anything, he moves the opposite direction and counters!"

My Brother the Boxer

"He's watchin' for that right-hand bomb of yours. You got him nervous, I can see it in his eyes," Doug said. "When he ties you up, keep your hands up at the break. He's hittin' you with those cheap shots the second the ref separates you!"

Terry spit out his second gulp of water and said, "He keeps hitting me with those punches behind the head when we're tied up too!"

The bell rang for Round Five and Doug said, "Snap those jabs, and hit him with some quick combos!"

Tom, Jeff, and Denny were not used to seeing their brother get hit with so many counter shots, and when Patterson exploded from his "peek-a-boo" style stance they didn't like seeing Terry's face marked from the punches.

With 30 seconds left in the fifth round, Patterson attempted to tie Terry up again, and head-butted him in the process. Blood began to trickle down from the top of Terry's head, giving him the appearance of a cut above his left eye. The crowd booed when the bell rang and the ref did not even give Patterson a warning.

The corner man applied a wet sponge to Terry's head and dabbed a towel on the small cut on the top of his forehead. Jeff turned to see his mother and Phyllis Burry get up from their seats and make their way to the exit. June was crying.

Then Jeff saw his dad on the opposite side of the ring – busy talking to the men around him, with a concerned look on his face. The fight was now at its halfway mark, and Jeff felt that everyone around him wanted to see the "Gallant Warrior from Willoughby" turn the fight around. He said a quick prayer for his brother.

The next two rounds were close, and Terry was showing signs of exhaustion. Then suddenly in Round Eight, he got a second wind and the crowd cheered as Terry connected with an uppercut to Patterson's jaw. Jeff could hear a radio announcer at a nearby table against the ring say, "Daniels landed a solid punch to Patterson's face. I think there's blood coming out of his mouth, at least, I don't think it's Daniels' blood."

In Round Nine, Terry came out of his corner with the determination to throw a big right-hand bomb to Patterson's face. He obviously had his corner tell him he was behind in the fight.

Although Terry continued to show signs of weariness, the crowd cheered his gamesmanship as he led with his jab and followed with three-and four-punch combinations. Patterson deflected most of them, and then unleashed a powerful left hook to Terry's right temple, sending him down.

The ref ordered the former champion to a neutral corner before starting his count. Terry took his time getting up. He put his left elbow on his knee and pushed himself off the canvas at the count of seven. He shook his head in disgust.

Patterson continued to tie Terry up in the 10th round, sticking his head into his face and throwing short punches to the back of his head. Several fans booed the former champion as the ref let it continue.

The bell rang several times, ending the fight as the house lights came on. Terry's brothers were cheering the loudest from the side of the ring. Jeff looked around to see that very few of the 5,000 people had left the arena, but his mother's seat was still empty.

When the announcer came back with a unanimous decision in favor of Floyd Patterson, the crowd responded with a mixed chorus of cheers and boos. Jeff and his brothers followed Terry back toward the locker room, and before he entered the tunnel, he turned back to the scores of fans still chanting his name and raised his hands. He wanted them to know he was all right, and could stay with the best of them.

He heard whistles and cheers in return.

In the dressing room, Doug looked at the cut in Terry's scalp and said, "We better have you stop by the emergency room on the way home."

The next day, all the papers had the fight as the lead article on the cover of the sports page. The title on the *News-Herald* read: "Daniels Retains Title Dreams" and stated – *The Willoughby slugger, due to an accidental butting of heads, fought the closing five rounds under a steady stream of blood from a scalp cut that required three stitches.*

But Daniels, who plans to rest at his mother's house for a week, should be encouraged that he is the only fighter to go the distance in Patterson's comeback campaign.

"Floyd's knocked out three guys before this fight," said Doug Lord, Daniels' manager. "Terry fought a good fight, I'm proud of him."

Patterson also told Lord that Daniels landed several effective punches, one that cut the inside of the 36-year-old veteran's mouth.

The article ended with: *Nothing to be ashamed of is an excellent way of summing up Daniels' showing. He took a needed lesson from an old pro – and accepted it with class.*

He brothers felt that Terry had actually made the former world champion nervous, and caused him to stay defensive for most of the fight – *their brother*, the fighting Rebel from Willoughby South High!

His mother had a different opinion, however. "I was a nervous wreck!" she said. "I couldn't sit there and watch you bleed like that, I had to leave. How can you stand to be in such a vicious sport, Honey?"

"It wasn't as bad as it looked, Mom," Terry replied. "I couldn't get a clean punch in on him. I never fought anyone like that before. He had moves I'd never seen."

He later spoke with his father, who did not have any words of encouragement either. "I know you were nervous in the ring with that guy. Hell, who wouldn't be?" he said in a stern voice. "But you know how I feel about the boxing. What more do you have to prove?"

Terry lay in bed that night with his eyes open while his wife slept soundly next to him. He couldn't sleep because his mind raced in different directions. He got up and stood in front of the bathroom mirror and mumbled to himself, "My son is 10 months old – what kind of future am I setting him up with? Karen loves and supports me; my brothers and sister do too. My manager and the promoters want me to continue, and my friends are behind me 100 percent."

He relaxed back in his bed and recited the Lord's Prayer. Again, he asked God to bless him in the decisions he was making for himself and his family, and to guide him with answers. *I've got the support of two major U.S. cities. Why can't my own parents support me?*

The next day, he got a call from Doug in Texas. "I just got off the phone with the promoter in Houston. He's linin' up a couple fight cards for some time in July. He's talkin' about havin' Frazier headline one, and Ali the other, and wants you to be in the lineup too. It would give ya' six weeks, which is plenty of time for trainin'. The payday would be good for us too – what d'ya say?"

"I'll be back in Dallas next week – have the contracts ready," Terry said.

CHAPTER 38

On June 3rd, Terry, Karen and Bret gave their goodbye hugs to the Daniels family and flew back to Dallas. The scrapes and bruises on Terry's face had subsided, but he still wore sunglasses in the airport hoping to avoid any fans. He just wasn't in the frame of mind to talk about the beating he took from Floyd Patterson.

He rested over the weekend in the warm Texas sun and was back in the gym on Monday. When he strapped on his headgear to spar a few rounds, he realized it had been almost two weeks since he was in the ring – it felt good to get back.

He was focused on snapping his jabs and moving his head quicker. He waited for his sparring partner to be the aggressor for a few rounds and countered quickly on every punch, something he learned a few weeks ago from the "old pro."

When he sat down with Karen for dinner that evening, he told her how good his workout went, but he could tell something was bothering her. "Is something wrong, Hon?" he asked.

"Oh, I wasn't going to bother you with it, but I just don't know what to do," she said in a worried tone, leaning against the kitchen counter and looking away.

"Don't know what to do about *what?*"

"Well, before we left for Cleveland last month, I had gotten a couple of phone calls from a guy who wouldn't identify himself. I told him he had the wrong number, but he said he didn't, and called me by name. Then he started talking about how good I looked in the papers, and what he wanted to do to me if I'd go to bed with him."

"*What the hell?*" Terry said in voice that he realized sounded like his dad when *he* got angry.

"Now watch your language in front of the baby," she said while glancing over to young Bret in his high chair. She continued, "I hung up, but he kept callin' back, so I took the phone off the hook. But you know how it makes that annoying continuous beeping? I'd eventually hang it back up, and then he'd call back a few minutes later."

"Why didn't you tell me?" Terry said, still angry.

"I didn't want you to worry with the big fight comin' up and all. Besides, I thought I could handle it by tellin' him I'd go to the police if he kept callin' back, but a day would go by and he'd call again. And every time, he said if I told you or anyone, that somethin' bad would happen."

"That motherfu–" he said, catching himself.

"He gave me the creeps," she confessed. "I didn't even want to take Bret outside until you got home. And that's the other thing, he always seemed to call when you were not around, which made me think he was watchin' our apartment.

"Anyway, we left for Cleveland and I tried to forget about it. I was hopin' he'd get tired of callin' and gettin' no answer. But I got another call, about an hour before you got home this evenin'."

"Well, this shit's not gonna keep happening – sorry," Terry said while monitoring his response. "I know a few cops from the PAL that I can call. They'll know what to do."

"No," she said with concern in her voice. "If he sees any cops patrolling around, he'll figure out a way to get to me or the baby. Can't we just change our number and get one unlisted?"

"I'm not gonna go to all that trouble over a little puke that makes obscene phone calls to girls, *especially my wife*," he growled. "Besides, there are lots of people that need to get a hold of me for interviews or publicity. No, let me talk to a few guys and we'll figure it out."

"Well, okay, I'm really sorry about not tellin' you, Honey," she said with tears in her eyes.

"Don't worry, Sweetie," he said as he hugged her gently. "He won't call or do anything while I'm around. You can bring Bret down to the gym, and maybe ride the bike while I jog in the park until we catch this guy. He'll screw up soon. Creeps like that always do."

Several days went by without any calls and their cautiousness seemed to be paying off. Then on Friday afternoon Karen got another call. She quickly covered the phone and whispered, "Terry, it's him!"

"Are you there?" came the voice on the other end.

"Yes, I am, I thought you finally gave up on me," she said.

She covered the speaker while the guy started with his insulting remarks and Terry whispered back, "Tell him to come over, that I'm out for a while and you want to meet him."

Her heart started pounding, but she managed to interrupt the guy and said, "Look, you always seem to know when my husband's not around. So, why don't you come over for a few minutes and let's meet. I'm tired of listenin' to you *tellin'* me what you're gonna do."

The guy stopped abruptly and listened to her. Then he said, "Now you're wisen' up! I'll be over in a few minutes, Baby, and don't worry, I don't plan on hurtin' you."

She hung up and told Terry what he said. Terry looked out the kitchen window and sneered, "He must have driven by and saw that my car was gone. I dropped it off at the dealer for a checkup and jogged home this morning, remember?"

"Oh yeah, jeez, I'm a nervous wreck," she said. "What'll I do, I mean, what do you want me to say to him?"

"Just have him come in when you answer the door and I'll be waiting around the corner right here," he said while pointing to the hallway. "And don't worry; I won't let him do *anything*. This is gonna end *today*."

A few minutes later, there was a knock on the door. "Wow, that was quick," Terry whispered. "He must have been at a nearby phone booth. Let him in and I'll take it from there."

Her hands were shaking as she opened the door. Standing in front of her was a thin, brown-haired man wearing sunglasses. He was in his 30s and weighed about 150 pounds. And even though it was 80 degrees out, he had on a thin white jacket with the collar turned up.

He boldly stepped inside and said, "It's about time you wised up and let me tell you to your face what I'd like to do to you."

But before she could respond, Terry walked around the corner wearing a tight black t-shirt that accentuated his muscular upper body.

The guy turned pale white and the smile left his face when he saw him. He stammered while saying, "Whoa! Hey man, I'm not here for any trouble. I meant absolutely no harm whatsoever!"

He reached for the doorknob behind him and said, "I was only foolin' around, I promise I'll get out of your life forever."

Before he could step outside, Terry grabbed his left arm and said, "Where ya' going so soon, man? I thought you had a few words to say to my wife!"

Karen stood by Bret, who was busy gnawing on a large pretzel in his high chair. She said, "Don't do anything in here with the baby, Terry!"

The guy was shaking as Terry held his arm and cautiously walked him out of their apartment. They went toward the parking lot and the guy kept saying, "I would never do anything to harm your wife, I swear!"

Terry got him to calm down by saying, "I would certainly hope not, but you've been calling her and I want you to stop!"

He faced the man and rested his right hand on his shoulder while the man blurted out, "You got it man, I swear, no more calls!"

Terry said, "Good," and punched the guy in the stomach with his left fist. The guy let out a scream and doubled up; in the process, his sunglasses dropped onto the pavement. He turned to run and Terry grabbed the collar of his jacket, but the guy slipped his arms out of his sleeves and took off running across McKinney Avenue.

Terry threw the jacket down and took off after him. Luckily, traffic was light that time of day. The guy zigzagged across the streets to the park, and Terry, who jogs several miles per day, stayed right on his tail. He wanted to see how long it would take before the guy quit – he was gassed in a matter of minutes.

He made a pitiful attempt to climb over a chain-link fence, and Terry grabbed him by the belt of his pants and pulled him to the ground.

The guy got to his knees and was sobbing between breaths, begging for mercy. "Please don't hurt me. I swear you'll never see me again, please!" he cried out while clasping his hands for forgiveness.

"You pathetic piece of shit!" Terry said, and for a moment, he actually felt sorry for the guy.

"You're a skinny little worm of a man," he continued, "who probably couldn't satisfy any woman with your pathetic little pecker. So you have to get your rocks off calling them on the phone? How stupid are you to pick the wife of a heavyweight boxer?"

The guy was still sobbing with his hands clasped to his chin, and Terry paused, as if he was going to let him go. Then said, "Sorry," and slugged him with a short left hook.

Blood splat out from the gash Terry made above the guy's right eye when he hit him. He let out a horrible scream and rolled over on the ground while holding his hand to his eye. Terry let him get up and watched him run in the opposite direction.

"Don't let me catch you *anywhere* in Dallas you creep!" he yelled as the guy quickly disappeared.

Terry checked his left fist from the punch he threw and realized he had his wedding ring on. He mumbled, "I must have cut him with that – oh well."

When he returned to the parking lot, he picked up the guy's jacket and sunglasses. He felt in the pocket of the jacket and found a set of car keys – they belonged to a Chevy. "Fuck him," he said, and threw the jacket, car keys and sunglasses in the dumpster.

A few days later, Terry was taking the trash out and noticed a tow truck hooking up a white Chevy Impala in their parking lot. He looked at the driver and said, "Marshal Dillon's gotta keep this town clean!"

CHAPTER 39

On the Fourth of July weekend, Karen made arrangements with her parents to watch Bret while she and Terry spent a few days together with some friends. They were invited to stay on a ranch outside of Dallas that was owned by the family of their friend, Bart. The property was spread out over 100 acres, and was used frequently as a place to entertain celebrities. It had a stable for horses, a large swimming pool, and accommodations for many people. It even had an indoor movie theatre.

"We entertained Richard Harris here a couple weeks ago," Bart said to Terry. "He stayed here last year too when he was shooting scenes for a western he starred in. My dad made the arrangements with him and some of his crew."

Terry enjoyed the two precious days off from the gym. He and Karen swam and tanned at the pool all day, and then dined under the beautiful Texas sky at night with steak dinners hot off the grill. They stayed in a bedroom that had a plaque on the wall which read: "John Wayne slept here." It was a truly magical weekend. They had a blast.

It seemed to go by with a blink of an eye, and the following week Terry was back to work training. Doug told him, "The promoter's got Frazier doin' an eight-round exhibition split between Cleveland Williams and James Helwig at the Astro Hall. There are four fights on the card and you'll be the last one up before the champ.

"I got you paired with Clyde Brown, outta Memphis, Tennessee. He had a pretty good amateur career, and has four wins in four fights as a pro, with three knockouts."

"Any idea what he looks like?" asked Terry.

"He's black, six-one, around 200 pounds and I don't think he'll give you any problem. You know I think you're more experienced and better trained than any other heavyweight in Texas right now, Terry."

James Helwig, who was now under Doug's management, was hitting the speed bag and stopped when he heard that.

Doug smiled and said, "But Helwig's right on your heels."

The fight card with Frazier was scheduled for the following week on July 14th, and Terry got a call from his brother Jeff on the 10th. "I'd like to come down and visit with you, Ter," he said. "I had my appendix out just before the holiday and thought I might as well spend some time with you since I won't be working for a while."

"Hey, that sounds great, Jeff. I've got a fight in Houston in a few days, so why don't you hop on a plane and get here tomorrow? You can go with us. It'll be fun."

Jeff wasted no time catching a late afternoon flight to Dallas the next day. Terry picked him up at the airport and drove him directly to the gym for his last workout before the fight.

"Doug got a deal on some space downtown that's been vacant for years," Terry said. "It's actually Jack Ruby's old nightclub."

"Jack Ruby, the guy that shot Oswald?"

"Yeah, the Carousel, it was called. I guess it stayed open for a few years after he got arrested, but closed down not long after he died in '67."

Upon entering, Jeff observed stacks of tables and chairs against one of the walls which opened to a large floor. Two heavy boxing bags swung from chains connected to the smoke stained ceiling, speed bags were erected on wooden braces attached to an open wall, and a 16 x 16 foot boxing ring was set up on an old stage.

Doug talked with Jeff while Terry went to change in one of the old dressing rooms which had been converted to locker rooms.

"I moved into this place last year," he said. "The owners of the buildin' didn't want to put any money into fixin' it up and offered it to me free of rent. I just pay for the air conditionin'. How could I turn that down?

"Plus, it's a good location for my boxers. And when it's filled in the late afternoons, you'd never know it was a strip club years ago."

"If it wasn't for the ring on that stage, I'd never know," Jeff said.

Terry spent the first half of his workout doing squat thrusts, push-ups and sit-ups. Jeff quit trying to count his reps and marveled at his endurance.

The last half of his workout was spent sparring four rounds each with Helwig and Cookie Wallace. This was the first time Jeff had seen either one of the boxers he had heard so much about, and was impressed with how hard they worked in the ring.

Later, Karen cooked them a dinner of spaghetti and meatballs and told Jeff about her experience with the obscene phone caller. Jeff said, "Wow Terry, you let that guy come to your apartment?"

"I know, but I was so pissed. I thought if he was stupid enough to do it, I'd rather be home and ready for him," he said. "Anyway, there hasn't been a problem since, so that's enough talk about that.

"Hey, don't bother to unpack because we're all driving down in my car to Houston tomorrow. The promoter got us an extra room for you and Doug's son, Richard, so you'll be able to hang out with the pros for a few days."

"Oh, cool. So, Frazier is doing an exhibition with Helwig and another guy?"

"Yeah, Cleveland Williams, he fights out of Houston and has been in the ring since the '50s. He's fought some pretty tough guys over the years, and he's still built like a brick outhouse," Terry said.

"What time do we wanna leave tomorrow, Terry?" Karen asked.

"It takes about four hours, so let's plan on heading out around 10," he said.

"That sounds good to me. I'll help with the driving too," Jeff added.

After several stops along the way, they checked into the hotel by the Astrodome. The promoter had scheduled a press conference at the Astro Hall at 5 p.m. and Jeff accompanied his brother while Karen entertained Bret at the pool.

Most of the questions from reporters were directed toward the champ, and Jeff watched as Smokin' Joe smiled and answered each of them. They were mainly centered on his condition and health, but when one reporter informed him that Muhammad Ali was due in town tomorrow for his upcoming fight with Jimmy Ellis, Joe replied, "I don't care, as long as he don't come around here shootin' his mouth off!"

Terry was asked by one reporter if he had learned anything from Floyd Patterson and he replied, "I'm physically able to go toe-to-toe with anyone in the ring, it's my mind that holds me back sometimes. That's what happened to me with Patterson – I psyched myself out. I learned a lot, though, and I'm ready for action this Thursday night in the ring."

Later that evening, Karen accompanied Terry and Jeff to the hotel lounge, where a live band was playing the latest hits. The lead singer was a Latino girl who belted out song after song, and before their second break, she asked everybody to get up and dance to Tina Turner's version of *Proud Mary*.

When she got through the slow part she said, "I'm gonna need a little help with the rest of this song, and let's see if I can get this man to help me. Ladies and gentlemen, let's welcome the Heavyweight Champion of the World, Mr. Joe Frazier!"

The crowd applauded as Smokin' Joe grabbed another microphone and sang along with her:

Big wheel keep on turnin',
Proud Mary keep on burnin'.
Rollin', Rollin', Rollin' on the river!

Terry and Karen were dancing while Jeff applauded and shouted to Terry, "Wow, this is something else! The guys back home are never gonna believe this!"

When the song ended, everyone cheered, and Joe graciously thanked them and left. Terry said it was curfew for him too and they all headed back to their rooms.

Jeff heard the TV going in his room as he entered and met Richard Lord for the first time. Richard was 16 years old, had short, dark hair and wore a smile on his face – just like his dad.

They hit it off the minute they met, and when Jeff told him that he just heard the champ sing in the lounge, Richard said, "I was talkin' with his corner man this mornin'. I'll see if I can get him to introduce us to the champ tomorrow."

Jeff said, "Wow, a chance to meet the Heavyweight Champion of the World. The hits just keep on comin'!"

* * *

After breakfast the next day, Richard made good on his word and introduced Jeff to Frazier's corner man. "Hey, Little Richard," the man said while giving them both a new jive handshake. "I'd be happy to introduce you to the champ, but he just left to meet with some friends across town. I do have a couple autographs I could give ya' though."

He reached into the pocket of his sport coat and pulled out two autographed postcard pictures of Smokin' Joe in a boxing pose. "We keep a few of these handy. He don't like to be bothered with the public always lookin' to get 'freebies' from him."

The boys thanked him and said they looked forward to seeing him the next night. Later, Terry told Jeff about Muhammad Ali being in town and said, "He's at a gym nearby. You wanna go and watch him workout?"

Ali had arrived in Houston to prepare for a 12-round fight with the former champion, Jimmy Ellis. The fight was scheduled for July 26th, and was to be held at the Astrodome. After resting from his brawl with Frazier, he did an eight-round exhibition in Dayton, Ohio, in June, and had just finished a seven-round exhibition in Charleston, South Carolina.

Terry was able to get them in to see "The Greatest" do his magic in the ring amongst a small crowd of reporters and spectators. Jeff was eager to see him live after watching him on television for so many years.

"He's incredibly fast for his size," Jeff said to Terry. "I see how he can truly, 'Float like a butterfly, and sting like a bee!'"

Ali ended his workout with three minutes of skipping rope, and before he was finished, a young man grabbed a microphone off a table by the ring. He turned it on and said, "Ladies and gentlemen, in the ring is the *former* Heavyweight Champion of the World, Muhammad Ali!"

The crowd chuckled as Ali dropped his rope; jumped out of the ring, and comically ran after the boy. His eyes widened and his mouth was open while yelling, "I'll show you who *the champ* is!"

Terry and Jeff learned that the young man was Jimmy Ellis' younger brother. Jeff said, "Hey, the kid is just sticking up for his big brother!"

On fight night, Jeff and Karen sat six rows back from ringside and watched Terry struggle in the first two rounds with his opponent, Clyde Brown. Brown had a stiff left jab and moved like Ali in a way. By the end of the third round, Terry had developed a bruise under his left eye.

"You're droppin' your hands too much," Doug said to Terry in the corner. "Focus on slippin' off his jab and set him up with a left uppercut."

The bell rang for Round Four, and Jeff couldn't stop his palms from sweating while watching his brother fight. No matter how much he believed in Terry, there was never a guarantee of the outcome. Karen didn't help by squeezing his arm every time her husband took a shot to the head.

With 1:36 left in the round, they saw Terry lead with a left uppercut and release a thunderous right hand to the jaw of his opponent. Jeff saw Brown's eyes rolling around in his head as he went down on the floor. The ref counted him out and the bell rang, giving Terry another victory.

The crowd roared louder than they had all night, and Karen and Jeff were leading the cheers. Brown had to be helped from his corner to come back to the center of the ring while the announcer boomed over the P.A., "The winner, by a knockout in Round Four – from Dallas, Texas, Terr-eey Dann-yels!"

Back in Terry and Karen's apartment in Dallas the next night, they watched footage of the fights on the evening news. The reporter said, "Two boxers from Dallas stole the show in Houston last night when Terry Daniels led with a knockout of his opponent in Round Four, and later, James Helwig actually gave the champ, Joe Frazier, a bloody nose in their four-round exhibition match!"

Jeff flew home two days later with a smile on his face. He looked out the window at the clouds in the air and seemed to be reliving everything that had happened to him in the past week. Then he grabbed his carry-on bag and desperately checked the pocket for something.

As he pulled out the autographed picture of Smokin' Joe Frazier he whispered, "Nope, it wasn't a dream – it really happened."

CHAPTER 40

On July 18, 1971, two days after Jeff's visit with his brother and sister-in-law, Terry called the family with more news.

"You guys aren't gonna believe this," he said. "I'm on the Ali/Ellis card at the Houston Astrodome on July 26th! Doug talked with the promoter and Ali's camp after the fights last week, and they told him they wanted Helwig and me to be in the preliminary bouts. He said Ali specifically requested *me* to be the fight before the main event!"

His siblings were elated with the news. Their big brother, at the age of 25, was going to be in a boxing ring before thousands of people for the biggest pro fight of his career. *And* on the same card as Muhammad Ali!

"I was also told that my fight will be included on closed-circuit TV with Ali's, so you'll be able to see it in Cleveland," he added.

"That's awesome, Ter. Who's your opponent?" Jeff asked.

"Manuel Ramos, he's the heavyweight champion of Mexico. Tell Denny to look up his record in the boxing encyclopedia I got him last Christmas."

Once they hung up the phone Jeff and Denny went immediately to the book. They were good at finding the history of boxers in *The Ring Boxing Encyclopedia*. It was the industry standard for researching information on professional boxers.

"Wow, Terry's got his work cut out for him with this Ramos guy," Denny said as he looked up his stats.

"He's four years older than Terry, stands 6' 4" and has been a pro since '63. He's been in the ring with some tough boxers – he beat Ernie Terrell in '67, lost to Frazier in '68 and beat Tony Doyle, in '69. That's the guy Terry lost to back in February."

"Yeah, but Terry's in great shape," Jeff said. "You should have seen him knock that guy out last week. The crowd went ballistic! I'd say that Ramos will be the one to have his hands full."

The day before the fight in Dallas, Karen had elected to stay home with the baby while her husband took to the Houston Astrodome battlefield. Terry's friend Bart had made arrangements to fly the two of them on the new Southwest Airlines.

"I like their stewardesses better," he said to Terry while boarding the plane.

"I see what you mean," Terry replied as he stared at the shapely girls in their "hot pants" walking up and down the aisles.

The hotels were full to capacity near the Astrodome, and the promoter had two rooms reserved for Terry. They were on the top floor and learned that Ali's room was three doors down.

"I guess you're movin' up after all, Daniels," Bart jokingly said.

When fight night arrived, Terry's brothers met up with their buddies at the Palace Theatre in downtown Cleveland to see the bouts on closed-circuit TV. The place was packed with boxing fans. The boys' father was nowhere to be seen, but no surprise to them. He didn't care for that kind of crowd anyway.

They were thrilled when they saw Terry on the big screen, and they began to cheer loudly when they saw a close-up with his name. The morning papers had a small article covering the fight, and stated: *Terry Daniels, who fought Patterson at the Arena a few months earlier, is also on the card. Cleveland fight fans will be watching to see if he learned anything from the lessons the old pro gave him.*

Terry's brothers felt like they were cheering for the underdog after they overheard doubtful fans suggest he wasn't ready for the big time.

Jeff Daniels

Jeff's stomach was in knots as the announcer introduced Terry to 35,000 people under the bright lights of the Houston Astrodome and the millions watching on closed-circuit TV. The bell rang and Terry came out of his corner in the first round with hands held up close to his head. Ramos got the first jab in, but Terry quickly countered with two of his own. With two minutes gone in the round, he hit Ramos with a left-right-left combination, snapping his head back.

The Daniels boys led the cheers in the crowd when they saw blood smeared on the end of Ramos' nose. Terry was not backing down from his bigger opponent and stayed in command right up to the bell ending the round.

In the middle of Round Three, the crowd let out a roar when Terry decked his opponent with a solid overhand right. Ramos got up at the count of four and nodded that he was OK after the standing eight-count. Jeff yelled for Terry to take him out, and by now, the people in the seats around them knew who they were.

Instead of tearing into him with a flurry of punches, however, Terry took his time and kept his guard up. Jeff felt a tap on his shoulder and the man behind him said, "That your brother?"

"Yeah, us three are Terry's brothers," Jeff said while pointing to Tom and Denny.

"I thought so. I could tell. You look like him. That boy is pickin' his shots and he's lookin' way better than he did against Patterson," the man said.

Terry knocked Ramos down again in Round Six, but the tough Mexican got up and finished the round standing. The announcers were impressed with Terry's boxing ability. They said he was in complete control of the fight.

When the P.A. speakers boomed, "This is the 10th and final round," the Cleveland crowd in the theater was joining Terry's brothers and friends in rooting him on.

"Terry looks awesome, doesn't he, Jeff?" Denny asked.

Another combination by Terry put Ramos against the ropes, and Ramos desperately used his long arms to tie him up. The ref separated them and Terry threw a stiff left jab that caught Ramos square on the nose. Speckles of blood splat out onto the ref's shirt.

The crowd in the theater heard the bell ring several times ending the fight as Terry was hitting Ramos with a flurry of punches. There was no question who won the fight.

When the announcer read the judges' decisions and said, "The winner, by unanimous decision, from Dallas, Texas, Terry Daniels!" the speakers in the theater boomed with the cheers from the crowd in the Astrodome. Jeff and his brothers were slapping each other on the backs, and were being congratulated by people around them. It appeared that Terry had proven his worthiness to the Cleveland boxing fans.

* * *

In the main event, Ali looked sharp as ever as he hit Ellis with some punishing blows in the sixth and ninth rounds, ending the fight in the 12th. The ref stopped it when Ellis showed that he could not continue, and awarded Ali the victory via technical knockout.

After the fights, Terry, Bart and an entourage from Dallas joined a private party back at the hotel. Among the many guests enjoying the cocktails and hors d'oeuvres in the conference hall was Yank Durham, Joe Frazier's manager. He approached Terry and introduced himself.

"I'm putting together a card in the Houston Coliseum next month, and I'd like to know if you would be interested in headlinin' it," he said.

"Sure!" Terry said, "My manager's right over there. Let me get him and the two of you can talk."

An hour later, Terry excused himself to go back to his room for a quick change of clothes. A guest, who had a little too much to drink, spilled a rum and coke on his pant leg. He got on the elevator and pushed the button for the top floor, when a voice called out, "Hey, hold that elevator!"

A man in a flashy white suit, carrying a briefcase stepped in, and behind him was Muhammad Ali. Ali smiled at Terry and said, "You looked good tonight, Daniels. I told people that next to me, you're the prettiest boxer in the ring!"

Terry smiled, shook his hand and said, "Thanks Champ, I'm doing my best to protect this face, but it's not easy. Are you leaving the party so soon?"

"I don't drink and I'm tired," he said. "I'm either in the ring, or got somebody shovin' a microphone in my face and askin' me some foolish question. I leave early tomorrow mornin' to go back and see my family, then I got some exhibitions in Caracas and Spain next month."

The elevator door opened and they walked down the hall together. Ali went to his door and said, "I like Texas, Daniels. I'll give ya' a call when I'm in town again."

The next day, on their way back to Dallas, Terry told Bart about the conversation with Ali. "Hah, I knew it," Bart said. "You're getting closer to the brass ring, Terry!"

"Yeah, well Doug told me he talked with Frazier's manager about getting me to headline a fight card he's putting together next month. He wants Helwig on it too. We're still workin' our way up the ladder, buddy," Terry said.

Two weeks later, Doug gave Terry the details about his opponent. "You'll be up against a guy named Jack O'Halloran," he said. "I checked him out; he's from New Jersey. He's a big guy; stands 6' 6" and weighs 265 pounds – they call him 'Giant Jack' O'Halloran."

"Yeah, I guess!" Terry said.

"Well, I don't think he's *that* tough. He's got a record of 19-12-2 with 9 KOs, compared to your 26-3-1 with 24 KOs. He may have the size and reach, but I think you've got the power to knockout any guy in the ring with that right of yours. Besides, Durham thinks you can handle him, too. Just concentrate on the basics like you did this last fight, and you'll do just fine."

Four days before the fight, Terry was sparring with Al when he caught one of Al's left hooks to his rib cage.

"Aahh!" Terry grunted, and backed up holding his side.

"Time!" yelled Doug. "What's the matter, Terry?" he asked.

"My rib's been bothering me."

"Okay, that's it for the day. Lemme take a look at it before ya' hit the showers."

Doug examined him as closely as he could and said, "It's a little black and blue, and from the looks of it, I'd say you might 'a bruised it. He didn't look like he hit you any harder than usual. Did you hurt it last week?"

"Oh hell, I was out on my motorcycle and took a spill over the weekend, and when I went to bed that night it hurt every time I rolled over on it. I'll be okay." Terry said.

"I told you, you're gettin' too old for that thing. We oughta get you x-rayed."

"No, forget it," Terry said. "Just tape it up good tonight, I'll take it easy until the fight. I don't want to cancel it if they find something in the x-ray, Yank's counting on me. I'll keep my elbow tucked in, and try to knock him out early."

The next day, Yank had the boxers in front of the cameras for pictures in Houston. He had them taken with him in the middle, and another with the boxers facing each other for the fans' program and the newspapers. O'Halloran towered over both of them, so Doug asked the photographer ahead of time to take the shots from the floor looking up. "That way, 'The Giant' wouldn't look so big in the picture," he said.

Terry went back to his hotel and tried not to think about being eye level with O'Halloran's hairy chest. To set his mind at ease, he did something that the guys would laugh him out of the gym for. He propped himself up on his bed, got out a couple of knitting needles, a ball of yarn, and started to knit.

A few weeks prior, he had taken lessons from a woman at the Methodist Church in Dallas. She told him that learning to crochet would be good therapy and would take his mind off things that could make him nervous before a fight.

He decided to give it a shot, and within a few minutes found himself knitting row after row. He didn't have anything in particular in mind. He was only interested in mastering the basics. When he stopped, he looked at his watch on his dresser and realized an hour and a half had gone by. He was amazed at how focused and relaxed he was.

The next morning he took the tape off his rib cage and rubbed his hand over his bruised rib. It was still tender, but better than a few days ago. He had a strategy and was sticking with it no matter what. It was fight night.

James Helwig got the crowd cheering early when he knocked his opponent out in the first round of their scheduled four-round fight. It was Helwig's third pro fight as a heavyweight and he brought his record up to 3-0 with two knockouts.

The other two fights were in the middleweight division, and the results were mediocre decisions. The 4,500 fans at the Houston Coliseum took a 15-minute break and came back looking for a brawl between the two heavyweights in the main event.

Yank was standing ringside with a big grin on his face while the announcer welcomed the crowd to the main event. The cheers started when O'Halloran entered the ring, and then elevated when Terry entered sporting his velvet "hot pink" robe and trunks.

The fighters stood at the center of the ring while the ref gave them his instructions. Doug looked at the difference in height for his boxer and said to his corner man, "Those ring lights make that guy look even bigger!"

The fighters traded punches throughout the first two rounds, and when the bell ended the third round, Doug asked Terry in the corner, "Did that hook hurt ya' in the last minute of the round?"

"Yeah, a little," Terry said. "I'm having trouble connecting with my right because the son of a bitch is so tall."

"Well, you're scorin' with that jab to his belly. Double 'em up and follow with some short right hooks," Doug said.

The bell rang for Round Four, and Terry stuck to his strategy. O'Halloran's corner must have told him he stung his opponent with the left hook to the body, as he kept up the heat with his body shots.

With a minute and a half gone in the round, O'Halloran caught Terry with a short left hook to the head and followed with another to his rib cage. Terry went down on the canvas.

The ref ordered O'Halloran to a neutral corner and started his count. Terry got up to one knee, and stood at the count of seven. The ref looked at Terry's eyes and said, "One more time is all I'll allow you to go down, son."

O'Halloran attacked when the ref said, "Box," after the standing eight-count, and hit Terry with a flurry of combinations. Terry covered up and deflected most of the punches, but the ref stepped in and waved the fight over. O'Halloran was awarded the TKO 4.

Back in the locker room, Terry didn't say much to Doug. He didn't have to – the pain was obvious. Doug felt his fighter made the right decision and didn't want him to feel any worse than he already did.

When Yank found out, he agreed but felt disappointed. He knew Terry's potential and wanted to see him "bring the big man down," like everybody else. But he understood and appreciated Terry's decision not to cancel at the last minute.

Over the next two weeks, Terry worked hard running three and four miles a day, and wore protective gear on his stomach when he sparred. He was feeling better, and was preparing for another match with the tough Sonny Moore on September 30th.

Doug told Terry, "Sue Moses said the fight is sanctioned by the Texas Boxing Commission as the 'Texas State Heavyweight Title' and she's really lookin' for a win outta you. I got a call from Don Elbaum in Cleveland too. He's puttin' together another show in October. He's gonna get back with me on your opponent. So keep workin' hard boy, you still got a lotta fight left in ya'."

Sue was pleased with the turnout for her boxing card. She knew the Dallas crowd wanted to see Terry overcome a loss and get back in the winner's circle. They were not disappointed. Terry and Moore fought to the end of a 12-round slugfest and Terry was awarded the win by a split decision.

"It was close, but *my* boy clearly won the fight," Doug told the reporters. "He leaves for Cleveland in two weeks for a fight with a top contender in the Cleveland Arena, and then we've got plans for Europe."

* * *

The fight card in the Arena was scheduled for October 19th, and Terry flew in three days early with Karen and Bret to visit the Daniels family.

"Wow, Terry, you let your hair grow; you look really cool!" Jeff said when they came in the front door. In 1971, the hair styles for men were the longest they had been in decades in the States. It all started with The Beatles in 1964, and the U.S. teenagers kept pushing the envelope with their parents each year. Jeff noticed Terry also wore bell-bottom pants and a wide-collared shirt, to keep the fashionable look of the '70s.

For black men, the Afro-styled hair with sideburns was the look made popular by the movie *Shaft* and other black entertainers. Jimmy Ellis sported the look when he fought Ali a few months earlier. If boys could grow sideburns and let their hair grow they were considered cool.

After dinner, Denny got out the boxing encyclopedia and looked up Terry's opponent, Ted Gullick.

"It says his record is 17 wins and two losses, with 14 knockouts at the end of last year." Denny said. "Don Bernard told me Gullick was a Golden Gloves National Champion as a light-heavyweight too."

Terry smiled and said, "Is that right? Well, I need to beat a national amateur champion in my career, so now's as good a time as any."

The next day, Terry took young Bret with him to visit his dad at the fuel-oil office. They were greeted by his Aunt Sal at the front desk, and she immediately wanted to hold her nephew.

"He's gotten so big! How old is he now?" she asked.

"He's 15 months," Terry said.

"Oh, he is so cute. I seem to remember you were a bit bigger at that age, though."

His father came out of his office and said, "Hey, Ace, good to see you!"

Terry smiled and said, "Likewise, Pop! I see you've got one of my posters on the front window. Tom called me in Dallas last week to wish me luck and said he was stuck down at school in Athens. But *you're* planning on going aren't you?"

"Yeah, I'll be there. I guess everybody wants to see if you can do better than you did against Patterson," Bill said with a harsh laugh. "This black guy you're fighting is pretty tough I hear. The paper said he's ranked in the top 10 – you think you can handle him?"

Terry didn't feel comfortable the way the conversation was going, but politely responded, "Sure. I'm in the best shape of my life. Hey, is Grandma Clara home? I'd like her to see Bret while I'm in Willoughby."

"Yes, she just got back from shopping a little while ago," Aunt Sal said.

Terry sighed and held Bret in his arms, walking across the street to the house that his Grandpa "Doc" built in the '30s. As he walked up the blacktop driveway, he thought of the conversation with his father and said to Bret, "Why couldn't he just say, 'You look good, son. The boys saw you on closed-circuit in front of millions of viewers and said you had a great match. I look forward to watching you get revenge in the Arena.' Nope, not *my* Dad. Why can't he just support my dreams?"

After spending some quality time with his grandmother, Terry dropped Bret off at home and headed over to South High. He had an appointment with a reporter from the *News-Herald*.

Mr. Heglaw met Terry at the main office and escorted him to the choir room. The reporter learned that Terry was in the choir his senior year of '64 when they placed in the top 10 in the state competitions. He wanted to do a story about a "choir boy turned heavyweight boxer" from Willoughby who would be stepping into a boxing ring the next night.

After the interview, he spent time catching up with his choir director and some of his other teachers. He made one more stop at the coach's office and met with Jeff and the rest of the Rebel football team to wish them luck in their game Friday night.

The article appeared in the paper's afternoon addition the next day with Terry's smiling face shown singing in a choir robe. It was on the front page of the sports section. The headline read: "Daniels – Melodic Boxer." In the story it stated: *Daniels fists, not his vocal chords, will be on the line tonight against heavyweight Ted Gullick at the Arena. Like preceding many of his professional 32 bouts, Daniels is exhibiting the same confidence that's helped him triumph 27 times (24 by KO).*

A crowd of 3,500 attended "Fight Night at the Cleveland Arena." Back in his dressing room, Terry was trying to keep his mind off the fight by talking with his new trainer and corner man – his boxing buddy, Ronnie Wright.

Ronnie had hung up his gloves as a fighter the end of '69 in exchange for a job as a claims adjuster in Oklahoma City. The constant travel around the surrounding states eventually took its toll on him, however, and he left the position and moved back to Arlington in August 1971.

Doug heard about him moving back to Fort Worth and asked if he'd be interested in being Terry's trainer/corner man. Ronnie said he would love to, and the two of them flew into Cleveland that afternoon for the bout. Terry thought it was a good move also. Ronnie seemed to know just what a boxer liked to talk about before a fight.

At the intermission, Jeff stood in the concession line with his good friend Chuck Mehalic and his brother Johnny. Neither of them had seen Terry fight before. "Terry ever given you and Denny any pointers, Jeff?" asked Johnny.

"Yes, on occasion," Jeff said, "but Denny's the one that's been going to the gym in Wickliffe. He's doing pretty well too. I might have some time to join him after football ends.

"Hey, maybe we all go together and start a gang," he said jokingly. "I'll be the leader – Jeff 'Boom-Boom' Daniels!"

The boys laughed and Chuck said, "How about you concentrate on opening me up some running room on the line tomorrow night, Boom-Boom?"

The house lights dimmed while the boys made their way back to their seats. The bell rang several times as the Arena announcer grabbed the microphone and said, "Ladies and gentlemen, welcome to one of the main events of the evening!"

Jeff and Denny saw their dad earlier when the lights were on. He was several rows back from ringside on one of the floor seats. The boys' tickets were for "General Admission," but were on the front row of the first level. They had a clear view of the ring, and once again their hearts beat faster as they watched their big brother climb through the ropes and start to loosen up.

"Where's this guy, Gullick, train at, Jeff?" asked Chuck as Gullick entered the ring.

"Some place in Akron. The paper said his manager is a guy named Don King. They said he was looking to be the other 'Don' of Cleveland boxing next to Don Elbaum," Jeff said.

The boys got quiet when the announcer read off Terry's record and said, "Please welcome, originally from Willoughby, Ohio, and now the Texas State Heavyweight Champion, Terr-rree Daniels!"

At the sound of the bell for Round One, Gullick met Terry at the center of the ring and led off with two quick jabs, both shy of their target. Terry had his gloves up while his opponent dropped his down a bit, and countered off of Terry's punches. Gullick had a menacing look of assurance on his face.

He kept popping his left and following up with left-right combinations. He was scoring two to every one of Terry's punches and Jeff wondered if his buddies were as nervous as he was for his brother in the ring.

When the bell ended the first round, a man sitting behind Jeff tapped him on the back and said, "You rootin' for that white boy?"

Jeff turned and said, "We sure are!"

The man said, "I got 20 bucks, says he don't last 10 rounds."

Jeff had never been in a position to consider betting money on his brother. He didn't even have $20 in his pocket, but he immediately said, "You're on!"

The bell rang for the second round and he, along with his friends, started to root "The Choir Boy" from Willoughby. By the end of the round, however, his bet didn't look promising.

"That motherfucker is hitting me at will!" Terry said to Doug when he went back to his corner. "I can't get a clear shot off at him, and I'm tired of waiting to counter his punches!"

Doug said, "Take your time and get yourself loose. You got eight rounds to go to turn up the heat." But Terry was beginning to see red – he didn't want another loss in front of his family and fans in Cleveland.

The man behind Jeff tapped him on the shoulder again and said, "Hey, man, tell you what. I got two tickets to the Browns game this Sunday. They're $15 a piece, and good seats. I say your boy don't last *five rounds!*"

Jeff turned to Chuck sitting next to him and asked him for money. Chuck said, "We just spent what little money we had at the intermission, Boom-Boom."

Jeff shrugged his shoulders to the guy as the bell sounded for the third round. Gullick came out with his hands held at his chest and Terry led with a short left jab and followed with a quick right hand that caught Gullick hard on the top of his forehead. BAM! His legs gave out and he fell in a heap on the canvas.

The spectators leaped to their feet with a roar as Terry went to a neutral corner. Gullick slowly got to his feet and nodded to the ref, and after the eight-count the fighters were ordered to the center of the ring. Terry charged out of his corner and hit Gullick again with two quick left-right punches, sending him down within seconds.

Jeff and the boys were still standing along with most of the crowd as Gullick slowly rose again and the ref repeated his actions. Terry wasted no time and slugged his opponent down for the third time. The ref waved the fight over. It was a third-round TKO for the "Choir Boy."

The man behind Jeff was laughing while handing him a $20 bill and said, "You shoulda bet me those Browns tickets!"

When the announcer introduced the last bout of the evening, Terry's father excused himself from his friends. He wasn't sure exactly where he was going, but he knew that he had to see Terry right away.

He went to the tunnel and got directions to his dressing room. As he walked, emotions were filling his head from what he had just witnessed, and for the first time in years, he was speechless.

Was it the way he watched his son take iron-fisted punches to his head that left him feeling helpless in the crowd? Was it his overwhelming feeling of guilt in *not* having a "man-to-man" talk about getting out of this crazy sport after Terry lost to Patterson? Or was he just overpowered with joy and swept up with the crowd cheering wildly for *his* boy, the same way they did for him in the football stands years ago?

He approached the door with the name, 'DANIELS' taped to it. Doug was exiting and said, "Hey, good to see ya,' Bill. Go right in."

Terry was standing with his back to the door and was starting to unlace his boxing shoes on a chair. He turned and stood face-to-face with his father. Bill started to tell him what he came in to say, "Terry, I'm –" but instead let loose with tears of pride and joy for his son. Terry hugged his dad tightly. He couldn't get any words out either.

CHAPTER 4

The next day, the sports sections of the Cleveland and La[ke] County newspapers had Terry's fight on page one, and [he] was now being treated as a true sports celebrity in Northeast Ohi[o]. Gullick was nationally ranked and Terry stopped him in his tracks [in] Round Three.

Jeff noticed the articles from the *Plain Dealer* and the *Cleveland Press* taped onto the window of the coach's office at school. Underneath them was a piece of paper with a message written in black marker: *Rebels don't give up – they fight!!*

Two photos accompanied the *Press* article: one showing Gullick being hit hard from one of Terry's punches with bold print underneath – **Going Down**, and the other showing Gullick on the canvas with Terry standing over him reading – **And Out!**

Every class that Jeff attended that day had classmates and teachers congratulating him on his brother's victory. He told a friend, "Man, now I know how Terry felt on the campus of SMU when he won the Golden Gloves."

Chuck and Jeff were bragging to their football buddies later that day about the exciting evening they had. Chuck asked the group, "Did you read where Elbaum said he will try to match Terry up against Frazier, Foreman, Quarry or Ali and have the fight in Cleveland?"

"Your brother's hit the big time, Boom-Boom," Johnny said to Jeff, using his new nickname in front of the group.

Back at the Daniels' house, Terry sat down at the dining room table with Karen and read the headline of the *News-Herald* sports section: "Knockout Punch Surprises Daniels." On page three they had a picture of Terry ready to unleash a powerful right with another headline: "Gallant Prince Valiant Floors 'em."

"Wow, Honey, look at that picture with those muscles of yours bulgin' out. You are *my* prince," Karen said as she put her arms around her husband's neck and gave him a kiss on the cheek.

She read the paragraph that stated: *Following a sobbing reunion in the dressing room with his father, Daniels discussed his 28th triumph in 33 professional fights.*

"What was that about?" she asked.

Terry smiled and said, "Just a little father and son time together. Dad finally said he was really proud of me. Someday maybe I'll be able to share my dream with him: I want to fight for the Heavyweight Championship of the World."

Karen hugged him again. She knew how much that meant to him.

* * *

On November 9th Doug told Terry that he got a call from Ali's camp. "He'll be in Dallas tomorrow to work out at a gym across town and wants you as one of his sparring partners."

After defeating Jimmy Ellis, Ali was now scheduled to fight Buster Mathis in the Houston Astrodome on November 17, 1971.

When Karen found out about the news she said, "Wow, a chance to get in the ring with 'The Greatest'? I wanna see that, Honey!"

She accompanied him to the gym the next day, and waited with Doug while Terry changed in the locker room. Karen rarely went with Terry to the gym, and this time she was a bit uneasy as she noticed stares from Ali's entourage.

Then she smiled when Terry came out of the locker room with Ali. They were talking while shadow boxing and warming up. She had her

Kodak Instamatic handy when it was Terry's turn to get into the ring and go three rounds with The Champ.

Ali continued to jab and dance as he had done with the first man in the ring and Terry was surprised to hear taunts as Ali pecked away at his head gear. It was his style of fighting, and one that Terry had never experienced before.

Karen took two pictures of her husband in the first round, but was frustrated that none of them were of Terry hitting The Champ.

In between rounds, Terry said to Doug, "This guy is three times faster than Patterson. I haven't been able to lay a solid punch on him yet! Hell, does he know this is just a *sparring* session?"

The bell rang to start the second round, and Terry bit down on his mouthpiece. He doubled up his jabs and quickened his pace in hopes of connecting with some punches. A minute into the round, Ali hit Terry with a stiff jab of his own and followed with a left to his jaw.

Terry decided he'd had enough and committed to a left-right combination, but his right would not go straight to Ali's head. Instead, he threw it to where he thought Ali's head would be, a foot to the right of the normal target. The punch landed solidly on Ali's nose and he went down!

Everyone in the gym was "shell-shocked," including The Champ. Karen fumbled to get her camera to her eye and snapped two shots – one of Terry standing over him, and one of Ali getting up from the canvas. His eyes were wide as saucers.

Ali smiled, got up and said, "It's okay, I just slipped," and continued to move as he had been doing, but this time with a little more caution.

After they finished the third round, The Champ smiled at Terry and said, "I may be seeing you for *big* money someday, Daniels."

Karen could barely contain herself, and all she could talk about on the drive home was how good Terry looked in the ring.

"He didn't slip," she said. "You knocked him on his butt and I took the picture to prove it!"

On Friday morning, November 12th, Terry had returned from a long jog in the park when the phone rang.

"Terry, this is Jim Woodruff from the *Dallas Times Herald*. I just hung up with Yank Durham. Were you aware that he chose you as Frazier's next opponent?"

Terry was caught off guard and said, "What? You mean for an exhibition?"

"No! I quoted Durham as saying, 'Daniels has the fight. We are going to close the deal today.' Apparently, he hasn't called you or Doug Lord yet. I'm doing a story for the evening edition and I got a deadline to meet. What do you have to say?" Jim asked.

Terry blinked his eyes and said what he'd always dreamed about saying if ever asked this question: "I'm the most underrated fighter in the world. Frazier is just a man. I know the computer would say he would annihilate me. But he can hit and I can hit. I really feel I have a great chance."

After the conversation, Terry hung up the phone and said to himself, "Did that just really happen? Did he just say I have a chance for the heavyweight title belt?"

Karen had taken the baby to her friend's house and wasn't available to hear the sensational news. So Terry picked up the phone to dial Doug's office.

Doug answered on the third ring and Terry gave him the news. Doug said, "I talked with Elbaum last week and he said Durham was tryin' to get Quarry for the fight, but I guess that didn't work out. Frazier beat the hell outta Quarry once already, anyhow!

"Well, that's good news, Terry," he continued. "Lemme give Durham a call to confirm the details. I'll call ya' back later once I know more."

Karen arrived home with Bret at lunch time. She found Terry sitting at the kitchen table, dressed and clean-shaven. "Wow, don't you look good! Y'all relaxed from your workout today?"

Terry smiled and gave her the news, and together, they anxiously waited for the phone to ring. It rang 30 minutes later, and it was Doug.

"The guy from the paper called me the minute I hung up with you, and I told him I hadn't heard from Frazier's camp yet. He told me that Durham said it was a done deal as far as he was concerned.

"I got a hold of Durham in Philadelphia. He said Quarry's manager gave him some kind of excuse, and he knew Buster Mathis had already committed to fightin' Ali, so he said the fight is yours if you want it. I said I didn't need to talk with you about it and told him to get the papers ready."

"Hell, yes!" Terry replied.

"He said the fight will be held in New Orleans, January 15, which would be Saturday, the night before the Super Bowl," Doug said. "I told him that might work out 'cause Dallas has a good chance to make the playoffs and we may have a nice hometown crowd to root us on if they go all the way."

When Terry hung up he gave Karen the details and said, "Doug and I will be on a plane to New Orleans next week to sign the papers."

Once the afternoon edition of the paper hit the news stands at 4 p.m., friends, neighbors, and everyone else that knew them called to see if the "Cinderella" story was true. The phone at their apartment started ringing and didn't stop until late in the evening.

Terry called the Daniels home that night and told Denny the news. Denny said, "Oh, wow! You're gonna fight for the Heavyweight Championship of the World? I knew it! Debbie and I are the only ones home tonight. Mom went to Jeff's football game; they're playing Mentor for the last game of the season. I can't wait to tell everyone!"

Meanwhile, on November 17th, Muhammed Ali kept 21,000 boxing fans in the Houston Astrodome focused on his fight with Buster Mathis. It was televised on closed-circuit TV in 106 U.S. locations and 21 foreign countries.

Ali continued to prove his showmanship to the world by proclaiming before the fight, "This will be Buster's last stand. I will do to him what the Indians did to Custer – I'm gonna wipe him out."

He made good on his word by knocking Mathis down twice in Round 11 and twice in Round 12. He was awarded the unanimous decision at the end of 12 rounds.

The following week, Terry and Doug flew to New Orleans for the press conference. The photographers were busy getting pictures they needed to promote the title fight in the Crescent City.

On November 23, 1971, United Press International released a story nationally. A picture of Terry and Joe Frazier bumping fists and smiling for the cameras accompanied the story. One of the headlines was titled: "Frazier to Risk Title against College Student Jan. 15."

The article stated: *Frazier, undefeated in 27 fights, including 23 knockouts, has been guaranteed a $250,000 purse. Daniels, who will graduate from Southern Methodist University in a few months with a degree in government, will get $40,000.*

Daniels, 25 years old and a native of Willoughby, Ohio, and now lives in Dallas has a record of 28 victories four losses and a draw. The former SMU football player has 25 knockouts...

Terry called his family to give them the details of his experience in being face-to-face with the Heavyweight Champion of the World.

"The photographer wanted us facing each other in our boxing trunks wearing bag gloves," he said. "Frazier was being nonchalant about everything, until the photographer told us to pose in our boxing stances and get within inches of one another. Then Joe starts to lightly flick a hook into my stomach.

"I just stood there with my guard up while he continued to poke me with his fist. When the photographer told us to hold still while he changed lenses, Joe put a little more power in his punch and I decided that was enough. I clipped his chin with an uppercut and stepped back to show him I was ready if he intended to keep that shit up."

Jeff and Denny were listening together on the phone in the basement, while Debbie and their mother listened on the kitchen extension. The boys chuckled and said, "Holy cow, Terry! What did Frazier do?"

"His eyes got wide and he looked at me – I thought, 'Oh, here we go' – then he smiled and said to the people in the room, 'He don't know I'm just messin' with him!'"

* * *

The "dream" continued for Terry when he got back to Dallas. The local news media featured his "Once in a Lifetime Title Fight," and he was loving every minute of it. The SMU *Daily Campus* even ran an article the first week of December.

One of the sportswriters decided to write a story about what it's like to box with a heavyweight contender. Don Gardner was an amateur boxer from Vancouver, Canada, and the title of his article was, "Requiem for a Neo-Fight."

When he was getting ready for the four-round sparring session he wrote: *I got Jim Dent, our sports editor, to tie on my gloves. At first, I wasn't going to wear the headgear because Gretchen Moser was taking pictures for the newspaper and I wanted to look cool. But when I saw Daniels strap his on, and a foul cup, I decided to put on the headgear, no matter how uncool it was.*

Terry went through the motions with him and took it easy in the first round, but when Don started to test his boxing skills in the second round, he got a taste of what it was like to be in the ring with a trained professional.

Terry landed mostly body shots on the reporter and did his best to hold back his thunderous right hand. After three rounds, Gardner wrote: *The round ended – and thus so did the sparring session – I wouldn't dare call it a fight. My ribs were a bit sore, my nose was tender and the one side of my face – where the left hooks landed – ached a little. But I was still alive.*

He ended the article by writing: *I will say this. Daniels, being as strong and powerful as he is, could put up a good fight against anybody. Including the world's champion.*

Sportswriters throughout the country were mixed on their opinions of Terry's ability to be a true contender for the heavyweight title belt. The majority felt it was too early in his career to challenge one of the most powerful sluggers in boxing history, but the sides evened up a bit when the WBA released the top 10 rankings for professional boxers in the December issue of *Boxing Illustrated* magazine.

The *Dallas Times Herald* reported the story on page three of the sports section with the headline titled, "WBA Ranks Daniels 10th" and stated, *The Dallas heavyweight who will fight Joe Frazier for the championship Jan. 15 is now the No. 10-rated challenger in the world in the December listings.*

With the pressure mounting, Terry maintained his sanity by working hard in the gym every day, combined with prayer to keep him centered. Crocheting calmed his nerves, and he also worked on the power of positive thinking by reading, "Psycho-Cybernetics: A New Way to Get More Living out of Life."

He shared his findings in the book with his brother, Jeff, in a call home one evening. "I start my day off with prayer and sections from the book," he said.

"The author has done a ton of research proving that positive results come after conditioning your mind to think a certain way. I feel more energized and focused on positive things that I come to *expect* every day. I know it sounds incredible, but I truly believe I can beat Frazier."

Jeff needed no more than that – he went out and bought himself a copy the next day. After reading the first three chapters, he could understand how his brother felt.

On December 25th, Terry and Karen spent Christmas Day opening presents with young Bret. They later joined friends and watched the Dallas Cowboys in the NFL playoffs on TV. It would be the first time

NFL games were played on Christmas Day, and the news reported that the general population was not in favor of it.

The Dallas fans didn't mind, however. They watched their Cowboys beat the Minnesota Vikings in chilly Bloomington, Minnesota, 20-12. Terry and Karen celebrated the victory with their friends, then went home to watch the Miami Dolphins beat the Kansas City Chiefs 27-24 in double overtime.

The next day, the San Francisco 49ers beat the Washington Redskins 24-20, setting the stage for an NFC Championship Game against Dallas. On the AFC side, the Baltimore Colts beat the Cleveland Browns 20-3.

On January 2, 1972, the Cowboys beat the 49ers in their new Texas Stadium 14-3, and the Dolphins upset the Colts in Miami 21-0. The Cowboys' victory allowed Doug Lord and Yank Durham's wish to come true – the kid from Dallas would have fans on hand to root him on as he fought the toughest heavyweight fighter in the world, Smokin' Joe Frazier.

CHAPTER 42

January 3, 1972, New Orleans – Terry checked into the Monteleone Hotel with his new trainer, Ronnie, late Monday afternoon. Doug and two sparring partners were due to arrive in the next several days while Terry's wife Karen was scheduled to fly in three days ahead of the fight.

Before leaving for the airport, Terry called Regis McAuley, a reporter for the *News-Herald* in Willoughby, to give him an interview that he'd agreed to. The article appeared in the evening edition and was one of many to follow. There was a picture of Terry making a "number one" sign with his finger while holding a newspaper featuring a story about his upcoming fight with Frazier on Super Bowl weekend. The headline was titled: "Slugger in Bayou – Daniels Remains Confident."

The Daniels family read the article before dinner that evening. The boys were pleased to read quotes from their big brother: *"Most people think that I don't stand a chance against Frazier, but I know that I do, and it doesn't make any sense to say that I am hopelessly outclassed...Frazier doesn't have more speed, strength or more intelligence in the ring as me...I can hit as hard as he can."*

Tom was home from Ohio University for Christmas break and spoke with his dad about the possibility of going to the fight on January 15th. He shared his conversation with the rest of the family at the dinner table.

"Dad said the cost of getting us all down there to spend the weekend would be ridiculous considering the crowd in town for the Super Bowl," he told the family. "He also said the city is 'full of nuts' as it is, and we would be just as well off to see the fight on television at home."

The Daniels boys were disappointed because they wanted to watch their brother fight Frazier in person.

The paper informed the public that the fight would be carried on national television with the only blackout area being New Orleans. Century Telesports Network made it possible to see the fight in the U.S. and many other countries.

When Terry's brothers first learned of the fight in November, it took several weeks to absorb the national attention he was getting – both good and bad. Denny encouraged the rest of the family to stay positive by referencing an article from the scrapbook he was creating.

The story was dated November 23, 1971 and appeared in the *Plain Dealer*. It had a picture of Terry admiring Joe Frazier's fist and the headline titled, "Daniels Eyes Glory, Not Gold."

Denny read the part that stated: *Frazier, 28, will be an overwhelming favorite, but the champion warned Monday about his challenger: "He's young, he's got two arms that knocked out a lot of people and he's ambitious."*

"That was Frazier talking," Denny added, "not some fruitcake reporter. He knows how strong Terry is – this isn't gonna be a dull fight!"

The next day in New Orleans, Terry and Ronnie found a three-mile trail to jog, then checked out the boxing ring set up for the fighters on the top floor of the hotel.

"Looks like they got everything we need, Terry," Ronnie said. "Why don't you get your jump rope and start warmin' up? I'll get ready to go a few rounds with ya' before the press starts comin' in."

After a good workout, the boys cleaned up for a night on the town. They had been given a schedule of interviews, dinners and other events by the promoters when they checked in. Tonight, however, was their "free night" and they intended to use every minute before the press cornered Terry again.

They walked a block to Bourbon Street and sampled several dishes of Louisiana cuisine. Before they knew it, people had surrounded them asking for autographs and taking pictures. Terry smiled and was pleased to accommodate everyone.

Ronnie laughingly said, "Ten o'clock is curfew for us folks, and we bid you farewell. Ya'll be sure to see him take on Smokin' Joe next Saturday!"

The next morning when Terry and Ronnie were jogging, they stopped at a newsstand on their way back to the hotel. Ronnie flipped to the sports section of the *Times-Picayune* and saw Terry's picture on the cover page. It showed him sitting between two models holding a mock newspaper for the camera. The headline read, "Daniels Cools Frazier in the Fifth, New Champ."

Ronnie chuckled and said, "Hah! That oughta rustle a few feathers in Frazier's camp today."

Doug checked into the hotel with Terry's sparring partners around 10 a.m., and had them in the ring by 1 p.m. "I brought Joe Byrd and Sonny Moore with me," Doug said to Terry. "They'll keep the heat on ya' just like Frazier will."

On Sunday evening, Doug told Terry, "I want you and Ronnie out early before breakfast. Do five miles tomorrow mornin'."

"Five? I'm feeling good with just three," Terry said.

"You'll do five, and then I want 40-yard wind sprints – 10 of 'em."

Terry did as he was told, and as he feared, his left knee started to throb. He told Doug about it and said, "I'm gonna take a ride to Tulane University after breakfast and see if I can use one of the whirlpools the players use. The treatment always worked when I was at SMU."

He took a hotel courtesy car to the entrance of the stadium where the Cowboys and Dolphins were practicing and approached the guard at the gate.

"Who are you here to see?" the guard asked.

Although Terry knew some of the Cowboys that were playing, he figured they would be prohibited from letting outside friends into their private workouts. Instead, he said, "Tell Coach Shula that Terry Daniels from Riverside High School is here to see him."

Even though he'd never met Don Shula before, Terry thought he'd try to appeal to Shula's hometown values since they both attended high schools in Painesville, Ohio, and hoped that might get his attention. Shula played football and graduated from Harvey High. Terry attended Riverside before transferring to Willoughby South, and he knew Shula's roots were in Painesville.

Within a few minutes, Don Shula walked out and squinted into the sun to see if someone was playing a joke on him. He smiled as they shook hands and said, "Terry, how are you? It's a pleasure to meet you."

"Fine, Coach," he said. "I hope you don't mind that I came unannounced, but I wasn't sure how to get a hold of you."

"No problem at all," the coach replied. "I read about you growing up in Lake County, and I believe I met your dad at a Booster's luncheon a few years ago. He owns a fuel-oil company, right?"

"Right! Listen, I was wondering if I could use one of the whirlpools if they're available. My knees are throbbing from all the running I've been doing lately."

"Sure, no problem, c'mon in."

They spent a few minutes talking about Terry's upcoming fight with Frazier on Super Bowl weekend and how they both were considered underdogs.

"Well, listen, I gotta get back to work," Shula said. "But feel free to drop by around 9:30 or 10 in the morning any day you want. We'll still be on the field and practicing. I'll leave a note for the guard to let you in. Good luck to you next Saturday."

When Terry got back to the hotel, he told Ronnie where he'd been. Ronnie said, "Don Shula let you in? How the hell do ya' know him?"

"I don't," Terry replied. "It all comes from the power of positive thinking, my friend."

* * *

Back in Willoughby, on January 11th, the fans in Lake County read the cover of the sports section in the *News-Herald* with a picture of Terry slugging Ted Gullick the previous October. The title read, "History Favors Daniels" and the story was about Gentleman Jim Corbett upsetting John L. Sullivan in the last title fight held in New Orleans.

Jeff was filled with pride and confidence for his big brother while reading the story. He especially got pumped when he read a headline next to it titled, "Frazier Looks Sharp." It stated: *Heavyweight boxing champ Joe Frazier felt, "Good and strong" today for his title bout here Saturday night against young Terry Daniels.*

Frazier put in nine rounds Monday… "He's punching harder and sharper, and his reflexes are better," stable-mate Ray Anderson said.

Daniels quit for the day after eight rounds, including five with Sonny Moore. Daniels bounced Moore around the ring with lightning combinations of solid left hooks and right leads. Moore, who was successful last week in keeping Daniels on the ropes, couldn't do it this time.

"He was moving faster and punching harder," Moore said. "He stayed off those ropes. He's getting himself up."

Newspapers throughout the country had stories about the fight every day. On Friday afternoon, a teacher brought a copy of the *Painesville Telegraph* with him to lunch, and showed Jeff and his buddies the story about Terry's big night coming up.

"Look, you were quoted," he said to Jeff.

Jeff smiled as he read out loud, "He's got me thinking that you can do anything you want to do, and do it well, when you put your mind to it."

When he got home after school, he called his brother Tom in Athens and told him about the article.

"Hey, that's cool," Tom said. "Would you believe the OU paper interviewed me too and ran it in today's issue?" Both of them had a tough time realizing that the whole world was learning who their big brother was.

On Saturday morning, the Daniels household realized it wasn't a dream. All the papers in Northeast Ohio had the story on the sports pages with headlines: "Tonight it's Daniels-Frazier; Tomorrow it's Dallas-Miami;" and "Oh, Whatta Super Weekend!"

The cover of the sports page in the *Plain Dealer* had a headline titled: "Frazier is Star of Home TV Tonight," and had a picture of Terry reading his positive-thinking book. The story stated: *The fight will be shown on nationwide television and will also be viewed in Canada, England, France, Hong Kong, Italy, Austria, Yugoslavia, and parts in East and West Africa.*

Jeff's stomach had butterflies developing by 10:30 that morning. When he read that the fight would be on Channel 5 at 10:30 p.m. he said to Denny, "How am I going to get through the day? The minutes are gonna drag on and on – it'll seem like *forever* until the fight starts!"

The *Dallas Morning News* had an article titled, "Daniels, Goliath Toe-to-Toe." It stated: *Terry Daniels will step into the ring here in New Orleans Saturday night as the biggest underdog in the heavyweight championship fight in 15 years.* It was accompanied with a picture of a smiling Smokin' Joe Frazier toting a heavy boxing bag.

The article also stated: *From all that can be gleaned from both partial and disinterested observers, Dallas' favorite son has prepared himself to the ultimate of his ability for the fight.*

A couple of boxing veterans emphasized it in one of the innumerable conversations about the fight which have spiced Super Bowl week.

"I'll tell you one thing," said a New Orleanian who has watched 10 days of workouts of the two fighters, "If conditioning could do it, Daniels would win. He's in fantastic shape."

Karen made arrangements with her parents to watch Bret while she flew into New Orleans on Thursday. She accompanied Terry to the weigh-ins Saturday morning and listened to her husband in his interview with Tom Harmon, the sports commentator. He handled himself well and she knew the audience back home would be proud of Terry.

She understood the pressure he was under after reading an article in the *Dallas Times Herald* the day before she left, titled: "Frazier Wary of Date with Daniels." The story mainly focused on Frazier's health and who he planned on fighting next. The last four paragraphs were given to Terry. It stated: *"I'm fighting possibly the greatest heavyweight who ever lived,"* said the 25-year-old Daniels thoughtfully, slowly. *"I've been living with this for eight weeks now. It creates a lot of pressure. You have a harder and harder time falling asleep every night. Joe Frazier?*

"I was always respectful of him. I consider him a machine, almost unbeatable. But I've come up in the three years I've been fighting. Why do I think I can beat him? I've got the body and the mind. I can do it. I played some football at SMU and I remember a sign on the wall of the locker room. It said, 'dreamers who work can make their dreams come true,' I believe in this."

Terry and Karen met Doug, Ronnie and his wife Sharon in the lobby of the hotel – it was time to leave for the fight. The place was filled with Dallas Cowboy fans. As the elevator doors opened, the crowd whistled and cheered, patting Terry and Karen on the back as they made their way to the limo.

People were smiling and saying, "Good luck Terry, we want Dallas to have two knockouts this weekend!" and "We know you'll give 'em your best Daniels, we've got ringside seats!" Terry smiled and shook as many hands as he could before entering the limo.

He closed the door and said, "Wow, now I know how Elvis feels."

Back in Willoughby, Jeff, Denny and Debbie joined their mother in the living room for *their* ringside seats. They had plenty of snacks and soda pop. It was 8:30 pm and coverage for the fight was to begin at 10:30 pm. "Fight Night" had finally arrived.

Their father chose to watch the fight with friends at LaVelle's on color television sets. The Cleveland Cavaliers were playing the Houston Rockets on Channel 5, and Bill asked the owner if he could turn the sound down. "We don't need to hear all that racket right now. Save that for when my kid's in the ring," he said.

Tom and Marcie entertained friends in their apartment off campus at Ohio University. Tom felt the tension continuing to build all week and the hundreds of questions that he and his brothers were asked by newspapers, friends and neighbors, would be answered in a few hours.

Before Terry went to his dressing room with Doug and Ronnie, he got one more "good luck kiss" from his wife. She looked at him and said, "Stick to your plan and don't give up; you're a winner. I love you."

She watched as he turned and walked down the tunnel. Soon she would be cheering him on as she had so many times before. Ronnie's wife Sharon approached her and said, "Let's go find our seats and join our friends. You've got to relax a little."

At 9:50 p.m., June looked at Jeff and Denny and said, "Will you two sit down? You look like a couple of caged tigers! Go outside and shovel snow if you need to get rid of some energy!"

The boys tried, but couldn't contain themselves. Jeff asked Denny, "What do you think is going on in Terry's mind right now? Will Frazier come out bobbing and weaving, looking to take Terry out early? Is he determined to show the world that he's truly the undisputed champion that beat Ali?"

Denny replied, "I'd love to see Terry catch him coming in with his powerful right hand and knock him out!"

At 10:32 p.m. the announcers for the Cavs game said, "We hoped you enjoyed tonight's basketball game and now join Century Telesports Networks for a show already in process."

The screen switched to a boxing ring and the commentators, Tom Harmon and Gil Clancy, welcomed the television audience in the United States and around the world to "The Heavyweight Championship of the World!"

Jeff turned up the volume, and Debbie screamed, "Jeff, look out – there's Terry!"

He stepped back and they saw a poster-sized photo of Joe Frazier and Terry squaring off in their boxing poses. They started cheering as the announcers continued their introduction, and then went to a commercial.

The phone immediately rang and Jeff quickly answered – it was Darrell Tibyash.

"Is this cool or what?" Darrell said. "We all wish him luck! I hope Terry knocks his block off! Later!"

Back in the dressing room, Doug put the final touches of Vaseline on Terry's face while Ronnie grabbed a bucket and slung a towel over his shoulder. Terry reached for the hood of his robe, but had trouble grabbing it with his boxing gloves on. Ronnie flipped it over his head as Doug opened the door and led them into the tunnel.

"Let's do this," Doug said.

The crowd at LaVelle's was focused on the television screens above the bar and in the dining area, listening intensely to the pre-fight interviews taken earlier at the weigh-ins. "What a difference in the way Terry talks versus Frazier, aye Bill?" one man said to Terry's father.

Bill took a swig of his *Jim Beam* on the rocks and said, "Frazier is the toughest son of a bitch on the face of the earth. I hope my kid can land one good solid shot early to knock some of that piss and vinegar out of him."

After a few commercials, the cameras were focused on the boxing ring and Tom Harmon said, "And here comes the champion – Smokin' Joe Frazier."

After focusing on the champ, the camera panned out and everyone could see Terry. Jeff listened with the rest of the family as the ring announcer read off Terry's weight of 191.5 pounds.

When Terry removed his robe, Denny said, "Man, look at him, he's ripped!"

The speakers of the television vibrated as the family heard, "Let's welcome the challenger from Dallas, Texas, Terry Daniels!" They cheered along with the crowd of 8,000 at the fight while Terry raised one arm in the air. He continued to bounce around in a small circle and kept a look of confidence on his face.

When June heard the announcer give Frazier's weight of 215 pounds she said, "How does Terry always manage to fight someone heavier or taller than him?"

"Anything over 175 pounds is considered heavyweight, Mom," Jeff said. "Terry's too heavy for a light-heavyweight and too light to be a true heavyweight – if that makes any sense."

"But there's a 24-pound difference," June said. *"That doesn't seem fair!"*

"Terry's never been afraid to fight someone bigger than he is," Denny said.

After the referee gave his instructions to the fighters in the center of the ring, Terry returned to his corner to get his mouthpiece and last-second instructions from Doug: "Keep him off ya' with that jab, and keep that right hand up – you'll do just fine!"

DING! The first bell rang and the fighters met each other in the center of the ring. Frazier appeared to pick up where he'd left off with Ali 10 months earlier in Madison Square Garden – aggressively bobbing and weaving while throwing short hooks and right hands.

Terry did exactly what Doug told him to do. He threw stiff left jabs, two and three in a row to keep Frazier at bay, not letting him get solid footing.

The television audience heard Gil Clancy say, "Tom, Daniels did the right thing just then – he threw two good punches to make Joe respect him."

As they listened to the comments, Denny said, "That's what Terry always told us to do when that first bell rings. Remember, Jeff?"

They watched as Frazier started to bore in with his pile-driving punches to Terry's midsection and head, but Terry countered with left jabs, not staying in one spot long. With less than a minute left on the clock, Frazier started to unleash his heavy artillery and connected with a few hooks to Terry's head.

"One thing I will say for Daniels, he is punching back, Tom," Clancy said as the two gladiators kept slugging it out. Suddenly, Frazier connected with a hard left hook to Terry's jaw and he dropped back against the ropes. The champion immediately followed with another and Terry went down, face first, to the canvas. The audience gasped.

Terry's father heard a man from the dining area in LaVelle's say, "Ah hell, I knew this fight wouldn't go past Round One!"

Bill turned with a scowl on his face, but the bartender said, "Don't worry Bill, I'll tell that guy to shut his mouth or I'll throw his ass outta here."

In the ring, the ref stepped in and ordered Frazier to a neutral corner, then started his count. Terry pushed off the canvas floor and got up at the count of seven. Doug stepped into the ring and grabbed the ref's hand – apparently he hadn't heard the bell ending the round.

The television audience heard Tom Harmon say, "The bell rang and the referee called the fighters together, but realized the round ended. You recall, there is no saving by the bell, and Daniels beat the count."

Frazier sat in his corner waiting for his mouthpiece to be cleaned. Yank told him, "You had him, but he beat the count. Go back out there and finish him!"

Ronnie put a stool down while Doug hit Terry with a cold sponge and said, "It's okay Terry, you took his best punch and got up. You're gonna need to hit him hard this round to slow him down – he *can't* keep that kinda' pace each round."

"Hit him hard? I haven't exactly held anything back!" Terry said.

The bell sounded to start the second round. Frazier came out of his corner like a crazed bull while Terry kept his double jab working. Harmon said, "Let's see if Daniels has recovered from that last round. He really took some hard shots from the champion."

Frazier kept bobbing his head up and down while continuing his left-right hook combinations. The crowd suddenly cheered and Harmon said, "Daniels connected with a solid right uppercut that jolted Frazier back!"

The crowd at LaVelle's cheered as Terry continued to throw hard left and right punches to Frazier's head. But Frazier showed the audience why he was the champion by not slowing down. The announcers were trading off on calling the action-packed round, then Terry hit Frazier with a solid right, and Clancy said, "Tom, this kid has all the courage in the world. He's made a brawl out of it! He's gonna go out fighting – *if* he goes out!"

The two boxers fought like it was a three-round fight in a Golden Gloves final. Neither one backed down. When the bell rang to end Round Two, the crowd at Rivergate roared with excitement.

Back in his corner, Terry said, "What the hell? I hit that son of a bitch as hard as I've hit anybody in my whole life, and all he did was snort!"

Harmon continued to give the blow-by-blow description of Round Three. The televisions in LaVelle's boomed his voice out in stereo throughout the restaurant: "Frazier comes right out leading with left and right hooks. Daniels is bobbing and weaving the punches, trying to fight back. Frazier lands a left hook, and another, he's got Daniels on the ropes. He's trying to take him out. Terry Daniels is fighting back. The kid from Texas is swinging!"

The crowd at Rivergate was cheering as Terry ducked under one of Frazier's deadly left hooks and shuffled his way out to the center of the ring. They loved that Terry was making it a fight.

"Joe Frazier, constantly boring in throwing lefts and rights; Daniels trying to punch; trying to get one in that will slow him up," came Harmon's voice in the Daniels' living room.

"Keep hittin' him, Terry!" Denny yelled.

"Quiet! I want to hear what the announcer's saying," June said.

"Daniels is really swinging, but he doesn't seem to be having any effect on Joe," Clancy said. "He just can't stop this freight train."

Terry continued his game plan – *jab, jab, straight right hand, side-to-side movement, don't give him a stable target.*

"Frazier is hitting him every bit as hard as he hit Ali," Jeff said.

The champion continued his relentless attack and unleashed another thunderous left hook that sent Terry back against the ropes and down. The ref motioned Frazier to a corner and started his count.

Karen was a nervous wreck. With tears in her eyes she screamed, "Get up Terry, get up!"

The boys at home were on their feet. They watched as their brother slowly rolled over to his elbows and knees, then to the astonishment of the Rivergate crowd and the television audience around the world, he pushed himself up as the ref counted to nine.

"What courage this boy is showing, Tom!" Clancy said. "This kid can't win the title; he's just in with a tougher man."

Terry protected his head with his gloves as the ref stepped away, and Frazier powered right back into him with another right-left combination sending him down again.

Harmon called the action: "We want to tell you that there is no stopping the fight at the bell. That is at the discretion of the referee. Terry Daniels struggles to his feet. The seconds are ticking away, and there's the bell."

The ref dusted Terry's gloves off and said to him, "You okay to continue, Terry?"

Terry muffled through his mouthpiece, "Yeah, bring him on!"

The crowd at LaVelle's watched both cornermen come into the ring and escort the exhausted fighters back to their stools. The men at the bar were shaking their heads and patting Terry's father on the back, while the women were saying things like, "I can't stand this! Bartender, may I have another, please?"

Karen watched as Doug and Ronnie talked to her husband. She turned to Sharon and said, "I hope they're tellin' him they want to stop the fight. I don't think I can take much more of this!"

The bell rang for Round Four and the television audience heard Harmon say, "Frazier continues to bore straight ahead pounding body shots as that extra 24 pounds seems to be making a difference, and bulls Terry Daniels around the ring."

Terry took another hard left to the head, but seemed to shake it off and kept shuffling around the ring with his guard up. When Frazier pushed Terry against the ropes Harmon said, "Terry Daniels, the youngster from Dallas, Texas, may not win this particular fight, but I guarantee you, he's gonna send some folks home convinced of his courage."

Terry continued to throw lefts and rights, most of which hit their target, and Harmon said, "His punches don't seem to have any effect on Joe. Daniels is trying to stay in this fight, but I don't know if he has enough steam left. Frazier continues to look for the opportunity to throw his big left hook...And there it is!"

The punch caught Terry flush on his jaw and down he went, face-first to the canvas. The ref knelt over him and started his count. The only way the audience could tell if Terry was alive was by the motion of his rib cage as he breathed in and out. Jeff and Denny stood motionless in front of their television set. Debbie and their mother didn't care that they were blocking their vision – they sat with their hands covering their faces.

"Oh, my God – he's getting up!" Jeff yelled.

The crowd in the auditorium went wild, roaring as Harmon continued, "And Daniels is up on his feet. The referee is talking to him, and he is nodding that he is all right. The ref signals for the fight to continue!

"Frazier goes right after his opponent leading with his left...He's hitting him with a left; right; left; pounding him through the ropes... And the referee is calling the fight off!"

Terry's father remained sitting down, while most of the people in the restaurant were on their feet. He watched as the ring filled with people and the camera focused on the heavyweight champion. Then it switched to a full view and he could see his son standing against the ropes with his trainer putting his robe around his shoulders.

In a brief moment, he could see the look of disgust on Terry's face. He watched as he slammed his fists against the ropes. He'd seen that look of frustration before.

A man patted him on the back and said, "He put up a helluva fight, Bill. I don't think anybody can stop Frazier."

Bill smiled and said, "You know, I'd seen that look of frustration many times while he was growing up – striking out at the plate, fumbling a handoff or missing a tackle in football. But he always hung in there…and never gave up. Just like now."

* * *

On Monday, Jeff went to school knowing that everyone would have an opinion about the fight. Most of the papers had a picture from United Press International showing Frazier knocking Terry into the middle of the ropes. The articles had mixed reviews. Some said the fight was a mismatch, but Jeff preferred the headline that read: "Frazier Wins Fight; Daniels Wins Fans."

Quotes were recorded from the post-fight interview and stated: *"I was a little overanxious,"* Frazier said. *"But I wanna say something about this fella,"* he went on, looking toward the weary Daniels, sitting a few feet away.

"He's got a very good right hand. I think the guy's got a good chance to be champ someday. He's got the heart and the punching power."

Daniels won the crowd of 8,000 completely over with the way he kept climbing back off the canvas and coming back.

He didn't just come back holding on, either. He stung Frazier several times with smart rights.

Jeff listened to teachers and classmates offer everything from congratulations to condolences throughout the day. But it wasn't until he attended his history class that everything was brought into proper perspective.

His teacher handed him a sheet of paper and said, "My wrestling coach in college loved this quote from Teddy Roosevelt. After watching your brother's fight Saturday night, it was obvious that he put his heart into winning, and that kind of passion you can never lose. I thought you'd like to share it with the class today and later, with your brother."

Jeff stood behind the podium in the room and read the quotation:

"It is not the critic who counts; not the man who points out how the strong man stumbles, or where the doer of deeds could have done them better. The credit belongs to the man who is actually in the arena, whose face is marred by dust and sweat and blood; who strives valiantly; who errs, who comes short again and again, because there is no effort without error and shortcoming; but who does actually strive to do the deeds; who knows great enthusiasms, the great devotions; who spends himself in a worthy cause; who at the best knows in the end the triumph of high achievement, and who at the worst, if he fails, at least fails while daring greatly, so that his place shall never be with those cold and timid souls who neither know victory nor defeat."
– Theodore Roosevelt.

Jeff looked up into the eyes of his classmates as they applauded for him and his brother. Tears welled in his eyes. He realized that even though his brother lost, he was determined to see his dream come true and never give up. And <u>that</u> is how he was able to step into the ring to compete for the Heavyweight Championship of the World.

* * *

Eight days later, Terry, Karen and Bret flew back to Cleveland to be with the Daniels family. They took the airport shuttle to the Holiday Inn in Willoughby and smiles came to their faces when they read the message on the marquee out front: "Welcome Home Heavyweight Contender Terry Daniels."

They were met in the lobby of the hotel with plenty of hugs, kisses and even applause from June, Jeff, Denny and Debbie. Terry's smile beamed from ear to ear as he took it all in, but Jeff noticed he was slightly distracted as Terry scanned for one person in particular. That was when his father walked into the lobby.

Terry looked at Bill, not knowing what to expect. He walked up to him and they shared a long-overdue hug. Jeff could see the tenderness in his father's eyes and knew that he wouldn't have shown up unless he was genuinely proud of his number one son.

Jeff and Denny took advantage of the moment and joined in with a group hug. Jeff said, "Sorry we couldn't get down there and see you in person, Ter, but we watched every second of it on TV – and so did Dad."

Terry sent a wink in Jeff's direction.

"That's right, Terry," Bill said. "And you proved to everyone that you're no quitter. You made us proud, and it's good to have you home."

- The End -

EPILOGUE
WHERE ARE THEY NOW?

Jeff Daniels, Author

Writing my brother's story was a monumental task. But over the years it became clear to me that honoring his legacy by documenting his rise to fame, including all his trials and tribulations, was a special story that needed to be told.

From a younger brother's perspective, I definitely felt the peer pressure when Terry fought Smokin' Joe on national TV with an audience spanning the globe at over 70 million viewers. As an impressionable senior in high school, starting to make my way into the world, I wondered how I could ever follow in his gigantic footsteps.

Lord knows I gave it a good try.

Our other siblings seemed to be established in their lives or were, perhaps, too young to be affected. At the time, our brother Tom was married and a senior at Ohio University. He made a name for himself on the OU golf team when they won three Mid-American Conference Championships. Denny and Debbie were in junior high, and didn't take note of the bar that big brother had set so high. As a result of Terry's fame, I worked harder in every sport just to keep pace with my buddies. And the hard work paid off.

After graduating high school in 1972, I played in the Lake County East/West All-Star football game in August and a week later, started two-a-day workouts on the football team at Heidelberg College (now Heidelberg University) in Tiffin, Ohio. It wasn't like Terry playing in the powerful Southwest Conference when he attended SMU, but I did have the experience of playing on an undefeated football team that won the Stagg Bowl that year for the Division III National Championship.

After one year of college, I decided to take time off and for the next two years worked for my dad and uncle's corporations. The peer pressure was still all around me, however, at work and in the bars with my friends. Anyone who has a famous sibling has had experiences similar to mine when being introduced to someone: "I'd like to introduce you to Jeff Daniels, he's Terry Daniels brother! You know, the one who fought Frazier?" Then the conversation goes on and on about Terry, how he's doing, will he go for the title again, etc.

Of course I was proud of all that Terry had accomplished but it gets a little old when it's 20 introductions in a row that go *exactly* the same way. Again, I've had friends whose older brothers made a name for themselves, but none of them came close to *fighting for the Heavyweight Championship of the World.*

It was Joe Topoly, one of the football coaches from Willoughby South (who sparred with Terry a few times), who convinced me to start training with Larry and Billy Wagner at the Shamrock Gym in Collinwood. As a result, in 1974 I won the city and regional Cleveland Golden Gloves tournament Novice Light-heavyweight Division. After enrolling at Ohio State University I won the Columbus regional Golden Gloves tournament in the Open Light-heavyweight Division in '76 and '77. The following year I stopped pursuing the sport, focused on my studies and obtained a Bachelor of Science degree in Finance and Accounting.

For the past 30 years I've led a successful career as an investment broker. I recently retired to follow my passion for writing and speaking.

The experience I received from amateur boxing came as an unexpected bonus when taking on the task of writing this book. My brother's words echoed as I spent years working on his story: "If a person wants to do something with their life, and does whatever it takes to be good at it, things go their way. My motto is: Always keep striving to be good at something."

And as you've probably guessed by now, I'm a fan of my brother's perspective on life. Terry has been an exemplary role model. He taught me that hard work and dedication pays off.

I am happily married (for 34 years) to my "Ann-Margret" look-alike wife. We live in the Cleveland area and have raised two girls and a boy who have grown up to be confident and considerate adults.

Terry Daniels, Professional Heavyweight Boxer

When Terry and his family settled down in Dallas after the title fight with Frazier, he took Doug Lord's advice and invested his winnings. He made a down payment on a new house and finished his degree in Political Science at SMU. At the time, Doug tried to convince Terry to give up boxing, but Terry wasn't ready to throw in the towel. After all, one of the greatest heavyweights told him "he had the punch and the heart to be champion one day."

Terry fought four more times in 1972, but was taking a pounding against tough opponents including Jose "King" Roman, the heavyweight champ of Puerto Rico, in the preliminary fight on the Muhammad Ali/Bob Foster card. I watched it on closed circuit at the Palace Theatre in Cleveland with my brothers and friends. Terry looked sloppy and was hit way too many times. My brothers and I felt it was time for him to give up the sport.

But Terry disagreed.

Although he was on the receiving end of so many punches in a fight, he always seemed to recover quickly. He was a scientific miracle.

Aside from having his nose broken in several places, he never got cut or suffered from headaches. He thought he was indestructible. For a while we did too.

Looking back, I realize he hung in there too long. He had a tough time letting go of the fame and attention he received whether he won or not. And the prospect of working at a "normal" job and taking orders from a manager who liked to order around the heavyweight boxer became unbearable for him.

Terry fought his last bout in 1981 after starting his own business, the Terry Daniels Legal Reporting Service, in 1979 with the help of his old buddy, Ronnie Wright.

After retiring from the sport, he still had his good looks and kept in shape, unlike some retired athletes that turned to alcohol or painkillers. By the late '80s, however, signs of head trauma appeared, and Terry was starting to tremble. It started slowly in his left hand and became very noticeable by the mid '90s. His doctor diagnosed him with Parkinson's disease in 1996. Eventually, he could no longer perform daily duties for his company in Houston, and after 22 years he closed the doors. He became eligible for Social Security Disability Income in 2002. He was 56 years old.

Although he went through two divorces, he raised three exceptional boys and in 2004 I convinced him to sell his house in Texas and move back to Willoughby. At the time, he lived with our father, who was 85 and a widower from his second marriage. Dad passed away in 2009.

Doctors told Terry in 1996 that he had approximately 10 years before becoming incompetent, but he fooled them all. He eventually moved into an excellent assisted-living facility where he lives as of this printing.

Tom and I visit Terry on a weekly basis. Terry is lucky enough to be surrounded by people who care about him. He uses a walker to get around and exercises regularly at the recreation center in his complex. He shows signs of dementia, and has good days and bad, but gives everyone a flash of his famous dimpled smile.

Note: Because of Terry's degenerative disease, he no longer takes interviews or makes public appearances. All correspondence is to be directed to Jeff Daniels, Power of Attorney: jd@jeffdanielscompany.com.

ACKNOWLEDGEMENTS

A special thank you goes out to Terry's friends and neighbors in Houston. They were generous with the task of helping us move him back to Willoughby and encouraged me to write this book.

In addition, a *huge* thank you goes out to the people who helped me complete my first book including Gary Palmer, John Luttermoser (editor), and the best writing coach, T.L. Champion of Champion Studios in Cleveland, Ohio.

I would also like to end by thanking everyone who played a part in Terry's life during this period:

- Doug and Opal Lord –When I told Doug, who is 87 that I was writing a book about Terry he said, "You better hurry up and get this book done before I die!"
- Ronnie and Sharon Wright
- Danny Iafelice and the alumni from Willoughby South High School. Danny was helpful in sharing great stories.
- Tom Morris – "Tommy" still remembers the boxing days like they were yesterday.
- Mike McCann – Mike retired with his wife in 2015.
- Eddie Joe "Dedo" Davis – Dedo is retired with his wife.
- Karen (Allison) Johnson – Karen divorced Terry, but is happily remarried.

- Billy Wagner – Billy had a great pro career. He helped me sharpen my skills in the ring and retired from the Cleveland Fire Department.
- Muhammad Ali – "The Greatest" also suffers from Parkinson's and head trauma. He brought boxing back to life in the '60s and '70s and generations of fans are glad he did.
- Smokin' Joe Frazier – A special thank you goes to Frazier, who fought Terry at the pinnacle of his career, and Terry wants to recognize him for that. Frazier passed away in 2011 and will be remembered as one of the greatest heavyweights of all time.
- Jerry Quarry – Always a favorite heavyweight of the Daniels family, Quarry passed away in 1999.
- Larry Wagner – A fantastic boxing trainer and brother to Billy, Larry passed away in 2014.

A Special Thank You to the Police Athletic League (PAL) of Dallas, Texas

The Police Athletic League (PAL) in Dallas sponsored Terry's first year in the amateurs in 1965. It's important to my brother that we acknowledge the role the PAL boxing program played in shaping the lives of many young men, helping them to develop life skills and giving them advantages when they had none.

As disclosed in the beginning of the book, some names were changed at the discretion of the author to respect the need for confidentiality. The names of some of the trainers and amateur boxers in the PAL stories were changed, but dozens of press clippings and pictures chronicle the real events throughout Terry's career. As the owner of this book you are entitled to a special password-protected archive of these pictures and press clippings when you go to: www.mybrothertheboxer.com. To access it, go to the site and use this information:

Login: JD
Password: smuboxer

Thank you,
Jeff Daniels, Author

* We want to hear from you. If you have questions or comments, please contact us. Jeff Daniels is available for speaking opportunities and can be reached at JD@jeffdanielscompany.com.

Made in the USA
Lexington, KY
13 June 2017